THE RISE AND FALL OF
INTELLIGENCE

To my students.

"There is, perhaps in every thing of any consequence, a secret history which it would be amusing to know, could we have it authentically communicated."

James Boswell, *Life of Johnson*

THE RISE AND FALL OF
INTELLIGENCE
AN INTERNATIONAL SECURITY HISTORY

MICHAEL WARNER

GEORGETOWN UNIVERSITY PRESS
WASHINGTON, DC

Library of Congress Cataloging-in-Publication Control Number

2014000378

∞ This book is printed on acid-free paper meeting the requirements of the American National Standard for Permanence in Paper for Printed Library Materials.

15 14   9 8 7 6 5 4 3 2 First printing

Printed in the United States of America

CONTENTS

ILLUSTRATIONS

PREFACE

This book represents the product of two decades of reading, writing, and teaching intelligence. Those efforts shaped me in many ways, changing my outlook on recent and ancient history. I felt a need to make sense of what I was seeing, and to do so in a way that others could share and debate the conclusions that seemed to press themselves on me. Needless to say, even attempting such a project looked daunting at first, as so many fine authors and exceptional researchers have dug into intelligence history and connected larger events to developments in the intelligence realm. I cannot match their acumen or stamina. The literature really has flowered over the last generation, and I stand on some very large shoulders to view the field. Nonetheless, I felt that hitherto unnoticed patterns were emerging in what these authors had found. Events in one country seemed to echo simultaneous events in another, for instance. Pivotal moments for the course of intelligence, like Lenin's reconceptualization of revolutionary organization in 1903, suddenly took on new significance when viewed as problems of clandestine operations. Whole areas of endeavor, like the prodigious campaign to improve computer security that began in the 1960s, revealed unsuspected significance for intelligence policy and organization. The possible links between just these two examples—not to mention many others—came to fascinate me.

If I wanted to read an explanation of such things and others like them, it seemed to me that I would have to write it. That was the task that I set for myself in 2010. I wanted to remain faithful to the details, to adapt a multinational perspective, to keep events in chronological order as much as possible, and to discuss recent archival revelations. Most of all, I hoped to place intelligence developments in their proper diplomatic, technological, and ideological contexts. Doing so gave me many surprises, which I have done my best to convey. The reader may judge how well I succeeded.

I should explain that I finished this book just as the recent spate of leaks about US intelligence and allied efforts broke in the media, leaving observers surprised and a little bewildered about how to make sense of so many revelations. Viewing the reports and the ensuing controversy, I felt conflicting emotions. First, I wondered why so many seemed shocked, given the many leaks over the last decade. My second sensation was a curious regret; I would rather have been mistaken about the trend toward the unilateral declassification of sensitive intelligence matters in democratic nations.

Recent events have confirmed for me the urgency of imparting a clearer understanding of intelligence to the public of this country and others. The goal of this book is to contribute to that understanding. Intelligence has gained unprecedented powers to invade the privacy of anyone, anywhere. Those powers have devolved from states to groups and even to individuals. In the process, they have become less, not more, accountable in many places. The only remedy I can foresee is to continue the decades-long project of bringing intelligence under law. If that project lapses, whether through a lack of insight or a lack of courage, then intelligence will continue to serve ideologies that view law itself as the problem, and which in effect destroy not only privacy but conscience as well.

ACKNOWLEDGMENTS

The prepublication review staffs of US Cyber Command, the National Security Agency, the Central Intelligence Agency, and the Office of the Director of National Intelligence all reviewed this work for potential security concerns. CIA's reviewers asked me to note that all statements of fact, opinion, or analysis expressed are those of the author and do not reflect the official positions or views of the CIA or any other US government agency. Nothing in the contents should be construed as asserting or implying US government authentication of information or agency endorsement of the author's views. This material has been reviewed by the CIA to prevent disclosure of classified information.

Writing a book must be the surest way of learning how little one knows of a topic. In writing this one, I found that the pieces of the story lay all about, as it were, in plain sight, though scattered and twisted and long out of order. Determining that order was something far more difficult than I had imagined it would be for someone who had been researching and teaching intelligence for almost two decades. Doing so, moreover, took a lot of help. I wish to thank those who assisted me, some of whom I cannot name. You have all contributed to this work, and its errors are mine alone. I offer special regards and thanks to Robert Betz, Philip Costopoulos, Cynthia Efird, John Ehrman, Ben Fischer, Tom Fogarty, John Fox, Michael Goodman, David Hatch, Will Keezle, Paul Maddrell, Jon Rosenwasser, Rene Stein, Mark Stout, and Tom Warner. I also express my gratitude to Don Jacobs and the staff at Georgetown University Press for turning what came to them as a roughhewn manuscript into something worthy of their exacting standards. My students at American University and Johns Hopkins University merit my praise and thanks as well, for probing and questioning my ideas; I suspect I learned more from them than they did from me. Finally, I save my warmest thanks for Dorothy, the wise and patient Mrs. Warner, and our four children. Your love and your faith make everything possible.

ABBREVIATIONS

BI	Bureau of Investigation, US, 1908–35
C3I	Command, Control, Communications, and Intelligence
C4ISR	C3I, plus Surveillance and Reconnaissance
CCP	Communist Party of China
CIA	Central Intelligence Agency, 1947–
CPSU	Communist Party of the Soviet Union
CPUSA	Communist Party of the USA
DCI	Director of Central Intelligence, US, 1946–2005
DIA	Defense Intelligence Agency, US, 1961–
DRV	Democratic Republic of Vietnam
FBI	Federal Bureau of Investigation, US, 1935–
FLN	National Liberation Front, Algeria, 1954
FMLN	Farabundo Marti National Liberation Front, El Salvador, 1980
FSLN	Sandinista National Liberation Front, Nicaragua, 1961
GC&CS	Government Code & Cypher School, UK, 1919–46
GCHQ	Government Communications Headquarters, UK, 1946–
GRU	Main Intelligence Directorate, General Staff, USSR and Russia, 1942–
HPSCI	House Permanent Select Committee on Intelligence, US, 1976–
HUMINT	human intelligence
HVA	Main Directorate for Reconnaissance, East Germany, 1952–90
IBM	International Business Machines, US (corporation)
IC	Intelligence Community, US, informally since 1952
ICBM	intercontinental ballistic missile
IDF	Israeli Defense Force, 1948
IRA	Irish Republican Army, 1922–69
ISC	Intelligence and Security Committee, UK, 1994–
ISP	internet service provider

JIC	Joint Intelligence Committee, UK, 1939–
KGB	Committee for State Security, USSR, 1954–91
MACV	Military Assistance Command, Vietnam, US, 1962–73
MfS	Ministry for State Security, East Germany, 1950–90
MGB	Ministry of State Security, USSR, 1946–53
MI5	Security Service, UK, 1909–
MI6	See SIS
MID	Military Intelligence Division (various countries)
NATO	North Atlantic Treaty Organization, 1949–
NIE	National Intelligence Estimate, US, 1950–
NKGB	People's Committee for State Security, USSR, 1941, 1943–46
NKVD	People's Commissariat for Internal Affairs, USSR, 1934–54
NRO	National Reconnaissance Office, US, 1961–
NSA	National Security Agency, US, 1952–
NSC	National Security Council, US, 1947–
OPC	Office of Policy Coordination, US, 1948–52
OSS	Office of Strategic Services, US, 1942–45
PAVN	People's Army of Vietnam, DRV, 1944–
PFLP	Popular Front for the Liberation of Palestine, 1967–
PIRA	Provisional IRA, 1969–2005
PLO	Palestine Liberation Organization, 1965–
RAF	Royal Air Force, UK, 1918–
RAT	Remote Access Trojan
RFE	Radio Free Europe, US, 1950–
RHSA	Reich Main Security Office, Germany, 1939–45
RU	Intelligence Directorate, General Staff, Russia and USSR, 1918–42
SAM	surface-to-air missile
SD	Secret Service, Germany, 1932–45
SIGINT	Signals intelligence
SIS	Secret Intelligence Service, UK, 1909–
SOE	Special Operations Executive, 1940–46
SS	"Protection Squadron" (Nazi Party), Germany 1925–45
SSCI	Senate Select Committee on Intelligence, US, 1976–
SVR	Foreign Intelligence Service, Russia, 1991–
TSP	Terrorist Surveillance Program, US, 2001–7
UN	United Nations, 1945–

UNITA	National Union for the Total Liberation of Angola, 1966–
USSR	Union of Soviet Socialist Republics, 1922–91
WMD	weapons of mass destruction

TIMELINE

1881	Czar Alexander II assassinated—founding of the Okhrana
1901	Marconi makes radio commercially viable
1909	Secret Service Bureau founded in Britain; soon becomes SIS and MI5
1914–18	World War I
1917	Russian Revolution, followed soon after by the founding of the Cheka
1926	Machine encryption: Germany's military adopts the Enigma machine
1933	Hitler takes power in Germany
1936–39	Spanish Civil War
1939–45	World War II
1947	National Security Act reforms US intelligence
1949	Mao and his Communists win China's civil war
1950–53	Korean War
1954	France leaves Indochina; Algerian revolt gathers steam
1960	First intelligence satellites launched by the United States
1962	Cuban Missile Crisis
1964–72	Heavy US military involvement in Indochina
1969	"Urban guerrillas"; violent radicalism gains momentum
1975	Church and Pike Committees investigate US intelligence
1979	Revolutions in Iran and Afghanistan; Sandinistas take power in Nicaragua
1981	The IBM PC transforms the market for personal computing

1983	President Reagan announces the US will develop advanced ballistic missile defenses
1985	Gorbachev takes power in the USSR
1989	Democratic revolutions in Eastern Europe
1991	Coalition forces liberate Kuwait from Iraqi rule; USSR dissolved after a failed coup against Gorbachev
2001	9/11; al-Qaeda attacks in America, followed by a coalition invasion of Afghanistan
2004	Intelligence scandals and reform in the United States; investigators conclude Iraq had no weapons of mass destruction; credible allegations of the torture of prisoners
2006	Western leaders publicly accuse China of condoning widespread hacking
2011	US military and intelligence operation finds and kills Osama bin Laden

Introduction

Secrecy has this disadvantage: we lose the sense of proportion; we cannot tell whether our secret is important or not.

— E. M. Forster, *A Room with a View*

This book shows how the world changed intelligence and how intelligence changed the world. A century ago, almost any state, large or small, could be competitive at espionage. Fifty years ago only the Cold War alliances clustered around the two superpowers could run credible intelligence activities to understand and influence events outside their own borders—and sometimes not even there. Today, however, many states can do so once again; and what is more, private entities and even individuals (some with criminal motivations) can gather secrets and manipulate events around the globe. Indeed, many of these new intelligence actors feel they have a need to do so, lest worse be done to them than they do unto others. The skills needed to "do" intelligence have diffused around the world and across societies; they can literally be purchased online. The problems caused by this spread of intelligence, moreover, now reach beyond the security services to corporate offices and private homes. In short, intelligence has traded uniqueness for ubiquity. How and why that evolution happened is our story.

From Espionage to Intelligence

Spying might be as old as history, but what we call intelligence is much newer. Only in the last century has the grim imperative of espionage—long regarded in many lands as a loathsome necessity—been revamped as the profession of intelligence and a suitable concentration for government agencies and college classes. That conceptual shift happened for a series of reasons. Before we tell this tale, however, we must define intelligence and its scope.

Intelligence in its essence pertains to the ways in which sovereign powers create, exploit, and protect secret advantages against other sovereignties. A sovereignty, of course, need not be a modern state; it might be a warrior tribe on the steppe, a Greek *polis*, or a colonizing empire in South America—whether run by Incas or conquistadors. Sovereignties thus comprise people who have the will and the means to use force to control territory, resources, and other people. In our day, most sovereignties are indeed states, but today, as in ages past, various "nonstate actors" aspire to sovereignty and have the will and the means to fight insurgencies or to mount terrorist attacks to drive out an occupying army or an entrenched regime.

By definition, all of these sovereign actors seek to reduce risks, to mitigate threats, and to create and use opportunities to win and preserve what they see as their interests. They also seek to influence other actors. Until recently, there was no binding international law (or, needless to say, no world police to enforce it) that might protect them against their opponents, and thus their safety lay in the strength they could muster and the friends they might recruit. Sovereignties thus operate in something that can only inadequately be described as a competitive environment; the Enlightenment concept of the "state of nature" seems more apt. They are locked in a struggle in which the rules are unsettled and in which the stakes can be life and death. Historically, sovereignties that failed to defend themselves or find strong patrons were destroyed, with their rulers ousted and even killed.

No one should be surprised if sovereignties sometimes use secret as well as open means to protect themselves. Where sovereigns can do their business aboveboard and face-to-face, most indeed do so, because it is cheaper, faster, more reliable, and entails less risk of embarrassing them. Where those conditions do not apply, however, and the stakes are life and death, sovereigns resort to secret means. Opening a courier's dispatches can aid one's diplomacy; a few gold bars can deprive an enemy of his ally; and a spy can spot conspirators plotting against the prince. These measures are cheaper and safer than mobilizing the army and sending it into the field to fight, or allowing plots against the palace to ripen. Though hardly risk free, they are far less risky than the alternatives. They might not work, but they might gain time to devise something that does.

Such means that sovereign actors employ in protecting themselves and their interests might well entail espionage—properly understood as spying, or the clandestine collection of other people's secrets. Intelligence and espionage are not exactly the same thing. But intelligence as it came to be seen in the twentieth century meant something far more than eavesdropping at keyholes or steaming open envelopes. Indeed, intelligence took on a multiplicity of meanings, some of them only barely overlapping. It remained a synonym for espionage, of course, but it also came to mean any sort of information that decision makers might need to select a course of action. It also came to mean the overall system that manages the state's espionage (and counterespionage) function, its collection of secrets and nonsecrets for ministers and commanders, its interaction with friendly intelligence services, and the work product of these functions. In short, those secret activities had become systematized as intelligence, in both a professional and an institutional sense, and they worked collectively—if not always consciously—for strategic effect.

Telling the story of intelligence feels odd because it is a story that desperately did not want to be told. Over the last century, thousands of people have worked to ensure that secret operations and findings would stay secret. Nonetheless, our understanding of the patterns of secret practices has grown dramatically in recent years. Ancient authors like Sunzi in China and Kautilya in India succinctly described the business of espionage in their times, doing it so well that we recognize what they depicted even now—but they had few if any reliable facts to offer their readers. Only in the last half century have leaders and scholars begun to be able to study intelligence services and operations, still less to compare them across nations and time periods. In recent years, intelligence agencies, more or less voluntarily, have begun releasing secrets and even files. Though such projects remain incomplete to say the least, what we have learned from these revelations resembles the partial excavation of an old but still-inhabited city. We can see enough to map its earlier landscape and explain how people lived there long ago. Its living portions can be explored only with sufferance and care, of course, but an overall picture of the life of the place has emerged, even if many events and details may always remain hazy. That in turn has helped to transform intelligence from a hobby of kings and commanders into not only a staple of popular culture but also a proper subject of academic discourse. It has also begun to make it somewhat less bloody, less scandalous, and more accountable. That in itself makes a tale worth telling, and is a significant part of the story that follows.

Indeed, the releases and the work devoted to interpreting that newly available evidence now present us with an opportunity to understand intelligence as a whole—in its origins, its workings, and its effects. Political scientists and historians have debated the meaning and bounds of intelligence, adding a measure of theoretical rigor to studies of the topic. This is not a book of theory except in the applied sense of the term, but it helps to understand what it is that serious and objective observers have devised to apply to intelligence activities across countries, cultures, and time periods. What remains the same when so many other things change, it might well be argued, is the essence of intelligence. Various scholars have engaged this author over the last decade in a collaborative project to explore the nature of secret activities. There seems to be a rough consensus that intelligence activities should be examined not only as sets of organizations and processes, but also as the interactions between decision makers and subordinates and adversaries. Intelligence can be studied much as astronomers view the solar system—as a set of entities in motion that constantly influence one another.

Those entities, moreover, are devised and conducted by intentional actors—that is, by people, with all their foibles, predilections, and genius. Thus intelligence should be viewed as a "reflexive" activity, one involving complex, disproportionate, and inherently unpredictable interactions and outcomes. Intelligence operatives and agencies are under scrutiny by competitors and they always interact with other operatives and agencies (and with the world around them). The people involved in intelligence and the regimes that employ them might be quite professional but still they possess tendencies to biases, habits, and nonlinear reactions to events.[1]

This is not to say all is chaos. Intelligence is a way for sovereign powers to use secret means to protect their own and further their interests—it is a quintessentially Realist enterprise. By it, sovereigns transfer risk and uncertainty to people who do not suspect they have been deceived, tricked, or lightened of their plans. Intelligence is a way of mitigating potential disasters, and, perhaps, of guiding the future. The imperative to employ secret means for such purposes seems universal, as we find it in cultures as far from one another as ancient Greece and China, and as far removed in time from each other as they are from us.

The ways in which sovereignties organize their secret functions, moreover, appear to follow certain patterns. Knowledge of the factors behind these patterns gives us a basis for defining and comparing intelligence systems, both across countries and over time. Of these factors, the ruler's strategic objective ranks first in importance. Is he friendly or hostile, defensive or aggressive, toward his strategic rivals? The goals he wants to achieve dictate the sorts of tasks he assigns to his secret agents: whether to fend off an expansionist neighbor, to prey on a weak one, or merely to watch for potential threats at home and abroad. Such motives are timeless, of course, but the sorts of rulers who hold them, and the technology they can employ (or might have used against them), changed greatly with the rise of modernity. The term "modern" means different things to various observers, but there can be no disputing the global importance of the changes in European thought and life going back to the fifteenth century. Mobile artillery and moveable type for printing presses, along with a host of inventions in agriculture, navigation, and manufacturing, suddenly made European arms and products superior at the same time that European religious and intellectual ferment changed governments and cultures. These changes in technology and ideology would revolutionize espionage and ultimately transform it into intelligence. Thus we see three factors—strategy, technology, and regime type—as determining the types of intelligence systems that sovereignties build for themselves.

Why Study Intelligence?

In January 1943, soon after Allied fortunes in World War II had turned decisively for the better, President Franklin Roosevelt stood before Congress to deliver his annual State of the Union address. The tide of war over the previous year had threatened to swamp the Allies, with the conquests of Nazi Germany and Imperial Japan reaching their greatest extent. But in Russia, in North Africa, and in the Pacific, the Allies had contained the Axis drives and counterattacked. Thus, the president urged his listeners to "exercise a sense of proportion" in considering the events of the year past and the seeming chaos in Washington as the government mobilized itself for the conflict. Members of Congress should realize this one great thing: "The Axis powers knew that they must win the war in 1942—or eventually lose everything. I do not need to tell you that our enemies did not win the war in 1942." Surveying the ongoing campaigns of this most gigantic war in history, Roosevelt turned to the struggle against Japan: "In the Pacific area, our most important victory in 1942 was the air and naval battle off

Midway Island. That action is historically important because it secured for our use communication lines stretching thousands of miles in every direction."[2] Midway proved every bit as important as Roosevelt hinted, but he did not divulge how that battle came about. He merely tipped his rhetorical hat "to all the loyal, anonymous, untiring men and women who have worked in private employment and in Government" to foster the progress of the last year. He was indeed wise not to add that the battle, which involved dozens of capital ships, hundreds of aircraft, and thousands of men, would not have been fought in the way it was, and might not have been won at all, but for the efforts of a handful of US Navy codebreakers in a basement office at Pearl Harbor known to its denizens as Station Hypo. The new business of intelligence, which had scarcely existed when Roosevelt himself had been a young man, had helped in a small but vital way to change the course of history.

Intelligence is not an end in itself. It supplements other measures, seeks to fill in their gaps and extend their reach. Its reliance on means that are both vulnerable to an enemy's countermeasures and likely to provoke a response bespeaks a calculated desperation to find some effective source or method to influence events when other means do not quite work. But granting that its effects are often marginal, they are also real, as Franklin Roosevelt could testify. Whole branches of economics and engineering rest on the study of marginal effects, and economists and engineers know quite well how seemingly trivial things can matter a great deal. The marginal but real effects of intelligence merit our attention; indeed, their very secrecy creates an imperative to study them, not only to spot their impact, but also to guard against the opposite error of attributing too much influence to them.

Understanding such effects affords us a new and slightly disorienting view of a familiar historical landscape. If history is philosophy teaching by example, to paraphrase Thucydides, then such an understanding is sorely needed because there exist few things as well known and as misunderstood as intelligence. Obviously there is overlap—a gray area—between the overt policies that intelligence supports and the covert or clandestine means it employs. It is not always easy to distinguish "quiet diplomacy" on one hand from "covert action" on the other. Or to tell a spy from a military attaché on vacation. Such overlaps make it easier to understand why, as hinted above, smart and well-meaning people differ over the very definition of intelligence. That is why we must study intelligence with greater insight and greater attention to the facts of the historical record—the only source of data points we have for stepping beyond theory or speculation (take your pick) and learning the truth about how intelligence has developed.

This book seeks to tell this story from a worldwide perspective using original documents where possible (and elsewhere via reliable secondary works based on primary sources). It takes something of a stratospheric view in order to glimpse the larger decades-long patterns that can get overlooked in studies of a particular leader, operation, or conflict. At the same time, it seeks to remain scrupulously faithful to such details, striving wherever possible to allow inductive conclusions drawn from the facts to correct and guide its generalizations. It does not speculate on what might remain in the vaults, but tries to work from the sources already available so that other researchers can verify its findings. I contend that intelligence now has plenty of detail-rich history—even though not enough of that was based on original sources and written with a consistent commitment to objectivity. What the study of intelligence has lacked is the sort of synthesizing larger perspective that does not explain away the details but rather seeks to show them in a new relief and a different proximity to one another. Think of the effects of infrared light on mineral specimens—it does not show new rocks but it reveals more than previously known about familiar ones.

This account perforce has to be a British, and an American, and a Russian (and Soviet) story. That is so for two reasons. First, these three nations have so far yielded up the bulk of reliable documentation on intelligence currently available to scholars. The second reason is that these three nations have produced more than their share of intelligence developments over the last century. Others contributed significantly: France, Germany, China, and Israel, and of course the Commonwealth partners in the Anglo-American intelligence alliance. All appear in the pages ahead. It may well be that the century to come will see these or other states in the lead of intelligence evolution. Be that as it may, there is no denying that intelligence developments over the last century more often than not followed events and innovations in Britain, Russia, and the United States.

This is not a history of the last century, though intelligence is tightly wound with the central developments of the twentieth and (so far) the twenty-first centuries. The pages to come narrate many of those events. Our account, moreover, views that history from the inside out, as if from behind a cracked lens that shows some incidents in distortion and others with a startling clarity. Conspiracy mongers tend to like conspiracies that cannot be disproved, that is, plots that remain undiscovered because the plotters are just so secretive that they leave no trace. This book describes real conspiracies in the very words of the conspirators where possible. So much intelligence history has been released in recent years that a field once notable for its dearth of sources now is moving toward plenitude. This book is partly a way of making sense of the new information, and also partly a guide to the mysteries that remain to be solved by declassifications yet to come.

How to Read This Book

A number of factors combined, beginning in the late 1800s, to transform spying into intelligence. Recent technological progress is shifting the world toward a situation in which "state-like" intelligence methods are increasingly accessible (and needed) by groups and even individuals. Intelligence thus emerged from an obscure appendage of statecraft and war into something with a widespread if often marginal influence on world affairs, and then saw its uniqueness blur as states lost their monopoly of intelligence skills and capabilities.

Explaining how this happened is tantamount to sketching a roadmap to the book. The explosive progress of technology during the Industrial Revolution made the craft of war and spying into an industry, while also fomenting ample discontent and motivations for ideological violence against the leaders and then the "ruling classes" of the industrializing world. In response, the means of collecting and compiling secrets and the organizations for doing so grew rapidly in scope and sophistication so that soon only the great powers could operate them. World War II further raised the "barriers to entry" in the intelligence field; after 1945, only the superpowers and their closest allies could afford the best intelligence. These superpowers split the wartime Grand Alliance along ideological lines during the Cold War, and that long struggle saw both further refinements of the means of intelligence and their diffusion in the developing world, as each camp sought allies in the newly independent colonies. In the end, the Soviet side of the Cold War could not keep up, either in developing new technology or in frustrating the technologically enabled intelligence of the West. Western dominance of intelligence, however, would prove fleeting. The same technology that gave the liberal democracies clear economic and intelligence advantages over the progressive camp spread globally in the 1990s, making far more states and even well-armed extremist groups competitive in intelligence—and placing potentially anyone under surveillance—by the first decade of the twenty-first century.

Someone born before 1970 probably holds a clear, adult memory of privacy as a fact of daily life. Unless you lived behind the Iron Curtain or became a celebrity, you could expect to live without people watching your every action. That is no longer the case. Few of us are actually observed, of course, but almost all of us can be, at almost any time and in more ways than ever before. We are learning to live as if constantly under observation. Those who might be observing us can range from states to multinational corporations to petty criminals, with all sorts of actors of more or less malevolence in between. At the same time, groups and organizations well outside of intelligence organizations and even states now have to adapt to the torrent of data—both sensitive and "open source"— that they collect and that sometimes comes to them unbidden. New laws and oversight mechanisms have already arisen in many lands to keep these activities within ethical bounds, but of course, many of the people now exploiting intelligence methods to invade the privacy of others are also people with little oversight and fewer scruples.

This is vital to understand because intelligence is a business that should not be glorified. It carries physical and moral costs, even when performed in a just cause. Even as necessary wars are themselves bloody and brutish when seen up close, spying is often a bad thing in and of itself, and only defensible in light of the alternatives. Is it also necessary? Plenty of statesmen who are now lauded as national heroes and renowned figures have thought so. As Sunzi argued over two thousand years ago, he who blinks not at disrupting his whole state to fight a war but is too fastidious to pay spies when he needs them is neither prudent nor humane. It does indeed seem odd that we might have few qualms about spearing an enemy soldier, or dropping a bomb on him, but would blanch at noting his chatter about his unit's destination. One conclusion fairly leaps from even a casual reading of history: intelligence will continue to be employed by people who have no scruples about using it to harm others. States that neglect to understand it—if only to thwart it—do so at their peril.

The way in which the world has been transformed to place us all at least potentially under intelligence-like surveillance makes an important tale, for it is the history of our age, told from the inside out. It began in the mists of time but gathered its fateful momentum almost within living memory. This tale is still being composed, moreover, and the greater consciousness we have of its plot so far might enable some leaders and citizens to change its narrative. Read this book, then, with a sense of proportion and a concern for avoiding mistakes of the past as well as for honoring the occasional genius and plentiful sacrifices of our forebears. Read it most of all with an eye toward building a world in which intelligence is less often needed.

NOTES

1. Michael Warner, "Intelligence and Reflexivity: An Invitation to a Dialogue," *Intelligence and National Security*, 27:2 (April 2012): 167–71.
2. Franklin D. Roosevelt, State of the Union Address to Congress, January 7, 1943.

CHAPTER 1

From Ancient to Modern

For where the lion's skin will not reach, you must patch it out with the fox's.

"Lysander," in Plutarch's *Lives*

Spying dates to the dawn of civilization, but in the past two centuries it has taken on a new character. In short, it has been professionalized. That evolution began in Europe in the last half of the nineteenth century, and the factors that drove it were overwhelmingly technological and ideological. Along the way, the unchivalrous arts of espionage and letter opening began to be seen in a different light in the West. In Christian civilization they were long considered loathsome—a necessary evil justified only by the exigencies of wartime. The lion, not the fox, was the model for the ideal commander. Even some non-Western authors who advocated the use and generous payment of spies rationalized their employment as being preferable to defeat and death in war. These attitudes began shifting with the wars of religion and the Industrial Revolution. Confronted with steam-driven enemies armed with undreamed-of destructive power—and by radicals who wanted to overturn the capitalist order—the Western states tried desperately to adapt and to find methods of fending off internal enemies, and each other. Espionage became intelligence, and this would change the course of history.

Initial Reflections

Before there was history there were spies. Ruins of the Sumerian city of Uruk have yielded the earliest-known examples of writing; they also offered up hollow balls of baked clay, made to hold marked tokens in tamper-proof containers. These *bulla* from before 3,200 BCE are even older than the city's cuneiform tablets and monumental inscriptions, and they suggest that techniques to protect valuable information from prying eyes actually predated

11

attributes of civilization like writing and mathematics.[1] The walls around Uruk also showed that rulers were already organizing warriors and learning how to fight en masse.

Spies appeared all across the ancient world. Writings from cultures as distant as Rome and China record the deeds of spies and their fates. Espionage even factors in the Old Testament; the patriarch Joseph tested his unwitting brothers by accusing them of having come to spy out the weakness of Egypt. In two instances recounted in the book of Numbers, Moses sent his own spies to scout the land of Canaan. By the time the conqueror from the West (Alexander) met the future conqueror from the East (Chandragupta) near the Indus River, sages in the lands that would become China and India were beginning to reflect on what it was that spies did and how they could be employed more effectively. Some basic understanding of the craft and significance of espionage has continued ever since. That is where we must begin.

Over two thousand years ago, an Indian who styled himself Kautilya penned perhaps the most detailed of the ancient reflections on spying. We do not know the man's real name but Kautilya (or Chanakya) was one of Chandragupta's advisers. He was long dead before the second century BCE, when an author appropriated his illustrious name to add credibility to a tome on statecraft called the *Arthashastra*. This second Kautilya described the workings of a model principality in elaborate detail, down to the ministries and offices of the regime and the laws it should promulgate. He included in those offices a bureau for spies, for he judged them useful to the prince in all aspects of statecraft. Spies could watch the prince's ministers to see who was industrious and who was corrupt; they could listen for discontent and plots among the prince's relatives who might covet the throne; and they could eavesdrop in the marketplace for stirrings of dissent. Of course, they could also detect enemy spies and collect secrets from rival kingdoms. When necessary, they could not only listen but also act to defend the king, by stirring up dissension or whispering false counsel to his rivals, or by poisoning opponents.[2]

In China, another author had even hinted at a seemingly god-like power for spies. The figure we call Sunzi (or Sun Tzu) wrote *The Art of War* about a century before the *Arthashastra*, but like his Indian counterpart he had also employed a famous name to burnish his argument. At the time, China resembled India in having a common civilization but no common polity; squabbling principalities covered its landscape, and the more powerful and astute of them were busy consolidating their neighbors into larger kingdoms. *The Art of War* focused on the qualities and knowledge that a ruler or a general required in order to win when disputes between these principalities turned violent. The work's first sentences set the tone: "War is a matter of vital importance to the State; the province of life or death; the road to survival or ruin. It is mandatory that it be thoroughly studied."[3] That study meant achieving a complete understanding of one's enemy, oneself, and the circumstances likely to result in victory or defeat. *The Art of War*'s final chapter brought the argument to its climax: "the reason the enlightened prince and the wise general conquer the enemy whenever they move and their achievements surpass those of ordinary men is foreknowledge," which cannot be had from divination, spells, or horoscopes, but only from "men who know the enemy situation."[4]

Both Kautilya and Sunzi suggested that spies were more useful to a leader than even supernatural guides. "Delicate indeed! Truly delicate! There is no place where espionage is not used," proclaimed Sunzi.[5] After all, spies could tell the commander what transpired in the enemy's camp, could find and neutralize enemy spies, and could even whisper poor counsel or assassinate a foreign general. According to Kautilya, they could pretend to be gods, hiding inside idols to give bad advice to hostile kings.[6] Indeed, for Sunzi, the fates of dynasties and their many subjects might depend on a spy's actions: "Of old, the rise of Yin was due to I Chih, who formerly served the Hsia; the Chou came to power through Lu Yu, a servant of the Yin." In other words, spies could alter the very mandate of heaven. Thus, *The Art of War*, which opened with the assertion that war is the most dangerous and important activity a state undertakes, closed by arguing that spies are vital to success in that most important of activities: "secret operations are essential in war; upon them the army relies to make its every move."[7]

Kautilya and Sunzi independently articulated an understanding of the craft of espionage that has transcended cultures and millennia. It endured in the West as well as the East, in a remarkable symmetry of understandings among peoples who viewed the world in diverse ways. The cunning ruler or wise general might offer sacrifices to divine the will of the gods, but he relied on spies who could bring him information or even harm his enemies from a distance. Spies could do both jobs, reporting on events and affecting them by stealth. To those who regarded such work as low and dishonorable,

Sunzi had a subtle retort. War is a perilous and expensive business, he noted. A general who is too foolish to part with a little gold for accurate information "is no general; no support to his sovereign; no master of victory." Who is more humane, Sunzi implied: the ruler who puts his kingdom and subjects in harm's way without understanding the risks, or the one who does all he can to ensure he wins? Is it more honorable to triumph, or to lose and see your kingdom ransacked and your family destroyed? Fortune favors the well prepared.

The Coming of Modernity

This understanding of spies and their craft endures today among peoples who have never heard of Sunzi or Kautilya, but over the last century, it has encountered a rival notion of how leaders use secrets and those who bring them. The ancient world is long gone, and today leaders usually consult newspapers and books and databases rather than oracles and horoscopes to learn what might happen tomorrow. Principalities have given way to complex, bureaucratic governments. And the leaders of those governments oversee specialized ministries, departments, and offices to bring them information and implement their decisions to enforce laws and execute policies. Each one of those ministries and departments and offices has its own sources of data that it gathers and processes to make "actionable" information for decision makers, both at local or ministerial levels and at the national level as well.

Indeed, this devotion to the collection and processing of information for leaders to use marks one of the distinguishing characteristics of modernity itself. The ancients knew well enough how to levy taxes, but they did not amass data on people and things to anywhere near the scale that we moderns do in our governments and businesses and institutions. And they could barely dream of subjecting those data to analysis for trends and anomalies. Those data and information come from all manner of sources that require some degree of privacy to protect their accuracy and availability. Scholars today have a word for this ability and penchant for amassing information and, hence, power; they call it *surveillance*, after the French term (rather than its English cognate). It is used "not in the narrow sense of 'spying,'" explains Christopher Dandeker, but more broadly "to refer to the gathering of information about and the supervision of subject populations in organizations."[8]

Such capabilities, however, took a very long time to emerge; indeed, espionage remained largely unchanged well into the modern age. Christian Europe officially wanted little to do with the sins of lying and betrayal (Dante consigned traitors to the lowest pit of the Inferno, with three infamous exemplars—Judas, Brutus, and Cassius—there to be perpetually gnawed by the Arch-Traitor himself). Chivalry in the Middle Ages had heightened this repugnance of spies, who did not seek honor in battle against worthy opponents but skulked in the shadows to betray their betters. Gunpowder blew up mounted knights as a force on the battlefield, of course, but that did not vanquish the chivalric ideals—sometimes honored more in the breach than the observance—that innocents and prisoners were to be spared, armies to be disciplined, and spies to be hanged. And yet, the ancient arts never died out, and the religious and political conflicts of the Renaissance and Reformation cast new light on them. Niccolo Machiavelli of Florence in 1513 advised the astute among his readers that "since a prince is compelled of necessity to know well how to use the beast, he should pick the fox and the lion."[9]

Herr Gutenberg's printing press in 1437 made it possible for the secret arts to step at least partway into the light, turning a hobby into a craft that could be mastered. Methods for using and detecting secret writing had been explained since at least the fourth century BCE in Aeneas Tacticus's manual on siege craft. Around 1467, a true Renaissance man, Leon Battista Alberti, advanced the art greatly by inventing the polyalphabetic cipher and even a simple machine—a cipher disk—for manipulating it.[10] With the spread of printing, authors like Johannes Trithemius could explain in his *Polygraphia* (1518) how to hide the meaning of a text so that seemingly no one but the intended reader could divine it. Indeed, the rage for secret writing spread across Europe that same century, providing rulers and diplomats with Alberti's new ciphers, which would remain the standard mode of securing message texts through the nineteenth century. States also dabbled in cipher breaking, creating offices like Giovanni Soro's in Venice (1506) to read other states' mail. The Florentine diplomat and *consigliere* Francesco Guicciardini advised anyone carrying on a state intrigue to above all things "[Be] careful not to communicate by letters; for these are often intercepted, and furnish proof which cannot be controverted. And though nowadays there be many cautious methods of writing, there have also been discovered many aids for their interpretation."[11]

Prying eyes seemed everywhere. The death of Queen Elizabeth's spymaster Francis Walsingham in 1590 drew a contented sigh from the world's most powerful man, Philip II of Spain. When an informant in London reported that "Secretary Walsingham has just died, which has caused great sadness here," Philip made a note on the report's margin: "There of course," he wrote, "but here, we are very relieved."[12] A new word, "intelligence," found its way into English. Shakespeare used it in several plays; in *King John*, for instance, where the king starts at news of a French invasion: "Where hath our intelligence been drunk?," he rages. "Where hath it slept?" For armies, the business of espionage continued looking much as it had in Sunzi's time; indeed, Renaissance writings unwittingly echoed *The Art of War*. "The army that enters enemy territory must use spies and discoverers who will give news of its intentions," explained the Spanish jurist Jeronimo de Cevallos in 1623. Englishman Edward Cooke wrote in that same decade: "Provide you good espials, which espials are so necessary in the wars as anything else, for by them you shall understand how your enemie will fight." The English provided themselves with a Decyphering Branch a generation later. Such examples show that secret practices were common, but with little or no effort to systematize their work or institutionalize their functions beyond the personal magnetism of their chiefs. Spymasters came and went, as did their offices. In short, espionage and cipher breaking remained amateur, ad hoc, and unaccountable.

New Worlds

"Thus in the beginning all the world was America," wrote English philosopher John Locke in 1690.[13] The dynastic and religious conflicts of the Renaissance and Reformation convinced some of the best minds in Europe that law had to have a firmer foundation than the arbitrary will of the prince, and the new world across the Atlantic prompted reflection on man in his essence, in what was styled "the state of nature." Two men who thought deeply about such matters have a special claim on our attention. The first, John Locke, bade readers consider the ends of society to understand its means and its institutions—and to do so by conceiving of man's situation before civilization, in places like pre-Columbian America. Even without governments, people can organize spontaneously, Locke believed, creating order out of their exchange of goods, and doing so even faster when they consent to use something as money. The resulting commerce can lift them from penury as if, as Adam Smith later suggested, an Invisible Hand had molded the common good from the self-interest of many individuals.[14] People institute government to protect their property (expansively defined as their lives, liberty, and estates), and they consent to its rule so long as that government functions by law—through "settled standing rules, indifferent and the same to all parties." When government abandons law and fails to respect property, however, it becomes tyranny.[15] Locke's American followers a century later devised a mechanism for preventing such arbitrary governance; "ambition must be made to counteract ambition," wrote James Madison in *Federalist* 51.

Locke's ideas helped drive the Industrial Revolution in Britain, as well as political revolutions in America and then France. Locke did not, of course, get the last word on man and nature. "Man is born free, but he is everywhere in chains," wrote a citizen of Geneva named Jean-Jacques Rousseau in 1762.[16] Man once lived in blissful ignorance, at least until the invention of property: "The first man who, having enclosed a piece of land, thought of saying "This is Mine" and found people simple enough to believe him, was the true founder of civil society."[17] Society was *not* the solution, Rousseau had argued in 1755. Society itself was the problem.[18] It was an imposture to protect the interests of the powerful, and ideas like those of Locke only justified the resulting exploitation: "What is one to think of a system in which the reason of each private person dictates to him maxims contrary to the maxims of which the public reason preaches to the body of society, a system in which each finds his profit in the misfortunes of others?"[19] Such illusory freedoms only stir dissension and "mutual hatred in different social orders through conflict between their rights and their interests, and by these means strengthen the power that subdues them all."[20] True freedom lay not in special interests but in the General Will, the people's ultimate expression and the sole reliable guard of their interest. Only a democracy founded on it, changing constantly as needed to meet new circumstances, can legitimately claim the citizens' allegiance.[21] The citizen should thus surrender all rights and property to that General Will, for only thus would each citizen receive those rights back again with the powerful protection of the whole society: "Each of us puts his person and all his power in common under the supreme direction of the general will; and in a body we receive each member as an indivisible part of the whole."[22] In all, Rousseau captured the spirit of a new age that was dawning, one in which tyranny over societies and minds could finally be cast aside. "Man will never be free," declared Rousseau's friend and rival Denis Diderot, "until the last king is strangled with the entrails of the last priest."

Locke and Rousseau and their followers had fomented an argument over human freedom that continues to this day. Is man naturally brutish, and only civilized by society; or is he fundamentally good, but debased by property and its attendant vice? Is the answer to the universal scourges of oppression and want the enactment of good laws, or is it the overthrow of legalistic forms and rule by the people themselves? Both Locke's and Rousseau's ideas found expression in the French Revolution. Locke's ideas would spread faster and farther in the nineteenth century, which witnessed the flowering of the ideal of liberalism, defined in the continental sense as a society self-organizing toward a collective order very different from traditional norms. Such was the ideological underpinning of the capitalism that gave the world the Industrial Revolution and more wealth than humanity had ever seen. Liberalism was never completely or purely practiced, of course, but it prevailed more consistently in Western Europe and the Anglo-Saxon world, and it reached enough people in Europe to exert a powerful influence on the continent's periphery, particularly the Ottoman Empire and Czarist Russia, which had to scramble to keep up with Western Europe's ferment of scientific and political ideas. That liberalism also created the temporary advantages of wealth and technology that allowed the spread of mercantilist and capitalist states across the world—into territories with no traditions of city dwelling and book learning, like central Africa and the hinterlands of the Americas—and even to the ancient cultures of India, China, and the Islamic lands. Indeed, liberalism proved arguably more destabilizing than steel or steam when it reached traditional societies.

Rousseau's response to liberalism took longer to spread in the West and longer to reach the non-Western lands. It traveled in the ideas of his philosophical heirs—men such as Comte, Proudhon, and Marx. These Enlightenment ideas, of course, never fully established themselves anywhere, and they are still working themselves out today in mutual contention. Their indirect effects on espionage, however, would be profound. They would change the ways in which rulers spied on one another, whom they spied on, and the ends for which they did so. Combined with the results of the Industrial Revolution, these ideas would lead to the creation of intelligence as it has been understood in our day—as a systematized and state-based way of organizing secret activities. Sunzi might have recognized the sorts of espionage practiced in the Enlightenment when Locke and Rousseau penned their thoughts, but he would not recognize what had become of espionage by the second decade of the twentieth century.

The Industrialization of War

Liberal ideals spread rapidly around the Earth because they rode in railroad cars or steamships, and pulsed over telegraph wires. After about 1800, the world witnessed an astounding technological upheaval and a military revolution to accompany it. At the dawn of this era, during the Napoleonic wars, changes that most immediately and directly affected the business of espionage began with the military staff work that assisted generals in commanding the huge patriotic armies of France (the *levée en masse*) and the masses that France's enemies mobilized in response. Such forces required specialized staffs to plan and prepare commanders to make decisions—and then to ensure those decisions were properly implemented. These staffs consumed information voraciously, and they initiated a rationalization of warfare that continues today.

Carl von Clausewitz, a Prussian general who spent much of his life fighting the armies of the French Revolution and Napoleon, became one of the most prominent intellectual guides for this military revolution. In his later years he pondered what made for victory and defeat for all generals, leaving a manuscript that his widow published soon after his death as *On War* (1832). Clausewitz regarded information as vital but saw it as inherently suspect and thus only one factor to be considered by a battlefield commander who had to be a wise and imperturbable rock against the shifting emotions and alarms of all campaigns and battles: "Many intelligence reports in war are contradictory; even more are false, and most are uncertain. What one can reasonably ask of an officer is that he should possess a standard of judgment, which he can gain only from knowledge of men and affairs and from common sense. He should be guided by the laws of probability. *On War* nonetheless implicitly raised the expectation for military intelligence by defining it as "every sort of information about the enemy and his country—the basis, in short, of our own plans and operations."[23] If steady generals were rare in any army, however, Clausewitz thus hinted that another answer to the problem of fashioning such leaders was to improve the information that reached them, thus reducing the uncertainties of command.

The Prussian army was first to apply the new rationality to war and did so most thoroughly; and as a result they beat the Austrians in 1866—and the French in 1870—with stunning efficiency and dispatch. "Prussian" methods thereafter became the rage in Western armies for two generations to come. Most armies (although not France's) faddishly adapted some variant of the Prussian *pickelhaube* (the famous spiked helmet), but trained eyes would also notice new features in the armies' organizational design and ethos. The Prussians were famous for their diligent preparation and meticulous attention to the details of modern war, all of which came under the all-knowing General Staff, but what impressed keen observers were changes in the weaponry that the major powers introduced to match or surpass each other's fighting prowess. Smooth-bore muskets had already given way to rifles; that invention was followed in short order by breach-loading rifles and field guns, smokeless powder, machine guns, and then, just before World War I, by airplanes and self-propelled transport. Journalists and army officers surely wearied of chronicling all the innovations, sorting the dead ends from the breakthroughs, and forecasting what they meant for the next conflict. Someone had to take notes, however, and this chore fell to the new army intelligence bureaus created for the purpose from the 1860s on. Armies planning to fight on foreign soil, moreover, needed maps of where they might have to march, and those maps had to be kept current as new roads, rail lines, and industries reshaped the landscape. It was no accident that the first military information bureaus were usually in charge of map-making offices as well, or were at least quartered near the cartographers.

The armies of revolutionary France had also found a new way of scouting; they lofted observers in tethered balloons as early as 1794 to observe the positions of their Austrian enemies (and doubtless proved for Austrian recruits that the revolution was indeed diabolical in its origins). Decades later, Union troops used balloons to monitor the Confederates early in the American Civil War, and the major European armies occasionally employed them as well. The use of balloons to watch an opposing army is more reconnaissance than espionage, of course; there is nothing stealthy about a huge, silk bubble floating above a battlefield on a sunny day. Enemies could shoot at it (usually with no effect), or hide from its gaze under the trees. The latter response indeed frustrated the observations of the young Union cavalry officer and reluctant aeronaut, George Armstrong Custer, in 1862. Summer came early during the Peninsula Campaign in Tidewater, Virginia, and Confederate soldiers wisely spent their waking hours in the shade, giving Captain Custer, in his balloon, few glimpses of their positions. What Custer did, in turn, crossed over an invisible line distinguishing reconnaissance from something new. He had his balloon lofted before dawn, and beheld thousands of cooking fires glimmering, creating a perfect map of the Confederate army.[24] Union generals wasted this insight from advanced overhead collection, however, and Custer soon found himself other pursuits.

A similar demand for information developed almost overnight in the rapidly modernizing navies of the great powers. With the race for naval supremacy caused by steam and steel ships, a surprise innovation could deliver victory or defeat. Just such a thing happened in the Civil War with the debut of the CSS *Virginia* in 1862. Essentially a self-propelled and ironclad battery built atop a captured wooden hull, the *Virginia* was invulnerable to cannonballs and dispatched two of the United States' best warships in a single afternoon. Had she not met her match the following day in the form of a more advanced ironclad—the USS *Monitor*—*Virginia* might have chased the US Navy from Tidewater. The inconclusive duel between these two armored monsters put the world on notice. Every navy with modern aspirations now had to watch the shipyards of neighbors and rivals. Ever bigger iron- and steel-hulled ships with longer-ranged guns could potentially sweep the seas of all opponents and impose crushing blockades on foes; a navy that found the best design first could enjoy naval supremacy for years while rivals scrambled to copy its ships.

Naval thinkers in France would hit on a different understanding of technology and strategic vulnerability. They could not match Britain in building the new battleships, but they had cheaper means of making the English pay if war came again. By the 1890s, French armored cruisers, and soon even submarines with self-propelled torpedoes, could dodge the Royal Navy and prey on British shipping, driving up maritime insurance rates and effectively cutting overseas trade. The United Kingdom in the course of industrializing had rearranged its economy; the British Isles were no longer self-sufficient in foodstuffs, and indeed imported many of the raw materials used in their factories and workshops. British leaders and naval strategists took note and began pondering just how vulnerable they might really be to the new French naval strategy.[25]

While Clausewitz and contemporary military theorists gave a general idea of the types of information needed by commanders and of how to attain it, later authors would fill in the details. In 1895, a British colonel, George Furse, pursued just that goal in publishing his *Information in War*. Furse's generation was perhaps the last to cherish the traditional distaste for the very business of spying. Indeed, he readily conceded the conventional wisdom: "The very term spy conveys to our mind something dishonourable and disloyal. A spy, in the general acceptation of the term, is a low sneak who, from unworthy motives, dodges the actions of his fellow beings, to turn the knowledge he acquires to his personal account." Nevertheless, Furse argued for the necessity of espionage and the obligations it entailed:

> In war spies are indispensable auxiliaries; and, when we are precluded from obtaining information by any other means, we must discard all question of morality. We must overcome our feelings of repugnance for such an unchivalrous measure, because it is imposed on us by sheer necessity. Necessity knows no laws, and means which we would disdain to use in ordinary life must be employed in the field, simply because we have no other that we can turn to profitable account. Information has been sought through spies in all wars, and we can plead in our favour that the enemy will not scruple to employ them in his behalf.[26]

Though Furse almost certainly never read Sunzi (whose work would not appear in English until 1910), his case could have been excerpted from *The Art of War*.

The world when Furse wrote was dominated, for the only time in history, by European empires. Russia's sway reached from Poland to the Bering Sea; from the Arctic to Persia. France held possessions on almost every continent. Germany was in Africa and the Pacific. Spain and Portugal and the Ottoman Turks clung to remnants; even Italy and little Belgium owned large African territories. Austria-Hungary had no overseas empire but by any definition its dominions on the continent were vast. The United States and Japan had not yet set out abroad in search of new lands to rule, but they soon would. And then there was Britain, controlling the British Isles, India, Canada, Australia, New Zealand, vast tracts of Africa, and too many other places to list. Her Royal Navy was seemingly everywhere in an era when the sun literally never set on the Union Jack.

The military methods invented in Europe gave its Westernized forces advantages over local rulers everywhere—advantages that translated directly into diplomatic and mercantile power. The ageless civilizations of India and China were soon eclipsed by Western ideas and technology; European, American, and then Japanese gunboats patrolled the Yangtze, while no Chinese gunboats reached the Thames. Latin America was a collection of fiefdoms, diplomatically shielded from recolonization by the Monroe Doctrine and practically kept independent by the Royal Navy. Africa was tribal and animist—many parts had been raided by slavers for centuries, but other parts had never seen a European or American face. All these peoples had warriors and martial traditions but they lacked the amazing weapons of the West. The Vietnamese battled the French with wooden cannons in 1862. The Japanese confronted Commodore Perry's men with arquebuses in 1854, and quickly copied Western arms and methods—and turned them on their neighbors. Indeed, the Chinese Army equipped some soldiers with repeating crossbows to fight the rapidly modernizing Japanese in 1894. Everywhere, Western arms and trade proved all but invincible, as the Westerners could control and concentrate force when they needed it to break local resistance. A small Anglo-Egyptian army wielding rifled cannons and Maxim machine guns destroyed a much larger force of Sudanese at Omdurman in 1898, mowing down waves of charging Muslim holy warriors with minimal loss to itself. If liberal ideals of property rights, trade, and the rule of law had gained wide influence in the West, the prosperity they helped to create ensured that the introduction to such ideas in the rest of the world was often announced by cannon fire. After Omdurman, the English writer Hilaire Belloc penned some famous lines to clarify the situation: "Whatever happens we have got / The Maxim Gun, and they have not."[27]

Say It with Dynamite

Liberal ideals were not always followed at home either. Liberalism and the Industrial Revolution brought unimagined economic progress but also uprooted millions of humble people. The Industrial Revolution's mantra of self-help and self-generating order seemed to militate against collective welfare, while its free-market emphasis stymied even good regulations—and that fit nicely with fatter profits for monopolists who could influence regulators to suit their interests. Once in power, moreover, the new capitalist elites found new sources of raw materials and created new markets for their goods by colonizing much of the globe. Liberal visions of prosperity and law looked hollow to many observers.

The responses to liberalism came in many stripes: traditionalist, religious, socialist, anarchist, nationalist, ethnic, and racial. They shared a suspicion of the Lockean ideal of spontaneous social order organizing around commerce and property, seeing in that ideal a stalking horse for elites who sought to oppress whole peoples on behalf of their own racial, ethnic, or economic coteries. Indeed, adherents of various branches of the new science, which studied society itself, such as Marx, Proudhon, and Comte, claimed to see through the hypocrisy of the bourgeois, liberal order. In Darwin's ideas some saw a biological corollary to the development of society, with superior races outcompeting their inferiors. The scientific study of society, experts claimed, had exposed the essential fact of history: that it was a perpetual evolutionary struggle for mastery between classes, or races. Paris had been a hotbed of such ideas almost since Rousseau had lived there; after Germany's humiliating defeat of Louis Napoleon in 1871, Parisian workers and citizens, with socialist and anarchist leaders, proclaimed a Commune and fought the French army for autonomy. The army's bloody suppression of the Communards spread revolutionary sentiment across Europe.

"Two months of fighting have done more than twenty-three years of propaganda," wrote socialist Paul Brousse about the Commune in 1877.[28] The time had come to take direct action against the ruling elites and goad the masses to throw off their chains. But how? By "the propaganda of the deed," said Brousse. Soon would-be liberators struck directly at the tyrants. A new word—"terrorism"—arose in many languages. One of its early practitioners, the Russian anarchist Sergei Kravchinsky, proclaimed: "The terrorist is noble, irresistibly fascinating, for he combines in himself the two sublimates of human grandeur: the martyr and the hero. From the day he swears in the depths of his heart to free the people and the country, he knows he is consecrated to death." The terrorist's daring blows would liberate his people from despotism, and he would see that "enemy falter, become confused, cling desperately to the wildest means."[29]

Kravchinsky knew of what he wrote; he had knifed the chief of Czar Alexander II's small secret police unit in a Saint Petersburg park in 1878. Three years later the socialist group The People's Will blew up the Czar himself—the emancipator of the serfs, ironically enough. In the course of the generation that would come, anarchists, socialists, and other radicals would kill seven heads of state and almost murder eight more.[30]

Ι ΔΟΛΟΦΟΝΙΑ ΤΗΣ Α.Μ. ΤΟΥ ΒΑΣΙΛΕΩΣ ΤΩΝ ΕΛΛΗΝΩΝ
ΓΕΩΡΓΙΟΥ ΤΟΥ Α. ΕΝ ΘΕΣΣΑΛΟΝΙΚΗ·

L'ASSASSINAT DE S. M. LE ROI DES HELLÈNES
GEORGES I. A SALONIQUE

1.1 The Propaganda of the Deed. This lithograph by artist Karl Haupt depicts the assassination of King George I of Greece in Thessalonika by an anarchist in 1913. *Wikimedia Commons, public domain*

Such ideologically driven zealotry was something new in Western society—or at least something forgotten since the wars of religion. Violent radicals could hide in plain sight, and some were willing to die in their assaults—a huge complication for the bodyguards posted to stop them. Though they usually targeted prominent persons, ordinary people sometimes died in their assaults. Indeed, terror and terrorists came close to blaming not only autocrats and capitalists but entire classes of society as well: "There is no innocent bourgeois," proclaimed Emile Henry after he bombed a Paris railway station cafe in 1894 (just days earlier another anarchist, Auguste Vaillant, had cried "*A mort la société bourgeoise et vive l'anarchie!*" as he awaited the guillotine for throwing a bomb in the National Assembly). Such dedication and deeds required organization as well, not merely for spreading ideas and propaganda, but also for coordinating actions—even anarchists have to schedule meetings. Thus was born an "underground"

(Kravchinsky's term), or parallel international network of conspirators and conspiracies, facilitated by the modern technologies of rotary printing presses, telegraphic communications, and steam-powered travel. That degree of organization expanded the reach and power of the radicals, but it also created certain weaknesses, soon to be exploited by the rulers they threatened.

The Police Response

For whoever conspires cannot be alone, but he cannot find company except from those he believes to be malcontents; and as soon as you disclose your intent to a malcontent, you give him the matter with which to become content.

—Machiavelli, *The Prince*

European nations responded to the violence by expanding the powers and capabilities of their largest police forces. London's metropolitan police—the closest thing to a national police service in Britain—formed its Special Irish Branch in 1883 to combat a Fenian bombing campaign. The office had its duties expanded to deal with other threats and took its present name, the Special Branch, in 1888. France's Sûreté Nationale was even older; under its reforming prefect, Louis Lépine, it pioneered forensic methods of investigation. Czar Alexander II, in St. Petersburg in 1880, reformed his regime's secret police into the Department for Protecting the Public Security and Order—better known now as the Okhrana—under the Ministry for Internal Affairs. All of these bureaus and their counterparts in other Western states worked in law enforcement agencies and specialized in operating, as it were, undercover—and soon at exploiting their powers of arrest and detention in order to turn radicals into cooperating agents within the revolutionary underground itself.

These special branches grew, along with more professional policing, and the two trends can barely be disentangled for the purpose of analysis. Innovative forms of technology assisted their efforts. Anarchist bombmakers had habits that could be forensically analyzed for clues to their haunts and identities (New York City's Police Department established a bomb squad in 1914 for just this purpose).[31] The Paris Prefecture of Police began photographing criminals in 1872 and, in the 1880s, adapted Alphonse Bertillon's method for recording the body measurements of offenders;

a fingerprint classification scheme created under the aegis of Edward R. Henry in the Bengal police soon made biometric cataloging even more efficient. Improvements in office machines made these nascent databases possible. Previously, official records and record keeping had been limited by what could be handwritten and searched with the naked eye.

Industrialization began lifting these barriers in the 1870s, giving shop clerks and ministers of state new systems for recording, storing, retrieving, and sharing information. Typewriters, index cards, and file cabinets expanded the extent and precision of the records that governments and industry could produce, store, and analyze, and this in turn created a hunger for new sorts of records. Suddenly, it became possible to compile databases on customers, market segments, or an entire population. Indeed, in 1890, Herman Hollerith's machines for reading punch cards tabulated the decennial United States census in only a year—versus the eight years taken to tabulate the 1880 census (Hollerith's company would later become International Business Machines—IBM for short). Before about 1870, it had been possible in some societies for a fugitive, or a spy, to simply move and never be found. After the data revolution, a state could follow its citizens more closely than ever (as anyone researching her family tree today can attest).

The new Western security units could also share leads faster than ever; that helped the fight against anarchists and revolutionaries, changing the possibilities for intelligence work as they did so. The security units could tie colonial to internal police and intelligence functions, surveilling suspects across borders.[32] The telegraph had been invented in the 1830s; in 1866, an undersea cable linked Europe to North America. The telephone came along a decade later, and was soon used in offices, businesses, and even homes. Both inventions immediately raised issues of security: as soon as telegraph wires followed armies, adversaries found ways to tap their enemy's messages. The Union and Confederate armies in the American Civil War, for instance, intercepted each other's telegrams and resorted to enciphering at least some of their own communications.[33] The telegraph and telegram also raised privacy concerns. Who owned the information transmitted along a wire strung by someone else? Who had a right to hear it or view it? For the purpose of law enforcement, was it public speech, or private? Each country's jurists had begun to wrestle with such questions by 1900.

Face-to-face liaison contacts supplemented the remote sharing of leads among police forces. The Russians creatively deployed the Okhrana

abroad in 1883, establishing a station in Paris that swapped information of mutual interest with French authorities while keeping an eye on
Russian émigrés across Western Europe. The Okhrana in Paris initially
hired French detectives to do its sleuthing but soon turned to direct intelligence gathering, developing its own leads and eventually graduating to
covert action against the more-radical émigrés. The French tolerated such
a presence in their country because it was useful. Okhrana officers had
leads to barter with the Paris police, they usually kept out of sight and out
of trouble, and the émigrés they watched were a quarrelsome lot who (in
French minds) needed close supervision. Such feelings only strengthened
when the Third Republic struck an anti-German alliance with Imperial
Russia in 1903. Even the Okhrana station's graver misdeeds—like its
occasional *agents provocateurs* planted to foment feuds among the revolutionaries—never caused the French to expel the station or to curtail
intelligence sharing. The French government finally ordered the station
closed in 1913 but turned a blind eye as it swiftly reopened under cover as
a private detective agency.[34]

The new information techniques found application overseas as well,
though not against radicals but rather against restive natives imagining an
end to the colonial order. French colonial administrators and commanders skillfully collected and exploited local information and political intelligence; General Joseph Gallieni, working to pacify Indochina in the 1890s,
explained that an officer "who has successfully drawn an exact ethnographic
map of the territory he commands is close to achieving complete pacification, soon to be followed by the form of organization he judges most appro-
priate."[35] The United States used the new methods to beat down sparks of
insurrection in the Philippine Islands after 1898. The Americans in Manila
were able to import their new technologically assisted methods in full—
having just taken over the islands from Spain, they had no established habits or institutions of their own to set aside. Furthermore, in the Philippines,
the Americans were not constrained by the constitution's Bill of Rights—a
fact that allowed them latitude for experimentation with surveillance and
law enforcement techniques.[36] The British, in India, applied the new methods through political and military intelligence bureaus assembled in the
last decades of the nineteenth century. They began reading telegrams that
were passing in and out of India in 1906; this worked tolerably well in urban
areas, ensuring that neither domestic conspiracies nor Russian and German

plots could shake the Raj (it would take Gandhi and a new mode of anticolonial resistance to accomplish that in later years).[37]

In places like the northwest frontier of India, however, far from the cities and any "softening influence of Christian civilization," as George Furse
put it, standard methods worked less well for the police or the army: "In
wars of this nature there is little to go upon. We cannot form an estimate
of the enemy's numbers, for very little is known about his military system
or spirit; all we can be almost certain of is that every male adult will bear
arms against us. We cannot surmise where the bulk of the hostile forces
will assemble, and what other tribes may not be induced to make common
cause with our adversary. The country is very superficially known to us."[38]
A few years later, another British officer, Major Charles E. Callwell, published his own reflections on the importance of intelligence in such "small
wars." A commander in uncivilized lands would do well to understand
that he was constantly being watched. News could spread though the local
"social system" in "a most mysterious fashion"; the natives might have no
formal intelligence mechanisms but nonetheless were so observant that by
"a kind of instinct they interpret military portents even when totally deficient of courage and fighting capacity."[39]

As a result of all this effort in a dozen or more countries, by 1900
the outlines of an international surveillance system had taken shape. Police
liaison and police agents caused serious problems for radical conspiracies
of all varieties. The anarchists might share the advantages of spontaneity
and obscurity, but, being anarchic in all senses of the term, they also suffered the weaknesses of factionalism and disorganization. Police agents,
inspired by Pyotr Rachkovsky, head of the Okhrana in Paris and later in St.
Petersburg, plagued their efforts. The socialists might be equally factious,
but they had no such congenital aversion to organization. Indeed, in 1902,
a Russian Marxist who had recently begun calling himself Vladimir Ilyich
Lenin, writing from exile in Munich, offered the Russian secret police a
backhanded compliment for their effectiveness: "The government, at first
thrown into confusion and committing a number of blunders . . . very soon
adapted itself to the new conditions of the struggle and managed to deploy
well its perfectly equipped detachments of *agents provocateurs*, spies, and
gendarmes. Raids became so frequent, affected such a vast number of people, and cleared out the local study circles so thoroughly that the masses
of the workers lost literally all their leaders, the movement assumed an

amazingly sporadic character, and it became utterly impossible to establish continuity and coherence in the work."[40]

Lenin had hardly exaggerated. Portions of the Okhrana's archives would soon reveal battalions of spies. In Moscow alone, the small and secretive revolutionary organizations unwittingly hosted fifty-five police agents in 1912, including seventeen among the Socialist Revolutionary (SR) party and twenty more with the Mensheviks and Lenin's Bolsheviks. The chief of the SR's terrorist arm, Yevno Azev, spied for the Okhrana, as did Father Georgiy Gapon, one of the instigators of the revolution of 1905.[41] At least one Bolshevik member of the Tsarist Duma, Roman Malinovsky, served on the party's Central Committee and also as an Okhrana agent; he may have had a fellow revolutionary, Josef Stalin, sent to Siberia.[42]

Lenin feared the Okhrana so much by 1903 that he argued for a new form of revolutionary organization. The workers would not or could not arise on their own to establish the proletarian order. They needed a vanguard, and specifically they needed a core organization of revolutionaries "who make revolutionary activity their profession."[43] These men and women would work with absolute dedication, and with security that could not be penetrated by police agents: "The only serious organizational principle for the active workers of our movement should be the strictest secrecy, the strictest selection of members, and the training of professional revolutionaries." They would not worry much about "democracy" within the movement, but instead would do their duty for the revolution: "They have not the time to think about toy forms of democratism (democratism within a close and compact body of comrades in which complete, mutual confidence prevails), but they have a lively sense of their *responsibility*, knowing as they do from experience that an organization of real revolutionaries will stop at nothing to rid itself of an unworthy member. Moreover, there is a fairly well-developed public opinion in Russian (and international) revolutionary circles which has a long history behind it, and which sternly and ruthlessly punishes every departure from the duties of comradeship" (emphasis in original). This meant endless conspiracy, secrecy, and rigorous intercell security. Indeed, professional revolutionaries had no use for fruitless talk and "resolutions about 'anti-democratic tendencies' [that] have the musty odour of the playing at generals which is indulged in abroad." Only something new and ruthless could hope to overcome the imperialists and their spies.[44]

1.2 Vladimir Ilyich Lenin, ca. 1920. *Library of Congress*

The Enemy Within

Two results came from all this ferment. First was the popularization (and romanticization) of the secret agent in an age of mass literacy and cheap publishing. Those last years before the cataclysm of the Great War saw the emergence of spy fiction—some English-language examples of which even achieved lasting literary value. Joseph Conrad found in the shadows a set-ting for *The Secret Agent* (1907), in which apparently Russian provocateurs sought to shock Britain out of its sentimental attachment to civil liberties through a blow to the heart of civilization, delivered by a staged bomb-ing of the Greenwich Observatory. Rudyard Kipling's *Kim* (1903) was far more than a depiction of the British Indian secret service in action against Russian spies, of course, but espionage lay at the heart of its plot. Spies also appeared closer to home. The vanishingly small possibility of a German invasion of England had diverted English writers since the Franco-Prussian War in 1870.[45] An Anglo-Irish sailor and budding politician, Erskine Childers, adapted this unlikely scenario in *The Riddle of the Sands* (1903), which follows two young Englishmen on a sailing holiday who stumble into a German invasion plot—and worse, find a renegade countryman assisting the Kaiser's henchmen. Childers's novel rode the crest of a wave of pulp spy fiction, and it had an influence on British sentiments (Winston Churchill credited it with a shift of the Royal Navy's attentions and redeployment from its historic focus on the Channel—guarding against the French—to the North Sea, watching Germany's growing fleet). Another novelist, William Le Queux, raised the invasion novel to even more breathless heights with his thriller *The Invasion of 1910* (1906)—which sold a million copies in two dozen languages. He followed it with an allegedly factual exposé of the enemy in England's bosom, *Spies of the Kaiser* (1909).

The fear of foreign enemies in the midst of society, of course, must be as old as mankind. After all, what were witches if not agents of the powers of darkness, working undercover for the ruin of souls? What the *fin de siècle* spy mania accomplished was to give those enemies faces—and an arsenal. In England or France they were Germans (or French or English, in Germany). Of course, they might be thought to be French Jews working for Germany, as the unfortunate Captain Alfred Dreyfus discovered. Court-martialed for treason on suspicion of passing secrets, Dreyfus endured years on Devil's Island before finally being cleared in 1906. Spies were not merely eavesdroppers and tale bearers, or sometimes poisoners or knife-wielding assassins, like Kautilya's exemplars of old. If anarchists and revolutionaries, they now employed modern weapons in an age when ordnance powerful enough to maim dozens of innocents—or to kill a king and his queen—could be carried under a coat. If they worked for a foreign government, they had the resources of a modern state behind their perfidy. With such power, spies might divine the hidden weakness of an entire society—finding not just a secret tunnel into a castle, but a landing beach for an army descending upon a sleeping England. In an era when military technology had been transformed in a single generation and then transformed again in the next, such fears of secret weapons and surprise attacks were exaggerated—but not groundless. Spies in ages past had been low, skulking fellows. Now they had become tactful but ruthless engineers, quiet but lethal.

Policymakers, senior commanders, and prominent businessmen knew how dependent industrialized societies had become on regular trade, communications, and finance—and consequently how vulnerable they seemed to disruptions of the intricate web of services and infrastructure that kept their teeming cities supplied with food, power, credit, and news. Indeed, by 1908, the Royal Navy was actively incorporating this insight into its planning for a conflict with Germany.[46]

The spy mania softened British leaders to the idea of a professional intelligence and security service. London had done away with its Decyphering Branch in 1844, and the opening of diplomats' mail—though still practiced with "notorious frequency" in Europe—was beginning to look dated and foolish by the 1850s.[47] But half a century later it seemed that spying could be done for good motives, and as Erskine Childers imagined, the methods of spies could be turned against them by gentlemen. Such ideas eventually overwhelmed official hesitancy concerning the threat of foreign subversion. Though the War Office had established a small counterespionage office in 1903, the Liberal government quietly determined in 1907 that there was no chance of a surprise German invasion. As popular concern about the Anglo-German battleship building race and the Kaiser's intentions mounted, however, the government of Prime Minister Herbert Asquith revisited the issue in the spring of 1909. A panel convened by the Committee on Imperial Defence considered the possibility that German saboteurs could delay mobilization in a crisis—members heard dubious but worrisome reports that the Germans planned to wreck bridges, docks, arsenals, railways, and telegraph lines. The idea was not wholly illusory— at least one actual German spy contemplated sabotage of British infrastructure.[48] While discounting much of the supposed evidence of enemy agents roaming the countryside (some of it helpfully provided by Le Queux), the panel nonetheless found it advisable to create a "Secret Service Bureau" to improve foreign and domestic security.[49]

The Secret Service Bureau lived only a few months and was never publicized, but its impact can be felt more than a century later. Two innovations explain the bureau's importance. First, it answered to both the army and the navy, having a senior officer from each service as its cochief. In this way, it secretly supplemented the work of the intelligence bureaus in both services without directly impinging either; indeed, part of its job was to procure intelligence while allowing each service to "be freed from the necessity of dealing with spies," as well as to make it tougher for adversaries to spot "direct evidence" of British intelligence work. Second, the bureau's money came from neither service but from the Foreign Office in the form of "Secret Vote" funds—the provision of which not only helped hide the entity from prying eyes but also gave the Foreign Office a voice in its work. The bureau thus took on a permanent and "national" character from the outset, answering to the needs of the nation as a whole as well as to those of its parent services.[50] That character was passed down to its institutional heirs in 1910 when the bureau was split into an office for domestic security and counterespionage, MI5, and another for intelligence collection abroad, soon to be titled the Secret Intelligence Service. They would each attain a serviceable maturity just in time to help Britain's war effort in the First World War.

Spy scares were only one influence on war planning in the years before 1914. Wireless telegraphy (soon called simply "radio") had shown its promise in the 1890s by linking transmitters on land with ships at sea. This invention had opened the possibility of real-time control of naval forces at a distance, and farsighted officers in the Royal Navy were struggling as early as 1905 to put new ideas about naval warfare into service. By 1909, wireless sets had improved to the point where every capital ship could carry one; the Royal Navy's summer maneuvers thereafter featured opposing fleets of battleships talking to their bases ashore (and each other) via radio—at least insofar as they could keep up with the volume of messages sent and received. The exercise also featured widespread cheating, as both the "Blue" (British) side and the invading "Red" force eavesdropped on each other's signals and sought to use the information to gain a competitive edge.[51] If British ships could listen in on other British ships in exercises, they could also eavesdrop on German ships in a war—there would be no scruples about invading the privacy of enemies. And the young first lord of the Admiralty, Winston Churchill, had glimpsed a future in which control of forces could be centralized, informed by intelligence that might be only hours or even minutes old, and exercised over hundreds of square miles in real time.

Conclusion

By 1914, the world had changed enough to bring the visions of Sun Tzu and Kautilya hazily to reality. In the imperial capitals of Europe, two key things had happened to the craft of spying. One was obvious and public, the other was apparent only to a handful of people who were both old enough to remember earlier days, and who had also traveled enough to see how other nations had coped with the need to build up their secret services. The result of all this change was that spying had taken on a character that is now familiar to people everywhere. In Europe, at least, it was beginning to be professionalized. Whereas for the rest of the world spying remained pretty much a hobby of princes as it had always been, in the industrialized states, at least, espionage was changing in a specific direction and in a specific way. The investigating capacities accumulating in the military and interior ministries were being constructed to meet the particular decision needs of their ministers. In other words, espionage had developed dramatically and rapidly, but only at the ministerial level. Heads of state in America or Germany or Russia might still employ the occasional spy, but no sovereign or president had the time to oversee the secret service bureaus of his ministers. No one, however, had noticed the imbalance that was thus created, nor had anyone seen and answered the need for a head of state to have his own way of checking the suddenly copious information available to him; and no one had thought about administering the organs that provided that information to ensure they collaborated in the best interests of the nation. The insights and powers offered by the military information bureaus and police special branches were still different and separate things.

Yet within five years they would be one thing: intelligence. Even before 1914, the needs of governments and militaries to gather and concentrate information by all available means were beginning to transform spycraft into intelligence. As the Industrial Revolution reshaped armies and navies in the late nineteenth century, the intelligence complements to those military systems changed as well. States also built special branches to police their old and new empires, and to ward off the threats posed by anarchists and revolutionaries. Technological change gave the growing bureaus new targets and concerns as well as new tools to employ. The types of regimes building intelligence systems inevitably colored the resulting systems. Czarist Russia, beset by enemies without and within, created a capable spy service that worked both overseas and at home. Imperial Britain, concerned about unrest in its far-flung dominions but relatively peaceful at home, fashioned intelligence capabilities to watch foreign navies and colonial unrest, and came only late to the business of watching enemy agents and saboteurs at home. The United States' concerns mirrored those of Britain only to a much lesser degree, and hence its intelligence capabilities remained small and crude. All of this meant that a large difference was beginning to open between the states that did little in the intelligence arena and those few that were beginning to build intelligence systems. That opening gap would become a widening gulf during World War I.

NOTES

1. See the Schoyen Collection's range of *bulla* from the ancient Near East. The Schoyen Collection is based in London and Oslo; accessed September 1, 2012, at www.schoyencollection.com/math.html#4631.
2. Kautilya, *The Arthashastra.* trans. L. N. Rangarajan (New Delhi: Penguin Books India, 1992). See especially books I (chapter 11) and XII.
3. Sun Tzu, *The Art of War*, trans. Samuel B. Griffith (New York: Oxford University Press, 1972 [1963]), book I:1.
4. Ibid., XIII:3–4.
5. Ibid., XIII:14.
6. *Arthashastra*, XIII, 1:3–6.
7. *Art of War*, XIII, 22–23.
8. Christopher Dandeker, *Surveillance, Power and Modernity: Bureaucracy and Discipline from 1700 to the Present Day* (New York: St. Martin's Press, 1991), vii.
9. Machiavelli, *The Prince*, trans. Harvey Mansfield (Chicago: University of Chicago Press, 1985), chapter 18.
10. David Kahn, *The Codebreakers: The Story of Secret Writing* (New York: Scribner, 1996 [1967]), 126–29.
11. Francesco Guicciardini, *Counsels and Reflections of Francesco Guicciardini*, trans. Nanine Hill Thomson (London: Kegan Paul, Trench, Trubner, 1890), maxim 193.
12. Diego Navarro Bonilla, "'Secret Intelligences' in European Military, Political and Diplomatic Theory: An Essential Factor in the Defense of the Modern State," *Intelligence and National Security*: 27:2 (April 2012): 295, 298.
13. John Locke, *The Second Treatise of Government*, Thomas P. Peardon, ed. (New York: Bobbs-Merrill, 1952), chapter 5, paragraph 49.
14. "Find out something that has the use and value of money amongst his neighbors, you shall see the same man will begin presently to enlarge his possessions." Ibid., paragraphs 48–50.
15. Ibid., chapter 7, paragraphs 87–88, 91; also chapter 9, paragraphs 123–31.
16. Jean-Jacques Rousseau, *On the Social Contract*, trans. Judith R. Masters (New York: St. Martins Press, 1978), book I, chapter 1.
17. Jean-Jacques Rousseau, *A Discourse on Inequality*, trans. Maurice Cranston (London: Penguin, 1984), part II, 109.
18. "Men are wicked; melancholy and constant experience removes any need for proof. Yet man is naturally good." Ibid., 147, footnote I.
19. Ibid.

20. Ibid., part II, 134.

21. Rousseau, *On the Social Contract*, book III, chapters xi–xviii, 99–107.

22. Ibid., book I, chapter vi, 53.

23. Carl von Clausewitz, *On War*, trans. Michael Howard and Peter Paret (Princeton, NJ: Princeton University Press, 1989 [1976]), see book I, chapter 6 on "Intelligence War," 117.

24. Lawrence A. Frost, "Balloons over the Peninsula: Fitz John Porter and George Custer Become Reluctant Aeronauts," *Blue and Gray Magazine* 2:3 (January 1985): 6–12.

25. Nicholas A. Lambert, *Planning Armageddon: British Economic Warfare and the First World War* (Cambridge, MA: Harvard University Press, 2012), 23–28.

26. George Armand Furse, *Information in War: Its Acquisition and Transmission* (London: William Clowes & Sons, 1895), 238–40.

27. Hilaire Belloc and Basil Temple Blackwood, *The Modern Traveller* (London: Edward Arnold, 1898), 41.

28. Alex Butterworth, *The World That Never Was: A True Story of Dreamers, Schemers, Anarchists, and Secret Agents* (New York: Vintage, 2010), 126.

29. S. Stepniak [Sergei Kravchinsky] and Petr Alekseevich Lavrov, *Underground Russia: Revolutionary Profiles and Sketches from Life* (New York: Charles Scribner's Sons, 1885), 39–41.

30. Other assassinations included those of the French president (1894), the Spanish prime minister (1897), the empress consort of Austria (1898), the king of Italy (1900), the president of the United States (1901), the king of Portugal (1908), the Russian prime minister (1911), another French president (1911), the Spanish prime minister (1912), and the king of Greece (1913). Attempts included those against the Kaiser (1878), the Prince of Wales (1900), the king of Belgium (1902), and the king of Spain (1906).

31. Thomas J. Tunney and Paul Merrick Hollister, *Throttled!: The Detection of the German and Anarchist Bomb Plotters* (Boston: Small, Maynard, 1919), 1–3.

32. Martin Thomas, *Empires of Intelligence: Security Services and Colonial Disorder after 1914* (Berkeley: University of California Press, 2007), 211–14.

33. A. W. Greely, "The Military Telegraph Service," in Francis Trevelyan Miller and Robert Sampson Lanier, eds., *The Photographic History of the Civil War*, vol. 8, *Soldier Life, Secret Service* (New York: Review of Reviews, 1911), 360–64.

34. See the preface of Ben B. Fischer, ed., *Okhrana: The Paris Operations of the Russian Imperial Police* (Washington, DC: Central Intelligence Agency, 1997).

35. Quoted in Paul Rabinow, *French Modern: Norms and Forms of Social Environment* (Chicago: University of Chicago Press, 1996 [1989]), 147.

36. Alfred McCoy, *Policing America's Empire: The United States, the Philippines, and the Rise of the Surveillance State* (Madison: University of Wisconsin Press, 2009), 26–56.

37. Richard J. Popplewell, *Intelligence and Imperial Defence: British Intelligence and the Defence of the Indian Empire, 1904–1924* (London: Frank Cass, 1995), 5, 317, 331; Thomas, *Empires of Intelligence*, 37.

38. Furse, *Information in War,* 80.
39. C. E. Callwell, *Small Wars: Their Principles and Practice* (London: Harrison & Sons, 1903 [1899]), 35.
40. V. I. Lenin, *What Is to Be Done?: Burning Questions of Our Movement,* 1902, from the V. I. Lenin Internet Archive, chapter 4, on "The Primitiveness of the Economists and the Organization of the Revolutionaries," section A; accessed June 28, 2012 at http://marxists.org/archive/lenin/works/1901/witbd/iv.htm.
41. Victor Serge, *Memoirs of a Revolutionary* (New York: New York Review of Books, 2012 [1951]), 113.
42. Simon Sebag Montefiore, *Young Stalin* (New York: Alfred A. Knopf, 2007), 231.
43. Lenin, *What Is to Be Done?*, chapter 4, section C.
44. Ibid., section E.
45. See, for instance, George Tomkyns Chesney's 1871 novel *The Battle of Dorking: Reminiscences of a Volunteer.*
46. Lambert, *Planning Armageddon,* 497–98.
47. E. C. G. Murray, *Embassies and Foreign Courts: A History of Diplomacy* (London: G. Routledge, 1855), 133–45.
48. Armgaard Karl Graves, *The Secrets of the German War Office* (New York: McBride, Nast, 1914), 175–76.
49. Christopher Andrew, *Defend the Realm: The Authorized History of MI5* (New York: Alfred A. Knopf, 2009), 5–28. See also Nicholas Hiley, "Re-entering the Lists: MI5's Authorized History and the August 1914 Arrests," *Intelligence and National Security* 25:4 (August 2010): 441.
50. Keith Jeffery, *The Secret History of MI6: 1909–1949* (New York: Penguin, 2010), 5–8.
51. For an idea of the information revolution's effects on operations, see Nicholas A. Lambert, "Strategic Command and Control for Maneuver Warfare: Creation of the Royal Navy's 'War Room' System, 1905–1915," *Journal of Military History* 69 (April 2005): 395–99.

CHAPTER 2

A Revolutionary Age

For the first time the entire mechanism of an authoritarian empire's police repression had fallen into the hands of revolutionaries.

—SERGE, *MEMOIRS OF A REVOLUTIONARY*

I n the days of Napoleon or George Washington, a commander, or even a head of state, could essentially run his own spy network. Not much had altered that possibility since the time of Sunzi and Kautilya, but that was about to change forever. Napoleon lost at Waterloo in 1815 and never fought again, hardly knowing that his armies, and the turmoil they caused, had provided the catalyst for a revolution in the way militaries and even nations would transform the secret services and their operations. By the turn of the twentieth century, the ancient craft of spying was becoming institutionalized in bureaucracies. A generation later, these bureaus were transformed again into something that no one in Washington's time could have imagined.

This new thing sprang into being almost without notice, in response to two world-altering forces. The Industrial Revolution had taken hold in Europe and North America and was spreading across the Earth. At the same time, the misery and dislocation in its wake stirred passions and intellects, with no small number of radicals proclaiming that only violent struggle could halt political and economic oppression. New ways of gathering information and of influencing events by stealth were fashioned to meet the needs of states to combat technologically enabled and ideologically motivated enemies. When these forces collided under the guise of militant nationalism in 1914, the most advanced nations found new ways to spy on each other. Three new capabilities would arise in the major states: sustained and dedicated technological collection and analysis for commanders and decision makers; interactions of analytical products and operations specifically intended to create more intelligence; and the consciousness, among leaders, of the national significance of the secret arts. States that could not follow the leaders in this new field fell too far behind to catch up.

Into the Maelstrom

On June 28, 1914, a young radical in Sarajevo finally succeeded where the anarchists and socialists had failed in their efforts to rock Western civilization. Ironically it was a Serb, Gavrilo Princip, striking a blow for Slavic nationalism rather than world revolution, who assassinated the heir to the throne of the Austro-Hungarian Empire. When war came a month later, the world's most advanced nations opened their astonishing arsenals to equip armies of conscripts who could be mobilized in days. In keeping with the war's ironic and unexpected origin, no one knew quite how the conflict would unfold. For a few weeks it resembled what people remembered of the Franco-Prussian War. Indeed, the war's initial campaigns were fast-paced affairs, with colorful uniforms and massed cavalry formations. At sea, German cruisers added another touch from the nineteenth century, preying on allied shipping for a few months before the Royal Navy hunted them down.

Commanders in those early battles, however, had tools undreamt of by Napoleon: radios and aircraft. The massive armies of 1914 were deployed according to precise railroad timetables and carried wireless transmitters to help their senior officers monitor and control formations in the field. The Germans marched first and fastest, crashing through neutral Belgium in a calculated gamble that they could fall on the flanks of the French army before Russia could bring its strength to bear on the Eastern Front. Everything depended on speed and firepower and timing. If there was too much delay in beating the French, the Russians would invade Germany itself.

It almost worked, but from the beginning things started to go wrong. The Belgians fought hard, and their fortresses had to be flattened with Krupp's huge guns, giving the French precious days to prepare for the German tide. Worse yet, the British set aside their neutrality when Germany invaded Belgium, and sent their own contemptible little army (in Kaiser Wilhelm's unfortunate phrase) to France's aid. Worst of all, the Russians moved faster than anyone had thought possible, pushing into Prussia with two armies, and threatening to crush the smaller German force left to guard the frontier.

The Russian commanders coordinated their advance by radio, which everyone, by 1914, knew was being intercepted by the enemy. It was for that very reason that every modern army was already encoding tactical radio traffic. The two Russian armies had gone to war with incompatible code-books, however, and their generals threw caution to the wind and transmitted vital messages in the clear. The result was disaster. The German Eighth Army, rallied by Paul von Hindenburg and Erich von Ludendorff (who was rushed straight from pounding the Belgians to serve as Hindenburg's right hand), saw from the Russian transmissions how to defeat the invading armies separately before they could join forces. Hindenburg and Ludendorff did just that at the battles around Tannenberg and the Masurian Lakes in late August, thrashing the Russians so thoroughly that it would be 1916 before they mounted another serious offensive.[1]

A new method of watching the enemy's movements assisted the French just days later. With help from the British Expeditionary Force, the French army counterattacked at the Marne in early September, dealing the Germans their first major defeat and pushing them back. The "Miracle of the Marne" was famous at the time for the Parisian taxicabs used to ferry fresh troops to the battle, but it should have been noted for the French and British use of reconnaissance aircraft to spot a fatal gap between two German armies. The pilots aloft on those September days witnessed sights that would never be seen again: enormous Napoleonic columns of soldiers and cavalry rushing to and fro across the countryside and grappling for position before Paris. In that dawn of military aviation there was as yet no way to transmit reports to the ground, and so the pilots did the best they could, landing on convenient fields, fueling up, and heading aloft again for more. One pilot recorded his day: "Saint-Dizier, Reims, Fismes, Bergeres-les-Vertus, where we descended to report to General Foch, who is in command, it is said, of three army corps, forming the IXeme Armée which is from this time to come between us and the army of Franchet d'Esperey on our left. We saw four German army corps today marching in order of battle across the camp of Chalons and the neighborhood of Reims. What feelings it aroused! But what a splendid spectacle!"[2]

The French army had also pioneered the use of units to intercept and analyze radio signals. Sloppy radio procedure by German cavalry units helped to confirm the observations of the pilots, convincing French commanders that the hour for a counterattack had arrived. Though there is no way of knowing quite what information was reaching generals like Ferdinand Foch, it is clear that he and his colleagues gained increasing confidence in what they were doing. Foch's legend also owed something to his quip at the Marne: "Hard pressed on my right. My center is yielding. Impossible to maneuver. Situation excellent. I attack." By October the intercept units' hypotheses about German formations and plans were even more useful to the French generals in "the race to sea," as the two sides sought again to turn the other's flank.[3] Each of the opponents in the growing conflict had thus learned painful lessons about the methods for gathering intelligence, and had set about improving their own.

Within weeks the Western Front in France and Belgium bogged down in interminable trench warfare. The Eastern Front remained more fluid, but its ebb and flow obscured the strategic stalemate between the Russians on one side and their German and Austro-Hungarian adversaries on the other. For two years the Germans and Austrians won battlefield victories that seemingly got them no closer to winning the war, as the Russians raised new armies to replace their appalling losses. Observers then and now attributed the stasis and carnage on both fronts to the deadly troika of the machine gun, rapid-firing artillery, and poison gas; not until almost the end of the war could the generals figure out how to overcome the defenders of fixed positions.

The Strategic Chessboard

A few months of total war in 1914 left every combatant stunned and running low on war stocks. Europe settled in for a continent-wide siege, as the trenches were deepened, factories geared up to full production, and fresh recruits trained for new offensives in the spring. German agents dabbled in stirring up trouble in the British and French empires, with little success.[4] Both sides turned to the United States for supplies; America had stayed neutral but remained open for business, its banks loaning money and its farms and industries eager for sales. Soon America would unexpectedly find itself the world's biggest creditor nation, but its loans and products went predominantly to the Allies, as the Royal Navy's blockade of the continent meant the Germans and Austrians could not ship what they had bought in the States. This imbalance would have strategic consequences, as it made the United States a covert battleground between the warring sides. The French, the Russians, and especially the British sought to preserve and expand their access to American credit and production, while the Germans and Austrians hoped to curtail it.

The good opinion of Washington and the American public thus became perhaps the war's greatest prize—the warring side that convinced the Americans to back it might well be the ultimate winner. Here was a situation tailor-made for intrigue. The Germans tried first, displaying a casual disregard for the perils of antagonizing Americans. Their ambassador in Washington and several of his attachés received authorization from Berlin to undertake a range of covert activities to assist the Kaiser's war effort. A fair number of German-born citizens of military age residing in America were already German army reservists, and Ambassador Johann von Bernstorff's embassy staff conspired to procure US passports that could take them safely past the Royal Navy to the continent. This scheme was unmasked by the American government in a few months, causing Berlin embarrassment that surely outweighed the advantage of adding a few hundred men to the German muster rolls. The Germans' next step was far more consequential. Exasperated by Washington's refusal to embargo arms to both sides in the conflict (which would have the effect of hurting the Allies far more than it hurt Germany and Austria-Hungary), Berlin in late 1914 authorized a small but noisy campaign of sabotage against war supplies bound for Britain, France, and Russia.

When German diplomats in Washington and New York bungled the campaign, and sabotage proved an unproductive and diplomatically risky tactic, Berlin doubled its bets. Germany found more capable saboteurs, who kept mostly out of sight as they turned their attentions to targets in New Jersey. Their most noteworthy successes were setting fires at a pier laden with munitions for Russia and at a plant for packing artillery shells. The pier was called Black Tom; it sat on the New Jersey side of New York City's harbor, and one night in July 1916 it went up with a roar that broke windows in Times Square and was heard in faraway Maryland. The shell factory was even closer to Manhattan, just across the Hudson River in a neighborhood called Kingsland, and a fire there raged in broad daylight in January 1917. Neither incident took many lives, but their audacity (both were watched from New York City) helped convince many in the United States of Berlin's contempt for the sentiments and the very lives of Americans.[5]

Despite prewar fears, the use of saboteurs elsewhere in the Great War had tactical success but little strategic impact. The experience of anarchist bombings, and years of lurid fiction, seem to have convinced people, at least in Britain, to expect a wave of sabotage. Within a month of the war's outbreak, authorities were guarding 800 militarily sensitive sites in Britain with 20,000 volunteers.[6] Arrests of suspected German agents by British police and the young MI5 in August 1914 had the effect of forestalling any chance that the Germans might have had of mounting a campaign akin to that launched in America.[7] Elsewhere saboteurs only seemed more effective. Italian authorities claimed that Austrian agents sank two Italian battleships at their moorings (the *Benedetto Brin* in 1915, and the *Leonardo da Vinci* the next year), though the fact that several navies lost warships to accidental powder-magazine explosions during the conflict suggests negligence rather than sabotage. Indeed, sabotage campaigns were difficult to run against serious intelligence opposition anywhere. Even where the local security services were weak, as in America, sabotage caused trouble but did little real damage.

The reason sabotage campaigns usually failed was that it was too dangerous to run agent networks in an enemy's homeland. Most citizens remained loyal in deed if not in thought, and even if they had wanted to spy they would have no opportunity to contact diplomats or intelligence officers in the service of an enemy power. The police special branches that had been created for fighting radicals now showed their worth. Foreigners, especially enemy aliens, were scrutinized too closely by the authorities and their fellow citizens to accomplish any sort of intelligence mission. Everywhere counterintelligence services relied on the sharp eyes of landladies, dockworkers, and constabularies for most of their leads. Britain's MI5 developed postal censorship to an art.[8] In the United States, the bomb squad of the New York (City) Police Department posted German-speaking plainclothes officers in taverns frequented by German sailors, but probably got the bulk of its information from police colleagues in New Jersey who talked to local chemists (national agencies had little part in the campaign; sabotage was not a federal crime until after America declared war in 1917).[9] Sometimes more imaginative tactics had success. As it had against anarchist and socialist rings, Russia's Okhrana penetrated at least one German operation and fed its controllers fanciful tales of the death and destruction its agents were supposedly causing in Russia.[10] The British also tried their own twist—reading intercepted German diplomatic telegrams for clues to the Kaiser's agents, and then either intercepting the agents en route aboard neutral ships or passing subtle leads to American authorities (who were not to be told how His Majesty's Government read foreign communications—including America's).

Sabotage or intelligence-gathering agents could, on the other hand, operate for a time on the soil of gullible neutrals—as Germany proved in the United States. Such networks might also, moreover, survive in territory overrun by a hostile army. In occupied Belgian and French territory, for instance, most locals hated their German conquerors. A few had the courage to pass information to the Allies when they could. Britain's new foreign intelligence service ran such a network of Belgian "train watchers" from neutral Holland; called *la Dame Blanche* (the White Lady), it remained a thorn in the German army's side for years, despite the loss of several of its assets. Human agents would never come close to being a strategic weapon that could break the deadlock on the Eastern and Western Fronts, though *la Dame Blanche* passed some information of strategic value to allied commanders. Its ultimate contribution, however, might have been in convincing Britain's intelligence chiefs that agent networks in occupied territory were not only possible but potentially valuable—a lesson learned for the next war.[11]

The War at Sea

Time favored the Allies in this continent-wide siege because the Royal Navy (with help from its French counterparts) controlled the sea lanes to Europe and thus the flow of crucial supplies to the Germans and Austrians. Coal and iron the Germans had in plenty, and foodstuffs, too, for a time, but certain minerals and materials that their industries needed could only come from over the sea. Thus Germany grew determined to circumvent or lift the blockade.

Enforcing that blockade depended on one of the largest intelligence operations in history. In Napoleonic times, the blockade would have been attempted by fast cruisers along the German coast. In this modern age, the weather would have beat the cruisers down, or German battleships, submarines, and mines would have sunk them. Now enforcement could be done by diplomatic consuls and insurance agents in distant ports, supported by battalions of postal censors, intercept operators, file clerks, and analysts in England who monitored the shipping news, correspondence, and telegraph circuits for clues to shipments bound for neutral ports in Holland or the

Baltics; from there they would be sent on to Germany. Though the blockade was never airtight, it was not necessary to stop many actual ships on the high seas to convince shipping agents and sailing masters that a quiet warning from a British consul meant their cargoes really would be taken as prizes and their ships and crews impounded—or sunk.[12]

Berlin had three options for breaking the stranglehold. The battleships of the Kaiser's High Seas Fleet might defeat the Royal Navy's larger Home Fleet. If they did, the Germans would be able to range the oceans themselves to protect German shipping. Alternatively, Germany's U-boats might evade the allied navies and try to impose their own blockade on British and French ports. Finally, the Germans might take the war home to British subjects, inflicting on them with bombs what the blockade was threatening to do to German and Austrian civilians by slow starvation. Berlin ultimately tried all three of these measures, but once again, British intelligence did much to frustrate German plans.

Radio helped to ensure the Royal Navy would always fight German battleships on at least an even footing. This was crucial—losing a sizable portion of the Home Fleet to a German trap was something that London especially dreaded. First Lord of the Admiralty Winston Churchill described Admiral Sir John Jellicoe, the Home Fleet's commander, as "the only man on either side who could lose the war in an afternoon." The British had worked hard on this problem for a decade, with naval visionaries like First Sea Lord Jacky Fisher grasping the opportunity that radio offered to centralize nearly real time information on opposing fleets and so guide an admiral in the North Sea toward an enemy squadron. The new methods took time to perfect—they failed more than once because of bad weather and tactical mistakes—but by early 1915 the British perceived correctly that they would not be surprised by a significant sortie of German capital ships into the North Sea.[13]

What made this strategy effective was the hard work of what came to be identified as Room 40, the Admiralty's codebreaking apparatus. Headed by William "Blinker" Hall, head of Naval Intelligence and a nervous genius (he apparently had a habit of rapid-fire blinking which perhaps accounted for his moniker), Room 40 was named after its original and short-lived home in the Admiralty block. It held the keys to German naval communications and much else besides. Poor German security practices early in the war gave Hall and his office time to learn the business of signals intelligence through

2.1 Admiral Reginald "Blinker" Hall, 1919.
Wikimedia Commons, public domain

trial and error, and thus, as the Germans improved Hall had a trained work-force able to follow each increasingly sophisticated step. The Admiralty in London accordingly had ample warning of the High Seas Fleet's most daring sortie in July 1916; the Germans used stereotyped wireless patterns that told the British something was afoot. The result was the Battle of Jutland, the greatest clash of big-gun ships in history. The Home Fleet had been alerted by its intercept operators and analysts in time to sortie en masse from its base at Scapa Flow, and the British intercepted the High Seas Fleet and fought it to a draw. The Germans sank more British ships than they lost that day, but the Royal Navy had more ships to lose, and the bloodied German navy never again attempted a breakout.[14]

The Kaiser's battleships in practice proved less of a threat to Britain's survival than his slow and tiny submarines. These submarines became by default the chief naval menace to the allied cause in World War I, and their influence on the course of the war, was immense. Early in the war, in 1914, when the submarine conflict began, the Germans played by the old rules of armed conflict—an intercepting U-boat would surface and allow its victim's crew to man the lifeboats before sending it to the bottom with a torpedo or a few shells—but after the British began hiding deck guns on freighters, no more warnings were given. By the spring of 1915, the U-boats would torpedo anything they saw in British waters, a policy that Berlin soon revoked after the U-20 torpedoed the liner *Lusitania* off the Irish coast, killing hundreds of people, among them 128 Americans, and angering Washington. Even with more restrictive rules of engagement, however, the U-boats sank so much shipping by early 1917 that, had the British not implemented the convoy system, their island might have starved.

The campaign to stop the U-boats called forth prodigious efforts by allied intelligence services. SIS had a man in the German navy and he provided clues.[16] Once again, however, signals intelligence led the way, particularly with the help of radio direction finding the signals transmitted by U-boats on the surface. Where they could, the British also broke the coded messages sent between the submarines and their bases to divine procedures and destinations. To do so meant the Royal Navy had to exploit every opportunity to get codebooks out of sinking submarines, or to send divers down to wrecks in shallow waters in the North Sea or the English Channel. Both jobs were as dangerous and unpleasant as could be imagined, but repaid the effort through the insight they gave into U-boat operations. The U-boats' attacks were never entirely halted; they sank ships until the end of the conflict (costing the Allies 11 million tons of shipping in total), but 178 U-boats were lost, allied ships were warned away from the submarines' patrol areas, and their depredations were lessened.[16]

Germany also broke the taboo against direct attacks on cities. In 1915, the Germans started bombing London from Zeppelins, huge and rigid-framed "air ships." The Zeppelins were slow and unwieldy in high winds, and their bombs did little damage, but they could fly for hours at altitudes beyond the reach of most aircraft, and their looming appearance over London was shocking. Britain hastily organized air defenses for England like those its army was building on the Western Front; quick-firing guns provided point defense for valuable targets, while fighter planes sought to intercept the raiders before they dropped their bombs and escaped. Such defenses relied on a web of spotters, and on coordination nodes to pass warnings to likely targets and interceptor bases in range. Everything depended on timing, and that meant signals intelligence again played an

2.2 A British recruitment poster from the Great War showing German Zeppelin dirigibles over London. Signals intelligence played a key role in halting their air raids. *Library of Congress*

important role, hearing the Zeppelins check in with their bases as they lifted off, and plotting their calls for direction-finding assistance as they closed on their targets. During one night raid in 1916, for instance, the winds picked up unexpectedly and British defenders heard multiple Zeppelins radioing home for direction checks; realizing the Zeppelins were being driven off course, central control took a calculated gamble and ordered London's searchlights switched *off*, so as not to give the straying airships any help in finding their target. Nine Zeppelins were lost that night—a significant share of the total fleet. Britain's air defenses could not stop the nuisance raids, especially after the Germans abandoned Zeppelin raids in favor of those by huge aircraft (Germany's *Riesenflugzeuge* bombers, for instance, had wingspans greater than a jet airliner). Nevertheless, air defense took a toll on the raiders and demonstrated the government in London's commitment to guarding civilians against air attack—not a trivial point, as the appalling casualties in France began to undermine popular morale. By the last months of the war, intelligence and operations had been effectively fused in Britain's air defense system, which could track every aircraft over southeast England within ninety seconds, using only observers, telephones, wireless, and hand plotting.[17]

This nearly real-time monitoring of friendly and enemy forces dispersed over hundreds of square miles represented something new. Combined with the Admiralty's analogous capabilities to surveil and command forces at sea, it presaged a new era in warfare—one in which communications and intelligence would have more importance and influence over tactics, operations, and strategy than ever before.

Trench Warfare

The stalemates endured in both East and West, despite efforts on both sides to break the deadlock. In the West, the armies were essentially locked in their positions after autumn 1914 and could not advance by any means other than grinding and brutal attrition. The fronts were tactically more fluid in the East, and traditional means of scouting, such as cavalry, still proved useful, at times. On all fronts, machine guns and field artillery ruled the battlefield. All sides, moreover, swiftly grasped the value of tactical intelligence even on the most static battlefields. Intelligence could not break the stalemate—though it did assist in some local victories—but it ensured that none of the armies could be decisively defeated.

Gathering intelligence in the trenches was a matter of constant observation, at multiple points, combined with continual evaluation of the take. Observation meant literally watching the enemy, who naturally kept out of sight as much as possible, at least within range of bullets or shells. Even so, all sorts of indicators of enemy activity would reveal themselves to a trained eye; fresh dirt and sandbags around trenches, smoke from cooking fires, new barbed wire, and a myriad of other clues could be seen without undue risk. Noise helped, too; machinery and vehicles could not be run near the forward trenches without being heard. Crude but effective technology, like giant sound-magnifying artificial ears, assisted in locating artillery batteries behind the lines. Telephone and telegraph wires snaked across the moonscape behind and along the front line, and even if they could not be directly tapped, they still were not safe from eavesdroppers. Under cover of darkness, soldiers slipped out into No Man's Land and drove stakes into the ground that could pick up faint induction signals from the wires of enemy field telephones and carry those echoes back to a friendly trench. Of course, observers close enough to do such work were also close enough, at least briefly, to hear enemy soldiers moving about and even talking.

A potentially more profitable—though bloodier—way of gathering intelligence was by raiding the enemy's trenches. This meant creeping as close as possible at night and then rushing forward with enough men to capture and briefly hold a short segment of trench. Once there, the raiders could hurriedly round up any prisoners able-bodied enough to be marched back, scour the dugouts for anything of value, and beat an orderly retreat to the cover of their own line before the inevitable counterattack. Both sides perfected these techniques, and front-line soldiers were drilled to resist such incursions, which were sometimes performed with special units brought in for the purpose. A successful raid netted prisoners at a modest cost in friendly lives, along with enemy weapons, equipment, and documents such as maps, manuals, messages, and codebooks.

Here was where reconnaissance became intelligence. Information from all these sources had to be assembled, collated, evaluated, and studied for its significance. Prisoners had to be searched thoroughly and interrogated, preferably soon after capture while they were still psychologically stunned. This was work for trained intelligence officers who could talk to prisoners in their own language and probe their answers. Anything on their persons, and any materiel carried out of enemy trenches, was to be examined and cataloged, and not left behind with the raiding party for souvenirs. Logs of such finds were kept and passed back to higher headquarters so trends could be observed and new weapons recognized. Every Western army learned to be meticulous about such work, and circulated standards and innovations for doing it that soon crystallized into doctrine, imposed on all formations down to the lowest tactical units. The British Second Army developed an illustrative model, which is noteworthy because it was adopted as a pattern for tactical intelligence doctrine across the entire British Expeditionary Force (and later by the American Expeditionary Force as well).[18]

Airplanes constituted one of the Great War's major contributions to intelligence. Scouting is as old as warfare itself, and it had been performed by all sorts of means, chief among them the cavalrymen who had made up sizable portions of armies for the last millennium. Reconnaissance did not qualify as "spying" (though it certainly produced information called "intelligence") because it was conducted by armed soldiers in uniform, who ran all the risks of the battlefield but relied on speed and stealth to avoid a fight rather than mass and firepower to win one. Scouts held a certain status in the army for their resourceful daring, but the cavalry surpassed all other soldiers in the romantic esteem with which they were held by the public. When captured in uniform, scouts and cavalrymen could usually expect to be accorded the rough courtesies due to prisoners of war (instead of being hanged like petty criminals—the age-old fate of spies).

Conducting reconnaissance from "overhead" quickly came of age as an intelligence tool in World War I. Traditional observation balloons served throughout the conflict, but soon the airplane joined the fray as well. By the end of 1914 all sides were flying reconnaissance aircraft, first with observers taking notes but soon with increasingly sophisticated cameras. The airplanes could not only take pictures for later reference; they could also vector artillery shells onto targets of opportunity, first by dropping notes near friendly batteries and later telegraphing messages on airborne wireless sets. Imagery intelligence pioneer Edward Steichen explained to his superiors in the US Army that "[i]t would be well for every soldier to know that the enemy observation planes flying high overhead are a much more dangerous enemy to them than those that come with bombs or harass them by machine-gun fire."[19] It was to chase away such threats that other aircraft—called fighters—would soon be armed with machine guns and then custom-designed for the work of pursuing and downing enemy reconnaissance planes.

Airplanes quickly supplanted cavalry for reconnaissance, at least on the Western Front (the horse soldiers still proved useful in the vast expanses of the Eastern Front, and on minor fronts like Palestine). As George Custer had learned in 1862, reconnaissance from aircraft crossed the line into intelligence work at the point where the observer could see more than those on the ground imagined. In World War I, that line was bridged when trained photo interpreters started studying the pictures that the airplanes had carried home. Armies in the past had dug in, slipped behind hills or woods, or somehow obscured their positions from line-of-sight scrutiny, but they had never had to worry about hostile eyes directly above them. How much could the interpreters really see, and what did it mean? These were carefully guarded secrets, as even a hint might cause the enemy to change practices (though such leaks were probably rarer than the security officers feared). In reality, the fact that British or French or German photo interpreters could learn so much from seemingly indistinct blurs on black-and-white prints was quickly shared with British and French and German commanders, who studied those images and ordered their armies to hide from aerial observation. Henceforth, the ancient practice of camouflage had to be developed anew, this time with scientific rigor (and sometimes even by scientists recruited for just this purpose).

Aerial reconnaissance never lived up the hyperbole of the US Army's Chief Signal Officer George Scriven, who wondered aloud in late 1914 whether aircraft had made surprise impossible in war.[20] For starters, it was expensive in terms of aircraft, pilots, observers, and ground crew, as well as the entire basing infrastructure required at even the simplest grass landing fields. Photographic missions were often frustrated by weather and were pointless at night. The job was also dangerous. Pilots took their lives in their hands just taxiing to the flight line in such rickety craft; once airborne, they were prey for increasingly deadly and determined antiaircraft fire, not to mention ever-faster enemy fighters whose chief task and relish was downing vulnerable observation planes. Bringing back a fresh roll of film meant still more work on the ground for camera technicians, developers, interpreters, analysts, editors, supervisors, mapmakers, publications specialists, and briefers. For all this trouble and expense, however, aerial reconnaissance ensured that a great number of secrets could not be kept. Aerial imagery had become vital to commanders on both sides.

The paramount source of intelligence for the World War I battlefield, however, came from intercepted electronic communications. Opposing armies had been cutting or tapping each other's telegraph lines since at least the American Civil War, forcing generals to encode their transmissions and devote some of their smartest officers to the chore of puzzling out the enemy's ciphers. What set the Great War apart was the hitherto unimaginable quantity and quality of electronic transmissions that exploded into the ether as the warring powers worked to direct and inform their generals, admirals, and even their new pilots. The head of the French cryptologic service estimated that his people intercepted more than 100,000,000 German words over the course of the conflict.[21] The volume, timeliness, and precision of information gained from radio intercepts, at all hours and in all weathers, could not be matched by any other intelligence source. Radio intelligence, moreover, also bridged the tactical and strategic realms, making it of importance along the front lines, and for planners and commanders in the rear, as well as for ministers and diplomats at home.

The armies relied on three methods of collecting intelligence from enemy signals. In order from the simplest to the most demanding, these amounted to (1) direction finding, to pinpoint the physical location of radio transmitters; (2) "traffic analysis," to glean all sorts of clues from the "externals" of enemy messages; and, where possible, (3) cryptology, to produce plaintext versions of the coded and enciphered messages themselves. The French pioneered direction finding, or "goniometry," from the war's opening days; it was a fairly simple but laborious process of monitoring the airwaves for transmissions and keeping detailed logs at multiple points to allow the triangulation of signals.[22] Traffic analysis ranged in sophistication from the simple counting of the enemy's messages (which might, for instance, increase as his troops prepared for an offensive push), to scrutinizing the addressing lines of the messages themselves to identify enemy units and determine his command structure. Cryptology constituted the most difficult and time-consuming method of exploiting intercepted messages, but it held out the promise of a break into enemy communications that could reveal his plans and vulnerabilities wholesale.

Radio's early successes in battles like Tannenberg would not be repeated in this war, at least on such a scale. All sides rapidly improved their communications security, imposing discipline on commanders and radio operators. The Germans came later to the business of systematically analyzing enemy signals, but by 1916 all the major combatants were refining their devices and practices for exploiting the enemy's inevitable lapses, and finding ways to exploit messages sent even with his best codes.[23] The resulting race between "defense" and "offense" lasted for the remainder of the war, with no side developing a clear and lasting lead in signals intelligence for the armies.

The basic problem became that of devising secure communications systems that could be ever more readily adapted to the importance of the content they carried and the circumstances of their use. Codes and ciphers, of course, varied in their complexity and in the skills they required of their users, but the code and its accompanying cipher are only parts of the larger system created to ensure the timeliness, accuracy, volume, and security of messaging. A minister or an ambassador needed a lengthy codebook and the best cipher to withstand prolonged attacks by the best foreign code-breakers, and an embassy could also employ trained specialists, working in secure offices, on the tasks involved in handling messages (they also had comparatively ample time to do their work). At the opposite end of the scale, a "trench code" for the front lines could be expected to be used under dire conditions and even to be captured. It did not have to be "unbreakable" as it was not to be trusted with messages of more than local and passing importance; it might be just a simple cipher disk of the sort recommended by Alberti in the fifteenth century, for all it had to do was to obscure basic tactical information long enough for the information to be useless to the enemy. Such a code also had to be flexible and simple enough for junior personnel to use quickly and correctly; if it was not, a commander who needed to call for help might toss it aside and broadcast his demand in the clear. Worse yet, front-line units that disliked or distrusted their codebooks and cipher wheels might be tempted to make up their own, substituting cinema or sports terms, as some American units did in 1918. These homemade codes were probably even less secure than clear text transmissions, as the illusion of security made their users careless.

The kinds of information that could be gleaned from the ether by taking advantage of the enemy's communications security lapses were many and varied. The closing campaigns on the Western Front witnessed a classic example of the seesaw competition between codemakers and code-breakers—and the risks inherent in even the smallest lapses in communications security. In early 1918, the Germans gathered their forces from the relatively quiet Eastern Front (after the new Bolshevik regime in Moscow had signed a separate peace with the Central Powers in March 1918) and massed them in the West for one final drive to knock France out of the war before American troops could swing the balance in the Allies' favor. Allied intelligence across the line knew something was brewing—it is not possible to prepare a major offensive without the enemy noticing something. A German wireless operator helped them just before the start of the big push by obligingly keying a message in his army's sophisticated new "Schluesselheft" trench code and then repeating it moments later in the old code. An alert American intercept station noticed the duplication and made the initial breach in the cryptographic system, which French and British codebreakers soon widened.[24]

The subsequent attack, Operation Michael, was a surprise mostly in its magnitude and ferocity. The Germans nearly broke through the British and French lines, separating formations from one another and forcing them to counterattack against heavy odds or retreat for miles in order to gain time and space to regroup. The Germans were not able to sustain the momentum of their assault, however, and allied troops sealed the dike in time. The Germans at almost the same time had introduced a new cipher—they called it "ADFGX" —for the use of their rear-area headquarters units. It stumped French codebreakers for weeks, until the volume of message traffic had accumulated to the point where the *Bureau de Chiffre*'s Georges Painvain surmised that the enciphered text had to be based on a transposition table set up like a checkerboard. By June, he and his colleagues were reading German messages only hours after they had been transmitted—fast enough, for instance, for the French to blunt Ludendorff's final blows before the German army gave up the offensive for good.[25]

A young American codebreaker in G2/A6, William Friedman, wrote an epitaph for German trench codes shortly after the war: "But no code, no matter how carefully constructed, will be safe without trained, intelligent personnel. A poorly constructed code may be in reality more safe when used by an expert than a very well constructed one when used by a careless operator, or one ignorant of the dangers of improperly encoded messages."[26] Marcel Givierge, who headed the French army's cipher bureau for much of the war (and afterward returned to it and created its training course), admonished students of cryptography to "encode well or do not encode at all. In transmitting in clear text, you give only a piece of information to the enemy, and you know what it is; in encoding badly, you permit him to read all your correspondence and that of your friends."[27]

The War to End War

One nation—Great Britain—was clearly the best at seizing the opportunity to glean strategic insight and cause strategic effects through the control of communications (both its own and its foes). The breakthroughs of its code-breakers came only at the price of backbreaking analysis, but they repaid the investment and far more. British military and political leaders, and the managers of their intelligence services, fleetingly glimpsed the future and used that insight strategically to guide strategy and diplomacy. They even scored perhaps the greatest intelligence coup of all.

Late in 1916, Berlin determined that its best course lay in starving England through unrestricted submarine warfare. Russia was faltering but still tying down great numbers of German troops in the East (along with almost the entire Austrian army). Something had to be done to split the Anglo-Russian-French alliance, and Britain was vulnerable. A resumption of the unrestricted campaign that the U-boats had launched and then hastily dropped the previous year (after the sinking of the *Lusitania* had angered Washington) might do the trick. The Kaiser's counselors knew their torpedoes would sooner or later claim American lives—and might even provoke the United States into declaring war and joining the allies—but the small US Army was distracted by revolution in Mexico and seemed unlikely to make much difference even if sent to the Western Front. To hedge Germany's bets, however, Foreign Minister Arthur Zimmermann devised a way to distract the Americans and divert their war supplies from the allies. He had his embassy in Washington pass along an offer to the Mexican government: Declare war on the United States, he urged the Mexicans; once they joined the fight, Berlin promised to see that Germany's ultimate victory resulted in the return of territories that Mexico had lost to the Americans in 1846.

The government of Mexico spurned the offer, of course, but not before Zimmermann's telegram had landed in the delighted hands of Britain's Admiral Hall. How it got there made a tale for the ages, and one moreover that encapsulates the ways in which the intelligence business was evolving faster than all but a handful of people grasped at the time. Hall's organization had been reading German diplomatic telegrams intercepted from neutral-owned cables since early in the war, and had been reading American diplomatic traffic as well since 1914.[28] Telegram 5747 on January 16, 1917, represented a combination of both—a German diplomatic message hidden inside a telegram sent by the American embassy in Berlin to the State Department in Washington. That in itself proved an interesting story. In essence, President Wilson had been engaged in secret talks with Germany to find an end to the war, and he did not want leaks of his dealings to the press from talkative or obstreperous State Department officials. Wilson thus used ciphers of his own (childish) design in State telegrams, and he promised the German Foreign Ministry that their correspondence on the negotiations with their ambassador could be sent across the Atlantic on American-owned cables (which in his touching way he assumed the British would not dare to tap). Telegram 5747 was thus an abuse of Wilson's misplaced trust—it was Foreign Minister Zimmermann's use of an American cable to prepare a knife for America's back.

Admiral Hall at once recognized the opportunity and the hazard that the telegram represented for Britain. Used correctly, it could convince Washington to declare war, bringing the world's largest economy and a vast pool of capital and manpower into the conflict on the Allied side. Mishandled, Zimmermann's offer to the Mexicans could give ammunition to Britain's many detractors in the United States. All that Zimmermann had to do was to deny the telegram and call it a British hoax. In the event, British diplomats could hardly be expected to argue its authenticity and demonstrate how Room 40 had pulled the message from a decoded State Department telegram.

His Majesty's Government had to work swiftly and carefully. First, a cover story was needed to explain how London had innocently come into possession of Zimmermann's telegram without mentioning they had found it in a sensitive State Department message. Britain's diplomats rapidly answered this need, obtaining a still-enciphered copy of the telegram from the telegraph office in Mexico City. Now the Foreign Office could call the American ambassador in London and let his aide read Zimmermann's fantastic proposal. To add verisimilitude, the British even handed him their reconstructed German diplomatic codebook and let him decode the unenciphered message by hand. The story held up, utterly convincing the American ambassador, Walter Page, and through him Wilson and his advisers, that the treacherous Zimmermann was plotting against the United States, and moreover that Britain had done nothing contrary to American interests in uncovering the conspiracy.[29]

News of the Zimmermann telegram thus broke upon the American public with great force. It answered the political need of the Wilson administration for dramatic and objective proof of the danger inherent in German militarism. While it was still derided as a British trick by some in the United States, Zimmermann's own avowal on March 3 of his (figurative) paternity to an American journalist soon clinched the matter. Congress declared war on Germany on April 6, 1917, thus handing Admiral Hall and his colleagues the intelligence coup of the war. The affair was a combination of codebreaking skill and timely foreign intelligence in Mexico City contributing to a "covert action" (a later term, but apt here) that earned the Allies formal American backing and the promise of fresh troops for the Western Front.

World War I had already been the most revolutionary conflict in history, at least for intelligence. This revolution meant that the United States, when it came late to the war, was woefully backward in this rapidly evolving field. American officials had to learn a lot in a very short time. The extent and pace of their forced education over the next eighteen months was testimony to how much had changed.

The first agency affected was the Department of Justice's small Bureau of Investigation—the nation's first true federal law enforcement agency. The bureau had been created in 1908, not long after Congress decreed that the Department of Justice could no longer hire private detectives or Secret Service agents from the Treasury Department to fulfill its occasional need for investigators. Congress formally made peacetime espionage and sabotage federal crimes and gave the job of stopping them to the bureau when it passed the Espionage Act in April 1917. The bureau's performance in World War I proved valuable more for the precedents it set than the contribution it made to final victory. With a slate of tasks inherited from its peacetime work and fewer than 400 agents to cover the entire country, it spent much of its energy chasing "slackers" (draft dodgers), and did little against German agents.[30] By this point, furthermore, most or all of the Germans had decamped for Mexico, fearing that the penalty for wartime espionage or sabotage would be a quick death sentence.

A still more intense education in the new ways of intelligence forced itself on the US Army when it arrived in France. The army had been small but tough in 1914, with senior commanders who had proved themselves in the war with Spain and the Philippine insurrection (some, like Brigadier General John J. Pershing, had fought Apaches and the Sioux). Three years of modern war had passed the army by, however, and by 1917 the Americans needed sustained tutoring before they could be trusted to hold trenches opposite German troops. Indeed, the US First Infantry Division arrived in France to fanfare not long after Washington declared war, but it was a pick-up outfit comprising veteran regiments that had been scattered along the Mexican border and filled out with green draftees. (The division, nick-named the Big Red One, would not be fit for front-line duty until January 1918, and most army divisions would not enter the line before the follow-ing summer.) The US Army's intelligence function had been similarly left behind. The army had intercepted radio signals in pursuit of Pancho Villa but had no fixed doctrine for intelligence work before 1917.[31] The disci-pline of intelligence had led an impoverished and precarious existence in the rudimentary General Staff, and the army's standard reference on the topic (Arthur Wagner's *Service of Security and Information*, reprinted fif-teen times between 1893 and 1916) retained chapters on cavalry patrol-ling and Indian scouts. Commanders of the American Expeditionary Force (AEF) learned swiftly under British and French mentors, however, adopting the French army's staff system, borrowing intelligence regulations and doc-trine from the British, and building a Military Intelligence Division (MID) in Pershing's General Headquarters. MID grew rapidly into a capable ser-vice providing "theater-level" intelligence services (including signals and imagery intelligence, counterespionage, and even small-scale agent opera-tions in neutral Switzerland).[32]

The American intelligence ordeal typified the experience of every major combatant in the war. The difference was the compressed timeline in which it occurred, which made it for the Americans a perfect crystallization of what was happening. Pershing's officers brought this experience back to Washington when the war ended, reforming the War Department's own MID along the lines they had utilized in France in the early 1920s.[33] As a result, the Americans' intelligence doctrine took on a decidedly British coloration.

Back at home, the Americans had to develop some sort of strategic codebreaking capability. They also had to improve their own codes, and swiftly, for the British now had quietly informed the embassy in London that the ways in which the Americans were encoding their cables con-stituted a menace to allied security. All this gave opportunity to a State Department clerk, Herbert O. Yardley, an inveterate tinkerer who loved a good puzzle. The department's crude encipherment system posed only a brief obstacle to his curiosity, as he easily solved it and warned his superi-ors of its vulnerability. As a result, he gained a reputation as a codebreaker and the army hired him shortly after the declaration of war, giving him license to establish a branch in the Military Intelligence Division (MI-8) in Washington that would be dedicated to unlocking the coded messages of

German spies who tried to set up new operations in the United States.[34] By the end of the war, Yardley and MI-8 had run out of German secret writing and moved on to reading the diplomatic telegrams of several countries, sharing the take with the State and War Departments. He and his office did not make much of a difference to the American war effort before the Armistice in November 1918, but it was a beginning for the United States in the field of strategic cryptology.

The Information Revolution in War

World War I forced progress in every field of technology with a military application. Airplanes, ships, and automotive vehicles all improved rapidly, along with chemistry and electronics. War had become an insatiable consumer of materiel during the Industrial Revolution, and now it became a geometrically greater consumer of information as well, with the possibility of real-time transmission of orders and reports almost immediately becoming the imperative—to do so faster than the enemy. Furthermore, as noted above in the context of Britain's blockade of Germany, the war demanded the creation and management of vast new data sets, which would be useless without sustained collation and evaluation—and progress in the techniques and the organization of analysis.

The sudden and urgent need to exploit radio signals and photographic images created wholly new intelligence disciplines. Men (and soon women as well) with little or no prior training in these crafts became specialists, and the services that gathered them together to parse intercepted transmissions and scrutinize aerial photographs applied the maturing principles of organization to create, as it were from whole cloth, new information processing bureaus where nothing of the sort had existed before. The goal was intelligence fusion. Prisoners and documents taken in raids told what units were across No Man's Land and hinted at the enemy's physical and moral condition. Direction finding could pinpoint the locations of headquarters and other targets behind the lines; traffic analysis revealed the enemy's order-of-battle and thus offered more hints about his plans. French cryptanalysts occasionally suggested artillery barrages and feigned attack preparations on the German lines to goad the Boche into talking more on the radio, thus yielding more "intercept" for analysis.[35] Actual codebreaking might reveal his orders to the troops, and their readiness to execute those commands. All these clues in turn allowed the analysts to form hypotheses about the enemy's plans, which cued the pilots and photo interpreters where to search for his preparations. When working properly and together, each intelligence "discipline" supported the others, making a whole greater than the sum of its parts, and providing astute commanders with a system not only for constructing mosaic pictures of the enemy's situation but also for actively winkling out his capabilities and intentions.

Each of the armies on the Western Front had to follow suit in developing such a system. Espionage had traditionally shunned organization and method, as the handful of people engaged in it had little need for formal processes. As espionage morphed into intelligence, however, the armies' analysts and technicians had to be organized in increasingly sophisticated offices and staffs, complete with intricate divisions of labor, precise support and logistical services, hierarchical management structures (and sometimes with around-the-clock production cycles) to process data and disseminate reports and briefs to their patrons and "customers." Furthermore, someone had to manage these workers and offices—hence American cryptologist Herbert Yardley's lament that "it began to look as if the war had converted me into an executive instead of a cryptographer."[36]

Making sense of quantities of data as fast as possible transformed military operations as well as military intelligence. Since, for the most part, the new organizations created to process signals or imagery were situated in military structures, this need for analysis and analysts caused something of a cultural shock to those same militaries, which were forced to hire and also to protect and promote all sorts of distinctly unmilitary persons.[37] Official reflections on this topic during World War I sound amusing in hindsight. The head of the American Expeditionary Force's SIGINT section (G-2/A-6), Frank Moorman, noted in 1917 that the army suddenly needed men of the sort who had "spent their lives studying hieroglyphics, cuneiform characters and the like."[38] One can imagine how such advice must have struck some of his superiors, trained as they were for an era of black powder and cavalry charges.

Information processing drove an imperative to share information across national lines with allies. This was also something new for militaries, as it involved sitting down beside foreign intelligence officers not in some smoky bistro but at conference tables, with maps and charts and statistics—and increasingly with intercepts and aerial photographs. Intelligence "liaison" magnified the power of the British and French services. Even in its rudimentary and wary beginnings it helped each side understand which problems the other had already solved—thus economizing both their efforts—and it allowed for at least a rough division of labor, increasing the collection resources and brainpower applied to problems from multiple angles. Both the British and French came to the game with comparable skill levels and facing similar issues. By 1917 they were enormously more skilled than the Americans who joined them, but both Britons and Frenchmen by this juncture were convinced of the value of intelligence liaison and rolled up their proverbial sleeves at once to tutor the Americans (the consequences for American fighting power, if they neglected this chore, were too grave to imagine). American energy and resources soon created a three-way intelligence-sharing arrangement.

Intelligence liaison also worked at the strategic level. British authorities tipped their still-neutral American counterparts to a German conspiracy with Hindus that was seeking to undermine the Empire, and also ran agents in the United States with the tacit acquiescence of the Justice Department.[39] But in this field the most important efforts might have been those of a young Englishman in Washington, DC. William Wiseman had served briefly in France in 1915, and after being wounded and sent home, he joined the new SIS. His bosses there sent him to New York to run SIS's growing station, and he was soon in Washington, where he impressed Colonel Edward House, confidant of President Wilson. House, like Wilson, prized Wiseman for his candor and earnest willingness to make himself useful in all matters that concerned the new and novel Anglo-American alliance. This "plausible little man" (in First Lady Edith Wilson's estimation) was not exactly an agent with covert influence over American war policy, and so it is a bit of stretch to call his business an intelligence operation at all. Wilson and House liked having in Wiseman a second line of communication with decision makers in London (a line that was moreover outside the control of Britain's ambassador in Washington, Cecil Spring-Rice). It probably would not have overly concerned them to know that their special line to London ran through the Ministry of War instead of the Foreign Office, or that every favor Wiseman seemed to do for them placed American policy ever more tightly in Britain's orbit (as well as complicating Britain's own policymaking process toward the United States).[40] William Wiseman was thus a very well-placed liaison officer rather than a spy. As such, he was an early exemplar of a kind of intelligence officer that would become far more common in the latter half of the twentieth century.

Impacts

In World War I, the quiet arts of divining the enemy's secrets and influencing him by stealth graduated to become strategic and technological forces in their own right. Intelligence helped drive tactics, technological change, and even strategy. The airplane, between 1914 and 1918, was far more important as an observer (to find the enemy and target the artillery) than as a weapon. Radio was an instrument of command and control with huge intelligence applications—its effects as an intelligence tool shaped not only tactics and campaigns but also influenced how radios were built, fielded, and employed. Britain's strategically important blockade of Germany was only possible with signals intelligence. These and other examples showed how intelligence became a force not only for affecting people and events but also for transforming entire fields of national endeavor.

What difference did intelligence make in the war's outcome? It is clear that the Allies defeated the Central Powers because their armies and their blockade bled the Germans white. Both of those factors were enabled by intelligence. The Allies' ability not only to halt Germany's spring offensive in 1918 but also to gain ground on the German army during the following summer—which finally convinced the Kaiser's high command it could not continue—was made possible by the Americans finally entering the line. The Americans had arrived not a moment too soon—and almost too late. The French and British might have stopped the German drives in 1918 without American aid; but they could not have taken the offensive that summer without it. The French had learned the operational art—the way of stringing together a series of well-prepared offensives that consumed German reserves—and the British had at last deployed the manpower and materiel to work in Marechal Foch's new system. The Americans freed up sectors of the front and enabled the more formidable French and British armies to concentrate their forces and take the offensive in late summer. Timing was everything. President Wilson was inclining toward war early in 1917 and might well have entered without the goad of the Zimmermann telegram. But when? Would the doughboys have had enough time to go "Over There" while they could still make a difference in 1918?

Perceptive leaders soon after the war recognized the strategic importance of intelligence. What is fascinating from the perspective of later ages, inured as they are to the demands of secrecy, is how open the leaders of World War I soon became in talking about their wartime sources

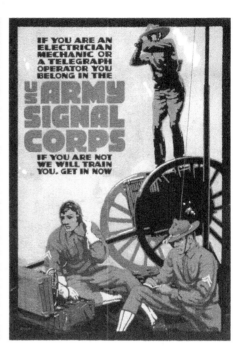

2.3 and **2.4** The Great War created enormous demand for communications specialists—those who eavesdropped as well as those who transmitted. Radio was a cutting edge technology at this time. These two recruitment posters are from the US Army Signal Corps. *Library of Congress*

and methods. Several commanders in the 1920s discussed the advantages that radio triangulation and intercepts had offered them. Admiral William Sims, who had led the American fleet in European waters, talked about locating U-boats by their transmissions.[41] German commanders proved no more circumspect. "We were always warned by the wireless messages of the Russian staff of the positions where troops were being concentrated for any new undertaking," bragged German general Max Hoffmann in his 1924 memoir. "Only once during the entire war were we taken by surprise on the Eastern Front by a Russian attack."[42] The strategic advantage of codebreaking worked its way out into the public eye as well. A British official hinted at it in a speech in 1926, and American attorneys followed that lead in building their public case for the German government to pay damages for the Black Tom sabotage.[43] As a result, the fact that the British government had systematically exploited German diplomatic traffic was revealed, causing considerable attention in Germany in the late 1920s.[44] That leaders and experts across the advanced nations could infer that fact was significant to the course of the war. One of those experts was the American cryptologist William Friedman, who divined the truth behind the Zimmermann telegram and published his findings in 1938.[45] Those revelations fed the general conclusion across the West that messages sent in military and diplomatic communications had to be made secure, and that the power of machines had to be harnessed to cloak sensitive messages from prying eyes.

The combatants also learned another lesson in the Great War: that the methods of controlling forces at a distance were vulnerable to being exploited by adversaries. "The radio is a last resort that no prudent commander, particularly of the higher units, will use as long as any other means remains," noted US Army signals officer Parker Hitt in a lecture to other officers shortly after the war. "The enemy is sure to copy all radio messages sent out and at the same time will locate accurately the position of the sending station and usually tell what kind of a headquarters it is serving."[46] All the industrialized states set to work after World War I to fix that vulnerability with improved communications security. The key, so to speak, was in letting machines do the laborious chore of enciphering messages. Codebooks were awkward enough to use, both for sender and receiver. Printed encipherment tables and cipher disks compounded the complexity and burden on code clerks, and further lengthened the time required to prepare messages for secure transmission. In the 1920s, all the major powers investigated machines that promised to encipher and decipher their coded messages swiftly and reliably—important considerations for a commander on the move in a ship, a field headquarters, or even an airplane.

The Germans found their answer in an electromechanical device called Enigma. A Swiss invention, it was marketed from the early 1920s to far-flung business enterprises feeling a need to keep trade secrets from their competitors. The German Navy soon adopted it and the army followed suit, adding improvements that the *Kriegsmarine* acquired in turn in 1934. A simple machine to use, the Enigma was durable, portable, and quite secure when properly employed. Messages that it enciphered through a series of rotor wheels and a plugboard like that of a telephone switch seemed (and practically were) invulnerable to a "brute-force" attack on all its 3×10^{114} possible key configurations—a sum greater than the number of atoms in the observable universe.[47] Enigma was such a good tactical encryption system that the

Germans frequently used it for strategic messages as well as battlefield communications. They would also force it on their Italian partners when the two nations began operating in conjunction in early 1941. The Italians had decent communications security and signals intelligence of their own, but the Germans assumed theirs was superior, and had their way.[48]

Other Western militaries also shopped for enciphering machines. The Americans dabbled with a device offered to them by inventor Edward Hebern, until the US Army's William Friedman unlocked the machine's secrets and realized that others could as well. In the late 1930s, the British refined the Enigma into something better, which they called Typex. A Swede, Boris Hagelin, built his own Enigma rivals and sold them to the French, the Americans, the Swedes, and others. Friedman's team with his navy counterparts designed a machine to beat them all: the ECM Mark 2 (or SIGABA), the state of the art in rotor enciphering, which, while adopted by both the army and navy just before World War II, weighed far more than the Enigma and thus was suited mostly for ships and higher headquarters. The US Army made do on the battlefield with simpler devices, like the Hagelin-designed M-209. The encipherment of diplomatic messages in many countries followed suit, with the foreign bureaus also adopting machines to secure their telegrams, which of course had to travel over wires that were in the complete control of host nations.

As all sides adopted machine encryption, they also tried to break the new ciphers of their rivals. Several succeeded. The British, Germans, French, Poles, Estonians, Finns, Japanese, Americans, and Italians all made progress against the codes and ciphers of the countries of concern to them. In Italy, that success owed much to a campaign of burglaries against foreign embassies mounted by the army's intelligence bureau.[49] The most successful were the British, in part because they had built up a great deal of capacity in signals intelligence during the Great War. Just after the Armistice, Britain's armed services had merged their respective cryptologic arms in a new organization called the Government Code & Cypher School (GC&CS), housed first in the Royal Navy, then under the Foreign and Commonwealth Office, and finally, from 1923 on, under the Secret Intelligence Service (once again, the subtle influence of Winston Churchill played a role in bringing this to pass). GC&CS soon showed its power even in peacetime, handing British diplomats and statesmen decrypted messages from many nations of concern to London, including France, Russia, Japan, and the United States.

Despite the finding that the codebreakers seemed to be odd chaps with "somewhat peculiar temperaments," leaders in Whitehall appreciated the service they rendered. A British senior negotiator at the Lausanne conference (1922) complimented the help his team had received from them: "the information we obtained at the psychological moments from secret sources was invaluable to us, and put us in the position of a man who is playing Bridge and knows the cards in his adversary's hand."[50]

The Americans came right behind, however, and for the first time in that nation's history were building a world-class intelligence capability. Herbert Yardley's codebreakers in the US Army's MI8 kept on working after 1918, with an infusion of money and attention from the State Department. They soon repaid the investment, reading Japanese diplomatic cables and helping State negotiate a favorable ratio of capital ships vis-à-vis Japan at the 1922 Washington Naval Conference. Not only was Yardley working under joint diplomatic and military sponsorship (as with GC&CS in Britain), he unwittingly reached for a similar metaphor to describe his triumph over his Japanese counterparts: "Stud poker is not a very difficult game after you see your opponent's hole card."[51] But Yardley's day was passing. His native intuition and the manual methods employed by his "Black Chamber" were no match for the enciphering machines on the horizon, and were already yielding diminishing returns when in 1929 a new secretary of state, Henry Stimson, withdrew his department's support. "Gentlemen do not read each other's mail," Stimson wrote years later, in a quip that unfairly became proverbial for naiveté. Yet Stimson was no fool; he had few qualms about the US Army reading diplomatic telegrams; he simply did not want the State Department and Yardley doing so. He might indeed have sensed that Yardley was not only out of ideas but a loose cannon as well. If he did, then Yardley soon proved him right by publishing the secret story of the Washington Naval Treaty in a potboiler titled *The American Black Chamber* (1931), which sold well in the United States but twice as well in Japan.

The men (and increasingly women) of the future for American cryptology were already in harness by the time Yardley got the sack. William Friedman led the way for the US Army. Born to Russian Jewish immigrants from Odessa and trained as a plant geneticist, he was neither a mathematician nor an electrical engineer. But he was a genius of sorts at identifying a problem and motivating the right people to solve it. He also found machines to help with the work of decrypting mechanically enciphered

2.5 William Friedman in an undated photo.
National Security Agency

messages, persuading the army to buy IBM tabulating machines in 1936. The US Navy's Laurance Safford played a similar role for his service; his staff had experimented with IBM tabulators for codebreaking four years earlier.[52] By the early 1930s, both services were having modest but growing success against the military, naval, and diplomatic codes of various nations, especially Japan. Unfortunately, these achievements were achieved almost in spite of the disorganization of American cryptology. Unlike Britain, where GC&CS was a joint entity from the start, and had firm guidance from the diplomats and entrée to SIS from 1923 on, the army and navy cryptologic arms in America remained separate and (after 1929) comparatively isolated not only from each other but from the State Department as well. They occasionally shared leads and findings, such as material copied in burglaries of the Japanese consulate in New York ("a never-failing source of supply" of diplomatic ciphers and keys, recalled Safford), but they did not do so smoothly or consistently.[53] The divide between them would be a continual puzzlement to their British partners in World War II, and a limitation on their performance.

Shaking the World

Europe and much of the planet suffered the trauma of the First World War. Over 35 million fighting men were killed, wounded, or missing at the conflict's end. Disease killed more inclusively; at least 50 million men, women, and children died in the 1918 influenza epidemic. Vast wealth and productive capacity had been lost, either destroyed outright or diverted to war production. The catastrophe created the conditions in which the challenges to liberalism at last had a chance to flourish. Resulting dislocations also allowed challenges in the empires—challenges from elites who had imbibed the new Western notions to use against their colonial overlords. The challengers in the West and East, and the ideas they espoused, ranged from democratic to radical, and some happily embraced violence. The pre-1914 anarchists could kill, but they could not shake the world order. That changed in 1917, and from then on liberalism came under siege from more lethal threats.

The first and greatest challenge came from Russia. The collapse of the Czarist regime in February 1917 opened the road for revolutionaries of many stripes. The subsequent rise of the Bolsheviks the following autumn owed no small debt to their proficiency with the clandestine arts, learned during their long repression by the Czar's Okhrana. The fact that the Bolsheviks under Lenin held on to power in the face of a sea of troubles was in turn owed partly to their creation of the "All-Russian Extraordinary Commission for Combating Counter-Revolution, Profiteering and Corruption"—or "Cheka" for short. The Cheka began in Petrograd (Saint Petersburg) within weeks of the October Revolution and spread to become a collection of local Chekas or Extraordinary Commissions charged with rooting out the counterrevolution in their towns and districts. In their collectivity, all the Chekas soon became something new—a modern intelligence organization that worked for a party and a cause rather than a ministry.

Headed by Felix Dzerzhinsky ("a sincere idealist, ruthless but chivalrous" recalled one colleague), the Cheka was powerful and secretive—as were the several European secret services, of course—but soon it was also relatively autonomous.[54] The Cheka had busy executioners who were arbitrary and unchecked, answering nominally to the Bolshevik interior ministry and the revolutionary tribunals but in effect answering only to Lenin and the People's Commissars. Clemency could be obtained by personal appeals through party officials to Cheka leaders, who did not always prove merciful or effective: "While I was away they shot the poor devil," shrugged the president of Petrograd's Cheka to an inquiring comrade in one case.[55] Such men constituted the "sword and shield" of the revolution, attacking enemies within and ultimately without, while paying especial attention to progressive (as opposed to reactionary) but still-suspect allies and rivals of the revolution. Mensheviks, Socialist Revolutionaries (SRs), and anarchists all fell under suspicion and worse as the "Red Terror" ground them down after an SR named Fanny Kaplan shot Lenin in August 1918. The Extraordinary Commissions thus had a key role in protecting the revolution from several possible counter-revolutions, which would surely have offered the Bolsheviks no more mercy than the Bolsheviks had shown their foes and rivals.

In the grim winter of 1918–19, a young revolutionary who called himself Victor Serge happened to oversee the archives of the Czar's now-defunct Okhrana in besieged Petrograd. Though important records had escaped the Bolsheviks' grasp (those of the Okhrana's Paris branch soon found their way to America), the Petrograd trove included files amassed on 30,000 to 40,000 "agents provocateurs" active over the preceding two decades. The revolutionaries pored over them and made plans to guard the archive intact until the last possible minute before the city fell to the counterrevolutionary Whites, as the records "would provide precious weapons for tomorrow's hangmen and firing squads." The People's Commissars and the Cheka learned rapidly from the Okhrana archives—which included "excellent historical dissertations on the revolutionary parties"—using them to root out former Czarist agents and track leftist rivals.[56] Identifications proceeded apace, but the local Chekas were not fastidious about guilt, innocence, and due process. Loose organization and no standards but revolutionary fervor made them drunk with power and desperate to save the revolution—and themselves. They even defied Lenin's 1920 decree ending the death penalty. The Petrograd Cheka solved this problem by preemptively executing its prisoners. One of its leaders told Serge "if the People's Commissars were getting converted to humanitarianism that was their business. Our business was to crush the counterrevolution forever, and they could shoot us afterwards if they felt like it!"[57]

With the Cheka's help, the Russian Revolution soon became totalitarian—and seemingly irreversible. This upheaval sent a new and unforeseen intelligence challenge all across the world: revolutionaries with the fervor of anarchists but also with real discipline, as well as a state to train and finance them. The anarchists were still dangerous; authorities in the United States discovered a plot to mail bombs to three dozen prominent American businessmen and officials in April 1919, and weeks later, eight simultaneous bombings injured Attorney General A. Mitchell Palmer and others. A huge bomb left in a wagon on Wall Street killed thirty-eight and injured another 400 that September—the crime was never conclusively solved, but imputed to anarchists. But the long-term subversive threat, such as it was, came from Russia. By 1920 British codebreakers were reading (and British officials were leaking to the press) messages of the Soviet Trade Delegation in London that showed the Soviets were working against all odds to stir up revolution among the workers and soldiers of Britain.[58] Moscow's attempts to foment and organize revolutionary cells in the British and French militaries continued into the 1930s.[59]

The Communists' ability to hold power and wage this intelligence struggle in the West testified to their ferocious counterintelligence apparatus, which itself depended on the Communist Party's penetration of all segments of society with its members, agents, and ubiquitous informers. After the revolution, the Soviet regime had gained virtually absolute control of its population, ensuring that Russia would remain for foreigners the proverbial riddle "wrapped in a mystery inside an enigma" (Churchill's phrase, in 1939). Russia's Communists took a long perspective, and sought to raze the "little platoons" of society, leaving no intermediary authorities between the individual and the state. The result was a system of social control that Kautilya might have envied, of which George Orwell one day projected the logical extension in *Nineteen Eighty-Four*. Such a system, of course, required its own apparatus of institutions; the Cheka and its successor organizations soon ran the largest and most comprehensive secret police and intelligence organizations the world had ever seen, a state within the state, complete with its own string of prisons in Siberia that Solzhenitsyn later dubbed the Gulag Archipelago. Not for nothing did the Cheka adopt the label of "sword and shield" of the revolution.

Chekists not only ensured that no threats could arise to Communist control from inside the regime and the nation. After 1919, the Communist Party of the Soviet Union reached out and transformed other national Communist parties, making of them loyal instruments and platforms for evangelization (or subversion, from the point of view of local authorities). Red uprisings (or at least agitation) across Europe resulted in pitched battles in Germany and Hungary just after the end of the First World War. These only lasted a season, but their effects lingered throughout the West. Where the party could not impose its discipline on foreign comrades, Chekists sometimes gave it the wherewithal to silence some of those whom Moscow deemed threats to the revolution. The Russian Revolution thus sparked a civil war on the Left that would not end until the assassination of Leon Trotsky in 1940, as Communists fought socialists, anarchists, and syndicalists—and each other. Some of those socialists, like Italy's Benito Mussolini, made common cause with radicals from the opposite end of the political spectrum, the demagogues and their followers who blamed the disasters of World War I on scheming capitalists, politicians, and Jews. Internationalist, Red violence in the streets of Europe was met in Italy, Germany, and elsewhere by nationalist black- and brown-shirted violence. For a few years after the Great War it seemed the center could not hold, though only Italy succumbed (in 1923) to a full-fledged dictatorship under Mussolini and his "Fascists"—an appellation that the Communist International quickly gave to all of Soviet Communism's national socialist opponents.[60] But while the Right matched the Left in Europe in streetfighting and violence, the Reds, so it seemed, had no peers at the art of subversion.

The Bolshevik revolution in Russia put a party in charge of a state's resources—and a party moreover that had little patience for the bourgeois norms of contract and diplomacy. A wave of fear spread through the continent and across the seas, as the architects of the revolution in Russia had hoped. Leon Trotsky, the people's commissar of the armed forces, justified the new "terrorism" in 1920 in his rejoinder to the German Marxist Karl Kautsky (a friend of Marx's coauthor Friedrich Engels). Trotsky insisted the goal of socialism justified the Cheka and the means it used not only against counterrevolutionaries but also against the classes they putatively represented. He merits quoting at length; this translation appeared in a pamphlet that the Worker's Party of America published in New York:

> War, like revolution, is founded upon intimidation. A victorious war, generally speaking, destroys only an insignificant part of the conquered army, intimidating the remainder and breaking their will. The revolution works in the same way: it kills individuals, and intimidates thousands. In this sense, the Red Terror is not distinguishable from the armed insurrection,

the direct continuation of which it represents. The State terror of a revolutionary class can be condemned "morally" only by a man who, as a principle, rejects (in words) every form of violence whatsoever—consequently, every war and every rising. For this one has to be merely and simply a hypocritical Quaker. "But, in that case, in what do your tactics differ from the tactics of Tsarism?" we are asked, by the high priests of Liberalism and Kautskianism. You do not understand this, holy men? We shall explain to you. The terror of Tsarism was directed against the proletariat. The gendarmerie of Tsarism throttled the workers who were fighting for the Socialist order. Our Extraordinary Commissions shoot landlords, capitalists, and generals who are striving to restore the capitalist order. Do you grasp this . . . distinction? Yes? For us Communists it is quite sufficient [punctuation in the original].[61]

Conclusion

Nothing like the Great War had ever happened before. Never before had leaders controlled such means of destruction to allow them to kill so many people in so many places and in so many ways. The scale of the conflict stunned the world, leaving statesmen, commanders, and ordinary folk uncomprehending and all but unable to find their way through the moral thicket that enmeshed them. It also witnessed an erosion of the international conduct and order that had more or less prevailed in Europe since the Peace of Westphalia in 1648. States no longer felt themselves quite so bound by principles like noncombatant immunity, and the new Soviet Russia hardly conceived of itself (yet) as a state at all—let alone one bound by bourgeois conventions and rules.

The war gave rise to intelligence properly speaking. In 1900, a local potentate in India might have secret sources and capabilities roughly comparable with those of the czar or the president of France. Between the states, moreover, the most and least powerful of them (in the clandestine field) were not that far apart in their abilities. By 1918, that was no longer true. Three new capabilities had arisen in the major states: sustained and dedicated technological collection and analysis for commanders and decision makers; the interaction of analytical product and operations intended to create more intelligence; and the consciousness among leaders of the national significance of better intelligence, as exemplified by Britain's skillful exploitation of the Zimmermann telegram to bring the United States into war on the allied side. Only a handful of states could produce a Blinker

Hall or a Herbert Yardley, and by 1918, every state that could not was distinctly second rate in terms of international power.

The war had done something else as well. Centuries earlier, Sunzi had said the objective of victory justified the means of espionage (and even assassination) against armed enemies. Trotsky and his comrades, as seen above, sought a transformation of the social order and advocated total espionage, and the execution of class enemies fighting against the proletariat. The new justification not only had revolutionary ends; as a result of World War I it acquired new and much more sophisticated technological means of gathering, analyzing, and disseminating intelligence. This subjective definition of spies and terrorists as those who opposed the revolution (i.e., by their alleged ends and thus their intentions, rather than by their actions), and the indictment of class enemies instead of individuals, amounted to the imputation of collective guilt against the state. Its logic justified the employment of the new state instruments, like intelligence, against whole segments of society. The world would never be the same.

NOTES

1. David Kahn, *The Codebreakers: The Story of Secret Writing* (New York: Scribners, 1996, [1967]), 622–27.
2. Brindejonc des Moulinais, quoted in Terence J. Finnegan, *Shooting the Front: Allied Aerial Reconnaissance and Photographic Interpretation on the Western Front—World War I* (Washington, DC: National Defense Intelligence College, 2006), 24–26.
3. Kahn, *The Codebreakers*, 304; Finnegan, *Shooting the Front*, 25–26.
4. Martin Thomas, *Empires of Intelligence: Security Services and Colonial Disorder after 1914* (Berkeley: University of California Press, 2007), 38, 79–80.
5. We will probably never know just how these two operations unfolded. After World War II the West German government admitted that German agents had been responsible for them, although American claimants did not start receiving damages for the attacks until 1953. Jules Witcover, *Sabotage at Black Tom: Imperial Germany's Secret War in America, 1914–1917* (Chapel Hill, NC: Algonquin, 1989), 310.
6. Nicholas Hiley, "Re-entering the Lists: MI5's Authorized History and the August 1914 Arrests," *Intelligence and National Security* 25:4 (August 2010): 447.
7. Christopher Andrew, *Defend the Realm: The Authorized History of MI5* (New York: Knopf, 2009), 48–79.
8. Ibid., 63–65.
9. Michael Warner, "The Kaiser Sows Destruction: Protecting the Homeland the First Time Around," *Studies in Intelligence* 46 (2002).

10. Rita T. Kronenbitter (ps.), "Okhrana Agent Dolin," in Ben B. Fischer, ed., *Okhrana: The Paris Operations of the Russian Imperial Police* (Washington, DC: Central intelligence Agency, 1997), 69–78.

11. Keith Jeffery, *The Secret History of MI6, 1909–1949* (New York: Penguin, 2010), 78–82.

12. Nicholas A. Lambert, *Planning Armageddon: British Economic Warfare and the First World War* (Cambridge: Harvard University Press, 2012), 263, 274–76, 376–85, 396. John R. Ferris, "Reading the World's Mail: British Blockage Intelligence and Economic Warfare," conference paper, "The Military History of Canada," Kings College London, June 22, 2010.

13. Nicholas A. Lambert, "Strategic Command and Control for Maneuver Warfare: Creation of the Royal Navy's 'War Room' System, 1905–1915," *Journal of Military History* 69 (April 2005): 404–8.

14. Christopher Andrew, *Her Majesty's Secret Service: The Making of the British Intelligence Community* (New York: Viking, 1986), 103–6.

15. Jeffery, *The Secret History of MI6*, 84.

16. Andrew, *Her Majesty's Secret Service*, 121–22.

17. John Ferris, "'Airbandit': C3I and Strategic Air Defence during the First Battle of Britain, 1915–1918," in Michael Dockrill and David French, eds., *Strategy and Intelligence: British Policy during the First World War* (London: Hambledon, 1995), 24.

18. Jim Beach, "Origins of the Special Intelligence Relationship?: Anglo-American Intelligence Co-operation on the Western Front, 1917–18," *Intelligence and National Security* 22:2 (April 2007): 235.

19. Edward Steichen, Headquarters Air Service, American Expeditionary Force, "Aerial Photography: The Matter of Interpretation and Exploitation," December 26, 1918, quoted in Finnegan, *Shooting the Front*, 477.

20. "The War and Aviation," *The Nation*, November 12, 1914, 573.

21. Kahn, *The Codebreakers*, 300.

22. Ibid.

23. Ibid., 313.

24. Ibid., 334–36. See also *The Friedman Legacy: A Tribute to William and Elizebeth Friedman* (Ft. Meade, MD: National Security Agency, 2006), 116.

25. Kahn, *The Codebreakers*, 340–47.

26. *The Friedman Legacy*, 117.

27. Quoted in Friedrich L. Bauer, *Decrypted Secrets: Methods and Maxims of Cryptography* (Berlin: Springer, 2006), 217.

28. Lambert, *Planning Armageddon*, 263.

29. The story of the Zimmermann telegram is well told in Thomas Boghardt, *The Zimmermann Telegram: Intelligence, Diplomacy, and America's Entry into World War I* (Annapolis: US Naval Institute Press, 2012), 19, 104–5. See also Peter Freeman, "The Zimmermann telegram Revisited: A Reconciliation of the Primary Sources," *Cryptologia* 30:2 (2006); and Jonathan Reed Winkler, *Nexus:*

Strategic Communications and American Security in World War I (Cambridge, MA: Harvard University Press, 2008), 104–5.

30. Federal Bureau of Investigation, *The FBI: A Centennial History, 1908–2008* (Washington, DC: Federal Bureau of Investigation, 2009), 2–4, 8–12.

31. David A. Hatch, "The Punitive Expedition: Military Reform and Communications Intelligence," *Cryptologia* 31:1 (January 2007): 38–45.

32. For the story of how this rapid tutorial came about in practice, see Beach, "Origins of the special intelligence relationship?," 232–35.

33. Bruce W. Bidwell, *History of the Development of the Military Intelligence Division, Department of the Army General Staff: 1775–1941* (Frederick, MD: University Publications of America, 1986), 250–56. See also Brian Graff, "American Expeditionary Force Intelligence Sections in World War II: A Failure to Adapt to Open Warfare," unpublished master's thesis at the Joint Military Intelligence College, Washington, DC, 2006, 1.

34. Herbert Yardley, *The American Black Chamber* (Indianapolis: Bobbs-Merrill, 1931), 35–50.

35. Kahn, *The Codebreakers*, 307.

36. Yardley, *The American Black Chamber*, 48.

37. See, for instance, Christopher Andrew's description of the cast of characters recruited for Room 40, the Royal Navy's cryptologic enterprise in World War I, in *Her Majesty's Secret Service*, 94–97. See also Jim Beach, "'Intelligent Civilians in Uniform': The British Expeditionary Force's Intelligence Corps Officers, 1914–1918," *War and Society* 27:1 (May 2008): 7–11.

38. Frank Moorman, Office of the Chief of Staff, American Expeditionary Force, "Notes on Personnel Required by Radio Intelligence Service, AEF," no date [1917], National Archives and Records Administration, Record Group 120, American Expeditionary Force, Entry 105, Box 5765, unnamed folder. I thank Mark Stout for this reference.

39. Richard B. Spence, "Englishmen in New York: The SIS American Station, 1915–21," *Intelligence and National Security* 19 (Autumn 2004): 518–19.

40. Jeffery, *The Secret History of MI6*, 110–16.

41. See, for instance, William S. Sims with Burton J. Hendrick, *The Victory at Sea* (Garden City, NY: Doubleday, Page & Co., 1921), 125–26.

42. Quoted by David Kahn in *The Codebreakers*, 633. William Friedman was citing Tannenberg as an object lesson for National Security Agency employees more than four decades later; *The Friedman Legacy*, 123.

43. Sir Alfred Ewing spoke at the University of Edinburgh on the decoding of German diplomatic messages in 1925; see Henry Landau, *The Enemy Within: The Inside Story of German Sabotage in America* (New York: G. P. Putnam's Sons, 1937), 153.

44. Marcus Faulkner, "The *Kriegsmarine*, Signals Intelligence and the Development of the *B-Dienst* before the Second World War," *Intelligence and National Security* 25:4 (August 2010): 526.

45. William F. Friedman and C. J. Mendelsohn, *The Zimmermann Telegram of January 16, 1917: And Its Cryptographic Background* (Washington, DC: Government Printing Office, 1938).

46. Parker Hitt's lecture to the Army War College on September 21, 1923, is quoted in Betsy Rohaly Smoot, "Pioneers of US Military Cryptology: Colonel Parker Hitt and His Wife, Genevieve Young Hitt," *Federal History* 4 (January 2012): 94.

47. A. Ray Miller, *The Cryptographic Mathematics of Enigma* (Ft. Meade, MD: National Security Agency, 1996), 12.

48. Donald P. Steury, *The Intelligence War* (New York: MetroBooks, 2000), 80. See also Jeffery, *The Secret History of MI6*, 500.

49. Brian R. Sullivan, "Soviet Penetration of the Italian Intelligence Services in the 1930s," in Carlo Rastelli, ed., *Storia dello Spionaggio* (Associazione Europea degli Amici degli Archivi Storici, 2006), 87–89.

50. Jeffery, *The Secret History of MI6*, 196, 209–13.

51. Yardley, *The American Black Chamber*, 313.

52. Kahn, *The Codebreakers*, 576. See also Frederick D. Parker, *Pearl Harbor Revisited: United States Navy Communications Intelligence, 1924–1941* (Ft. Meade, MD: National Security Agency, 1994), 32.

53. Laurance F. Safford, "A Brief History of Communications Intelligence in the United States," part 1, SRH–149, March 27, 1952, National Security Agency, 6–11.

54. Serge, *Memoirs of a Revolutionary*, 94.

55. Ibid., 95.

56. Ibid., 105–6, 113, 115.

57. Ibid., 116.

58. Jeffery, *The Secret History of MI6*, 211–12.

59. Andrew, *Defend the Realm*, 161.

60. Paul Johnson, *Modern Times: The World from the Twenties to the Eighties* (New York: Harper & Row, 1983), 102.

61. Leon Trotsky, *Dictatorship versus Democracy: A Reply to Karl Kautsky (Terrorism and Communism)* (New York: Worker's Party of America, 1920); accessed September 1, 2012, at www.marxists.org/archive/trotsky/1920/terr comm/index.htm.

CHAPTER 3

As Good as It Gets

War is thought, and thought is information, and he who knows most strikes hardest.

The House on 92nd Street, 20th Century Fox

The First World War had hardly ended before all the combatants started preparing for the sequel. The Great War unleashed national and ideological passions and destabilized entire economies and social orders. France's greatest soldier, Ferdinand Foch, prophetically quipped after the Treaty of Versailles in 1919, "This is not a peace. It is an armistice for twenty years." The industrialized powers recovered from the war, to some extent, during the economic revival of the 1920s, but soon the Great Depression strangled finance and production around the world. The crisis helped turn a rabble rouser into a would-be national savior, bringing Adolf Hitler to power in Berlin in 1933. Where extremists of the Left and Right had fought one another in the streets in the 1920s, now they could prepare for war on a national scale. Indeed, Hitler began immediately, blaming the Communists and citing their treachery in his imposition of dictatorial rule and a remilitarization of Germany in defiance of the Treaty of Versailles. In the Soviet Union, Josef Stalin reciprocated, soon declaring a Popular Front with progressives and socialists against the common fascist enemy, but also attempting to maximize this opportunity to control the international Left. From thence began a weird symbiosis, with each tyrant exploiting the fear of the other to consolidate power at home and foment violence abroad.

The Second World War would be the most horrendous conflict in history, killing perhaps 70 million combatants and civilians. The war changed the map of the world, as had the First World War, but it also presaged the end of the European empires, the rise of Asia, and a two-generation stalemate between the Communist world and the West. The new business of intelligence played vital roles in these outcomes. The soldiers, sailors, and pilots won the war's battles, of course, and farmers and factory workers and scientists provided the wherewithal to do so, but secret insights and means guided the decisions of policymakers and commanders to a perhaps unprecedented degree. The winning side, moreover, gradually developed stunning advantages in the clandestine arts. While still developing, those advantages helped the Allies stave off defeat; when mature, they hastened the collapse of the Axis. Perhaps the greatest testament to the contribution of intelligence to final victory came in the separate and joint decisions of the Western Allies not only to break precedent by preserving significant portions of their new intelligence capabilities but also to maintain a novel and powerful collaboration in signals intelligence after the war had ended.

The effects of World War II for intelligence linger still. By 1918, states dominated intelligence because only states could afford the new capabilities that gave them the collection capacity and the ability to exploit what was collected through intercepts and photo reconnaissance. But what kind of states, and what kind of intelligence, would prevail? Not every advanced nation had the insight and the wherewithal to remain competitive in this arena. Fortune would favor science and ideology—and the ability to organize them.

Ideological Challenges

The aftermath of World War I brought demobilization and retrenchment in every military, yet the new intelligence capabilities, if sometimes neglected, were nonetheless preserved. Those capabilities suddenly had more work to do. The new enemy within was not the vanguard of an advancing army or a surprise invasion, but rather of a proletarian revolution or a Leninist uprising. The "cold war" between the Russian intelligence services and their Western rivals really began in September 1918, when the Cheka murdered the Royal Naval attaché in Petrograd as he defended his embassy from intruders seeking evidence of British espionage. Britain's new SIS took a measure of revenge the following year by mounting torpedo boat attacks from Finland on the Soviet fleet.[1] For most of the next sixty years, communism would be the primary concern of Western intelligence services.

The British and French services also had much more ground to cover, monitoring events in their own empires while also trying to keep order in formerly German and Ottoman possessions that fell to them in the Treaty of Versailles. Britain and France were weaker in relative terms than they had been in 1913, but they remained powerful enough to accept the League of Nations mandate to govern the Holy Land, the Levant, Iraq, and Syria after the Ottoman Turks retreated. These regions became even tougher to pacify once the Balfour Declaration (1919) endorsed increased Jewish emigration to Palestine, sparking Arab-Jewish violence. The wonder is not that the information and security services of the British and French had a tough time keeping order across the Middle East; it is that London and Paris had intelligence organizations and skills good enough to give them the confidence to attempt the feat at all—and to accomplish it with middling success for almost three decades.[2]

In Britain, all this meant a decade of halting steps, culminating in a major intelligence reform in 1931. The result was not bigger services, but better-organized and better-governed ones, with clear lines of demarcation between foreign and domestic work. The "Secret Service" that had run agents overseas in World War I gained a permanent home under the Foreign and Commonwealth Office in the early 1920s, but then was caught spying on British trades unionists suspected of working for the Soviets in 1927. The Special Branch of London's Metropolitan Police (Scotland Yard) continued in its counterespionage and antisubversion missions until it proved itself incapable of monitoring its own ranks for undercover Soviet agents. In 1931, the British government settled upon a simple and lasting solution to these ills. The Secret Intelligence Service was restricted to the foreign field.[3] The delicate business of countering clandestine threats at home and in the empire (still a large portion of the Earth's surface), from both espionage and subversion, was given to MI5, which had done well in World War I but since then had mostly watched for foreign agitators in the armed services. MI5 also received a new institutional home in the Home Office and a new name: the Security Service. It would have no law enforcement powers but would pass its leads to Special Branch and local police forces for action.[4] This arrangement would see Britain through another World War, a Cold War, and well into the next century.

All that institutional reform passed with little public notice in the United Kingdom, which published virtually nothing about the organization and work of its intelligence agencies. In the United States, by contrast, intelligence reform (though it was not called that) proceeded mostly in the open. The intelligence bureaus of the army and navy had worked to counter German subversion in World War I, but (with some exceptions) withdrew from this field after the war. "Secret Service methods carried on by military agencies cannot be justified in time of peace," explained the head of the army's Military Intelligence Division, Brigadier General Marlborough Churchill, to his colleagues in 1920.[5] The Justice Department's Bureau of Investigation, moreover, had given creditable war service but had hardly distinguished itself. In the war's chaotic aftermath, the bureau fell into disrepute, with its agents exposed for corruption and some of its investigations launched for partisan purposes at the personal behest of congressmen. The bureau's security counterparts in the armed services, moreover, occasionally turned their warrant to investigate radicalism into a license to probe progressive leaders and labor organizers. Congress, the White House, and the public soon reined in the federal and military investigators. The latter were limited to defending the facilities and personnel of the army and navy. The former gained a new broom at the top. An energetic acting director, J. Edgar Hoover, took over the Bureau of Investigation in 1924 and applied what he had learned at the Justice Department during the war in the form of a new doctrine. Now the bureau would only investigate crimes, and thus would no longer be available as a sort of hired lance to help congressmen against their political opponents or as a source of corrupt income for special agents. Reformed in this fashion, and through scientific standards of evidence gathering and professional ethics and training for its agents, Hoover's bureau laid the foundation for a world-class internal security and counterintelligence service.[6] Even these reforms, however, did not go far enough for some officials. Supreme Court Justice Louis Brandeis, dissenting in a 1928 case that upheld federal agents' authority to use wiretaps without a warrant, warned that "Discovery and invention have made it possible for the government, by means far more effective than stretching upon the rack, to obtain disclosure in court of what was whispered in the closet. The progress of science in furnishing the government with means of espionage is not likely to stop with wiretapping."[7]

The Western intelligence services also began talking to each other more than ever. In part, this came about because the individual services remained small. Britain's Secret Intelligence Service typically had about 200 employees during the 1920s, with most of them overseas. Even as war loomed in the late 1930s, its chief Sir Hugh Sinclair reminded his bosses that SIS's budget roughly equaled the maintenance outlay for a single Royal Navy destroyer in home waters.[8] MI5, before its mission was expanded in

1931, made do with two or three dozen employees.[9] In America, by 1929 the Bureau of Investigation had dwindled to 339 special agents and a couple hundred more support staff, and the bureau's primary focus remained domestic law enforcement, not intelligence.[10] The nature of the subversive threat forced the agencies to cooperate across national borders. A revolutionary movement based in Moscow that both controlled and influenced planning and action by the citizens of at least a score of countries was not something that any nation's domestic or foreign service could handle alone. Tentative cooperation among the Western services against Bolshevism, therefore, began even before the Treaty of Versailles, and gradually broadened and deepened. Near the center of this web of secret liaison arrangements stood Britain's SIS, with ties to the French, the Americans, the Baltic States, and even the Germans (indeed, limited intelligence sharing on Soviet topics continued in Berlin until 1937).[11] Such sharing of information on subversives was by no means limited to intelligence channels, as the diplomats and security officials swapped names and leads as well. Two developments would compel these loose contacts to grow much closer and more intense during the 1930s: Adolf Hitler's revival of Germany as an aggressive power, and the nearly contemporaneous shift in communications technology discussed above.

The British lead over everyone else in codebreaking increased still more because SIS (with Foreign Office encouragement) courted the cryptanalytic experts of other nations, especially after Hitler came to power in 1933. The greatest liaison effort was a de facto collaboration of the Poles, French, and British against the German Enigma cipher machine. The French had a well-placed agent, one Hans-Thilo Schmidt, inside the Wehrmacht's communications section. They passed his information and documents on to Polish cryptographers, who made the initial break into traffic transmitted on early versions of Enigma from 1932, and with this breach were able to keep pace with German improvements to the machine. The French also brought in the British via the colorful SIS station chief in Paris, Wilfred "Biffy" Dunderdale (who in later years apparently inspired a Naval Intelligence colleague named Ian Fleming). British, French, and Polish experts opened trilateral discussions on the Enigma in 1938.[12] There had never been anything like this coalition intelligence effort in peacetime. It paid dividends during the coming war, and would pay even more in the war that followed.

Dictators on the March

The subtle kinship between Soviet communism and German fascism extended to the intelligence realm as well. The rise of ideological regimes meant the emergence of something new: party intelligence—services that began as organs of the Nazi and Communist parties and morphed into institutions of their respective states. Each dictatorship needed utterly loyal security organs to guard the revolution and its leaders, and also to permeate the surrounding society and state institutions with informants listening for heresy, dissension, and coup plots. In short, the party organs enforced ideological purity and suppressed the revolution's natural enemies (whether capitalists, Kulaks, and anarchists, or suspect racial groups and social "parasites"). Where possible, these party security organs also harassed the revolution's enemies abroad. They grew to become virtual states within their respective states. Germany's *Schutzstaffel* (SS) had civilian and military arms; the latter built its own army, while the former protected Hitler's person, ran racial policies, did some police work, and manned concentration camps—and ultimately administered the Holocaust. The Cheka of revolutionary Russia evolved into successive entities in the Soviet Union, most notably (in 1934) into the People's Commissariat for Internal Affairs (NKVD); it ran internal security, border guards, and the *gulag*.

The party security systems also ran intelligence operations, with important consequences for their respective regimes. The hybrid state-party intelligence organs existed alongside the standard ministries and offices of the state but answered to high party officials, and operated outside legal review and oversight by the state's conventional authorities.[13] They collectively made up a "counterintelligence state" (in the words of a later scholar), and duplicated and competed with the work of the ministries' intelligence agencies—as the Cheka and its heirs did with the Red Army's intelligence directorate, the RU (after 1942, the GRU).[14] In Germany, the SS's intelligence arm (the *Sicherheitsdienst,* or SD) ultimately supplanted the military's *Abwehr*. Indeed, the secret arm of the German state police (or Gestapo) and the SD were federated under *Reichsführer* Heinrich Himmler in the Reich Main Security Office (RHSA) in 1939, thus making the Nazi party almost indistinguishable from the German government in security and intelligence matters. Western intelligence agencies had long competed with one another, of course, and sometimes in destructive ways. What was different in the totalitarian states was that the competition could not be adjudicated—the party always got its way. That was not a recipe for long-term success.

As the revolution matured in the Soviet Union, the NKVD also took on a sanguinary new function: purging the party itself to ensure loyalty to Lenin's self-appointed heir, Josef Stalin. The Nazis were brutal in their maintenance of revolutionary purity, creating party and state apparatuses at war with Hitler's ethnic and racial enemies at home. Nonetheless, their hunt for what they deemed alien elements mostly left in place traditional social structures and groupings. Churches, businesses, universities, and clubs, while abused and under siege in the Nazi order, nonetheless survived and managed to provide some manner of shelter to their denizens from the pervasive reach of the Nazi regime (Italy's Fascists were even less meticulous about such matters than the Nazis). The Communists in the Soviet Union, by contrast, far outdid the Nazis in using intelligence as a means of social control. Under successive chiefs, the NKVD in the 1930s conducted a campaign of denunciations, arrests, show trials, and executions to cleanse the party, the army, and the intelligence agencies themselves of independent thought. Stalin declared that terrorists were assassinating party leaders and German spies had infiltrated everywhere.[15] But his NKVD operatives always got their man: "Listen, let me have him for one night, and I'll have him confessing he's the King of England," joked the NKVD's last chief, Lavrenti Beria. Another of Stalin's favorites, Nikita Khrushchev, later conceded that Moscow had become "constipated" with "non-workers, parasites, and profiteers" —and therefore needed a strong purgative—but later complained that Stalin's purge had harmed the party: "since every promotion had to be made in accordance with directions from the NKVD, the Party lost its guiding role. It was disgraceful."[16]

Could ideology translate into immediate intelligence capability? The record was mixed. The Nazis inspired a certain ideological sympathy in lands once included in the German and Austro-Hungarian empires. The new Germany also had an attraction for some German Americans. Several of them volunteered to spy for the fatherland in the late 1930s; with a few dozen friends and associates they secretly contributed American industrial secrets to the German war effort.[17] The Italians seem not to have thought much about exporting their brand of autocracy.[18] Fascism of the German and Italian type was, indeed, pointedly particular in its appeals—only certain peoples need apply. Hitler might have inadvertently assisted the British in this struggle. He had largely restricted German intelligence from recruiting Britons to work as agents in the United Kingdom from 1935 to 1937, in effect guaranteeing the *Abwehr* (and later the SD) would have to scramble to make up lost time when war loomed.[19]

The Communists, however, became the uncontested champions at ideological recruitment abroad. The Bolsheviks had already established an underground in Europe before the revolution, and thus as the new Cheka came into being it included the beginnings of a foreign espionage and recruiting apparatus. The ideological gravity of Marxism increased after the rise of Hitler in 1933 and Moscow's announcement of the Popular Front (1935) made communism apparently the world's leading opponent of fascism. Soviet intelligence services recruited, moreover, in all walks of Western society. After all, Marxism was by definition a global force—it was meant to unite all proletarians, and it had no inhibitions about signing on progressive artists and writers and scientists who wished to join the winning side of history. Marxist socialism seemed both a march toward a more solidarist and scientific society and a promise of personal liberation from stifling traditionalism in art and morality. The result was a powerful cultural multiplier effect, adding a *frisson* of novelty and daring to communism that compounded its appeal in certain sets, even after the NKVD's assassination of Leon Trotsky in Mexico in 1940 eliminated Stalin's last living rival in the Marxist pantheon. Soviet operatives in the West remained the main concern and target of most European intelligence bureaus during the interwar years, just as penetrating those societies and their governments remained the prime (foreign) occupation of the Soviet services. The West paused in this struggle when war with Hitler loomed in the late 1930s, but the Soviets barely slackened their efforts against all the Western powers, as they viewed Hitler and fascism as but more virulent strains of the capitalism dominating Europe and the Americas.

Communism had some appeal outside the European world as well. China's revolution actually predated Russia's, but took much longer to reach its conclusion. The last emperor of a string of dynasties stretching back two millennia had abdicated in 1912, and the regime that followed him never controlled all of China. That new regime also had European ideals and props; the nationalists under Sun Yat-Sen spoke of transforming China's ancient culture, and of throwing off the foreign experts and financiers whose counsel they needed to modernize that vast nation. Chaos resulted; war, famine, and exhaustion probably claimed millions, and the hated influence of the Westerners—and increasingly the Japanese—only grew. After Sun, Chiang Kai Shek's Guomintang government talked of radical reforms and cooperated with the Communist Party of China (CCP)—both accepted Soviet aid in the 1920s—until Chiang turned on the Communists in 1927 and sparked a two-decade struggle for mastery. The Communists were poorly armed and easily defeated in the cities; in the countryside, however, they rallied under the leadership of Mao Zedong and other commanders who instilled discipline and treated the peasantry with relatively more respect than the Guomintang and local war lords had done. Peasants accordingly shared more of their meager stores with the Communists, and provided them with intelligence. Success bred success on both the political and military fronts. Mao contended for CCP leadership and dominated the party after 1936. On the battlefield, his troops defeated Chiang's middling formations, and induced enough desertions for his troops to arm themselves. By the time Chiang took their threat seriously and sent his best troops (and their German advisers) against them, Mao's forces were too strong to destroy. They rarely relinquished the initiative on the battlefield to either the Guomintang or the Japanese, who invaded central China in 1937.

Most significantly for what followed, Mao crafted a doctrine for insurgency warfare, an amalgam of Marx, Sunzi, anti-imperialism, and nationalism, that inspired generations of revolutionaries to come.[20] From his base at Yan'an, he called his guerrillas to fight a protracted struggle against a stronger and better-equipped foe—what modern theorists call "asymmetric" contract. Key to everything was the unity between the guerrillas and the populace; that was what distinguished a true people's war in Mao's thought from the sorts of counterrevolutionary guerrilla campaigns that even the Japanese occupiers attempted. Mao's guerrillas would move secretly and with "supernatural rapidity," concentrate at key points, and shift their strength continually in order to catch the adversary where he was weak and off guard. In short, Maoist doctrine called for hitting dispersed enemy forces and driving them to concentrate in ever-larger garrisons—and thus to leave the countryside and its people to the guerrillas, who could create the conditions for a decisive, conventional war. Such a strategy required constant vigilance on the part of guerrilla leaders at all levels: "To conduct one's troops with alertness is an essential of guerrilla command. Leaders

must realize that to operate alertly is the most important factor in gaining the initiative and vital in its effect on the relative situation that exists
between our forces and those of the enemy. Guerrilla commanders adjust
their operations to the enemy situation, to the terrain, and to prevailing
local conditions. Leaders must be alert to sense changes in these factors and
make necessary modifications in troop dispositions to accord with them."
This strategy required intelligence, and indeed, Mao's organizational advice
included creating intelligence sections in units from companies up through
battalions, regiments, and divisions.[21] People's war was not only something
modern from a political standpoint; it likewise adopted the latest Western
ideas on military intelligence.

Under Mao, China also became the first great importer of Stalinist
methods for internal security. The CCP had already proved a capable opponent of Chiang on the clandestine front; penetration agents more than
once tipped CCP leaders to Guomintang plans. During World War II, Mao
Zedong's ally Kang Sheng (who had lived in Moscow during the Great
Purges) developed local variations on NKVD methods for inducing con-
fessions and conformity to use in Mao's Rectification Movement to cleanse
party cadres of outmoded notions. That same Rectification Movement also
gave history a word for "the washing of brains."[22]

The Communists everywhere had their opponents, of course, but it
was Hitler who had the effect of creating and motivating enemies in such a
way as to drive some of the world's great talent toward communism or the
liberal West. The competition for brains was thus lost by the "Rome-Berlin
Axis" before World War II even began. This would be particularly costly
for the Reich in the sciences, such as physics. Furthermore, the intelligence
sharing among the Western and Eastern European nations that began mod-
estly after World War I broadened and deepened after Hitler and Mussolini
began their campaigns of conquest in the mid-1930s—and were joined by
Imperial Japan, another state with a racial theory of history and a distaste
for liberal decadence. Britain's SIS quietly acknowledged the shift in priorities from traditional targets and began cultivating new opportunities
in 1938, dropping its handful of agents in America and judging correctly
that "it is for us to consider whether our Air and Naval work against the
U.S.A. is of sufficient importance to maintain against the potential advantages of a satisfactory liaison."[23] SIS's outreach on the continent paid further
dividends a few months later when, with SIS help, the small but capable

Czech military intelligence service (including its precious files) decamped to London as Hitler occupied Czechoslovakia.[24]

The Western states also intensified their internal security work (and sharing) against German agents. More money helped in Britain; MI5 and SIS slowly gained resources and people after 1933.[25] More authority helped in the United States; President Franklin Roosevelt quietly authorized Hoover and his special agents to watch Reds and Nazis in 1936. Hoover's organization, recently renamed the Federal Bureau of Investigation (FBI), had probed Fascist activities on requests from the White House and State Department in the past, but the president's new order marked a watershed, providing a general mandate for intelligence gathering in addition to law enforcement investigations.[26] The key to much of the later success on both sides of the Atlantic, however, would be MI5's growing proficiency in penetrating radical organizations by using double agents. A secretary that the Security Service planted in the Communist Party of Great Britain provided leads that pointed to a Soviet spy in the Woolwich Arsenal. Another agent, a pilot in the Great War named Christopher Draper, briefly passed to the *Abwehr* information carefully selected by MI5. The mailing address he used in Hamburg, Box 629, was used moreover by another German agent in Scotland, who in turn posted messages to agents in the United States. Soon these investigations led toward respective Soviet and German spy rings in America; MI5's doubles therefore helped stymie active operations on British soil, and helped British intelligence convince the FBI's J. Edgar Hoover of the need for more sharing.[27]

The Western intelligence coalition was still forming, however, as Europe staged a dress rehearsal for World War II in Spain. A new republican government had ousted the ancient Spanish monarchy in 1931, and imposed a wave of social and economic changes upon the deep traditionalism of many Spaniards and their institutions. The disturbances that had shaken Central Europe a decade earlier now rocked Spain, as both sides turned to violence and extremists in each camp fed on the chaos. General Francisco Franco led an army uprising in 1936, sparking civil war, and to boost his chances he turned to Germany and Italy for modern arms. The republic and its Loyalists in turn took weapons and intelligence help from Moscow, and enlisted volunteers from all over Europe and North America. Both sides extracted vengeance and made atrocity their policy. Franco's forces, however, had better weapons and a unifying cause; the

Loyalists were a crowd of warring factions, with Communists and anarchists openly fighting each other. Britain and France held aloof, seeing no clear right or advantage on either side, and Franco finally conquered Madrid in early 1939.

From this, Stalin concluded that the West was irredeemably irresolute and would not help him against Hitler, and so he determined to strike the best deal he could with Berlin while he still had time. Thus came the Nazi-Soviet nonaggression pact, announced to a stunned world on August 23, 1939. The Weimar Republic in Germany had secretly used the expanses of Soviet Russia to test its forbidden tanks in the 1920s, but mutual assistance had ended once Hitler came to power. Now the new pact gave both Hitler and Stalin something each craved: strategic depth, and time to deal with other enemies. Suddenly the two mortal enemies were bosom buddies; "It felt like being among old party comrades," recounted Hitler's Foreign Minister Joachim von Ribbentrop about the impromptu celebration in Moscow after he signed the pact. Stalin toasted Hitler in absentia and claimed he "knew how much the German people loved the Führer."[28] Overnight the balance of power in Europe shifted. The countries of Eastern Europe were now prey for the Wehrmacht and the Red Army, and the killing began with Hitler's invasion of Poland a week later on September 1, 1939.

Early Rounds

The second global conflict would differ from the first in important ways. Western militaries drew from World War I the imperative to restore the ability to maneuver to modern warfare. The Great War had hardly ended when military thinkers began pondering the possibility that the trench systems could now be breached and bypassed by massed tank formations—which had not really been possible given the numerical and mechanical limitations on tanks during the war. Airplanes seemed to be part of the answer as well, both for observing enemy movements and for acting flying artillery ahead of the tanks. Every major army invested in improving its tanks and learning to coordinate the tanks' action. In addition, air power enthusiasts like Giulio Douhet in Italy and Billy Mitchell in the United States glimpsed the strategic effect that larger and faster bombers could have on enemy warships, troop concentrations, and even cities. "The bomber will always get through" against interceptor aircraft and antiaircraft artillery, or so it seemed to Conservative leader (and future prime minister) Stanley Baldwin in 1932. The Germans in the 1930s would develop a way of combining aircraft and tanks with mobile artillery—all controlled by radio— and observers called their new doctrine the *blitzkrieg*, or lightning war. The concepts for controlling and concentrating forces at sea would now be applied on land as well. If the Great War had marked the beginning of military intelligence doctrine in modern armies, then the interwar period marked its codification. The modern militaries also sought to inculcate the war's lessons not only of intelligence gathering and analysis, but also its lessons of producing useful information from all sources, particularly signals intelligence, for battlefield commanders.

The new war commenced where the last one left off in 1918, with the Germans against the French and British, and the Russians on the sidelines awaiting the main chance. The initial strategies on both sides looked similar as well; the Western allies sought to blockade Germany and hold on in fortified positions, while the Germans sought to keep Britain at bay and defeat the French. The big difference between 1918 and 1939 was that the Americans were not "Over There," and thus the French and British had to bear the might of the German army on their own. It was not a fair fight. London and Paris, having declared war over Poland, had little prospect of defeating a Nazi Germany that could—as soon as it divided Eastern Europe was divided with Stalin—devote its strength to fighting them.

The Germans conquered Warsaw in four weeks and rested the following winter—the Phony War. The Soviets had mounted their own invasion of eastern Poland that September, and then seized the Baltic States and bullied Finland into terms. In April 1940, the German dragon stirred again. Hitler swallowed neutral Denmark in a few hours and mounted a daring gamble to seize another neutral, Norway, with its deep fjords and access to the North Atlantic. The main blow in the West fell on May 10. The Wehrmacht surged into the Low Countries as the Allies had expected, and the French army with the British Expeditionary Force moved forward into Belgium to stop them. Within days, however, a disaster loomed. Unlike 1914, the real German push was not across Belgium's plain at all, but concentrated in an armored thrust through the thinly held Ardennes forest. German panzers thus slipped around the best French troops and raced for the English Channel, bagging the main Allied force and compelling the British to evacuate what men they could (minus their weapons, vehicles, and supplies) at

Dunkirk. The French army was not beaten yet, however, and the formations that remained fought hard to save Paris, but to no avail. France's once excellent military intelligence was little help. Its old reconnaissance planes were easy prey for the Messerschmitts, French signals intercept units not infrequently monitored their own army's transmissions so commanders could find friendlies on the battlefield, and the precious decrypts of German Enigma messages piled up with no one to exploit them.[29] By late June it was over. What had seemed the world's best army had fallen to a smaller force, and Marshal Pétain, hero of Verdun in 1916, made a separate peace with Hitler. To add a final fillip to the catastrophe, Mussolini's Italy threw in its lot with Germany just before the armistice. A great liberal democracy was gone, the victim of Hitler's ruthlessness and skill and, it seemed, of its own fractious corruption and lassitude.

Hitler had won much of Europe in mere months with no clear intelligence advantage. Indeed, the two sides in the secrets war were fairly matched at the outset. Neither side could learn much about the other with human agents. The French, Czechs, and British all had a few sources reporting to them from inside the Reich before 1939, but the Germans erased this advantage through improved counterintelligence as the war loomed. Indeed, the Gestapo and the *Abwehr* humiliated Britain's SIS, neutralizing its best agents in Germany and capturing two officers of SIS's Dutch station by enticing them to a border post called Venlo in late 1939.[30] But German agents did nothing of consequence in Britain, which rounded up Nazi sympathizers, even catching one (code clerk Tyler Kent) in the American embassy in London.[31]

Temporary intelligence successes gave several military advantages to the Germans (and later the Italians and Japanese) between 1939 and the end of 1941. Each of the Axis powers had early wins, and for a time had some success against neutrals like the United States. The Allied break into Enigma was too small to be much good before the latter half of 1940. The German navy had enough insights from reading British naval codes to bloody the Royal Navy off the coast of Norway and cause heavy losses to British merchant shipping, though its U-boats never came as close as they had in World War I to breaking the blockade or starving Great Britain.[32] The German army initially had very good tactical SIGINT support—historian John Ferris has called it "the finest signals service of any army on earth" at the time.[33] German battlefield SIGINT would prove the most productive and reliable source for the Wehrmacht in Russia, giving commanders a sense of Soviet deployments and strength, if not as much of Soviet intentions.[34] The Japanese were reading American diplomatic cables and also had a good idea of US naval deployments and movements.[35] They had a consul at Pearl Harbor charting the berths of the Pacific Fleet and investigating whether its capital ships were protected by torpedo nets (the US Navy felt such nets were unnecessary in the shallow harbor). The Italians showed proficiency at codebreaking, and also read US diplomatic traffic. Indeed, when the Italian campaign against the British in North Africa was taken over by the Germans in 1941, *Afrika Korps* commander Erwin Rommel called the American military attaché in Cairo (then under British military governance) "my good source." He greatly valued the insights that Major Bonner Fellers, US Army, gained from his British hosts on the state of the Eighth Army, and then cabled home to Washington. Fellers had no idea that the Italians and Germans were decoding his messages thanks to the theft of another American attaché's codebook by the *Servizio Informazioni Militairi* in Rome in August 1941.[36] What the Germans did not have in 1940, however, was the dreaded "Fifth Column" of spies and saboteurs to raise havoc in the rear of the French army—but legends about German agents spread anyway, creating their own reality in the minds of Allies and neutrals who expected similar waves of subversion to presage Hitler's future aggressions.

With the fall of France, only Britain and some frightened neutrals on the continent remained outside Hitler's orbit. The luxury of an existential crisis gave London the opportunity to do something new; the British had no choice but to coordinate their institutionally scattered intelligence efforts and analyses. Ultimately, they also had more time than they expected to have in June 1940, when the long-dreaded cross-channel invasion seemed likely that very summer. In short, British intelligence leaders had to experiment, and fast, but as events unfolded they had months and then years—not weeks—to sort out the experiments and adapt means and procedures that made the collective effort more effective. This was a national intelligence priority. If Luftwaffe bombers could sink the Royal Navy, then Hitler could starve the island into submission with his U-boats. Barring that objective, if German fighters and bombers could extinguish the Royal Air Force as a fighting force, they could then blast British industry and ports at will, neutralizing Britain as an offensive power. For a few weeks the Battle of Britain raged in the summer skies of southern England, with RAF fighter squadrons merging the tactical, operational, and strategic levels of war in desperate dogfights to halt the Luftwaffe's raids on British airfields. For Britain, everything came down to a relative handful of pilots in their Spitfires and Hurricanes, flying day after day against armadas of Heinkels and Messerschmitts. The RAF won the campaign, however, forcing the Germans to abandon raids against high-value targets in favor of more lethal but less strategically threatening poundings of London and other cities.

The intelligence contest also shifted to the skies over southern England, which would witness a sequel to the German bombing offensive in World War I. This time, however, both sides had radar to detect incoming raids, though its deployment remained spotty in 1940. The British built their radars for air defense, integrating them well in a revived 1918-style network of observers, guns, and interceptors. The Germans built all kinds of radars, the cleverest being *Knickebein* ("the bent knee")—narrow radar beams only yards wide that could be crossed over a target in England from across the English Channel to give *Luftwaffe* bombardiers the proper azimuth and distance even on a cloudy night. How the British came to suspect and then to frustrate *Knickebein* in 1940 makes a compelling read that has been well told by its chief protagonist, R. V. Jones, who at the time was a twenty-eight-year old physicist. The *Luftwaffe* tried but soon abandoned costly massed raids in daylight, shifting to night bombing that autumn and trusting to its superb aircrews and *Knickebein* to smash English war production. Jones was able to convince Winston Churchill (now prime minister) and his advisers of the importance of detecting the beams. Interrogations of downed airmen, decrypts of puzzling Enigma messages, and careful examination of wrecked bombers had suggested the beams were a reality in spite of British doubts that the Germans even had radar, let alone that they could do something so technically daring with radar signals. After gaining Churchill's backing, Jones and his colleagues found *Knickebein* in a matter of days and devised ways to distort the signals heard by German bombers, throwing off their aim. The effort not only saved considerable damage to British industry but in effect forged a partnership between analysts and collectors to mold a process for "scientific intelligence" that made it highly effective later in the war.[37]

Fittingly, with the innovation that thwarted *Knickebein*, the British also used their early counterintelligence success for another step beyond what they had accomplished in the First World War. Once again they were

3.1 A present-day photograph of a German Wurzberg air-search radar installation in Douvres-la-Délivrande, Calvados, France, left over from World War II. Electronic warfare and intelligence came of age in World War II. *Yummifruitbat, Wikimedia Commons*

helped by German overreaching. Hitler began hasty preparations to invade England just after France fell in May 1940, and the *Abwehr* did its part that fall by parachuting two dozen ill-prepared agents into Britain in the hope that some of them could help the invasion. This was surely the first use of the parachute on a mass scale as a tool for espionage, and its result was disastrous for Germany. All the agents were swiftly rounded up as they wandered the countryside or blundered into English towns; but instead of being simply jailed or shot, many of them were evaluated by their captors for their suitability as double agents. MI5 took the idea of doing so from its earlier success with Draper and another double agent, a Welsh engineer named Arthur Owens (codenamed SNOW). Owens in 1939 had handed over his codebook and explained the procedures for communicating with the *Abwehr* and its chief for operations against Britain, Nikolaus Ritter (whom Owens knew by an assumed name). Four of the newly captured agents, given the choice of turning their coats or execution (a fate met by fourteen of their comrades), agreed to radio the *Abwehr* in Hamburg with messages that their British handlers dictated. The actual working of this rolling deception took sustained concentration, for a range of services, departments, and offices had to cooperate in offering and coordinating real but not seriously damaging information for the doubled German agents to transmit to their handlers on the continent. A "Double Cross" committee soon formed to do this job. By the spring of 1942, London had confidence that its counterspies had complete control over German human intelligence operations against Britain, and that Berlin was thoroughly fooled. For the rest of the war, the "Double Cross system" kept the leaders of the German intelligence services satisfied that they were getting something worthwhile out of the spies they sent to Britain. Ritter and his colleagues in Hamburg thus kept on doing what seemed to work, instead of examining those operations, discarding them as failures, and devising something more effective. Along with its regional franchises in Cairo and Italy, the Double Cross system also gave the British an ace in the hole to play at a later date, when they really needed Berlin to believe something that was not true.[38]

What the success against *Knickebein* and the double agents demonstrated was an inventive British intelligence system learning from its early missteps and improving rapidly. Two leadership changes helped. Hugh Sinclair, head of SIS (now called MI6 as well), died of cancer in late 1939. His successor, Stewart Menzies, was a veteran of the service who not only understood its business but also proved adept at dealing with senior commanders and cabinet leaders, particularly Prime Minister Churchill. He would soon impress his American colleagues as well. At the same time, early in the war, MI5 was roiled by a series of office moves and the sacking of its founder and only chief to date, Vernon Kell. The appointment of Sir David Petrie in early 1941 righted the ship. Like Menzies, he had also spent time in the service and proved not only a capable administrator but also a reassuring presence for senior policymakers. The two British agencies thus accomplished, in the midst of the wartime crisis, something that had so far proved difficult for other civilian intelligence agencies around the world— they replaced their leaders without bloodshed or internal chaos, and indeed, in both cases, with improvements in efficiency and effectiveness.[39]

Similar examples of fusion marked the overall British intelligence effort, desperate as it was to squeeze every lead and clue to stave off invasion or starvation. The scattered photo interpretation functions in the armed services gave up their analysts, who became part of a central imagery analysis bureau, where those interpreters collectively amassed copious files and expertise on the German war machine. They were aided by a nationwide campaign to accumulate captured materiel, particularly parts from downed aircraft, which when cataloged and studied yielded clues about German industrial and military capabilities. Last but by no means least, the "Joint Intelligence Committee," formed a few years before the war, came into its own. The committee benefited from a novel idea—that the armed services, intelligence agencies, and cabinet departments should send senior representatives to debate the meaning and import of the information available to the government, and then present policymakers with informed "assessments" of the war or its various aspects. The result was not clairvoyance but foresight. The intelligence brought to the table by the agencies could be seen in a fuller perspective when amalgamated, and the institutional positions of the various actors grew sharper and better honed for the debates.[40]

But Britain could not sustain this losing struggle. By April 1941, its gold reserves were depleted and London had to pay the interest on its growing debts by taking a loan from Belgium's government-in-exile. The British had few friends left on the continent. France was run by a regime in Vichy that hated the British after the Royal Navy crippled the French battle fleet at Mers el Kebir in July 1940 (on orders from Churchill, who feared French warships might fall into Hitler's hands). The Balkans was a hotbed of intrigue, as usual, but British attempts to stiffen Greek and Yugoslav resistance to the Axis merely resulted in German occupation of those nations in spring 1941. The continent was going Hitler's way; with patience, he would win.

The Grand Alliance

Across the Atlantic, however, the United States was stirring. The crisis of June 1940 forced dramatic changes in America's national strategy. Suddenly the Nazis controlled the continent from the Arctic Circle to the Pyrenees, and if the Royal Navy were sunk or bargained away—both seemed possible to American observers—Germany could own the entire eastern side of the Atlantic.[41] Once that happened, President Roosevelt believed, war would inevitably come to the New World, at a time and place of Hitler's choosing. The shock in Washington was profound. Realizing that traditional strategic assumptions were obsolete, Congress approved conscription and quadrupled the defense budget and military manpower in a single year, and authorized the president to "loan" arms and supplies to Great Britain through Lend Lease. As World War I had pulled American intelligence into the twentieth century, the June crisis caused another upheaval for the secret services. Indeed, that month marked a historic shift in America's conception of its role in the world. The United States was not officially a combatant, but Roosevelt concluded that America's first line of defense was now the English Channel, and resolved to help Britain by any means necessary. The British and American militaries secretly began sharing an amazing quantity of technical and intelligence data, inaugurating a strategic partnership that still endures.

The first fruits of that improved intelligence relationship emerged in the security field. This time there would be no hesitation in America about protecting the country against foreign agents seeking to sabotage war production. The FBI quickly and secretly gained new powers when the president and the Treasury Department reversed long-standing prohibitions on wiretapping and the scrutiny of bank transactions. Almost simultaneously, the State Department dropped its ban on direct contacts between American agencies and foreign liaison partners (State had insisted that intelligence liaison was a form of diplomacy, and that all such activities had to proceed through diplomatic channels). Finally, Roosevelt ordered the FBI into Latin America in June 1940 to stop Nazi infiltration, and the bureau did so by creating from scratch its own foreign intelligence capability, the Special Intelligence Service, to operate from American embassies in cooperation with local authorities. The June crisis thus ensured that American intelligence agencies had new tools to use against a wave of German espionage in the United States.

When Germany attempted to mount new operations in America, the FBI was ready. With a tip from Britain in 1938, the FBI had elicited information from an amateurish German spy, Guenther Rumrich, who fell into the bureau's hands and gave up several *Abwehr* agents (most of whom got away when the US government bungled its indictments). Indeed, the *Abwehr* seemed determined to squander its advantage in recruiting sympathizers in America. Its chief for British and American operations, Nikolaus Ritter, was able to keep in touch with his remaining assets in the States after the Rumrich affair through postal drops and seamen couriers, but he remained all too trusting of agents an ocean away from Hamburg.[42] A clumsy Gestapo attempt to recruit an American visiting his family in Germany just as the war began resulted in another disaster for Ritter's operation. The target recruit, a veteran of the Kaiser's army, William Sebold, immediately warned American authorities, complaining to the US consulate in Cologne of how he was being blackmailed into espionage. Bureau agents met him on his arrival at New York in February 1940. Together they established a dummy business near Times Square (complete with a movie camera behind a two-way mirror) where Sebold could meet *Abwehr* agents, and a clandestine radio to relay their reports to Ritter in Hamburg. The FBI sprang its trap on June 28, 1941, bagging thirty-three agents in a blaze of publicity. This time Justice convicted or took guilty pleas from them all, crushing German espionage in America for good.[43]

The US Army and Navy made progress as well, at least against the Japanese target, as Tokyo crouched to spring beyond its holdings in China and into thinly held French Indochina and the oil-rich Dutch East Indies. London and Washington warned that such aggression would mean war, and Roosevelt ordered reinforcements for American bases in Hawaii and the Philippine Islands. Though the United States had no spies in Japan, signals intelligence seemed to fill the gap. US Navy codebreakers had intermittently read Imperial Japanese naval codes for years and now verged on breaking the latest fleet system (which the Americans dubbed JN-25) when a codebreaking coup by William Friedman and his team of army cryptologists shifted their priorities from Japanese naval to diplomatic messages.[44] In September 1940, Friedman's protégé Frank Rowlett divined the secrets of the machine-enciphered cable traffic of the Japanese foreign ministry and its overseas missions. Rowlett and his colleagues replicated—sight unseen—the Japanese machine and codenamed it Purple, stamping the control label "Magic" on the intercepts it produced. Thereafter, they read Japanese diplomatic traffic almost as fast as Japan's diplomats did—indeed, they deciphered so many messages that they had to borrow linguists from the navy, repaying the loan by allowing navy officers to carry the precious Magic decrypts to President Roosevelt every other month. The breakthrough provided American codebreakers something important to share with their British counterparts when they met face-to-face in early 1941, and it also gave Washington strategic certainty that war was imminent the following December. But it also distracted the US Navy from JN-25 just as the Japanese Navy, with an eye to British successes in the Mediterranean, was considering new ways to employ its aircraft carriers against the US Pacific Fleet.

America could defend itself against Japanese ships and German spies, but Roosevelt knew that defeating Hitler ultimately necessitated extensive cooperation with Great Britain. This did not come automatically. The SIS station chief in New York, William Stephenson, proved an invaluable partner to Hoover and the FBI, once Hoover overcame his initial suspicion. The FBI maintained its taps on British intelligence officials in New York until at least the fall of 1940, and kept an eye on Stephenson's doings as well. A few weeks after Pearl Harbor, Hoover's boss, Attorney General Francis Biddle, called in British ambassador Lord Halifax to inform him (in Hoover's words) that "it was imperative that the present activities of the British Intelligence [sic] in the United States be materially and drastically changed and that they must conform to whatever procedure the Director of the Federal Bureau of Investigation determined was desirable and necessary."[45] The British complied, and despite this rocky beginning, the liaison arrangement promised to benefit both countries in the end.[46] Prime Minister Churchill was determined to make it work, even, in early 1942, showing to an aide to Army Chief of Staff George C. Marshall several British cables exposing London's earlier machinations to bring the United States into the war; "You won't like this," he told Colonel Walter B. Smith, "but I want no secrets" between the two allies.[47]

American and British planners set the overall war strategy in the spring of 1941, secretly outlining a plan for use if and when the United States entered the conflict. If events forced a two-front war with Japan, they agreed to concentrate on stalling the Japanese advance and defeating Germany first. To begin that task, the Allies would continue the naval blockade, expand aerial bombardment of German industry, and mount clandestine operations to spark rebellions in Nazi-occupied territory.[48] The British were already implementing all three parts of this strategy, and had created in their Special Operations Executive (SOE) a secret capability to "set Europe ablaze," in Churchill's famous phrase.[49] The latter requirement handed an opportunity to a New York corporate lawyer and globetrotting foreign affairs aficionado, William J. Donovan. In June 1941, he proposed to the White House a plan for an office to perform espionage, propaganda, guerrilla warfare, and even intelligence analysis. He offered to work with the British, who told Roosevelt—by no coincidence, on the very day Donovan submitted his plan—that they wanted to work with him. Donovan also assured a White House weary of interagency squabbles that

3.2 Winston Churchill helped anticipate and drive intelligence innovation over four decades. *Library of Congress*

he would leave domestic security to the FBI and military reporting to the armed services. The president approved his plan, and Donovan's new outfit soon became the Office of Strategic Services (OSS).[50]

Before OSS could do much, however, American intelligence of sorts was hard at work divining French intentions in North Africa. The Third Republic had signed an armistice with Hitler in June 1940; under its terms, a third of France remained unoccupied by the Germans. Indeed, the Vichy regime retained remnants of France's once-proud army and navy, and held the bulk of their strength out of Hitler's reach in North Africa. Much could depend on keeping Vichy from allying itself with Germany, and on cajoling the French to fight the Germans again. American diplomats in Vichy could cultivate private sources and even travel to North Africa to gauge the mood of French commanders there; the US Naval attaché (Roscoe Hillenkoetter) found, to Roosevelt's abiding interest, that the French army was determined to defend the national honor—and "the atmosphere over there is not comparable to the confusion in Vichy."[51]

This defiance in defeat would be perhaps the first of many times that Hitler's past and prospective victims sought allies in the West. Indeed, World War II was, in a vital way, a war of shadows and ambiguities. Several European states—Sweden, Switzerland, Spain, and Portugal among them—had been spared invasion by the Germans and retained a nervous and jealously guarded neutrality. Even the statelet of Vatican City, essentially a neighborhood surrounded by Rome, had a handful of Allied diplomats accredited to the Holy See who also kept watch on the Italian government, and (after the Italians deposed Mussolini and switched sides in September 1943) on the Eternal City's German occupiers. As long as they caused Hitler minimal trouble the neutrals were safe, but neutrality meant they still treated with the Americans (who until December 1941 were officially neutral themselves), and even with the British. Each of the neutrals represented a base for espionage and intrigue against the Reich; at the same time, their embassies in London and Washington harbored a worrisome quotient of Axis sympathizers.[52] Exploiting those ambiguities, and muffling those ears that listened on behalf of the Germans, would take daring and skill on the part of British (and soon American) intelligence—and took the disentangling of uncoordinated FBI and OSS operations against the Spanish embassy as well.[53]

In June 1941, Hitler made everything much clearer. He reneged on his pledges and invaded the Soviet Union and thereby pushed Stalin into an unlikely alliance with the liberal democracies. This in turn prompted a rethinking of principles, and the signing of the Atlantic Charter, through which Churchill and Roosevelt committed the British Empire and the American republic, to fighting for a world based on international law and self-determination. America was still neutral, but now it was explicitly ranged on the side of freedom—even though Britain's de facto ally, the USSR, was the world's second greatest tyranny. The Western alliance with Stalin would be a wary pact of necessity, with little sharing of secrets on either side. The alliance between Churchill and Roosevelt, by contrast, would endure and change both Britain and the United States, and their intelligence systems.

Once America was propelled into the war on the side of Britain and the Soviet Union by the Pearl Harbor attack, the eventual halting of the Axis was a foregone conclusion—if the Allies could hold together. They had superior numbers, resources, productive capacity, and strategic depth. If handled well, those strengths would translate into firepower, materiel, and manpower to stop the Axis offensives and eventually reverse their gains. Indeed, Churchill closed his eyes in weary satisfaction on the evening of that December 7, 1941, for he knew the Allies would win: "Being saturated and satiated with emotion and sensation, I went to bed and slept the sleep of the saved and thankful."[54] The greatest danger was exhaustion on the part of the Allies, especially the Soviets, as they suffered the horrific casualties required to defeat the Nazi invasion and force a surrender. Intelligence would play a key role in hastening victory before that point.

The Wizard War

World War I had linked science to intelligence. World War II ensured that science would forever be an element of all aspects of the intelligence field. The most important technicians—after the physicists who designed the atomic bomb—were the Allied mathematicians and engineers who delved into the secrets of Axis codes and ensured that the best codes of the Western Allies were impregnable. But other scientists and technicians played important roles on both sides, devising unprecedented new weapons, seeking methods to counter those of the enemy, and gleaning intelligence reports for clues to what new deviltries the other side was brewing.

Here was the heart of the Anglo-American intelligence liaison. The sharing had begun within weeks of the fall of France in June 1940, when the British reached out through their ambassador, Lord Lothian, offering President Roosevelt "an immediate and general interchange of secret technical information."[55] Roosevelt asked his army and navy chiefs what they thought of the vague idea, and, as London expected, the Americans promptly agreed. By February 1941, the cooperation had grown close enough for the US Army to divert a Purple machine intended for the codebreakers at Pearl Harbor to England instead. It sailed on the new HMS *King George V* on that battleship's return journey from America after delivering Lord Lothian's relief as ambassador. With the Purple machine traveled a contingent of American codebreakers from the army and the navy, who would be the first of many to visit and then to stay in the United Kingdom working alongside their British counterparts.[56]

The Anglo-American signals intelligence partnership had three strategic effects on the course of the war. First, clues from decrypted Axis cables—and the fact that the British and Americans shared security advice and innovations—eventually made the most important Allied codes and ciphers invulnerable, both to spies and to the Allies' own communication security lapses. Second, the operational picture that signals intelligence presented gave situational awareness and hence confidence to British and American commanders on land and at sea—there was no Allied theater of operations that was not assisted by SIGINT. Third, the quality of SIGINT as a source improved British decision making as a whole and ultimately American decision making as well. Let us examine these contributions in turn.

Axis spies had achieved little of significance in England or the United States in the war's early years. British and American counterintelligence did not have to be superb to defeat the *Abwehr's* energetic but clumsy attempts to plant agents in enemy territory. These initial victories, however, were accompanied by innovative Allied use of the German agent codebooks and transmitters that fell into friendly hands. By the beginning of 1942, the Allies had total control of the German espionage system as it reached into Britain and America. Signals intelligence supremacy enabled them to extend this advantage overseas to neutralize German spy nets everywhere outside Axis-occupied territory.

The beauty of SIGINT dominance was that it not only blinded the Germans but kept them stupid as well. In essence, MI5 and its double agents (with important support from SIS and the FBI) gave the *Abwehr* the illusion of success and kept it from hatching better ideas. In 1944, MI5's Section V had over a hundred double agents working with it in one fashion or another.[57] Its most famous was Juan Pujol Garcia ("GARBO"), a Catalan sent by the Germans to England. To the *Abwehr* he was a miracle worker, running as many as twenty-eight subagents and radioing advance warnings of Allied landings in North Africa in 1942, and even of the D-Day landings in France in 1944. To SIS and then MI5, however, he was another sort of marvel—a direct pipeline to his credulous masters in Berlin. The invasion warnings he flashed to the Germans were quite accurate, preserving his credibility with the *Abwehr*, but they arrived just late enough to assure that Hitler's High Command had no time to parry the coming blows. GARBO was one of many doubled agents, moreover, and Allied codebreakers monitored their effectiveness by reading German discussions about their agents' reports in the Reich's message traffic.[58] This control over German espionage dampened Berlin's influence in neutral states like Spain and Portugal, which fell in the portfolio of a smart SIS officer, Harold "Kim" Philby, who used the SIGINT clues to track the *Abwehr's* operations.[59] The advantage would allow not only counterintelligence success but strategic deception on a grand scale later in the war.

Another boon to the Allies from signals intelligence was its guidance to senior commanders. Though it first showed its value for the defenders, it was no miracle elixir that guaranteed victory. Even when it provided clear warnings of Axis intent, commanders still had to understand and use the hints it provided. The British on Crete failed to do so in April 1941, with the result that an audacious German parachute invasion over waters controlled by the Royal Navy routed the island's defenders.[60] The Germans also achieved surprise at the Battle of the Bulge in late 1944 in the face of overconfident Allied intelligence estimates. The Wehrmacht still had to be defeated on the ground. Against the Luftwaffe and the Kriegsmarine, Allied signals intelligence did better. By 1942, it had already helped to blunt the Luftwaffe's attacks on Britain and the Kriegsmarine's U-boat offensive. In both cases, SIGINT was but a part of an overall defensive system that came to rely on fine-tuned control of friendly forces. The Admiralty and the US Navy maintained constantly updated operational plots of Allied ship positions, and conjectured U-boat locations gleaned from sightings and signals intercepts. This mastery of information helped win the Battle of the Atlantic by steering convoys of supplies and troops to the United Kingdom around the U-boats, and concentrating British, American, and Canadian sub-hunting ships and aircraft where they would do the most good.[61] In the spring of 1943, the Atlantic campaign was largely won; thereafter, the U-boats were never a serious threat to the buildup of forces in England for the planned cross-channel invasion. The Allies had prevailed, moreover, just in time. New U-boats with radars, snorkels, and quieter propulsion were coming into service. Though too few to make a difference, they remained a menace; no fewer than eight U-boats still prowled off America's East Coast on VE Day in May 1945, despite sustained and well-coordinated antisubmarine patrols.[62]

In the Pacific, SIGINT was the only intelligence source of strategic importance. No source matched the ability of signals intelligence to show Japanese capabilities and suggest Japanese intentions. The Allied intelligence advantage over Japan was clear from the Battle of the Coral Sea (May 1942) until the end of the war. If Pearl Harbor in December 1941 seemed a consummate intelligence failure, the Battle of Midway six months later marked the opposite, a smashing intelligence success. The Japanese surprise at Pearl Harbor had owed more to the bumbling of American naval and military commanders on the scene than to an intelligence lapse, but lapses there had been—chiefly in the aforementioned diversion of US Navy cryptanalysts (in Hawaii and Washington) from monitoring Japanese naval traffic to helping the army process Tokyo's diplomatic messages. After the disaster, naval intelligence returned its attentions to the chief Japanese naval code (JN-25) and swiftly broke it, yielding insights that allowed the Pacific Fleet's aircraft carriers to gamble on an ambush of their Japanese counterparts off Midway Island in June 1942, and turning the tide of the Pacific war.[63]

After Midway and the naval battles in the Solomon Islands in fall 1942, the war in the Pacific was the Allies' to lose, or to win at greater cost— one which could have been horrendous. The Allied intelligence advantage became overwhelming once US Army and Australian codebreakers broke into Japanese army traffic in early 1944.[64] Signals intelligence successes collectively gave General Douglas MacArthur's "island hopping" campaign its brains and timing, showing MacArthur and his navy counterpart, Admiral Chester Nimitz, where the Japanese were and were not, and guiding aircraft and submarines to attack the transports that Japan's Pacific empire needed to supply its far-flung garrisons. The American submarine offensive foreclosed Tokyo's hope of shifting forces to meet emerging threats to its new empire. The Japanese army and navy wondered about the security of their radio traffic, but never changed their procedures, codes, or equipment enough to stymie the Allied advantage. Even Japanese diplomats unwittingly contributed to the harvest reaped by the Allies. The Americans had broken into the diplomatic code in 1940, as noted above, and exploited cables to and from Japan's embassies throughout the war. Hiroshi Oshima, the Emperor's ambassador in Berlin, unwittingly disclosed a trove of information on German capabilities and Nazi intentions, describing for Tokyo (and US Army cryptanalysts) the beach defenses in France before the Normandy invasion, and explaining the nearly successful assassination attempt against Hitler in July 1944. The Allies might well have won the Pacific war without intelligence dominance, given their materiel superiority over Japan. But the task would have taken years longer and a price in lives that Allied electorates might not have tolerated. That indeed was precisely the hope in Tokyo, whose strategists sought a series of sharp victories over the US Navy to force the Americans into a grinding island-by-island struggle before they could ever threaten Japan's Home Islands.

Signals intelligence showed its value for offensive action in Europe as well when the Allies gathered enough strength to mount their first attacks. The British and Americans, in the autumn of 1942, massed their growing forces in North Africa, pushing the Germans and Italians under Erwin Rommel back from Egypt for good, and invading the French possessions of Morocco and Algeria. By December, the Axis held only Tunisia, but German positions there were formidable, and the US Army was not yet up to the task of gaining ground defended by the Wehrmacht. Hitler gambled that he could thus maintain this foothold and thereby protect his Italian ally, but Ultra helped ensure he lost his bet. Swiftly decrypted German and Italian messages foretold the times and places of air and sea supply convoys for the Axis garrison, allowing Allied ships and aircraft to massacre the convoys. Indeed, the intelligence was so good that Allied commanders had to let some shipments through, lest the high commands in Rome and Berlin guess their messages were being read.[65] Axis commanders in Tunisia surrendered in May 1943, and 230,000 German and Italian prisoners were bagged—more than the Soviets had captured at Stalingrad three months earlier. The way to Italy was open, and with the invasion of the Italian mainland in September 1943, Mussolini was toppled in a coup and the new government in Rome quit its alliance with Hitler.

The production of strategic signals intelligence grew to industrial proportions in Britain and America, giving rise to an extended Anglo-American security empire, complete with its own authorities, institutions, customs, and mores. Senior American leaders prized the contributions of the Ultra and Magic codebreaking efforts, and their patronage allowed rapid growth and increased autonomy for the US Army and Navy signals intelligence branches—which in 1939 had been appendages of their respective services' communications bureaus.[66] Britain's Government Code & Cypher School had 8,000 employees in early 1944, though not all of them worked at its famous wartime headquarters at Bletchley Park.[67] Another factor in this growth was the need for more and better machines for breaking machine encipherment. The Polish *bombes* gave way first to Britain's more capable versions, and then to machines built en masse at National Cash Register's works in Ohio, and finally to an entrant for the title of the first real computer, GC&CS's

"Colossus." None of these devices yet fulfilled the potential glimpsed before the war by Bletchley's Alan Turing and others for a truly programmable, multipurpose computing machine—the exigencies of wartime forced technicians to improve on what worked, not to experiment with what they had glimpsed on the technological horizon—but they were amazing accomplishments all the same.[68]

The big cryptologic workforces, and the possibility of commanders acting on "hot" intercepts to parry imminent enemy moves, created a risk that the Germans or Japanese would realize that their signals security had been massively compromised. This was a worry that nagged Allied leaders throughout the war. Their remedy for it was twofold. First, the number who knew the secrets of the codebreakers was kept as small as possible, even though thousands of enlisted personnel had to have some degree of initiation to work the massive computing machines that crunched possible keys. The harshest of punishments were invoked to keep them quiet; young women reporting to the US Navy's processing facility in Washington, DC, were warned in stark terms: "They took us to the chapel and this navy officer got up to talk to us. And I thought we were going to have a little service, a little prayer. Instead he proceeded to tell us that the work we would be doing there was top secret. 'You will not discuss it, talk about it with anyone.' You couldn't even talk to one another in the barracks about it. And he said 'And don't think that because you're women you'll get special privileges. If you talk about what goes on here, you'll be shot.'"[69]

The second part of the answer was "compartments," restricting the distribution of the precious intercepts to commanders and staffers with a strict operational need to see them. F. W. Winterbotham's 1974 memoir, which after long silence divulged the fact that the Allies had read messages sent by German Enigma machines, described the practical considerations that led to this step just as the first Enigma traffic was decrypted in early 1940. The messages had to be correctly translated, and thus it would not do to have each service producing its own translation. They had to be transmitted securely to British (and later American) commanders and their staffs, and that meant via the SIS communications network rather than service channels. They needed an identifier to ensure that they could be readily segregated from less-crucial secrets, and so the label "TOP SECRET Ultra" was affixed to each page that contained information derived from the decrypts. Finally, those "Ultra" messages would be handled in the field by GC&CS-deployed "Special Liaison Units," to ensure that no security or operational risks were taken with the material.[70]

Despite its draconian trappings, this was a system designed to spread information rather than to hoard it. It was indeed the only way to make Ultra safely usable by Allied forces. Only a handful of commanders would know the scope and importance of the Ultra secret, and those commanders would have special intelligence liaison officers detailed from the cryptologic agencies sitting near their inner offices. In that way, the decrypts could pass directly to decision makers, bypassing most of their staffers and minimizing the possibility of leaks. This British-designed system was imposed on the American forces in Europe as a condition of their receiving Ultra decrypts, and it was then translated to the Pacific, where the Americans were already devising something similar on their own. Still, the problem remained that most intelligence analysts and lower-ranking commanders did not have the benefit of the Ultra intelligence. William Donovan and his OSS (with the exception of the office's counterintelligence branch and a few analysts in London), for example, did not have access. But security held. Not for nothing did Churchill dub the denizens of Bletchley Park "the geese that laid the golden eggs—but never cackled."

Guidance from the Top

Churchill himself proved to be a formidable factor in the success of Ultra and of Allied intelligence efforts more broadly. Early in the war, good reporting sometimes went unheeded; SIS, for example, found indications of the Nazi-Soviet pact in 1939, of Hitler's foray into Scandinavia in 1940, and of the Japanese invasion of Malaya in 1941. None helped the Allied defenders, for reasons ranging from incredulity to distraction in the ministries and services.[71] The new prime minister was not a model intelligence customer—being imperious with subordinates and famously stubborn—but he had decades of experience with secret reports, and most importantly, he knew how to cultivate his intelligence system to keep it prompting better decision making by the machinery of state. He regularly read not only Ultra decrypts but customized intelligence summaries from MI5 and SIS.[72] Churchill had glimpsed the future as first lord of the Admiralty before and during World War I, reveling in the control that radio gave over fleets at sea and the insight that signals intelligence offered about enemy intentions and capabilities.[73] As prime minister, he pored over Ultra intercepts, and waved them at his commanders and advisers who questioned his ideas or made excuses.[74] Britain's foremost military minds hated being second-guessed; General Sir Alan Brooke, chief of the Imperial General Staff, complained of constantly having to guard against the prime minister's notions: "Winston had 10 ideas every day, only one of which was good, and he did not know which it was." The discipline that Ultra imposed nonetheless made British strategic decision making more astute. It forced all parties to marshal facts and consider their opinions on major and minor questions—no inconsiderable feat in the crush of wartime. That discipline also forearmed British leaders and commanders in negotiations over grand strategy with their better-supplied but less-experienced American coalition partners. "We lost our shirts," complained a senior US planner who watched the British chiefs of staff wear down American arguments against a Mediterranean focus at the Casablanca conference in January 1943. "We came, we listened, and we were conquered."[75] For the next gathering of the combined chiefs at the TRIDENT conference in Washington (May 1943), the Americans were prepared—and won a British promise to invade France in the spring of 1944.[76]

Ultra cued the intelligence efforts to assist the Allied campaigns on enemy territory, like the imagery and analysis that assisted the Combined Bombing Offensive that the Allies launched over the Continent in 1943. Imagery and analysis were two inventions that had been influential at the tactical level in World War I, and they now guided the operational level of war as well. Early in the conflict, Allied bombers had grown so large and long-ranged that they promised to make a reality of prewar forecasts of the power of strategic bombing to choke an enemy's war-making potential. In so doing, aircraft technology had outstripped the vintage reconnaissance capabilities of the Great War that all sides used to guide targeting and damage assessment. In the midst of the national crisis that forced general reorganization in late 1940, Britain pioneered an interservice photo intelligence center to collect under one roof diverse sets of imagery expertise and intelligence sources. With a mania for files and details, the center's analysts (eventually based at Medmenham) did far more than interpret the photographs snapped by the bomber crews five miles up, and by modified fighter planes sometimes flying below tree-top level. The analysts, for example, learned to spot the latest models of German aircraft, which end of a factory was best to bomb, and how the Germans constructed jets inside a mountain.[77]

The British taught their newly acquired skills to the Americans, who appreciated the value added by Allied teams of expert photointerpreters who were supported by analysts like those of OSS's Enemy Objectives Unit in London. This team proved its value not only by analyzing the imagery but by linking intelligence and decision making in order to pick the indispensable sectors of the German economy to target—and to persuade commanders to risk precious crews and aircraft for the sake of hitting whole systems like synthetic oil production. By the war's end, imagery provided much of the tactical and strategic intelligence that Allied commanders employed against the Axis, and was a key to the bombers' success in crippling the German economy.[78]

The air war over the continent and the U-boat campaign in the North Atlantic turned on the struggle in the ether—or, more properly, the detection and analysis of radio emissions for the clues they gave to enemy capabilities, intentions, and vulnerabilities. Britain's thwarting of *Knickebein* in 1940 marked merely the opening salvo in this battle. When the Combined Bombing Offensive began in earnest, the shoe shifted to the other foot, with the Allies needing to coordinate waves of bombers over German-held territory, while the Germans watched for incoming formations to alert their defenses and allocate interceptors. Both sides invested heavily in detecting enemy emissions, analyzing them for weak points in one another's weapons and tactics, and devising countermeasures and counter-countermeasures.[79] At sea, most of Germany's U-boats (and all of their earlier models) had to spend much of their time on the surface, charging their batteries and awaiting target instructions. They could be detected by radar, by sonar (Asdic in Britain), and by the magnetic anomalies created by their steel hulls, so naturally the Kriegsmarine labored to divine whatever new detection devices the Allies had deployed and to move as quickly as possible to minimize the U-boat's telltale "signatures." The Allies, in turn, frantically studied and deployed ways to foil the glide bombs and guided missiles the Luftwaffe began launching at Allied ships in 1943.

The highest form of scientific intelligence, however, served the Anglo-American creation of the atomic bomb. Such a feat had been glimpsed in theory before December 1938, when German scientists found a way to "split" uranium atoms. Within weeks, physicists around the world grasped the significance of this discovery; if a fission chain reaction could be sustained, it could unleash sudden energy of seemingly boundless violence.

Every major combatant pondered the idea of finding some way for the scientists to build this power into weapons. Only the United States, however, possessed the surpluses of capital and supplies to build such an effort, and with prodding and assistance by British scientists, the Manhattan Project started its world-altering labors in 1942. In addition, the Allies tasked their intelligence services to spot any such preparations on the Axis side— an effort that led to bombing raids that smothered Hitler's meandering atomic program.

The Western Allies thus gained decisive advantages over the Axis in two fields of intelligence, SIGINT and imagery. These were combined at the operational level, with collection feeding analysis and vice versa. It was not as if the Germans, Japanese, and Italians were lazy or stupid in intelligence matters. All three Axis powers knew how to make serviceable codes and ciphers, how to break (some) Allied codes in return, to catch enemy spies in their midst, and to observe the battle space. Yet Axis intelligence efforts never achieved more than tactical significance. The Germans and Japanese, moreover, suspected from time to time that their tactical codes could have been compromised, and they worked throughout the war to improve their security. None of the Axis powers, however, proved able to penetrate the most important cipher systems of the Allies, and thus they never learned the truth—that after 1943 many of their most important messages (and by 1945, almost all of them) were being read by the Anglo-American coalition.

Historians will debate the significance of this crucial difference between the Axis and the Western Allies, but its origin seems to lie in the greater willingness of the Allies to share information and to consider unpleasant hypotheses. Simply put, the militaries of the United States and the Commonwealth nations produced true analysts and also decision makers who would listen to them. Those analysts—both the codebreakers and the photointerpreters—thrived in institutional cultures that allowed them to share data across organizational and even national lines, to form hypotheses, and to debate (politely) the assumptions and conclusions of military planners and commanders. That did not happen as often on the Axis side. The German, Italian, and Japanese militaries, despite their intellectual endowments, only rarely produced and never sustained comparable analytical prowess. German army intelligence analysts, for instance, "made a number of serious mistakes in analysis and estimation, which contributed directly to the defeat of the Wehrmacht in Russia," concluded one historian.[80]

The very idea of an independent role for analysis seemed offensive to some in the Axis camp. "Although staff of the Intelligence Department were not in the operation[s] room or in the battle, they try to refute the estimation of the operations staff. That's unforgivable," fumed a Japanese staff officer when his intelligence colleagues doubted the effects of Kamikaze attacks on the US Navy late in the war.[81] As a result, Axis analysts never marshaled genius on the order of that required to penetrate the secrets of JN-25, to spot the chokepoints in synthetic oil production, or to realize their own messages (and agent networks) had been laid bare to the enemy. Once having fallen crucially behind the Western Allies in this deadly competition, they could not catch up.

Set Europe Ablaze

Going on the offensive against the Third Reich presented the Allies with the same dilemma faced by the *Abwehr* at the beginning of the war—how to keep agents alive in enemy territory. Partisan warfare was an ancient art by 1940, of course, but the radio and the parachute gave it a new appeal to Allied and Axis spymasters alike. The problems with running operatives behind the lines had always involved the difficulty of reaching them with needed supplies and technical assistance, and in exfiltrating what information they collected. Aircraft and portable shortwave radios seemed to solve both problems.[82] The Germans pioneered this art, and the Allies followed, progressing through a painful and deadly learning process from bad to mediocre to useful with the help of the hatred that the peoples Hitler had conquered felt toward their occupiers.

As noted above, the *Abwehr* launched a hasty campaign to penetrate Britain with spies and saboteurs in late 1940. The genius of the British response (the Double Cross system) was that it throttled the German network, leaving it alive enough to convince its masters in Hamburg to send out more operatives to Britain and to America as well. More encouragement came from an operation mounted by J. Edgar Hoover's FBI when a German agent volunteered his services to the Americans in Montevideo. The FBI called him "ND98," and his identity remains locked in the bureau's archives. He had been sent to open a relay station for transmitting secrets from agents in America, but once in Uruguay he persuaded the *Abwehr* (still smarting from the loss of several dozen agents in the Sebold sting) to let him proceed on to the United States.[83] Using an FBI-managed radio on

Long Island, ND98 transmitted to Hamburg from February 1942 right up until the end of the Third Reich. When the Germans sent their last message to him in May 1945, they had already paid him a total of $55,000, providing the FBI a tidy profit on the operation.[84]

The *Abwehr's* head of operations for Britain and America, the ill-advised Nikolaus Ritter, knew that agents of the Kaiser had had some success in sabotaging war stocks in America during World War I. He and his colleagues also saw that they could indeed keep alive at least a few agents in the United Kingdom and the United States. After all, Ritter kept receiving a trickle of intelligence from ND98 and the Double Cross agents. That was enough. In June 1942, the *Abwehr* landed two teams of four agents each from U-boats off Long Island and Florida. Neither team survived long. All eight men were Germans who had lived in the United States, and such was the carefully burnished reputation of Hoover's FBI that two of their number felt they had no chance of carrying out their sabotage missions and quickly surrendered themselves in hopes of clemency. Within two weeks the bureau had bagged the rest; a month later, the six who had not turned coat went to the electric chair in the District of Columbia jail.[85]

Espionage and sabotage behind enemy lines could work only where outside agents could hide among a people resentful of their occupiers. The Germans gave some support to nationalists like the Ukrainian Insurgent Army when the Red Army began its inexorable westward advance after Stalingrad, but could never accomplish much given their alienation of the local populace and the savagery of Soviet internal security. The true masters of behind-the-lines operations, of course, were the Soviets. The Eastern Front saw espionage and partisan warfare on a scale that might never be rivaled. Where the *Abwehr* inserted hundreds of agents behind enemy lines—and had many of them doubled back by the Soviets—the Soviet intelligence services dwarfed what the Germans attempted. Moscow dispatched or recruited in place tens of thousands of agents to report back from German-occupied territory. Overwhelmed German counterintelligence personnel caught or neutralized many thousands of them but many remained to observe and penetrate Axis activities and organizations—a clear intelligence victory for the USSR.[86]

British operations in occupied Europe worked along a slightly different principle. As Hitler conquered nation after nation in the West, the intelligence officers of several vanquished regimes left, along with their refugee leaders, to establish governments in exile in London. These exile services, like France's *Deuxieme Bureau*, ran agents back into their homelands, collecting information on what the Germans were doing there, and better still, on the work their fellow citizens were conscripted to perform inside the Reich itself. British officers, alongside these exiled services, created networks of supporting agents to send those reports via couriers and radio to the Allies. SIS recreated *La Dame Blanche* in Belgium, and in France the service worked with SOE and local networks like the "Alliance" and its leader Marie-Madeleine Fourcade (later immortalized in the movie *L'armee des ombres* [*Army of Shadows*]).[87] The addition of the Soviets to the anti-Fascist cause in 1941 expanded espionage to networks of agents that the Germans called the *Rote Kapelle* (Red Orchestra). It also made guerrilla warfare possible, at least in rugged terrain like the mountains of Yugoslavia, where Josep Broz Tito's tens of thousands of Partisans sparred with the Wehrmacht for years, emerging from the war as the core of the armed forces of the new Democratic Federal Republic.

None of this could have worked without help from British (and Soviet) intelligence, working under Churchill's mandate to "set Europe ablaze" and keep the Nazis constantly stamping out the fires of resistance. The British had two arms for clandestine warfare: SIS, which grew from forty-two officers in April 1939 to 500 by January 1944; and the Special Operations Executive (SOE), formed in 1940.[88] The two organizations cooperated but did not always enjoy one another's company. After 1941, growing liaisons with US military elements and OSS added people, aircraft, energy, and resources to the mix.[89] Indeed, OSS's collaboration with Commonwealth services dictated that office's very structure; several of its major operating branches (particularly Morale Operations, Special Operations, and X-2 [counterintelligence]) were established specifically to shadow their British counterparts (Political Warfare Executive, Special Operations Executive, and SIS/Branch V, respectively). OSS eventually operated spies and commandos on three continents, in the process building substantial capabilities that would be revived in the latter day Central Intelligence Agency and US Special Operations Command.

In every country where a resistance movement took to arms (and especially in Yugoslavia), the dilemma for the Western Allies lay in discerning which factions to bet on. When Hitler was ascendant this calculation embraced primarily military factors, that is, who could do the most harm to the occupying Germans, or collect the best intelligence for the Allied cause. As the tide turned and victory seemed likely, however, political variables crowded for attention. In essence, the Allies had to decide not only who could kill Germans but which locals they wanted to deal with after the war. Once again, good work by SIS and the insights gleaned from SIGINT helped Allied commanders decide who merited support. This requirement also made Charles de Gaulle's Free French and other liaison services into legitimate intelligence targets themselves, at least for SIS.[90] By war's end the Americans, moreover, were intercepting the diplomatic messages of several neutral and allied powers, including the French and Chinese.[91] For Stalin, of course, the decision was easier. He backed the local Communists and did what he could to ensure that they did not stray from orthodoxy.

German energy and ruthlessness made espionage and sabotage deadly pursuits. The courage needed to defy the Nazis with deeds was incalculable, for the sufferings visited on those whom the Germans caught were indescribable. In 1942, SOE used Czech agents to assassinate Himmler's henchman Reinhard Heydrich in Prague, and Hitler had two villages (Lidice and Lezaky) annihilated in retaliation. The Gestapo harbored no civilized inhibitions about torture, and employed it methodically to crack networks and induce captured agents to switch sides. The dilemma for Allied agents and resistance leaders was whether to trust anyone; for their handlers in Britain, it meant wondering if a transmission from the continent was genuine or scripted by the Germans. Such deception was occasionally deadly to the operations of SIS, SOE, and OSS; the Allies more than once were persuaded to transmit clues and instructions (and to fly supplies and new agents) into the arms of the Gestapo.[92] Here was an unwitting German counter to the British Double Cross system, though the difference, once again, was Ultra. The Germans used their double agents for tactical, not strategic, deception, and Gestapo officers never had confidence that they had caught every Allied spy in their midst. Given time, they probably would have stamped out the agent nets, however, and thus the partisan war on the continent probably has to be accounted a draw, at least before the Normandy invasion in June 1944.

Partisan warfare had some effect against the Japanese, especially in rugged terrain. In Burma, Kachin tribesman, together with OSS's Detachment 101, worked alongside special operations forces from the British and American armies. In the Philippine Islands, a handful of American soldiers held on after the Japanese invasion and US surrender in 1942, eventually linking up with General Douglas MacArthur's advancing forces by radio and submarine and providing a lifeline to the growing resistance. Both countries were so large and difficult that the Japanese could never divert enough strength to fully pacify them (indeed, no one has). In China, moreover, the Japanese could not hope to stamp out resistance among the multitudes of peoples their army had ostensibly conquered. Both the Nationalists under Chiang Kai-Shek and the Communists under Mao Zedong kept the Japanese busy with guerrillas, although the Chinese also continued fighting one another. The US Navy backed Chiang's intelligence chief, Tai Li, who claimed to have thousands of agents of the Loyal Patriotic Army behind Japanese lines reporting back to his Investigations and Statistics Bureau, though OSS analysts doubted the wisdom of supporting this "Chinese Himmler."[93]

But generally the rule held in the Pacific as in Europe. Guerrillas and partisans, by definition, could only annoy an occupying force—they could not reverse Axis gains. The Germans and Japanese were too brutal to allow insurgencies more than temporary success. At some point the Western allies had to take and hold ground from the German and Japanese armies. They had to do so as soon as possible on the continent, lest Stalin cut a separate peace because he feared the British and Americans were waiting for the Germans and Soviets to exhaust one another. It is an unanswerable question whether it cost the Allies more resources and military power elsewhere to annoy the occupiers than it cost the Germans and Japanese in resources that they had to divert to keep their rear areas quiet.

Only when the battlefront (and in consequence the political situation) became more fluid after the Allied landings on D-Day could partisans, and the special operations forces supporting them, make a real contribution to the Allied war effort. It was then that the Resistance could rise in Paris and briefly force the German garrison to fight a pitched battle before French tanks arrived. The Poles had tried the same in Warsaw that summer, but Stalin halted his offensive to give the Nazis time to crush the resistance (and to slaughter those Poles who might be brave enough to resist a Soviet occupation in the future). Warsaw was thus a case in point. The blow to the Axis from the invasion of France came just in time for the partisans in both Europe and Asia—had the Allied counteroffensive been delayed by two or three more years, it must be doubted whether any organized resistance would have been left to greet the liberators.

One possible good that the Western Allies' visible support of partisan warfare accomplished only emerged after the war. In places like Northern Italy, Yugoslavia, and Greece, the fact that the West could put commandos and supplies on the ground for local resistance leaders like Tito gave a clear message that the Communists in Moscow were not the only force fighting fascism and able to help their friends. This would be remembered after 1945 in every place that the Red Army did not occupy. In East Asia, the memory of shared sacrifice in guerrilla warfare against the Japanese in the Philippine Islands helped convince Washington that the Filipinos deserved the independence that America had previously promised them. Partisan warfare thus gave the occupied peoples hope and a restored sense of dignity that helped them deal with the West after the war, and in the long run provided a certain moral grounding for national memories of the conflict.

The Dominance of Firepower

By 1943, the Allies' material and technical advantages were creating opportunities to go on the offensive and win ground back from the Axis. The Soviet steamroller lurched forward after Stalingrad and hardly stopped before reaching Berlin in the spring of 1945. The Western Allies had to land on the continent from the sea and gain positions that the Axis had to counterattack, thus bringing to bear Allied strength in firepower against German and Japanese forces seeking to dislodge them. This pattern held from February 1943 on in Tunisia, Italy, and France; when the Germans surged forward against Allied positions, British and American artillery and bombers flattened their attacks. In the Pacific, from August 1942 on, American forces proved able to hold their own on, above, and around the Solomon Islands, beating back almost every attack the Japanese threw at them (Commonwealth forces did the same in New Guinea). The Allies were even able to go on the offensive and advance in the Pacific without drawing too much combat power away from Europe.

The Allied intelligence and firepower advantage was all-powerful for the Normandy landing in June 1944. The Allies put ashore 160,000 men across a fifty-mile front in just one day, and then followed them with seemingly limitless supplies and reinforcements. German intelligence had not slept; Berlin knew an invasion was imminent by photographing the Allied buildup in southern England from above, and listening to the radio traffic of the units there. Indeed, US Army formations were notorious for their seemingly incessant on-air chatter—a bad habit that got more than a few GIs killed. But in France, the Germans did not know precisely where or when the cross-channel invasion was coming, and here the Allied advantages in cryptology and counterintelligence showed to their best. No genuine German spy operated in Britain in 1944—and thus the agent reports that reached Berlin were lies, designed to misdirect the defenders. The Germans could not decrypt the Allies' most sensitive communications, and they never knew their own were being read at Bletchley Park. As a result, the German defense of the French coast was dispersed, and its reaction time was slowed just enough to permit the Allies to seize a firm beachhead in Normandy. Even Allied disasters like the Rapido River assault in Italy the preceding January had worked some good; senior Allied commanders could read in Ultra that the Wehrmacht was diverting strength from France and the Balkans to the battlefield in Italy—meaning the upcoming Allied landings at Anzio (and ultimately Normandy) would have fewer German defenders to fight.[94]

To assist the illusions among Axis planners, the British in particular honed the occult science of military deception. The FORTITUDE campaign to mask the Normandy invasion was merely the largest and most important such effort. There were others, of lesser but still significant value to the war effort. The morbidly named Operation MINCEMEAT in 1943 helped confuse the Germans in the Mediterranean about the ultimate target of the Allied invasion fleet they saw massing in North African harbors. For MINCEMEAT, a British submarine released a corpse dressed as the fictitious Major William Martin, Royal Marines, just off a Spanish beach, near enough to where the local authorities would surely show him to a particular German diplomat. As expected, the neutral Spanish kindly helped both sides. They buried the poor Major Martin and returned his briefcase to the local British consul. Of course, they also copied its eminently plausible contents and passed them to their German friend. The files that Major Martin had supposedly carried hinted that Sicily was indeed not the target of the upcoming invasion, which was heading farther east. Generals in Berlin swallowed the bait, happily divining that Sicily was too obvious an objective for the Allies, and congratulating themselves for finding the missing clue that had kept them concentrating too much strength there. That delusion held right up to July 9, 1943, when British and American troops landed in Sicily.[95]

Allied ground and naval gunnery in Normandy, combined with air superiority over every landing beach and the battlefields beyond, meant the Germans could not mass the tanks and guns they needed to plow the landing force back into the sea. Their final attempt came at Falaise in Normandy in July; the panzers' counterattack turned into a massacre of German formations, the precursor to a country-wide rout like the Battle of France in 1940, only this time with German forces surrounded and broken. The Allies rushed to the very borders of Germany in a few weeks. Indeed, by the end of 1944, the Allied ability to mass firepower quickly on the battlefield was so devastating that the British and Americans could turn tactical defeats from Axis surprise attacks into operational victories, as they already had in Tunisia and at Anzio, and would again in the Battle of the Bulge. The Japanese suffered the same fate when they tried to take the offensive in 1944 in Burma, the Philippine Sea, and Leyte Gulf. Their formations were pounded by heavy artillery and their aircraft shot from the sky by superior Allied fighters and antiaircraft guns. In the East, the sheer weight of Russian manpower absorbed German counterattacks and hit back many times harder. The Axis has lost the ability to gain ground against the skillfully directed firepower of the Western Allies and the Soviet Union.

The Germans and Japanese responded in a remarkably similar fashion—by launching missile attacks. The idea, independently reached in both Berlin and Tokyo and deployed in the latter half of 1944, was to cause maximum casualties in hopes of sapping the Western Allies' will to fight. The Japanese made their attempt with Kamikazes—essentially manned cruise missiles aimed at Allied ships (they also ordered their troops to persist in suicidal cave fighting in the volcanic islands that constituted Japan's inner defense barrier). Hitler had a different concept, one enabled by Germany's more highly developed technological base. German scientists devised the V-weapons for use against British civilians: the V-1 was a jet-powered cruise missile, while the V-2 was an engineering marvel, a liquid-fueled, exoatmospheric rocket with a one-ton warhead. Neither was accurate, but they did not have to be to hit London.

Intelligence helped against the new German tactic, though less so against the Japanese. Imperial soldiers fighting to the death from caves had to be bombed or burned out; this was a nasty business that required remorseless courage (and flamethrowers), but one in which intelligence work had less to contribute. The Kamikazes similarly required little infrastructure, though Allied intelligence contributed marginally by locating their airfields. Intelligence offered far more to the fight against the V-weapons. Though temporarily confused by reports of their development, all source collection and analytical work by the British and Americans succeeded in locating V-1 launch pads and the V-2 test sites early enough for Allied bombers to disrupt their operations. Reports from the exiled liaison services (especially the Poles) were vital to the early work of identifying and analyzing the V-2 rocket program.[96] Allied bombers thereafter kept both programs on the run, hampering their production and deployment—which would have progressed with Teutonic efficiency and drive if left unmolested. British counterintelligence also devised a morally problematic but somewhat effective way of impairing the accuracy of the V-2 rockets, which could not be stopped once launched. The aforementioned Garbo fed his masters in Hamburg false reports of V-2 impacts, in effect convincing the Germans to shift their aim from Tower Bridge in the heart of London toward the city's less densely populated suburbs. This deception amounted to playing God with the lives of British civilians in the target zones, but it also kept fewer people from being killed by the V-2s.[97]

The new terror weapons imposed heavy costs on the Axis and Allies alike. The V-1s and V-2s caused about 32,000 casualties (mostly in Britain) from June 1944 until March 1945, when their bases were overrun by the advancing Allies. The Kamikazes sank dozens of Allied ships and caused thousands more casualties. Thousands of Allied guns, aircraft, and crews had to be diverted to defending against these flying bombs and, in the case of the V-2s, to hunting their launch sites. Both the Germans and the Japanese expended their dwindling strength on these programs. The Kamikazes used scarce planes, pilots, and fuel, while the V-2s were enormously expensive to build; all of these resources might have been devoted to more valuable military objectives. This fact, however, emphasized the truism that all war is political. Kamikazes and V-2s were military expressions of the totalitarian conceit that liberal societies were fractious and soft, and could be dissuaded by killing their civilians. Tellingly, Hitler aimed no V-1s or V-2s at Soviet targets. There was no point; Stalin ignored public opinion, and his security apparatus would easily cover up damage from mere missiles, so the Germans had no chance of influencing Moscow by causing civilian casualties. What happened in Europe thus marked a continuation of the pattern that began with British air defense efforts against the Zeppelin raids in

1915. Intelligence resources of the liberal democracies had to be diverted to guarding the civilian population. This shifting of military and intelligence power to provide warning of attacks on civilians and counters to enemy weapons of mass destruction would be a permanent trend going forward.

Collapse and Epilogue

As the war neared its end, the Allied material and intelligence advantages compounded each other's effects, helping to ensure that the Reich's downfall and then the Japanese collapse would be swift and final. Western strength could thus be used to pry the Japanese out of their island fortresses in the Pacific and to force Hitler to weaken his position in the East (thus giving the Red Army more opportunities to grind down the Wehrmacht). Stalin gave a toast at the Tehran Conference with Churchill and Roosevelt in November 1943: "Without American production the United Nations could never have won the war."[98] That production allowed the Allies to take the offensive on every front, and the Axis simply could not defend everywhere at once. All the same, World War II could have petered out, with a battered Hitler and Tojo fighting their opponents to an armistice that would have kept their regimes shrunken but alive as the Allies recoiled from the casualties required to roll back the Axis conquests. That the war did not end that way is a great boon to mankind, and it is also a credit to intelligence, which let the Western Allies pick their battles and their friends.

An early indicator of which way the wind was blowing could be seen in the increasing cooperation from neutrals who lost their fear of German invasion (and wanted to be counted on the right side when the Allies won). This paid off for Allied intelligence officers working from their diplomatic missions on the periphery of the Reich. Madrid, Lisbon, Bern, Geneva, and Stockholm all became world centers of intrigue. With the end of the war in sight in 1944, Ultra provided yet another benefit: it helped the Allies minimize the moral compromises they might otherwise have made with Nazis who were offering secrets and hoping to save themselves through clandestine cooperation. Some such offers were worth taking, like "Dictionary," an officer in Himmler's RHSA (which supplanted the *Abwehr* in 1944, in the final, Pyrrhic victory of party over military intelligence); and "Ecclesiastic," the pretty young consort of *Abwehr* officers in Lisbon. Both assets reported to SIS in the last year of the war.[99] Other potential recruits were better left alone. "We cannot do business with war criminals to save their necks," cabled

SIS headquarters in London to an officer in Stockholm who had proposed doubling the *Abwehr's* local representative, a high-living fellow who seemed vulnerable to blackmail. Ultra had helped SIS and MI5 chart the German's network of contacts and convinced the British the fellow in question was already doing more harm to the Reich than to the Allies. Hence London's explanation to SIS Stockholm: "There is surely nothing very important that this particularly unpleasant rat could give us if he was allowed to leave the sinking ship."[100]

In the end, old-fashioned espionage helped draw the war to its close. Contacts in 1945 between OSS station chief in Switzerland, Allen Dulles, and SS General Karl Wolff, commander of German forces in Italy during the final months of World War II, exemplified such discussions with tainted sources. Wolff brokered a separate surrender for his retreating but tenacious army—with Dulles as a key facilitator—thus ending the Italian campaign a week before the comprehensive surrender of the Third Reich (May 8, 1945) and saving hundreds if not thousands of lives on both sides. The fact that Wolff was dealing with OSS and Allied commanders at all, however, was withheld (ultimately unsuccessfully) from Stalin, who worried that his allies in London and Washington might negotiate their own peace with Hitler.[101] At roughly the same time, OSS's clandestine contacts with the government of Thailand in Bangkok also had to be held in tight secrecy for fear of provoking an outright Japanese occupation of the country.[102] Once again, OSS operators on the scene seized an opportunity to pull enemies apart from one another.

The end came four months later in the East. Japan had been isolated by summer 1945, or so it seemed. Allied submarines had wiped out its merchant fleet, and American aircraft carriers ranged along the Japanese coast, pounding targets at will. Japan's armies held on in China and Southeast Asia, but were harassed by US and British special operations forces. Giant B-29 bombers from the Mariana Islands firebombed Japan's wooden cities. And still Tokyo would not surrender. Indeed, thousands of Japanese troops were ferried across the Sea of Japan from the mainland despite the Allied blockade, stiffening the planned suicide defense of the Home Islands. Allied invasion planners forecast enormous casualties on both sides, and raised their forecast again that July when intercepts revealed the presence of reinforcements from Manchuria in the landing areas.[103] President Truman used atomic bombs in August almost in desperation, to avoid a bloodbath if the scheduled invasions went ahead later that year. The bombs, with the simultaneous Soviet invasion of Japanese-occupied Manchuria, forced the issue. They paralyzed the militarists in Tokyo who had demanded to fight on in hopes of better terms, and thereby gave the emperor a political opening to sue for peace. Diplomatic intercepts had already revealed to Washington a condition that might induce Tokyo to accept "unconditional" surrender: the emperor could retain his throne. And with that, the Japanese capitulated on August 14, 1945.

The Allied Supreme Commander in Europe, General Dwight Eisenhower, took a moment after VE Day to send a private note of thanks to SIS chief Sir Stewart Menzies, under whose purview fell not only the Secret Intelligence Service but also the codebreakers at Bletchley Park. Eisenhower asked for his gratitude to be passed along to the "members of the staff personally for the magnificent services" they had rendered: "The intelligence which has emanated from you before and during this campaign has been of priceless value to me. It has simplified my task as commander enormously. It has saved thousands of British and American lives and, in no small way, contributed to the speed with which the enemy was routed and eventually forced to surrender."[104] The general's note encapsulated the value and the scope of the Anglo-American intelligence cooperation in its allusion to the codebreaking, human intelligence, and analytic successes of the combined effort. The fact that such a note could be sent by a general of one nation's army to the secret intelligence chief of another nation also spoke volumes. A truly multinational intelligence instrument had been forged by the exigencies of war.

The Soviets, of course, were not members of that intelligence alliance. The end of World War II in 1945 saw the USSR and the Western Allies dominant in firepower, science, and industry. In a sense, that superpower status has endured. Only in rare cases since 1945 has anyone tried to stand up against a modern conventional force (whether Western, Soviet, or Israeli) and fight it on its own terms. In all wars but one (Korea), such a stand has resulted in swift defeat for the local forces who attempted it. World War II also created two intelligence superpowers. As a result of the First World War, by 1918 only states could control the most effective (and expensive) intelligence means. Axis intelligence had remained at World War I levels of proficiency—good enough to beat weak opponents and some good ones, like the French, and good enough to sustain a defense against the most powerful forces on earth, for a time—but not good enough to find the weak points and beat those strong powers. The Anglo-American intelligence alliance far surpassed World War I proficiencies, being superior not only in technical intelligence collection but also far more so in the information processing and analysis that magnified all other strengths. The Eastern half of the Grand Alliance—the Soviets—had battlefield intelligence that was comparable to that of the Axis, but defeated the Wehrmacht with gigantic manpower (supplemented by American production) rather than with finesse. But how could the Soviets rank as an intelligence superpower? Because their human intelligence was so much better than what the Axis had at the strategic level. It was so good as to rival Ultra in the richness of strategic insight that it offered Stalin. And that is the subject of the next chapter.

NOTES

1. Keith Jeffery, *The Secret History of MI6* (New York: Penguin, 2010), 175.
2. Martin Thomas, *Empires of Intelligence: Security Services and Colonial Disorder after 1914* (Berkeley: University of California Press, 2007), 4–6, 71–72, 244–56.
3. Jeffery, *The Secret History of MI6*, 209, 227.
4. Christopher Andrew, *Defend the Realm: The Authorized History of MI5* (New York: Alfred A. Knopf, 2009), 128–30, 137–38, 159; Jeffery, *The Secret History of MI6*, 151–52, 236.
5. Quoted in Mark Stout, "World War I and the Invention of American Intelligence, 1878–1918," unpublished doctoral thesis, School of History, University of Leeds, June 2010, 291.
6. The BI became the Federal Bureau of Investigation in 1935 in response to government reforms occasioned by the end of Prohibition a couple years earlier. Federal Bureau of Investigation, *The FBI: A Centennial History, 1908–2008* (Washington, DC: Federal Bureau of Investigation, 2009), 44.
7. *Olmstead v. United States*, 277 US 438 (1928).
8. Jeffery, *The Secret History of MI6*, 168, 246.
9. Andrew, *Defend the Realm*, 122, 127.
10. Federal Bureau of Investigation, *The FBI*, 17.
11. Jeffery, *The Secret History of MI6*, 192–97, 253, 302.
12. Ibid., 293–94.
13. Vadim J. Birstein, "Soviet Military Counterintelligence from 1918 to 1939," *International Journal of Intelligence and CounterIntelligence*, 25:1 (Spring 2012): 70, 95.
14. John J. Dziak, *Chekisty: A History of the KGB* (Lexington, MA: Lexington Books, 1988), 2.
15. Birstein, "Soviet Military Counterintelligence from 1918 to 1939," 72, 80, 87.

16. Nikita Khrushchev, *Khrushchev Remembers*, Edward Crankshaw, trans., and Strobe Talbott, ed. (Boston: Little, Brown, 1970), 28, 109.

17. David Kahn, *Hitler's Spies: German Military Intelligence in World War II* (New York: MacMillan, 1978), 330–34.

18. Mussolini's Fascism differed from its Soviet cousins and German imitators in one way that highlighted the immense danger that Hitler and Stalin posed. The Italian Fascists abused dissenters and even provided a dwindling subsidy to the British Union of Fascists (closely monitored by MI5); Andrew, *Defend the Realm*, 193. But they were nationalists first and racists only later in imitation of their Nazi allies. Their secret police bureau—the *Organizzazione per la Vigilanza e la Repressione dell'Antifascismo* (OVRA)—was not a party organ, and was far smaller than its counterparts in Germany and the USSR. Mussolini's Fascists did not cross over into actively seeking to liquidate entire categories of people.

19. Andrew, *Defend the Realm*, 209.

20. Paul Johnson, *Modern Times: The World from the Twenties to the Eighties* (New York: Harper & Row, 1983), 190–202, 315–17. Sun Tzu, *The Art of War*, in which see the essay by Samuel B. Griffith, "Sun Tzu and Mao Tse-Tung" (New York: Oxford, 1971 [1963]), 46–55.

21. Mao Tse-Tung, *On Guerrilla Warfare*, trans. Samuel B. Griffith (Champaign, IL: University of Illinois Press, 1961), 97, 101. See also the organizational charts in the appendix. Griffith translated the work, known in Chinese as *Yu Chi Chan*, while a captain in the US Marine Corps in 1940.

22. John Byron and Robert Pack, *The Claws of the Dragon: Kang Sheng, the Evil Genius behind Mao and His Legacy of Terror in People's China* (New York: Simon & Schuster, 1992), 174, 182. Kenneth Lieberthal, *Governing China: From Revolution through Reform* (New York: W. W. Norton, 2004), 51–52.

23. Jeffery, *The Secret History of MI6*, 254–55.

24. Ibid., 307–8, 399.

25. The figures cited in Jeffery's and Andrew's authorized histories suggest that both services by 1939 were larger than they had been a decade earlier; see Andrew, *Defend the Realm*, 180; Jeffery, *The Secret History of MI6*, 245–47, 475.

26. Don Whitehead, *The FBI Story* (New York: Random House, 1956), 157–62.

27. Andrew, *Defend the Realm*, 179–82, 210.

28. Quoted in Johnson, *Modern Times*, 360.

29. Martin S. Alexander, "Radio-Intercepts, Reconnaissance and Raids: French Operational Intelligence and Communications in 1940," *Intelligence and National Security* 28:3 (June 2013): 349–51.

30. Jeffery, *The Secret History of MI6*, 274, 300, 383–86; Andrew, *Defend the Realm*, 196–201.

31. Andrew, *Defend the Realm*, 224–26.

32. Donald P. Steury, *The Intelligence War* (New York: MetroBooks, 2000), 89. See also Marcus Faulkner, "The *Kriegsmarine*, Signals Intelligence and the

Development of the *B-Dienst* before the Second World War," *Intelligence and National Security* 25:4 (August 2010): 533–37.

33. John Ferris, "The British Army, Signals and Security in the Desert Campaign, 1940–1942," *Intelligence and National Security* (1990): 156.

34. David Thomas, "Foreign Armies East and German Military Intelligence in Russia, 1941–45," *Journal of Contemporary History* 22 (1987): 267–68.

35. Seishiro Sugihara, *Chiune Sugihara and Japan's Foreign Ministry: Between Incompetence and Culpability* (Lanham, MD: University Press of America, 2001), 56.

36. Steury, *The Intelligence War*, 77.

37. R. V. Jones, *Most Secret War: British Secret Intelligence, 1939–1945* (London: Hamish Hamilton, 1978), 93–105.

38. Andrew, *Defend the Realm*, 211–12, 248, 250–52. Jeffery, *The Secret History of MI6*, 432, 491.

39. Andrew, *Defend the Realm*, 236–38.

40. Percy Cradock, *Know Your Enemy: How the Joint Intelligence Committee Saw the World* (London: John Moore, 2004), 7–17.

41. Robert Murphy, *Diplomat among Warriors* (Garden City, NY: Doubleday, 1964), 55, 59. Also Walter Isaacson and Evan Thomas, *The Wise Men: Six Friends and the World They Made* (New York: Simon & Schuster, 1986), 183.

42. Kahn, *Hitler's Spies*, 330–34. Ritter was also in charge of *Abwehr* agents in England, and was simultaneously being taken in by SNOW and the Double Cross system; Andrew, *Defend the Realm*, 212.

43. Federal Bureau of Investigation, *The FBI*, 44.

44. Frederick D. Parker, *Pearl Harbor Revisited: United States Navy Communications Intelligence, 1924–1941* (Ft. Meade, MD: National Security Agency, 1994), 16, 49–50.

45. Federal Bureau of Investigation, running memorandum, "British Intelligence Service in the United States," January 1, 1947, 7.

46. Raymond Batvinis, *The Origins of FBI Counterintelligence* (Lawrence: University of Kansas Press, 2007), 62–63, 103, 204, 258, 284n9, 296n38.

47. D. K. R. Crosswell, *The Chief of Staff: The Military Career of General Walter B. Smith* (Westport, CT: Greenwood, 1991), 94.

48. Maurice Matloff and Edwin M. Snell, *Strategic Planning for Coalition Warfare* (Washington, DC: Department of the Army, 1953), 44–46.

49. J. R. M. Butler, *Grand Strategy*, vol. 2, September 1939–June 1941, in United Kingdom Military Series, *History of the Second World War* (London: Her Majesty's Stationery Office, 1964), 215, 549–50.

50. Douglas Waller, *Wild Bill Donovan: The Spymaster Who Created OSS and Modern American Espionage* (New York: Free Press, 2011), 69–71.

51. Murphy, *Diplomat among Warriors*, 66–76.

52. MI5 mounted a comprehensive campaign against the Spanish embassy in London, for example, utilizing intercepts, agents, and other means to monitor

what Spanish diplomats were doing that could be of assistance to Germany; Andrew, *Defend the Realm*, 259–62.

53. Waller, *Wild Bill Donovan*, 125–27.

54. Winston S. Churchill, *The Second World War*, vol. 3, *The Grand Alliance* (New York: Houghton Mifflin, 1985 [1950]), 544.

55. Sir Philip Kerr [Lord Lothian] to President Roosevelt, aide memoire, July 8, 1940 accessed April 3, 2013, at www.nsa.gov/public_info/declass/ukusa.shtml.

56. Cradock, *Know Your Enemy*, 273.

57. Jeffery, *The Secret History of MI6*, 569.

58. Andrew, *Defend the Realm*, 254, 285, 294, 297, 300; Jeffery, *The Secret History of MI6*, 569.

59. Jeffery, *The Secret History of MI6*, 491. See also Kim Philby, *My Silent War* (London: Granada, 1980 [1968]), 62–67.

60. John Keegan, *Intelligence in War: Knowledge of the Enemy from Napoleon to Al Qaeda* (New York: Knopf, 2003), 182.

61. Ladislas Farago, *The Tenth Fleet* (New York: Drum Books, 1986 [1962]), 18.

62. Ibid., 298.

63. Elliot Carlson, *Joe Rochefort's War: The Odyssey of the Codebreaker Who Outwitted Yamamoto at Midway* (Annapolis: US Naval Institute Press, 2011), 321–36.

64. They were aided in this task by the recovery of a trunk holding the Japanese Army's Twentieth Division's cryptographic library, dumped in a stream by retreating troops; Sharon Maneki, *The Quiet Heroes of the Southwest Pacific Theater: An Oral History of the Men and Women of CBB and FRUMEL* (Ft. Meade, MD: National Security Agency, 1996), 23.

65. Steury, *The Intelligence War*, 80.

66. Robert Louis Benson, "A History of US Communications Intelligence during World War II: Policy and Administration" (Ft. Meade, MD: National Security Agency Center for Cryptologic History, 1997), 45, 47, 147–48.

67. Jeffery, *The Secret History of MI6*, 475.

68. Colin Burke, "An Introduction to a Historic Computer Document: Betting on the Future—The 1946 Pendergrass Report on Cryptanalysis and the Digital Computer," *Cryptologic Quarterly* 13:4 (Winter 1994): 65–67.

69. Curt Dalton, "Keeping the Secret: The Waves and NCR Dayton, Ohio, 1943–1946" (1997); accessed August 7, 2011, at www.daytonhistorybooks.com/page/page/1482135.htm.

70. F. W. Winterbotham, *The Ultra Secret* (New York: Harper & Row, 1974), 17–22.

71. Jeffery, *The Secret History of MI6*, 312, 344, 575.

72. Andrew, *Defend the Realm*, 289; Jeffery, *The Secret History of MI6*, 347–48.

73. Nicholas A. Lambert, "Strategic Command and Control for Maneuver Warfare: Creation of the Royal Navy's 'War Room' System, 1905–1915," *Journal of Military History* 69 (April 2005); 395–99.

74. Winterbotham, *The Ultra Secret*, 63–66.

75. Rick Atkinson, *An Army at Dawn: The War in North Africa, 1942–1943* (New York: Henry Holt, 2002), 289.

76. Rick Atkinson, *The Day of Battle: The War in Sicily and Italy, 1943–1944* (New York: Henry Holt, 2008 [2007]), 12, 23.

77. Constance Babington-Smith, *Air Spy: The Story of Photo Intelligence in World War II* (New York: Harper, 1957), 192–94.

78. Alexander S. Cochran, Robert C. Ehrhart, and John F. Kreis, "The Tools of Air Intelligence: Ultra, Magic, Photographic Assessment, and the Y-Service," in John F. Kreis, ed., *Piercing the Fog: Intelligence and Army Air Forces Operations in World War II* (US Air Force, 1995), 85, 92, 93.

79. R. V. Jones helped to pioneer this field, both as a scientific adviser to the British high command and later as a memoirist; his reflections in *Most Secret War* provide an excellent introduction to the principles and patterns of this sort of work.

80. Thomas, "Foreign Armies East," 279–84.

81. Ken Kotani, *Japanese Intelligence in World War II* (Oxford: Osprey, 2009), 106–7.

82. Jeffery, *The Secret History of MI6*, 18, 481–82.

83. Federal Bureau of Investigation, *The FBI*, 45.

84. Ibid., 44. Whitehead, *The FBI Story*, 196–98. The *Abwehr* likewise dutifully transmitted to its Double Cross agents in Britain until the last week of the war, when British troops took Hamburg; Andrew, *Defend the Realm*, 316.

85. Whitehead, *The FBI Story*, 199–206. Himmler's SD landed two more agents from a U-boat in late 1944, with similar results when one of them called the FBI; Richard Willing, "The Nazi Spy Next Door," *USA Today*, February 27, 2002.

86. Thomas, "Foreign Armies East," 273–74. See also Robert Stephen, "Smersh: Soviet Military Counter-intelligence during the Second World War," *Journal of Contemporary History* 22 (1987): 601–2.

87. Jeffery, *The Secret History of MI6*, 388, 525–30.

88. Jeffery, *The Secret History of MI6*, 475.

89. Jay Jakub, *Spies and Saboteurs: Anglo-American Collaboration and Rivalry in Human Intelligence Collection and Special Operations, 1940–1945* (New York: St. Martins, 1999), 189–90.

90. Jeffery, *The Secret History of MI6*, 397, 435.

91. David J. Alvarez, *Secret Messages: Codebreaking and American Diplomacy, 1930–1945* (Lawrence: University Press of Kansas, 2000), 152.

92. The Germans, for instance, wiped out the British networks in Holland, which had long been rocky soil for SIS; Andrew, *Defend the Realm*, 906n34; also Jeffery, *The Secret History of MI6*, 395–96.

93. Milton E. Miles, *A Different Kind of War: The Unknown Story of the US Navy's Guerrilla Forces in World War II China* (Garden City, NY: Doubleday, 1967), 22, 290–91, 418–25. R. Harris Smith, *OSS: The Secret History of America's First Central Intelligence Agency* (Berkeley: University of California Press, 1972), 245.

94. Atkinson, *The Day of Battle*, 343, 516.

95. Ben Macintyre, *Operation Mincemeat: How a Dead Man and Bizarre Plan Fooled the Nazis and Assured an Allied Victory* (New York: Broadway, 2010). See also Andrew, *Defend the Realm*, 282, 286–87.

96. Jeffery, *The Secret History of MI6*, 533.

97. Andrew, *Defend the Realm*, 314.

98. "One War Won," *Time*, December 13, 1943.

99. Jeffery, *The Secret History of MI6*, 548, 570.

100. Ibid., 515.

101. A good summary of this episode is in Smith, *OSS*, 230–33. See also John Ranelagh, *The Agency: The Rise and Decline of the CIA* (New York: Simon & Schuster, 1987 [1986]), 78–82.

102. Thailand was an ally of Imperial Japan that had actually declared war on the United States and Britain in 1941. Washington had ignored the declaration at the request of the Thai ambassador; the British had not. Smith, *OSS*, 294.

103. Douglas J. MacEachin, *The Final Months of the War with Japan* (Washington, DC: Central Intelligence Agency, 1998); accessed September 12, 2011, at www.cia.gov/library/center-for-the-study-of-intelligence.

104. Eisenhower's letter is reprinted in Jeffery, *The Secret History of MI6*, 552.

CHAPTER 4

Cold War: Technology

You'll see, when I'm gone the imperialistic powers will wring your necks like chickens.

–KHRUSHCHEV, *KHRUSHCHEV REMEMBERS*

By the end of World War II, two intelligence systems capable of functioning on a global basis had come into existence. One intelligence system was the sword and shield of a Communist state that possessed a massive army but had suffered horrendous wounds in the war. The other system was made up of a confederation of agencies supporting the elected leaders of two allies, one of which was a huge state with a booming and unharmed economy; the other was an exhausted empire. The nature of these superpowers and the technology they wielded determined the course of their relations, making rivalry between them inevitable and conflict likely once it became obvious that they held mutually exclusive visions for the future of Central Europe—and that both sides would fight to maintain the boundaries established in 1945. The atomic bomb, however, raised the cost of a war between them to unprecedented heights. Both sides promptly armed themselves with H-bombs as well, and then with nuclear-tipped missiles that could hit any target in the world within minutes. Yet somehow they fought no war with one another, and indeed found a tense and costly peace, but a peace all the same.

The fact that East and West avoided direct conflict in the Cold War stemmed in part from the achievements of their intelligence systems. In 1946, both sides desperately needed knowledge of the other, and worked to get it through their respective strengths—the Anglo-Americans through signals intelligence, and the Soviets through spies. But those strengths quickly canceled one another out, and the services and techniques that had served well in World War II had to be modernized. In the West, that meant sustained and expensive investments of resources and scientific talent.

It also meant the US Intelligence Community, with all its flaws, became the world leader in intelligence by the 1970s. In the East, it meant the seeming perfection of all-pervasive surveillance at home, and the retargeting of already proficient espionage agencies. Out of this competition, both East and West gained a degree of certainty about their adversaries' intentions and capabilities, and a working confidence that their side could emerge from even a surprise attack to destroy the other.

The intelligence competition was not even, as the West clearly won it in the end. But that victory in strategic intelligence, for one of the only times in history, was used for peace. It enabled something unprecedented and so illogical that some observers at the time were not sure it was really happening. To wit, a democratic coalition and a Marxist pact made a series of arms control deals with their ideological and nuclear-armed nemeses, and those deals stood. How that happened makes for a barely believable tale.

The War at Home

Days after the end of World War II, Hollywood released an FBI-sponsored thriller, *The House on 92nd Street* (20th Century Fox), depicting Nazi spies in America and the special agents tracking them. In typical cinematic fashion, the movie's story veered close to the truth, but also featured a fanciful German effort to collect information on the Manhattan Project. Naturally, the G-men and their courageous operative inside the spy ring thwarted the plot in the nick of time, allowing the narrator to reassure audiences that "The atomic bomb—America's top war secret—remains a secret." These words were false, though the movie's producers could not know quite how inaccurate they were. Stalin's spies, not Hitler's, had already stolen key secrets from the Manhattan Project—enough to hasten the Soviet atomic program by years. This coup ranks among the greatest intelligence successes in history. How did it happen?

Put simply, spies gave Stalin strategic insights into the intentions and capabilities of his Western allies. The party's international bureau (or Comintern), the Chekists, and Soviet military intelligence (the GRU) had together managed sympathizers and spies well enough to glean information of strategic value to Moscow. The party espionage rings, even in countries where the party was not banned outright, functioned in parallel with (mostly) separate networks of agents and handlers, the former holding secret party memberships, and the latter having no visible connections to communism or any official Soviet activity. These "illegal" agent handlers proved to be the iron majors of the Soviet human intelligence system. In the 1930s, illegals like Arnold Deustch in Britain, Ishkak Akhmerov in the United States, and Richard Sorge in Japan had recruited or at least ran some of the most effective spies of the twentieth century. The groundwork that they and their colleagues laid made the spy system strong enough to survive Stalin's purges of his old Bolshevik colleagues (including several head Chekists). Their illegals functioned throughout the terror and the shock of the Molotov-Ribbentrop Pact in 1939. Indeed, the illegal networks did their work so well that the Western counterintelligence services did not fully understand their scope and significance until after World War II, by which time it was almost too late.

By 1944, Soviet espionage ranked supreme and unrivaled in its reach and success. In Washington alone that year, NKGB agents included an assistant secretary of the Treasury (Harry Dexter White), senior aides in the White House and State Department (Lauchlin Currie and Alger Hiss, respectively), and multiple penetrations of the Office of Strategic Services (Duncan Lee and Maurice Halperin, among others).[1] In Britain, the "Magnificent Five"—alumni of the University of Cambridge recruited during the previous decade—by 1944 had penetrated the Foreign Office (Donald Maclean and Guy Burgess), SIS (Harold "Kim" Philby and John Cairncross), and MI5 (Anthony Blunt); one of them (Cairncross) had recently served at Bletchley Park.[2] Their combined efforts ensured that Moscow not only understood the gist and the importance of Ultra, but also grasped the danger that Western codebreakers posed to Soviet communications. Stalin was notorious for distrusting unwelcome news, but these and other Soviet assets surely helped convince Moscow that the American economy was just as big as the Lend Lease program implied, that the Western alliance was ironclad and committed to the destruction of the Axis, and that the British had a wide intelligence lead over Hitler and had shared it with the Americans. This set of certainties in Stalin's mind probably helps explain some of his behavior toward the end of World War II (such as his willingness to incur massive casualties in the war's final weeks to ensure the Red Army controlled as much of Europe and East Asia as possible when the Nazis and the Japanese capitulated).

Espionage gave Stalin the atomic bomb, the greatest military innovation in history. The Soviet Union would have caught up eventually in this field, but thanks to spies around the Manhattan Project like Klaus Fuchs, the Rosenberg ring, and others, just four years after Hiroshima the Soviets detonated their own atomic device and proved they could rival the West militarily. The Germans, moreover, had shown how even a mediocre intelligence service like the *Abwehr* could collect industrial secrets in the United States; the GRU and the KGB had a longer period in which to work, and better methods; thus they stole far more than the Germans and used their booty for Soviet scientists and technicians to build upon. They also glimpsed how much the Americans were *not* giving them through Lend Lease. Ford trucks and Bell Aircraft fighter planes—and huge quantities of food and materiel—bolstered the Red Army's war-making potential against the Wehrmacht, but Washington had held its best weapons for its own use and shared them only with its Commonwealth allies. Soviet spying in the United States helped Soviet labs and factories close the technological gap with the Germans and the West.

The Soviet Union's intelligence services thus had a long lead over their Western rivals, which faced two substantial obstacles when they turned their attentions from the defeated Axis toward the increasingly problematic USSR. The time of Soviet espionage domination ended by late 1945, when the USSR became the prime target of the Western counterintelligence services, which could now close the wartime Soviet liaison offices and deploy their full strength against Moscow's diplomats and local party organizations. Even then, however, the earlier Soviet penetrations of the British and American services ensured that Western efforts to gather intelligence on the USSR, as they resumed or started on new efforts toward the close of World War II, would initially prove futile. The new, Soviet "target" proved impenetrable by means that had worked against the Germans and Japanese, as the Communist system of internal repression gave Moscow detailed knowledge of contacts between foreigners and citizens at home. Soviet moles, moreover, soon neutered the rapidly growing Anglo-American SIGINT effort against the Soviets; one in England (Kim Philby) and one in America (William Weisband) saw to it that this promising campaign hit insurmountable obstacles by 1948.[3] Finally, Kim Philby, the KGB's most famous mole in SIS, quietly hampered the West's exploitation of two knowledgeable defectors in September 1945, one each from the GRU and NKGB, thus holding the veil of ignorance of Soviet intelligence procedures and personnel over Western eyes a little longer.[4]

The only threat that Soviet security could not suppress was the past. Commonwealth and American files in the late 1940s bulged with leads on Communist Party leaders and members. In addition, the literal and figurative promiscuity of party intelligence gathering since the 1930s had made the spy nets too big for their own safety. Too many people knew too much, and a handful of defectors since Stalin's purges had given the Anglo-American services plenty of leads, at least to fellow Soviet operatives. Philby later claimed he lived in fear of a "nasty little sentence" in MI5's files that hinted at his own recruitment by Arnold Deutsch years earlier.[5] Japanese counterintelligence had pieced together Richard Sorge's ring from the interrogation of one his agents in late 1941, and courier Elizabeth Bentley exposed at least a dozen Chekists and agents to the FBI in 1945.[6] On top of these revelations, the US Army in 1946 scored a triumph: the decoding of NKVD and NKGB messages into and out of the United States during the war. As the messages were painstakingly read by British and American investigators and the breach expanded over the next few years, the FBI and MI5 amassed encyclopedic knowledge of Soviet operations, networks, organizations, and doctrine—including the "illegals" who had been working under their very noses. This sensitive set of leads—known to history as "Venona" for its dissemination compartment—acted as a sort of Rosetta Stone for Western counterintelligence for decades to come.[7]

By 1949, the clandestine struggle was well and truly met. The wonder here is that Soviet espionage had accomplished so much in the face of local control and counterintelligence that ranged from poor (in the prewar United States) to mediocre (Japan) to good (in Britain). The MGB (its new name) and the GRU had had espionage success all over the world, enough to counter the proficiency of the Anglo-American SIGINT alliance. But strength had blunted strength, and both sides would now have to change.

Reform and Stalemate

The Cold War can be dated from various points, with perhaps the best being March 1946, which marked the Soviet retreat from Iran in the face of Anglo-American opposition, and Winston Churchill's comment that Stalin had sundered Europe by imposing an "iron curtain" from Stettin on the Baltic to Trieste on the Adriatic. As rhetoric, this quip was masterful; as analysis, it was prophetic. Tensions between the allies who together had defeated Hitler were hardening into mutual antagonism. Within two more years, that antagonism had flared into active rivalry, as explained by Britain's Joint Intelligence Committee: "The fundamental aim of the Soviet leaders is to hasten the elimination of capitalism from all parts of the world and replace it with their own form of Communism." Nevertheless, noted the JIC, Moscow would move cautiously and incrementally: "Given the present balance of strength, the Soviet Union will wish her conflict with the United States and the capitalist world generally to be played out in the conditions most favourable to herself, that is to say, on a basis of Communist penetration, aided by economic distress, rather than on a basis of overt aggression; or, in other words, by "cold war" methods rather than by real war."[8] The intelligence services of both sides, of course, had long felt themselves on the front lines of such a conflict. When it came, however, the Cold War caught the British, American, and Soviet intelligence enterprises in the midst of reforming their organizations and missions. Ironically, all three powers felt, for their own reasons, that the intelligence tools they had used to win World War II required significant changes if they were to succeed against new challenges.

The Soviet system after the war still cannot be studied in detail, although it undeniably remained large, capable, and utterly under the thumb of party politics—particularly the ambition of its patron, Lavrenti Beria. One of history's great monsters, Beria had emerged from the purges of the NKVD in the 1930s and survived fifteen years at Stalin's side, which alone speaks volumes about the man. He did not head an agency between the end of the war and the last year of his life, but nonetheless exercised his influence over all of Soviet intelligence from his posts as deputy prime minister and curator of the organs of state security. Beria's shadow empire comprised the Ministry of Internal Affairs (the MVD) and the Ministry of State Security (MGB), the latter of which carried on the Chekist tradition. Not unlike the SS in Nazi Germany, the MGB's directorates oversaw foreign espionage, internal secret police and penetration work in civil, economic, and military institutions, covert action against counterrevolutionaries, and the protection of Soviet leaders. For a time it also handled signals intelligence (a portfolio later given up to the party's Central Committee), and served with the GRU under a short-lived umbrella organization for foreign intelligence called the Committee for Information (KI). Beria's apparatus also spent much of its energy investigating the Leningrad Affair and mounting minor purges as Stalin grew ever more paranoid and anti-Semitic. Beria's ambition ultimately proved his undoing. On virtually the day that Stalin died in March 1953, Beria orchestrated the takeover of the MGB by the Internal Affairs ministry, thus concentrating state power to a degree that had not been seen since the Great Purge and the darkest days of the German invasion. Beria's frightened colleagues felt their backs against the wall (figuratively), and quickly orchestrated his arrest and murder. The MGB was soon pulled back away from the MVD and demoted from a ministry to a committee. In 1954 it took on the name and acronym that would be the most famous moniker of all the Soviet intelligence organs: the Committee for State Security, or KGB.

The British did less postwar intelligence reorganizing, but faced perhaps the greatest adjustment of missions and attitudes. The war had left Britain bled white, and the granting of independence to India, in 1947, overnight dropped the United Kingdom from world empire to regional power. For a year or two its intelligence agencies devoted much of their attention to policing the colonies and mandates—such as doomed efforts to keep the peace between Arabs and Jews in Palestine—but by 1948 Britain's wartime ally, the Soviet Union, was Britain's main intelligence target.[9] The shift in priorities found British intelligence agencies well equipped in many ways but deficient in others. By and large, the maintenance done to the intelligence agencies after the war was constructive; at least it avoided schemes like the proposal by Field Marshal Bernard Montgomery, now chief of the Imperial General Staff, to transfer SIS from Foreign Office control to the Ministry of Defence.[10] Thus, in a sense, London heeded the advice of the Foreign Office's chief intelligence liaison, Harold Caccia, who warned "you get the Secret Service that you deserve."[11]

Britain's internal service, MI5, had emerged from World War II with well-deserved but hardly well-known honors. The incoming Labour government of Prime Minister Clement Attlee initially viewed the Security Service with suspicion that had lingered since MI5's work against the Left in the interwar years (legend had it that MI5 had fabricated a Soviet connection that cost the first Labour government its reelection bid in 1924). Attlee himself (though few of his ministers) knew that MI5 had crushed German espionage during the war, but within a year of taking office in 1945 he replaced its director general with a new one, the police constable Sir Percy Sillitoe. Regarded by his own deputies as a plodding cop (one noted that his appointment "puts the stamp of the Gestapo on the office"), Sillitoe nonetheless enjoyed Attlee's trust. Indeed, the fact that an opposition party could take power and choose a new head for the service had the salutary effect of demonstrating once again that intelligence agencies in democracies have to answer to the nation and not just to the party in power—and that the agencies had best remain both nonpartisan and clearly within the bounds of law. In a similar vein, various official observers quietly noted that MI5 needed a firmer legal foundation: its command relationship to the prime minister and his cabinet was muddled, and some of its practices, like the use of hidden microphones and telephone taps, had no statutory mandate. After another change of government in 1951—with Churchill's Conservatives coming back to power—the prime minister relinquished control of MI5 to the Home Office, but kept Sillitoe on for another two years.[12]

Britain's overseas intelligence service, SIS, underwent a different kind of transition. Whereas MI5's mission of suppressing subversion remained largely the same when the targets switched from Nazis to Communists, SIS's shifting foreign targets and methods forced significant adjustments. The Secret Intelligence Service remained under firm Foreign Office control, and (like MI5) remained publicly unacknowledged. It also absorbed significant components of Britain's demobilizing covert action arm—the Special Operations Executive (SOE)—particularly SOE's proficient training section and its technical services unit, which built "tricks and contraptions" for officers and agents in the field.[13] The service retained its chief, Stewart Menzies, until 1952, and he oversaw a professionalization and reorientation of SIS. Under him, SIS reaffirmed its identity as a truly clandestine service operating primarily against strategic targets; Menzies and his deputies worried by 1945 that the service had grown subservient to military requirements in the field and was entirely too well known to foreign liaison services.[14] He also found a *modus vivendi* with MI5 against the Soviet and Communist targets. The two organizations had worked well enough overseas but often clashed in London; Menzies and Sillitoe met in December 1948 and drew on the Christmas spirit to work out a more amicable relationship, greater sharing of information on hostile intelligence services, and joint operations in the Commonwealth (SIS continued its monopoly on work in foreign countries).[15]

Like SIS, the Government Code & Cypher School transitioned from war to peace with the burden of living up to high expectations.[16] SIS and thus the Foreign Office continued to run GC&CS until the mid-1950s, though that control was largely nominal and benign, as the codebreakers during the war had demonstrated their value and their ability to thrive without close supervision.[17] The greatest worry seemed to be that the miraculous codebreaking successes against the Axis might never be replicated: a study of SIS's prospects completed in the last year of World War II noted that technology was progressing to a point where it would be unwise for Britain to "count indefinitely on obtaining the bulk of our most valuable and secret information through the GC&CS."[18] The organization underwent a sharp demobilization of 80 percent of its staff (down to 2000) shortly after war's end, with a consequent consolidation and a move from Bletchley Park to Cheltenham; and in 1946 it also received a cosmetic name change to the Government Communications Headquarters (GCHQ).[19] Sir Edward Travis, who had taken over in 1942 from Alistair Denniston (who himself had served as the founding chief since 1919), remained in place as its chief until 1952. His successor, Sir Eric Jones, stayed until 1960, thus providing important stability. The key to GCHQ, however, was that it had long provided its government and military with both signals intelligence and communications security—it made codes and broke codes. The synergy between these activities under one roof (except for one interlude) made both better, and provided a model that the Americans would imitate as they built their own signals intelligence system.

Across the Atlantic, the United States worried about intelligence even in the flush of victory. Parts of its system had done well in the war, particularly the cryptologic and counterintelligence arms, which fought the conflict more or less as equal partners with their British counterparts. Others were merely adequate, like foreign intelligence and special operations, which had required prolonged British tutelage. Indeed, that debt to a foreign power concerned more than one American official. Lieutenant General Hoyt Vandenberg told Congress in 1947 that America should never

again find itself again confronted with the necessity of developing its plans and policies on the basis of intelligence collected, compiled, and interpreted by some foreign government. It is common knowledge that we found ourselves in just that position at the beginning of World War II. . . . For months we had to rely blindly and trustingly on the superior intelligence system of the British. Our successes prove that this trust was generally well placed. However . . . the United States should never again have

to go hat in hand, begging any foreign government for the eyes—the foreign intelligence—with which to see. We should be self-sufficient.[20]

By the time Vandenberg offered that advice, ironically enough, much of the
wartime intelligence enterprise had been demobilized. Truman summarily
dismissed OSS, ordering its liquidation a week before Japan surrendered.
Three pieces of the office floated free of the wreck: the counterintelligence
and foreign intelligence branches were warehoused in the War Department,
while the Research and Analysis Branch went to the State Department
(where it soon died of neglect). Other capabilities simply vanished in the
general rout. The sophisticated imagery analysis function that had supported the Combined Bombing Offensive in Europe wasted away, as did
the Joint Intelligence Center for Admiral Nimitz's Central Pacific Theater.[21]
A panel appointed by Congress to study the organization of the government warned in 1949 that the military intelligence arms had lost most of
the "skilled and experienced personnel of wartime," and that those who
remained had seen "their organizations and their systems ruined by superior officers with no experience, little capacity, and no imagination."[22]

The FBI emerged from the war with its luster burnished and its director, J. Edgar Hoover, at perhaps the height of his fame. The bureau had already begun shifting to the new Soviet target, and just after the war picked
up a key defector, a Connecticut-born courier for the Soviets named Elizabeth Bentley. Special agents also shared with their British and Canadian colleagues in the bounty delivered by Igor Gouzenko, a GRU code clerk in Ot-
tawa who defected to the Royal Canadian Mounted Police in 1945. Hoover's
public reputation did not, however, charm the new president, Harry Truman. The White House under Truman appreciated Hoover's value (and his
political invulnerability), but Truman did not share the late Franklin Roosevelt's zest for FBI reports. The new administration also divested the FBI of
its Latin American operations, ordering them to be transferred to a new organization called the Central Intelligence Group. To his discredit, Hoover
complied grudgingly, handing over the Special Intelligence Service's physical assets in Latin capitals but not its personnel, files, or contacts.[23]

Signals intelligence had served the Republic well in World War II.
But again, those in the know recognized that its success owed much to
the Anglo-American alliance, and that interservice rivalry diminished
the potential of both the army and the navy SIGINT arms. Some sort of

cooperation, or even a centralized organizational structure, seemed to be imperative, especially after the 1947 creation of an independent service (with its own SIGINT arm) in the air force. The first fruit of this trial and error was a new organization, the Armed Forces Security Agency (AFSA), in 1949. AFSA sought, under the Joint Chiefs of Staff, to harmonize the efforts of its three service components, and also took on the mission of securing American communications.[24] The arrangement did not work. By 1951, complaints from AFSA's customers (many of them indoctrinated into Ultra during World War II, and thus inclined to be dissatisfied with SIGINT's lesser accomplishments in the Korean conflict) had persuaded the secretary of defense and the president to intervene. The result was the creation of the National Security Agency (NSA) the following year. NSA was a hybrid, a civilian organization under a uniformed commander who answered to the secretary of defense. The secretary also served as executive agent for all US communications intelligence and security, and took his guidance from a special committee of the National Security Council comprising himself, the secretary of state, and also the new director of Central Intelligence in an advisory capacity.[25] The United States had thus created something new in its history—an intelligence agency designed specifically to make the signals intelligence system serve senior policymakers from multiple departments as well as combat commanders in the field.

That new director of Central Intelligence stood as perhaps the most significant accomplishment of the overall reform movement. Not long after taking office in 1945, President Truman realized he could not manage the military and intelligence enterprise using the studied chaos that Roosevelt had perfected. He desired a more rational decision process and a clearer flow of information to support it, particularly with regard to the cascade of operational cables and intelligence reports. His aides hit upon a "Director of Central Intelligence" (DCI) to make sense of it all for the president, and Truman endorsed the idea, directing moreover that the new DCI should not only review all information available to the government but also deconflict intelligence operations overseas. Truman secured acquiescence from the FBI and concerned members of Congress by assuring them that the new intelligence group would have no law enforcement powers and would only work abroad (thus preserving Hoover's monopoly on domestic intelligence and forestalling the creation of an American "Gestapo").[26] He enlisted the army and navy by guaranteeing they could continue to gather and analyze intelligence for their own needs.[27] Thus was born the Central Intelligence Group in January 1946; it was renamed the Central Intelligence Agency (CIA) and given a statutory foundation by Congress in the National Security Act of 1947.

The new CIA thus had a dual mission from the outset. It compiled intelligence reports for the president, sending a daily summary to the Oval Office from February 1946 on and soon writing longer analyses as well. In 1950, the fourth DCI, Lieutenant General Walter B. Smith, took inspiration from Britain's Joint Intelligence Committee for his new National Intelligence Estimates, which were technically collective products presenting the considered views of all the intelligence agencies (though they were often drafted in CIA). The agency's analytic functions would evolve into a worldwide warning and situational awareness capacity for two generations of national leaders who, like President Truman, held vivid memories of the surprise at Pearl Harbor.

CIA inherited its operational capability from OSS. Cadre from the OSS components warehoused in the War Department in 1945 quietly transferred into a new clandestine service the following year. CIA's resulting Office of Special Operations was smaller than the OSS, but it was led by officers who, like Menzies in SIS, viewed their capability as a national asset rather than a support agency for commanders in the field.[28] As the Cold War intensified in 1948, the office was joined by a covert action arm, the Office of Policy Coordination (OPC; the two offices merged in 1952 to become the CIA's Directorate of Plans).

This division of labor in the American intelligence system would endure for the Cold War and beyond. This meant that certain weaknesses in the intelligence system would take decades to resolve. Some were circumstantial, others structural. The National Security Act had made the DCI responsible for coordinating foreign operations and analysis, but it gave him few direct powers to do so, and it left the FBI and the armed services to fulfill their respective missions with little coordination with the DCI or each other. Even the weak but growing CIA, however, was still providing positive benefits for American commanders and decision makers. These arrived not only in terms of its analysis and clandestine reporting, but also in its role of sorting the functions of the intelligence agencies and supporting "services of common concern"—like reliable National Intelligence Estimates—that no one else had the inclination or the resources to provide.

Under the leadership of a forceful DCI—which CIA had finally received in the person of Walter B. Smith in late 1950—the agency grew in stature as the de facto leader of what was not coincidentally beginning to be called the "Intelligence Community."[29] Still, compliance with DCI policies and requests was mostly voluntary. At times, other agencies simply ignored the DCI's right and duty to coordinate overseas intelligence activities. The US Army in the mid-1950s, for instance, ran its own penetrations of the emerging West German intelligence establishment and offered unsolicited advice concerning them to Chancellor Konrad Adenauer without bothering to inform DCI Allen Dulles or the CIA.[30]

American intelligence efforts also had British help. This mutual aid manifested itself most significantly in the March 1946 "UKUSA" agreement to share signals intelligence—the foundation of the Cold War intelligence alliance. The collaboration it authorized was very broad, as one of the key bilateral memoranda noted:

> The parties agree to the exchange of the products of the following operations relating to foreign communications:
>
> - collection of traffic
> - acquisition of communication documents and equipment
> - traffic analysis
> - cryptanalysis
> - decryption and translation
> - acquisition of information regarding communications organizations, practices, procedures and equipment.

In short, the British and American codebreakers would share almost everything, from the raw take to their finished analytical products, and the equipment, services, and secrets that fed into their production. UKUSA, of course, left room for certain exceptions, but its spirit was captured in an oft-used phrase in its passages: "It is the intention of each party to hold such exceptions to the absolute minimum." UKUSA also excluded sharing with "third parties" except by mutual Anglo-American agreement, and it defined third parties to mean "all individuals or authorities other than those of the United States, the British Empire, and the British Dominions."[31] President Truman's senior military adviser, Fleet Admiral William D. Leahy, visited London in May 1946 to express the president's satisfaction with the intelligence alliance; he thanked MI-5's Percy Sillitoe "and all British Intelligence Services" for their wartime cooperation, and vowed to demand in Washington "that the United States do everything possible to have this cooperation continued."[32]

Some friction between friendly national intelligence systems was to be expected, partly because the long British lead in the field was giving way to a more equal partnership. British officials heard Vandenberg's desire for self-sufficiency expressed in various ways by their American counterparts; the SIS liaison officer in Washington reported in 1948 that a CIA colleague had insisted his own new agency "must stand on its own two feet or get out of the business."[33] Outside of signals intelligence, the sharing of secrets was not always smooth, at least for J. Edgar Hoover, who fumed and threatened until his men were allowed to question convicted atom spy Klaus Fuchs in Wormwood Scrubs prison in 1950.[34] For their part, the British did not always act within the spirit and the letter of allied collegiality, either. An SIS officer posing as a Canadian academic ran a rather unproductive station in Tokyo under the noses of the American occupation authorities, in defiance of General Douglas MacArthur's ban on all foreign intelligence presence in Japan. He noted that while the Americans had much to learn in Europe, they could not "safely be regarded as clumsy amateurs in any part of the Far East where they operated in the past or are operating today."[35] Despite irritants, however, both sides valued and nurtured the alliance.

Cooperation between the British and American systems meant that Soviet espionage against one of them often gave Moscow secrets from the other as well. Soviet penetrations negated some combined attempts to run covert action campaigns (modeled after those launched into Nazi-occupied Europe) against the Soviet "satellite states" in the late 1940s and early 1950s. Kim Philby sardonically noted that he had been close to the Anglo-American planning to parachute guerrilla teams into Ukraine in 1951: "In order to avoid the dangers of overlapping and duplication, the British and Americans exchanged precise information about the timing and geographical co-ordinates of their operations. I do not know what happened to the parties concerned. But I can make an informed guess."[36] Parachuting assets behind the Iron Curtain, said one frustrated case officer to a rising CIA manager, Richard Helms, accomplished little beyond proving that "the law of gravity was as strong in the Ukraine as it was in our parachute training areas."[37] Another Soviet mole, SIS officer George Blake, gave up the joint

Anglo-American operation to tunnel under the sector boundary in Berlin that was designed to tap underground telephone and teletype lines in the Soviet sector. Only upon Blake's arrest in 1961 did SIS and CIA realize that (in his words) "the full details of the tunnel operation had been known to the Soviet authorities before even the first spade had been put in the ground."[38]

Interallied cooperation also meant that countermeasures and tighter security, when instituted at last, heightened the security of both the British and the American systems. The allies cooperated extensively (if not seamlessly) in rooting out Soviet wartime spies; indeed, US Army Security Agency leaders briefed GCHQ on their Venona cryptanalysis coup well before telling their own countrymen in the FBI.[39] The British in turn used insights from Venona to insist that their Australian intelligence partners tighten security and follow MI5 guidance in the counterintelligence field. The creation of the Australian Security Intelligence Organization (ASIO) in 1949 sprang directly from this intervention.[40]

Korea

The net result of the intelligence struggle by 1950 was stalemate, with both sides in the deepening Cold War possessing atomic weapons but neither having a clear notion of the other's capabilities and intentions. The decision-making processes of Stalin in Moscow and Mao in Beijing remain almost as mysterious to historians today as they were to the West at the time. North Korean leader Kim Il-sung's full-scale invasion of the South on June 25, 1950, was naked aggression, however; that much was obvious, along with the fact that Kim could not have mounted such an assault without massive aid and the assent of Stalin and Mao. President Truman swiftly decided to meet force with force, and the United Nations agreed. Within days, the first American troops and aircraft were in combat against the North Koreans, followed soon by sizable contingents from Britain, Canada, Australia, France, Turkey, and the Philippines. The subsequent conflict killed and wounded almost two million combatants on both sides and probably even more civilians, making it one of the largest wars in history. For the United States, the invasion came as the second of three ugly intelligence shocks in a fourteen-month span (with the first being the Soviet A-bomb). Washington had indeed, inadvertently or not, left South Korea exposed outside the list of nations that America was prepared to defend. Still, seeing a Communist-armed and supported regime violate a neighbor so brutally, and so soon after the examples of Nazi Germany and Imperial Japan, served to prove every alarmist warning about the Red Menace. Once General MacArthur had routed the North Koreans and charged almost to the Chinese border that autumn, however, Mao's wholesale commitment of armies to halt the Americans in northern Korea almost threw the United Nations force into the sea. Indeed, the rout ranks among the worst battlefield defeats ever endured by American arms. The defeat was made all the more galling by the fact that both British and American intelligence missed the clues that Mao had decided to intervene.[41] These failures of strategic warning weighed heavily on subsequent reforms of US intelligence.

The Communists had intelligence problems as well. If US intelligence failed to provide warning, then the North Korean and Soviet and Chinese intelligence services were comparably deficient in failing to tell their respective masters what might happen once the proverbial die was cast. Stalin and Mao surely would not have abetted North Korean aggression if they had guessed it might draw in powerful US air, sea, and land forces, under a UN mandate and an implicit nuclear umbrella, to their very borders. This result was nearly fatal to Kim's regime, and it was at least costly and alarming to Moscow and Beijing.

Like World War I, Korea saw a tactically fluid phase in which battlefield signals intelligence aided commanders, at least on the UN side. AFSA and its army and air force components rapidly set to solving North Korean military communications systems, which fell to the attack with relative ease. Barely a month after the war began, the American general commanding the beleaguered Pusan redoubt, the last foothold on the Korean coast, could exploit the intercepted messages of his opponents to shift his troops to the perimeter's most endangered sectors. Pusan held, and when MacArthur landed a force in the enemy rear at Inchon that September, the North Korean army crumpled. The American cryptologic advantage over the North Koreans lasted until the following spring, when with Soviet or Chinese tutelage the Koreans upgraded their communications security.[42]

By then the main opponent of United Nations forces was not the North Korean Army but the Chinese. As the war settled into a phase reminiscent of the trench warfare of World War I, the Americans began relearning skills developed in earlier conflicts. The US Army reached back thirty-five years for tactical intelligence, rediscovering the trick of driving spikes into the earth near enemy outposts to eavesdrop on telephone lines.[43] The US Air

Force had to reconstruct, almost from scratch, the sort of intelligence support for strategic air operations it had enjoyed in 1945. When Lieutenant
General Matthew Ridgway took over the Eighth Army in late December
1950, he found that his command had scant knowledge of the sizes and
locations of the Chinese formations facing it. To add insult to injury, an
urgent reconnaissance campaign to locate those forces found few clues,
largely because the harried photo interpreters were relying in most cases on
imagery alone to spot camouflaged Chinese positions, without the aid of
other sources. Commanders who recalled the intelligence marvels of World
War II wondered what had gone wrong; Lieutenant General Otto Weyland
of the Far East Air Force complained "it appears that these lessons either
were forgotten or never were documented." Not until 1952 did theater command finally have at its call an all-source imagery intelligence, targeting,
and battle damage assessment capability.[44]

The Korean War resulted in a draw on the battlefield and in intelligence as well. Soviet and Chinese intelligence performance can only be
guessed at even now, but it seems safe to say that the tactical picture the
Communists had of the United Nations ground forces was about as good
as that which the UN had of the Communists (with the important exception of aerial reconnaissance, which American air superiority denied to the
enemy). Chinese and North Korean security and counterintelligence were
frightening in their efficiency, and seem to have had little trouble stifling
allied attempts to mount intelligence gathering and covert action north of
the 38th Parallel. British and American commandos had successes attacking Communist outposts and logistics along the coastline, but ambitious
operations to parachute Korean guerrillas behind enemy lines failed dis-
mally, at appalling loss of life among the agents.[45]

Only the air war over Korea saw true intelligence innovation. The Air
Force Security Service (AFSS) learned to provide near–real time cues from
signals intelligence to pilots on patrol. North Korean interceptors relied
on radioed directions from controllers on the ground to contest American
bombing raids; their Chinese and Soviet mentors, thrown into combat by
Beijing and Moscow, were equally dependent on "ground-controlled intercept." AFSS overheard these communications, disguised their information as radar plots, and sped it to American fighters in time to ambush
the ambushers. The program, codenamed Yoke, accounted for much of
the lopsided kill ratios that the air force's jet fighters racked up against

comparable Soviet-made machines.[46] A revived version of Yoke later helped the American air campaign over Vietnam.

Moscow raised the possibility of a negotiated end to the Korean conflict in June 1951, after battlefield reverses for the Chinese made it clear the UN could not be thrown off the peninsula. The talks dragged on while the killing continued, until Stalin's death in March 1953 made it possible for an armistice (not a peace treaty) to be concluded four months later. The war had kept South Korea from communism but the diversion of resources had the effect of cementing communism's rule in Eastern Europe, lending momentum to the North Atlantic Treaty Organization (NATO) and a permanent American troop presence on the continent, and prompting tacit American commitments to halting Communist encroachments against Formosa and southern Indochina. The crushing of the Berlin revolt in June 1953 showed that even a post-Stalin leadership in Moscow was willing to use tanks to suppress popular sentiments; seen in this context, the bloody end of the Hungarian Revolution in 1956 and the construction of the Berlin Wall in 1961 seemed foreordained. Communism would not expand by direct force of arms, but once subjugated, no peoples would be allowed to leave its orbit. The Cold War had entered its frozen phase.

The Korean War created three realities for the West that influenced the Anglo-American intelligence alliance for the remainder of the Cold War. First came the perplexities of defining a conflict, or "police action," in which UN and Chinese soldiers (and American and Soviet pilots) shot at each other while none of their governments had declared war. Second, sharp debates inevitably arose within Western electorates and between the Western coalition over what this conflict portended. Was it the prelude to a nuclear Armageddon or just a bloodier continuation of traditional power struggles in an atomic age? Such debates grew the more bitter for fear of the bomb and insinuations that policy missteps were hastening either Communist victory or world annihilation. Third, a general worry about surprise attack never entirely faded after Kim Il-sung's blitzkrieg into South Korea. The next surprise could be a nuclear one, with far more destructive results.

The Arms Race and the Collection Revolution

Director of Central Intelligence Walter B. Smith issued a stark assessment to the National Security Council in April 1952. He told his chief customers, in essence, that he could not do his main job:

[I]n view of the efficiency of the Soviet security organization, it is not believed that the present United States intelligence system, or any instrumentality which the United States is presently capable of providing, including the available intelligence assets of other friendly states, can produce strategic intelligence on the Soviet [sic] with the degree of accuracy and timeliness which the National Security Council would like to have and which I would like to provide. Moreover, despite the utmost vigilance, despite watch committees, and all of the other mechanics for the prompt evaluation and transmission of intelligence, there is no real assurance that, in the event of sudden undeclared hostilities, certain advance warning can be provided.[47]

Smith had hardly forwarded his memo when a summer storm in Texas highlighted for policymakers the precariousness of the nation's strategic defenses. Carswell Air Force Base housed the Strategic Air Command's (SAC) 7th and 11th Bombardment Wings—the core of America's capability to strike the Soviet Union with atomic weapons. On September 1, 1952, a tornado devastated both units, tossing their huge B-36 bombers like toys and damaging at least seventy of them. Only a miracle kept thousands of gallons of spilled aviation fuel from igniting and incinerating the crippled aircraft. Carswell was closed for days, and its bomber wings, which then comprised two-thirds of the air force's heavy bomber force, were grounded even longer. RAND Corporation researchers tasked by the air force soon pondered what could happen next time if the Soviets— instead of a tornado—launched a surprise attack on SAC bases. RAND's April 1953 report, assuming force deployments and defenses programmed for 1956, calculated that the Soviets could destroy most of SAC's bombers on the ground.[48]

Within months of the RAND report, the Soviets detonated their first thermonuclear device, thus making it inevitable that Moscow would soon join the Americans in deploying hydrogen bombs. President Dwight Eisenhower reflected on the future course of the Cold War with his Secretary of State, John Foster Dulles, in September 1953, arguing that it was the duty of the administration, and the West, to "point out that any group of people, such as the men in the Kremlin, who are aware of the great destructiveness of these weapons—and who still decline to make any honest effort toward international control by collective action—must be fairly assumed to be contemplating their aggressive use." It would then follow that

American strategy could not count on time to mobilize, should war come by surprise:

> Rather, we would have to be constantly ready, on an instantaneous basis, to inflict greater loss upon the enemy than he could reasonably hope to inflict upon us. This would be a deterrent—but if the contest to maintain this relative position should have to continue indefinitely, the cost would either drive us to war—or into some form of dictatorial government. In such circumstances, we would be forced to consider whether or not our duty to future generations did not require us *to initiate war at the most propitious moment that we could designate* [emphasis added].[49]

President Eisenhower did not desire a preventive nuclear war, and he said in public that war with modern weapons would destroy civilization. Some of Stalin's successors in the Kremlin publicly agreed, though the official line held that a nuclear cataclysm would only destroy capitalism and that H-bombs were useful for deterring imperialist aggression.[50] The stark future that Eisenhower foresaw—at best, a long, costly vigilance that could impoverish the nation or turn it into an armed camp—would be the basis for national security planning for more than a decade to come. In this climate, two imperatives drove Washington's planning. First, America needed to improve all aspects of its defenses against atomic attack (including the resiliency of warning functions and of command and control). Second, Washington and its allies desperately required intelligence on the modernization of the Soviet strategic arsenal—particularly the deployment of jet bombers and long-range missiles that could deliver H-bombs to American targets. The former imperative would lead toward a revolution in military and ultimately civilian communications; the latter toward an intensification of the intelligence revolution and its extension to outer space.

The Soviets were impervious to espionage for the time being and their most sensitive communications were secure. A review of the US Intelligence Committee in 1955 (the Clark Task Force) was so concerned about the lack of "high level communications intelligence" on the Soviet Union that it urged that "monetary considerations should be waived and an effort at least equal to the Manhattan Project should be exerted at once" to improve NSA's capabilities.[51] Soviet leaders added impetus to this concern with statements like that of Premier Khrushchev in April 1956: "I am quite sure that we shall have very soon a guided missile with a hydrogen-bomb warhead which could hit any point in the world."[52]

The Soviets were not exempt, however, from outside observation. Modern weapon systems emanated copious electronic emissions, which could be intercepted for analysis if one could find the proper vantage point. Aerial photography, moreover, could be quite valuable, if some way could be found to elude the USSR's aggressive air defenses. Both forms of collection were hazardous for the pilots and crew ordered to fly along and sometimes over the borders of the USSR. Several dozen British and American crew members were killed in the early Cold War, despite cautions like that of the Joint Chiefs' May 1950 policy that surveillance flights were to stay at least twenty miles from Soviet territory and could approach "particularly sensitive or heavily defended areas" only at night or in bad weather.[53]

In search of alternatives, President Eisenhower approved development of the U-2 reconnaissance aircraft in late 1954, in the hope that it could fly too high for intercepting fighters and missiles. Essentially a jet-powered glider, the U-2 was built and deployed under CIA supervision to ensure plausible deniability; Eisenhower worried that its violations of Soviet airspace would be even more provocative if undertaken by the US Air Force. U-2s directly overflew the USSR only two dozen times from 1956 until the Soviets finally downed one on May Day, 1960, but the frail aircraft contributed greatly to the strategic intelligence picture on Moscow's capabilities. DCI Allen Dulles summarized the program's accomplishments for Eisenhower four weeks after the shootdown. Despite the international incident that ensued when the Soviets displayed not only the U-2's wreckage but its pilot (Francis Gary Powers), Dulles argued the overflight program had performed splendidly. Its cameras and sensors had clarified knowledge of Soviet atomic and strategic weapons programs, saving the United States millions of dollars it might have spent on even more bombers and missiles, and had also located targets for SAC and charted the USSR's air defenses.[54] Perhaps best of all, collection by the U-2 had granted Washington "the ability to discount or call the bluffs of the Soviets with confidence," and in several international crises had provided the certainty that American "courses of action could be carried through without serious risk of war and without Soviet interference."[55] The U-2 had fulfilled initial expectations and did still more as well. The air force bought its own stable of U-2s starting in 1958 and made them available to theater commanders for peripheral coverage of the Soviet Union. In addition, from the Suez Crisis in 1956 on, Washington depended on U-2s for tactical intelligence and situational awareness during periods of international tension.

The plane is still in service today, making it one of the best investments in aviation history.

Collection from space provided the long-term solution for strategic reconnaissance. Military uses for satellites had been discussed since the 1940s, but Moscow's launch of Sputnik, the first man-made object in orbit, goaded the United States into a frenzy of satellite development. By 1960, two of the American-launched systems had secret intelligence missions. The CIA's CORONA "birds" took pictures from space and dropped the film down through the atmosphere to be snagged in air by waiting aircraft and rushed for interpretation. The navy's short-lived GRAB satellites (short for Galactic Radiation And Background, their scientific cover mission) collected Soviet radar emissions and radioed them to ground stations. By 1964 the Americans had also tested a spaced-based surveillance radar they called QUILL.[56] These early systems soon gave way to more sophisticated and durable successors that could collect communications signals as well as radar emissions.[57]

Satellites cost astronomical sums even when development and deployment went smoothly—the exception rather than the norm. The first dozen CORONA missions failed, as did three of the five GRAB launches.[58] Those that worked, however, collected hitherto unimagined quantities of data to be turned into intelligence. Khrushchev's 1959 boast that one Soviet factory alone was building "250 rockets with hydrogen warheads" per year was exposed as bluff.[59] Within a decade, the physical and electronic infrastructures of the USSR had yielded up many of their secrets to American satellites. The hybrid management form for signals intelligence that had worked at NSA provided the model for managing these systems, which had to serve both national and military decision makers, as not even the United States could afford to build duplicate and customized constellations. Thus the community saw the creation in 1961 of the National Reconnaissance Office—a then-secret CIA–air force–navy combine—to manage satellite acquisitions and operations.

Exploiting the voluminous take from the satellites taxed the US Intelligence Community to its limits. Computers were the key, but computer development was progressing by leaps and bounds, and such rapid progress was both blessing and curse. Digital equipment permitted analysts to store and retrieve far more data, and to manipulate them in new ways. The constant churn of computer technology, however, meant resources diverted into promising but dead-end hardware and software projects, and continual recapitalization of computer inventories as state-of-the-art systems rapidly reached obsolescence. The National Security Agency helped lead the world in deploying and networking computers, though even that agency fell out of the pack of hardware manufacturers as the processors transitioned from vacuum tubes to transistors to silicon chips in the 1960s.[60]

The new wealth of satellite imagery, moreover, forced the CIA to expand its small strategic reconnaissance interpretation capability, created to study photographs from the relative handful of U-2 missions, into an industrial-scale activity. The National Photographic Interpretation Center (1961) was the result; it was a CIA–Department of Defense hybrid to analyze imagery from "national systems."[61] The CIA was already growing in unforeseen ways to compensate for the weaknesses of the Pentagon's intelligence, which had trouble interpreting the data collected on new targets. The agency in consequence built a massive effort to understand Moscow's capacity for war; one observer told Congress decades later that "our intelligence community's quest to describe the Soviet economy absorbed enormous resources and marshaled considerable analytical talent: indeed, it may well have been the largest single social science research project in the history of humanity!"[62] The DCI's Board of National Estimates, moreover, drew together Intelligence Community–wide appraisals on the USSR, and in so doing managed and encouraged a process that forced arguments among the agencies over Moscow's plans—and led in turn to better collection and sharper assessments.[63] Some of the CIA's conclusions about the Soviet economy were shared with the public in the form of congressional testimony and press releases from 1959 on.[64]

National-level intelligence in the Pentagon continued to be a virtual service monopoly until well into the 1960s. Secretary of Defense Robert McNamara tried to remedy this in 1961 by creating the Defense Intelligence Agency to serve his needs for analysis and insight into the department's sprawling intelligence fiefdoms. DIA, however, had little authority over the service agencies, and took over a decade to mature in its own internal staffing and organization. Still, DIA's advent and eventual prominence fit with the centralizing trend in American intelligence and marked another increment of intelligence clout for the secretary of defense.[65] At roughly the same time, the British military undertook a similar reform as well, linking its service intelligence organizations under a new Defence Intelligence Staff.[66]

Western navies also joined the air forces as active collectors of intelligence. This stemmed from the comparatively more discreet nature of naval operations and the ability of ships to sail close to hostile shores. It also owed to the US Navy's, and the Royal Navy's, willingness to make their ships double as intelligence platforms, serving collectors and analysts abroad and in national capitals.[67] Real gains in understanding Soviet intentions and capabilities were being made in the 1960s, setting the stage for a revolution in Naval "OPINTEL"—which would have implications for both naval operations and national strategy by the late 1970s.[68] The US Navy also found, as the air force had in the 1950s, that real success came at a real price; pushing collectors like the USS *Liberty* and the USS *Pueblo* so close to their targets could be dangerous. These small ships were inspired by the seemingly ubiquitous Soviet trawlers that tailed NATO exercises, but where Western forces refrained from shooting at intelligence collectors, other countries objected to such vessels hovering nearby. The *Liberty* was accidentally strafed by the Israeli Air Force off the Sinai coast during the 1967 Six-Day War; North Korean ships captured the *Pueblo* near Korean waters the following year.

The collection and analytical revolution also shifted the center of gravity of the trans-Atlantic intelligence alliance. America's Commonwealth partners could not afford surveillance satellites of their own; nor could they keep pace with the scope and speed of computer development, despite quiet American subsidies in fields like communications security. By the early 1960s, the situation caused concerns in both Washington and London. "The Americans are becoming less dependent on us because they are getting better themselves," the Deputy Director of GCHQ told a review commission led by the Treasury to squeeze economies out of the ministries in 1962. GCHQ needed its budget allocation and even more, the agency contended, and argued that its contribution to the SIGINT partnership allowed Britain to enjoy the profits of "the much more expansive and extravagant effort of the Americans." Treasury ultimately agreed, boosting GCHQ's budget while trimming those of other government departments.[69]

The net result of the technological and organizational innovations was a better intelligence effort on the part of both the United States and its partners—one more responsive and helpful to civilian and military leaders alike. The linkages of SIGINT, imagery, and analysis, all of them influential at the operational level in World War II, now in the Cold War became influential at the strategic level as well. This in turn yielded creditable understandings of Soviet deployments and weapons progress, from which could be inferred statements about Moscow's capabilities and intentions. Though on-site verification in the USSR would not be permitted by Moscow until almost the end of the Cold War, the United States created unilateral means to ascertain the state of Soviet forces. By 1967, the Intelligence Community was able to report to the White House that, absent a massive, hypothetical Soviet program to deceive US intelligence, "we believe that we would almost certainly detect any extensive new deployment in strategic forces, although the Soviets could probably effect small-scale increases without our knowledge."[70]

The Soviets indeed remained capable of tactical surprise. They invaded Czechoslovakia in 1968, to the surprise of many Western observers who had watched the Soviet buildup on the Czech border but had doubted that Moscow would jeopardize improving relations with the West by invading.[71] But by now US intelligence still provided good situational awareness even when caught off guard. The Cuban Missile Crisis serves as perhaps the most striking example. American analysts had discounted the possibility that Soviet leader Nikita Khrushchev would introduce nuclear-armed missiles into Fidel Castro's Cuba, but émigré reporting and a U-2 overflight found in October 1962 that missiles had been installed despite American skepticism. The ensuing standoff between Washington and Moscow marked the closest the world came to a nuclear exchange; indeed, the crisis's several false alarms and chance mishaps, if anything, look even more frightening in hindsight than they did at the time. Nevertheless, timely intelligence gave President John F. Kennedy both the confidence to confront the Soviets and opportunities to prod Khrushchev toward a peaceful resolution.

This progress had important political effects on both sides of the Atlantic. Almost from the Cold War's beginning, European leaders and publics had wondered about Washington's tolerance for nuclear risk. Ideally, that tolerance could be neither too high nor too low. Not a few among America's allies, even in Britain, worried that American leaders and commanders might act recklessly and provoke a confrontation with Moscow.[72] As the majority of Soviet nuclear weapons were aimed at targets in Western Europe, any exchange could devastate America's allies, even if it left the United States unscathed. On the other hand, some in Europe worried that a future president might flinch in a crisis, fearing to lose Chicago in order to save Hamburg, Lyons, or Liverpool. American officials thus had to strike a careful balance, showing commitment and resolve along with patience and restraint. One part of the answer to this dilemma was arms control with the Soviet Union, pursued from the Kennedy administration on until the end of the Cold War. American administrations publicly embraced the peaceful resolution of superpower disputes and mutual, verifiable restraint of nuclear deployments. The collection revolution made such verification possible, and thus opened the possibility to arms control, thereby strengthening the NATO alliance.

The Spy Game

The collection revolution gave the Anglo-American intelligence alliance unmatched capabilities. But those capabilities did not, strictly speaking, have to be matched. Many of the intentions and capabilities of NATO's members were quite public; data on Western deployments, programs, and policies that would be state secrets in Russia or China were shouted from the proverbial housetops in the *Congressional Record,* on the BBC, or in *Popular Mechanics* magazine ("Written so you can understand it"). What Moscow needed most to know was precisely what the British, Americans, French, or West Germans were able to see and collect from behind the Iron Curtain, and then to limit as much as possible the take from Western collection. The Soviets and the Warsaw Pact developed technical intelligence collection techniques and systems of their own.[73] The KGB's signals intelligence department, for instance, reported to the Communist Party's Central Committee for 1967 that it had intercepted and exploited communications in 152 code systems from seventy-two countries—in all, 188,400 cables.[74] Moscow's main tool to restrict the access of the Anglo-American collection juggernaut, however, remained old-fashioned espionage.

The KGB and GRU could not repeat their prewar success with ideological spies. Indeed, after 1945, both of these Soviet services avoided local Communists in recruiting, and preferred their operatives and assets to have no obvious political ties. Some assets the Soviets cajoled (or more or less coerced) into working for them, like Heinz Felfe, a former Nazi and SD officer who rose in the counterintelligence staff of the West German intelligence service from 1953 until his arrest in 1961.[75] By the early 1950s, the Soviets had found the answer to their espionage dilemma; they would focus on the weakest link of the Anglo-American collection enterprise—its young, lonely, or disgruntled enlisted men doing the drudge work of intelligence in spartan environments far from home. Security vetting was still an immature science, even when it employed the most modern methods, like the polygraph, and the constant flow of new personnel rotating in and out of sites in places like Cyprus and West Berlin meant that even careful monitoring could not catch or deter all misdeeds. The KGB and GRU ensnared some in espionage, like William Marshall (arrested in 1952) and Douglas Britten (1968) of GCHQ, Jack Dunlap of NSA (1963), Nelson Drummond of the US Navy (1962), and Robert Johnson, a US Army courier (1964).[76] Others defected, like William Martin and Bernon Mitchell, who vanished together from NSA in 1960, as Brian Patchett did from GCHQ three years later. Martin and Mitchell gave a spectacular and humiliating (for Washington) press conference in Moscow, at which Martin announced that NSA and GCHQ had a secret partnership and claimed NSA was reading the coded messages of more than forty nations, including those of "Italy, Turkey, France, Yugoslavia, the United Arab Republic, Indonesia, Uruguay—that's enough to give a general picture, I guess."[77]

Still others volunteered to the Russians. Americans Al Sarant and Joel Barr had worked with Julius Rosenberg's spy ring during the Second World War and defected in 1950; the pair thereafter helped build the USSR's electronics and computer industries.[78] John Walker of the US Navy, with his friend, his brother, and his son, gave the Soviets a trove of cryptographic blueprints and keys, together with documents such as fleet operational plans. Walker volunteered his services during a surreptitious visit to the Soviet embassy in Washington in January 1968.[79] The KGB hired him on the spot—one of the best recruitments the service ever made. By coincidence, the KGB also accepted the help of a volunteer from GCHQ, Geoffrey Prime, that same year.[80] Working separately, the pair did grave damage to US and British security for over a decade.

Another strength of the system the Soviets built was its reach across the Warsaw Pact services. Relations between them and the KGB were not exactly intelligence alliances, as the KGB had trained their leaders in the USSR during the war and controlled each partnership, but the information sharing and division of labor nonetheless multiplied Moscow's intelligence power, and helped the security of each local Communist regime.[81] The Soviets maintained such arrangements from the mid-1950s on.[82] In addition, the Warsaw Pact nations ran effective operations against the West. The Poles had success in recruiting Americans beginning in the 1950s.[83] In the 1960s, the Czechs placed a low-level agent (Karl Koecher) in the CIA, the Bulgarians burgled codebooks and documents from the Italian embassy in Sofia (and shared them with the KGB in 1965), and the Romanians placed an asset in a French office in NATO.[84] The Hungarians ensnared the US Army's Clyde Conrad in the mid-1970s.[85] Success by one Warsaw Pact country bred success in the others, especially in counterintelligence.

The best of the lot was East Germany's Ministry for State Security (MfS). Ironically, its beginning as a world-class intelligence service dated from a pair of setbacks in 1953. The West Germans, with CIA help, had smashed an East German spy network that spring, and in June, state security was caught napping by riots in East Berlin (ironically enough, given what followed, the security forces had deployed too few informers in the populace). The MfS, soon better known as the Stasi, took these lessons to heart as it was rebuilt under Soviet tutelage.[86] The Stasi ranks as one of the most efficient security forces in history, playing on every human weakness in its quest for internal enemies and eventually seeding its own country with tens of thousands of informers. Its foreign intelligence arm, the Main Directorate for Reconnaissance (*Hauptverwaltung-Aufklaerung*, or HVA), ran under the icy genius of Markus Wolf. By the late 1950s, the HVA was having success against US targets in West Germany.[87] Wolf ran a spy (Rainer Rupp) in NATO headquarters in Brussels in 1977, and another, Günther Guillaume, in West German Chancellor Willy Brandt's inner office; the subsequent scandal forced Brandt's resignation in 1974. The HVA was already a fearsome opponent, probably better than the KGB at espionage; indeed, between 1970 and 1989, West Germany would convict 510 persons of espionage for the East Germans.[88] Far more surely escaped justice.

Like the KGB, moreover, the local services searched aggressively for real and potential foes in their own societies. After all, the services were the party's shield as well as its sword. One Stasi historian, writing for his colleagues, noted that their service "from the beginning could not be restricted to defending [against] the attacks of the enemy. It was and is an organ that has to use all means in the offensive fight against the opponents of socialism."[89]

The West did not sit idle in the spy game. After some initial caution about running operations against the Soviet Union, SIS and CIA gained proficiency in places like Germany, where big military establishments on both sides of the intra-German border and relatively free movement between

the Allied sectors in Berlin (at least before 1961) provided ample opportunities to hone the trade of espionage.[90] By the mid-1950s, the Western
services started getting volunteers of their own who were willing to stay
behind the Iron Curtain. Three of these volunteers reported from inside
the GRU: Pyotr Popov, Oleg Penkovsky, and Dmitriy Polyakov, though the
work eventually cost them all their lives.[91] Another, Michal Goleniewski,
sent anonymous letters from Poland's counterintelligence service before
turning up at the American consulate in Berlin to request asylum in 1961.[92]
With rare exceptions, the West could succeed at running these individuals
in place only briefly, and then only by employing the best possible "tradecraft" in meeting and corresponding with them. They could not produce
much, given the extreme caution with which they had to work, and the per-
vasiveness of Soviet counterintelligence (the KGB's annual report for 1967
boasted of 167,000 agents in its internal security networks).[93] But some
of their reports were pure gold, like the clues to the KGB's mole in SIS,
George Blake (arrested 1961), and technical manuals for Soviet missiles
that assisted CIA analysts during the Cuban Missile Crisis. The CIA also
obtained Soviet military secrets in other countries, through operations like
HABRINK, in the late 1960s.[94]

But the West also grew paranoid under the onslaught of Soviet-bloc
spies. Once the Venona leads dried up in the early 1950s, Western services depended on surveillance and defectors for key insights into KGB
and GRU operations. These means depended to some extent on serendip-
ity, like the wave of defectors from the USSR after Stalin's death in 1953;
they collectively made "outstanding contributions to US intelligence and
psychological warfare programs," supplemented by "the intelligence benefits from defectors received by various other friendly Western countries."[95]
Of course, suspicions lingered in Washington and London that not all the
wartime moles had appeared in the Venona messages. Guy Burgess and
Donald Maclean, after all, had held positions of trust in the Foreign Office
until 1951; had they not panicked and fled to Russia, their classmate Kim
Philby might have remained a senior SIS officer. It did not defy logic or
precedent to imagine that another wartime mole might have prospered in
a British or American service into the 1960s, by which point he could be
at the height of his career. Such a dangerous penetration would be worth
a great deal of counterintelligence effort to find. That effort was indeed
expended, though with meager results. By 1964, MI5 had quietly identified

all of the "Magnificent Five" recruited out of Cambridge thirty years earlier (Philby, Maclean, Burgess, Blunt, and Cairncross), and arguably only one of them (Philby) had found any secrets for the KGB for over a decade. Nevertheless, the Security Service did not finally believe it had reached the bottom of the matter until still another KGB defector (Oleg Gordievsky) listed all of the Five in 1982.[96]

A well-placed mole, so the reasoning went, could be so important to the Soviets that they might try anything to keep the Americans or the British off his scent. This sort of logic was worthy of a John LeCarré novel. It could tie an intelligence agency in knots, as the CIA learned.[97] The major victim was one Yuri Nosenko, a KGB officer who volunteered to the agency in Geneva in 1962. He had the misfortune to contact the CIA just after another defector, Anatoly Golitsyn, promised his debriefers that the KGB would soon seek to discredit him—perhaps by sending a fresh defector to debunk Golitsyn's testimony. Nosenko thus found a wary reception when he threw himself on the CIA's mercies in early 1964 and was taken to the United States. He raised suspicions further by claiming, among other falsehoods, that he had read the KGB file of President Kennedy's assassin, Lee Harvey Oswald, and that the file cleared the Soviets of complicity in the president's recent murder. Nosenko subsequently endured years of hostile interrogation and extralegal imprisonment as agency leaders debated what to do with him. Ultimately, his inquisitors in the CIA's counterintelligence staff and its Soviet division moved on to new assignments, and the CIA, unable to decide whether Nosenko was a genuine defector or a provocateur, hired him as a consultant. The dispute had sapped morale and efficiency in the Soviet division, as had Golitsyn's other claim that the agency unknowingly harbored several KGB moles. CIA counterintelligence chief James Angleton, a brilliant operations officer now past his prime, exasperated even the distrustful J. Edgar Hoover in hunting such phantoms. Similar suspicions wasted resources in the French and Canadian services, and surely rank as some of the most exquisite side effects of the Soviet's wartime espionage prowess.[98]

Thus the West could make but not keep a technical intelligence lead—the Soviets seemingly always found it out and minimized its revelations as much as they could. Because capabilities on both sides were known, a strategic surprise attack probably was not possible—though intentions remained in doubt in all the capitals. The Achilles heel of intelligence in

Moscow remained what it had been in 1950; Soviet leaders did not understand Western decision making, and this incomprehension was perhaps the largest source of instability in the balance of terror, as Khrushchev's Cuban blunder showed in 1962. Once the West committed to a mixed economic system and international trade after World War II, the Soviet system, after its brief spurt of recovery and industrialization, was doomed to be left behind. Soviet spies were crucial to keeping the USSR alive and competitive for two reasons: they stole enough industrial secrets to substitute for innovation in some sectors, and they kept Moscow apprised of where the West was reading Soviet secrets.[99] Commercial espionage is as old as commerce, of course, and the Industrial Revolution itself had spread with artisans carrying their employers' trade secrets to competitors who paid more. But the Cold War was different in an important way; now, the resources of powerful states and the latest intelligence tradecraft were placed at the disposal of industrial spying and social control. It would not be enough to save communism, but it helped to keep the USSR competitive against the liberal democracies.

Managing the Colossus

The collection revolution dramatically increased the size, complexity, and expense of intelligence, especially in the United States. The novelty was technical sophistication and scale; no one knew how to run such intelligence enterprises, with the parts working in secrecy and doing very different things for their respective departments and ministries. The first sign of serious issues came with the spiraling costs of launching satellites and building computers. Intelligence budgets were small in comparison with overall military spending, it was true, and good intelligence in theory at least impeded the tendency of what the departing President Eisenhower in 1961 dubbed the "military-industrial complex" to build for worst-case scenarios. Nevertheless, the growth of intelligence costs prompted concerns on both sides of the Atlantic. America's federalized intelligence structure did not satisfy the White House or its advisers during the administrations of John F. Kennedy and Lyndon Johnson.[100] In Britain, the 1962 government-wide budget review wondered if GCHQ's growing costs were "commensurate with the intelligence obtained." Indeed, Whitehall sought (in part) to cut the expenses of the service intelligence bureaus when it created the Defence Intelligence Staff two years later.[101]

The problem of managing intelligence was not only one of cutting costs. The collection revolution saw the development and deployment of systems that pushed the limits of scientific knowledge and engineering skill, and those systems forced a rethinking and reshaping of intelligence organizations and the relationships between them. The problem was two-fold, and it caused the most discomfort in the United States as result of the scale of the US Intelligence Community. Even the world's wealthiest intelligence system could not meet all the needs placed on it for support capabilities that were too sensitive and expensive to duplicate for all requesters. Both CIA and NSA felt conflicting pressures to maintain their traditional, strategic focus and to support the war effort in Vietnam. These strains were not always easily handled: one CIA analyst working that account remembered that his colleagues were always "overworked and undersupported," and told "too often that Vietnam was the Pentagon's problem."[102] The second aspect of the problem, at least in America, was that intelligence suffered from Washington's traditionally weak mechanisms for coordinating plans, operations, and findings across departmental lines. CIA, NSA, and NRO, for instance, helped build and manage national collection capabilities, but they still competed and duplicated one another's efforts at key points, such as the development of satellite platforms.[103] Nonetheless, presidents from Eisenhower through Johnson contented themselves with instructing the DCI to encourage efficiencies and collaboration in the Intelligence Community—though they did not augment his authority to do so.

Another problem was the analysis of the torrents of new data flooding into the Intelligence Community. In July 1961 alone, NSA received 17,000 reels of magnetic tape from collection sites. Automation of the agency's processes in the 1960s helped, though they also increased the speed and volume of material for processing and analysis.[104] The problem of strategic warning of a Soviet attack had been largely solved by 1967, but the incoming administration of President Richard Nixon also wanted to know how the United States could deal with the men in the Kremlin. On this, the analysts had few insights for the new occupant of the Oval Office. A note taker in 1970 recorded Nixon's resulting complaint:

> The President stated that the United States is spending a total of about $6 billion per year on intelligence and it deserves to receive a lot more for its money than it has been getting. He does not expect the intelligence community to provide the President with proposed courses of action; that is a

function for the National Security Council. He does, however, expect the community to present objective intelligence with an indication of majority and minority views where such exist. He said that he understands that the intelligence community has been bitten badly a few times and thus tends to make its reports as bland as possible so that it won't be bitten again. The result is that many reports are completely meaningless.[105]

President Nixon's National Security Adviser, Henry Kissinger, offered the president a more nuanced critique of the analyses. A former Harvard professor, Kissinger in late 1969 graded the community's latest National Intelligence Estimate on Soviet nuclear forces: "The most serious defect is the lack of sharply-defined, clearly argued discussions of the characteristics and purposes of Soviet strategic forces. . . . Instead, what discussion of Soviet objectives there is in the NIE is superficial. There is no analysis of the evidence, no systematic presentation of the alternatives. Indeed, there is not even a precise definition of what our people [in the Intelligence Community] disagree about and what evidence would resolve their disputes."[106]

The strains on the Intelligence Community caused by the Vietnam War and spiraling costs of new collection convinced the White House in 1970 to seek fundamental reform. Nixon detailed an aide from the Bureau of the Budget, James Schlesinger, to get to the bottom of the matter. Schlesinger's resulting report linked the issues facing the community in a sort of unified field theory of intelligence management. He developed a twofold critique of the Intelligence Community's problems, according to which agency leaders concentrated on controlling the unprecedented funds required by the new intelligence hardware, for "each organization sees the maintenance and expansion of its collection capabilities as the principal route to survival and strength with the community." Their analysts, however, were "swamped with data," and had insufficient training, imagination, or funding to make the most of emerging opportunities. Thus they showed little initiative "in developing the full range of possible explanations," and had failed "to acknowledge uncertainty and entertain new ideas."[107] In short, they were insufficiently analytical.

To solve these twin problems, Schlesinger proposed central management of the intelligence confederation. The Director of Central Intelligence should be empowered—perhaps as a "Director of National Intelligence" with greater budgeting and programming authority—to impose efficiencies upon intelligence spending, and to ensure that the community's systems and capabilities complemented one another.[108] President Nixon had no desire, however, to spend on amending the National Security Act any of the waning political capital he needed to conclude the Vietnam War. His answer was to give the DCI an unprecedented but modest warrant to draft a central budget for the intelligence enterprise, and concomitant access to the accounts of the Defense Department's seven intelligence services. When his DCI (Richard Helms) seemed unwilling to use those powers, Nixon replaced him with James Schlesinger. That did not work either, as Nixon quickly moved Schlesinger on to run the Pentagon as secretary of defense. Indeed, the indirect cause of that second shift—the Watergate scandal—soon consumed Nixon's presidency. Intelligence reform in the United States would await congressional intervention later in the decade.

Schlesinger's analysis would have lasting influence all the same. His centralizing prescription would prove to be the dominant mode of thinking about intelligence reform in America for decades to come. From 1971 on, the notion that the spiraling costs of collection were not well managed and were siphoning money and attention from analysis recurred in study after study of the US Intelligence Community. The corresponding remedy—central management of the system—would be recommended almost as frequently. Nevertheless, the strength of the department heads in America's executive branch would ensure that centralizing reforms could only happen incrementally—at least until a major shock to the system in 2001.

Conclusion

The early Cold War marked perhaps the most dangerous phase in the history of the world. The two superpowers fielded thermonuclear warheads on hair-trigger alert, with untested command and control links, little situational awareness, and inadequate warning intelligence. Both sides hoped for peace but expected war. The weapons of each superpower had to be employed early if they were to be used all, fostering in Moscow and Washington a feeling that war could come with terrible swiftness—and might just favor the side that struck first.

Intelligence helped to stabilize this perilous standoff. With the impetus provided by the Korean War, both sides learned much about the other's arsenals and realized that there remained enough mystery about their adversary's strategy and targeting to make brinksmanship existentially dangerous. For the Anglo-American intelligence alliance, the result of

technological and organizational innovation in intelligence was a creditable understanding of Soviet deployments and weapons development, from
which could be inferred statements about Moscow's capabilities and intentions. The Soviets could not duplicate the collection apparatus built by the
Americans with British help, but nor did they need to; spies and newspapers gave them enough insight into Western weapons progress and collection triumphs to keep the game honest.

The major players thus gained a sense of the other's red lines, and
decided that their adversaries would not risk nuclear war absent a significant shift in the correlation of forces. After the first two decades of the
Cold War, neither side seriously believed that even an imminent surprise
attack could render it helpless with no chance of retaliating. Indeed, by
that point, Washington had gained enough confidence in its estimates of
Soviet strength to promote (both politically and practically) arms control
and "détente." The Johnson administration hoped for arms control and the
Nixon administration achieved it—realizing not only a plateau in the arms
race with the Soviet Union but also a shift in the global situation by reaching out to Mao Zedong's China.

By the early 1970s the United States had become the undisputed world
intelligence leader—something it had never been before. But its lead was
a shaky one, and the American model for intelligence, with its expensive
collection platforms and sprawling agencies, was one that no other country could emulate. And it was not even fully effective at much of what
it did. Technology had made American intelligence better but not always
smarter. The Anglo-American partnership that worked in monitoring the
Soviets was not close at all in places where British and American interests diverged. Across much of the globe, Soviet-sponsored and local intelligence services remained competitive and even superior to the Americans.
The key role of the intelligence struggle in the Cold War was to prevent the
end of the world. But that was only a part of what intelligence was doing.
Its other role was to help determine what sort of world would emerge from
the Cold War.

NOTES

1. Robert Louis Benson and Michael Warner, eds., *Venona: Soviet Espionage and
   the American Response, 1939–1957* (Washington, DC: Central Intelligence
   Agency, 1996), xxiv–xxvii.

2. Christopher Andrew, *Defend the Realm: The Authorized History of MI5* (New York: Knopf, 2009), 341.

3. Benson and Warner, *Venona*, xxvii–xxviii. See also Thomas R. Johnson, *American Cryptology during the Cold War, 1945–1989*, book I, *The Struggle for Centralization, 1945–1960* (Ft. Meade, MD: National Security Agency, 1995), 159–60, 169, 184.

4. Andrew, *Defend the Realm*, 343–45, 348; Jeffery, *The Secret History of MI6, 1909–1949* (New York: Penguin, 2010), 561, 657–58.

5. Kim Philby, *My Silent War* (London: Granada, 1980 [1968]), 160.

6. Gordon W. Prange, with Donald M. Goldstein and Katherine V. Dillon, *Target Tokyo: The Story of the Sorge Spy Ring* (New York: McGraw-Hill, 1984), 465.

7. For an overview, see John Earl Haynes and Harvey Klehr, *Venona: Decoding Soviet Espionage in America* (New Haven, CT: Yale University Press, 1999).

8. JIC (48) 9 of July 23, 1948; quoted in Percy Cradock, *Know Your Enemy: How the Joint Intelligence Committee Saw the World* (London: John Murray, 2002), 27–28.

9. Jeffery, *The Secret History of MI6*, 690–94. Andrew, *Defend the Realm*, 352.

10. Jeffery, *The Secret History of MI6*, 629–30.

11. Ibid, 621.

12. Andrew, *Defend the Realm*, 321–25.

13. Jeffery, *The Secret History of MI6*, 628–29, 685.

14. Ibid., 604, 622, 697.

15. Ibid., 635–37.

16. Ibid., 656.

17. Ibid., 750–51.

18. Ibid., 601.

19. See GCHQ's official website, www.gchq.gov.uk/History/Pages/index.aspx; accessed October 26, 2011.

20. Quoted in Larry A. Valero, "From World War to Cold War: Aspects of the Management and Coordination of US Intelligence, 1941–1953," unpublished doctoral thesis, St. Catherine's College, University of Cambridge, 2001, 177.

21. Michael Warner, "The Collapse of Intelligence Support for Air Power, 1944–52," *Studies in Intelligence* 49 (2005). See also James D. Marchio, "Days of Future Past: Joint Intelligence Operations during the Second World War," *Joint Forces Quarterly* (Spring 1996): 122.

22. Commission on the Organization of the Executive Branch of the Government [Eberstadt study panel], "The Central Intelligence Agency: National and Service Intelligence," January 1949, 39–40; accessed December 12, 2011, at www.foia.cia.gov/helms.asp.

23. See, for instance, Hoover's complaint to Attorney General Tom Clark on August 12, 1946, reprinted in Department of State, *Foreign Relations of the United States, 1945–1950, Emergence of the Intelligence Establishment* (Washington, DC: Government Printing Office, 1996), 298.

24. Johnson, *American Cryptology during the Cold War*, book I, 32.

25. See the editorial note in Department of State, *Foreign Relations of the United States*, 1950–1955, *The Intelligence Community* (Washington, DC: Government Printing Office, 2007), 233.

26. See also Harry S. Truman, *Memoirs*, vol. 1, *Year of Decision* (Garden City, NY: Doubleday, 1956), 226.

27. Harry S. Truman, *Memoirs*, vol. 2, *Years of Trial and Hope* (Garden City, NY: Doubleday, 1956), 57.

28. Michael Warner, "Prolonged Suspense: The Fortier Board and the Transformation of the Office of Strategic Services," *Journal of Intelligence History* 2 (June 2002): 73–76.

29. The term "Intelligence Community" seems to have been in circulation by 1952 at the latest; see Ludwell Lee Montague, *General Walter Bedell Smith as Director of Central Intelligence: October 1950–February 1953* (University Park, PA: Pennsylvania State University Press, 1992), 74.

30. James H. Critchfield, *Partners at the Creation: The Men behind Postwar Germany's Defense and Intelligence Establishments* (Annapolis: US Naval Institute Press, 2003), 167–70, 189–98.

31. "British-U.S. Communications Intelligence Agreement and Outline," March 5, 1946, see 3–4; accessed November 4, 2011, at www.nsa.gov/public_info/declass/ukusa.shtml.

32. Quoted in Jeffery, *The Secret History of MI6*, 718.

33. Ibid., 720.

34. Andrew, *Defend the Realm*, 388.

35. Jeffery, *The Secret History of MI6*, 704.

36. Philby, *My Silent War*, 146.

37. Richard Helms with William Hood, *A Look Over My Shoulder: A Life in the Central Intelligence Agency* (New York: Presidio, 2003), 126.

38. George Blake, *No Other Choice* (New York: Simon & Schuster, 1990), 182.

39. Benson and Warner, *Venona*, xxii.

40. Andrew, *Defend the Realm*, 369–71.

41. Cradock, *Know Your Enemy*, 100–101.

42. David A. Hatch, "Before and After June 25: The COMINT Effort," in James I. Matray, ed., *Northeast Asia and the Legacy of Harry S. Truman: Japan, China, and the Two Koreas* (Kirksville, MO: Truman State University Press, 2012), 294–98. See also Johnson, *American Cryptology during the Cold War, 1945–1989*, book I, 43, 55.

43. Johnson, *American Cryptology during the Cold War, 1945–1989*, book I, 47–48.

44. Robert F. Futrell, "A Case Study: USAF Intelligence in the Korean War," in Walter T. Hitchcock, ed., *The Intelligence Revolution: A Historical Perspective* [Proceedings of the Thirteenth Military History Symposium], (Washington, DC: Office of Air Force History, 1991), 275, 284–88.

45. Richard J. Aldrich, *The Hidden Hand: Britain, America and Cold War Secret Intelligence* (London: John Murray, 2001), 284–85.

46. Johnson, *American Cryptology during the Cold War, 1945–1989*, book I, 49–51.

47. Walter B. Smith, Director of Central Intelligence, to the National Security Council, April 23, 1952, *Foreign Relations of the United States, 1950–1955, The Intelligence Community* (Washington, DC: Government Printing Office, 2007), 254; accessed November 13, 2011, at http://history.state.gov/historicaldocuments/frus1950-55Intel/d107.

48. RAND Corporation, *Vulnerability of U.S. Strategic Air Power to a Surprise Enemy Attack in 1956*, Special Memorandum 15, April 1953, ii.

49. Eisenhower to John Foster Dulles, September 8, 1953, Series *EM, AWF, International Series: Korea—Dulles, The Papers of Dwight David Eisenhower*, vol. 14, *The Presidency: The Middle Way*, Part III: *The Space Age Begins; October 1957 to January 1958*, Document #404, accessed November 12, 2011, at www.eisenhowermemorial.org/presidential-papers/first-term/documents/404.cfm#6.

50. David Holloway, "Soviet Nuclear History," *Cold War International History Project Bulletin*, Fall 1994, 14–16; accessed November 13, 2011 at www.scribd.com/doc/61520970/7/COLD-WAR-INTERNATIONAL-HISTORY-PROJECT-BULLETIN.

51. Quoted in J. Patrick Coyne, National Security Council, "Report on Intelligence Activities in the Federal Government," undated [early 1956]; quoted in Department of State, *The Intelligence Community*, 779.

52. "Is Russia Really Ahead in Missile Race?," *US News and World Report*, May 4, 1956; quoted in Gregory W. Pedlow and Donald E. Welzenbach, *The CIA and the U-2 Program, 1954–1974* (Washington, DC: Central Intelligence Agency, 1998).

53. Omar N. Bradley, Chairman, Joint Chiefs of Staff, to Louis Johnson, Secretary of Defense, "Special Electronic Airborne Search Operations," May 5, 1950, in Department of State, *Foreign Relations of the United States, 1945–1950, The Intelligence Community* (Washington, DC: Department of State, 2007), 10.

54. Raymond Garthoff, "Estimating Soviet Military Intentions and Capabilities," in Gerald Haines and Robert Leggett, eds., *Watching the Bear: Essays on the CIA's Analysis of the Soviet Union* (Washington, DC: Central Intelligence Agency, 2002), 140–41; accessed November 20, 2011, at www.cia.gov/library/center-for-the-study-of-intelligence.

55. Gregory W. Pedlow and Donald E. Welzenbach, *The CIA and the U-2 Program, 1954–1974*, 3–4, 23, 33, 37, 316–18; accessed December 12, 2011, at www.cia.gov/library/center-for-the-study-of-intelligence.

56. For more on QUILL, see the recently declassified packet of documents on the program at the website of the National Reconnaissance Office, accessed October 22, 2012, at www.nro.gov/foia/declass/quill.html.

57. Thomas R. Johnson, *American Cryptology during the Cold War, 1945–1989*, book II, *Centralization Wins, 1960–1972* (Ft. Meade, MD: National Security Agency, 1995), 410.

58. Robert A. McDonald and Sharon K. Moreno, *Grab and Poppy: America's Early ELINT Satellites* (Chantilly, VA: National Reconnaissance Office, 2005).

59. The Associated Press reported this on November 17, 1959, and it was widely carried in US newspapers the following day.

60. Johnson, *American Cryptology during the Cold War, 1945–1989*, book I, 200–204.

61. Pedlow and Welzenbach, *The CIA and the U-2 Program*, 82, 115, 189–91.

62. Testimony of Nicholas Eberstadt of the American Enterprise Institute for Public Policy Research on U.S. Policy toward North Korea before the US House of Representatives (Committee on International Relations), Hearing on "U.S. Policy toward North Korea," September 24, 1998; accessed November 20, 2011, at www.fas.org/spp/starwars/congress/1998_h/ws924982.htm.

63. See, for instance, National Security Council Report, NSC 5509, "Status of United States Programs for National Security as of December 31, 1954," March 2, 1955, part 7, in Department of State, *The Emergence of the Intelligence Establishment*, 606, 610.

64. James Noren, "CIA's Analysis of the Soviet Economy," in Haines and Leggett, eds., *Watching the Bear*, 19, 25, 27.

65. Michael B. Petersen, *Legacy of Ashes, Trial by Fire: The Origins of the Defense Intelligence Agency and the Cuban Missile Crisis Crucible* (Washington, DC: Defense Intelligence Agency, 2011), 5–7.

66. Pete Davies, "Estimating Soviet Power: The Creation of Britain's Defence Intelligence Staff, 1960–1965," *Intelligence and National Security* 26:6 (December 2011): 840–41.

67. Richard J. Aldrich, *GCHQ: The Uncensored Story of Britain's Most Secret Intelligence Agency* (London: HarperPress, 2010), 128–39.

68. Christopher Ford and David Rosenberg, "The Naval Intelligence Underpinnings of Reagan's Maritime Strategy," *Journal of Strategic Studies* 28 (April 2005): 380–83.

69. Aldrich, *GCHQ*, 211, 219–23.

70. Director of Central Intelligence, "US Intelligence Capabilities to Monitor Certain Limitations on Soviet Strategic Weapons Programs," Special National Intelligence Estimate 11-10-67, February 14, 1967; accessed November 20, 2012, at www.spacebanter.com/showthread.php?t=49729.

71. Cynthia M. Grabo, *Anticipating Surprise: Analysis for Strategic Warning* (Washington, DC: Joint Military Intelligence College, 2002), 115–16. See also Cradock, *Know Your Enemy*, 252–54.

72. See, for example, the impressions of Britain's Director of Naval Intelligence after visiting the United States in 1951, noted in Aldrich, *The Hidden Hand*, 327–31.

73. See, for instance, Ben B. Fischer, "'One of the Biggest Ears in the World': East German SIGINT Operations," *International Journal of Intelligence and Counterintelligence* 11:2 (Summer 1998): 142–53.

74. Raymond L. Garthoff, "The KGB Reports to Gorbachev," *Intelligence and National Security* 11:2 (April 1996): 228.

75. Critchfield, *Partners at the Creation*, 165–67, 170.

76. Aldrich, *GCHQ*, 185–89, 228–37. Frank J. Rafalko, ed., *A Counterintelligence Reader*, vol. 3, *Post-World War II to Closing the 20th Century* (Washington, DC: National Counterintelligence Center, 1998), 58, 185. Sandra Grimes and Jeanne Vertefeuille, *Circle of Treason: A CIA Account of Traitor Aldrich Ames and the Men He Betrayed* (Annapolis: US Naval Institute Press, 2012), 27.

77. James Bamford, *The Puzzle Palace: A Report on NSA, America's Most Secret Agency* (Boston: Houghton Mifflin, 1982), 144. See also Johnson, *American Cryptology during the Cold War*, book I, 284.

78. Steven T. Usdin, *Engineering Communism: How Two Americans Spied for Stalin and Founded the Soviet Silicon Valley* (New Haven, CT: Yale University Press, 2005), 159, 213.

79. John Barron, *Breaking the Ring: The Bizarre Case of the Walker Family Spy Ring* (Boston: Houghton Mifflin, 1987), 162–79.

80. Aldrich, *GCHQ*, 368–86.

81. Anne Applebaum, *Iron Curtain: The Crushing of Eastern Europe* (New York: Doubleday, 2012), 69–72.

82. David E. Murphy, Sergei A. Kondrashev, and George Bailey, *Battleground Berlin: CIA vs. KGB in the Cold War* (New Haven, CT: Yale University Press, 1996), 295.

83. Rafalko, *A Counterintelligence Reader*, 3:60, 190, 186.

84. Ibid., 270; Aldrich, *GCHQ*, 254–55; letter from Angel Solakov to V. Semichastni, "Acquired materials from the Italian Embassy in Sofia," November 15, 1965, Todor Zhikov Collection, Cold War International History Project, accessed November 27, 2011, at www.wilsoncenter.org/digital-archive.

85. Rafalko, *A Counterintelligence Reader*, 3:257–58; Grimes and Vertefeuille, *Circle of Treason*, 83–84.

86. Murphy, Kondrashev, and Bailey, *Battleground Berlin*, 139, 286–88, 293, 294, 300.

87. Rafalko, *A Counterintelligence Reader*, 3:63, 186, 187.

88. Jens Gieseke, "East German Espionage in the Era of Detente," *Journal of Strategic Studies* 31:3 (June 2008): 405.

89. Applebaum, *Iron Curtain*, 82.

90. Paul Maddrell, "British Intelligence through the Eyes of the Stasi: What the Stasi Records Show about the Operations of British Intelligence in Cold War Germany," *Intelligence and National Security* 27:1 (February 2012): 60–62, 67. See also Jeffery, *The Secret History of MI6*, 659, 668.

91. Popov and Penkovsky have been discussed at length; see William Hood, *Mole* (New York: Norton, 1982), and Jerrold L. Schecter and Peter S. Derabian, *The Spy Who Saved the World: How a Soviet Colonel Changed the Course of the Cold War* (New York: Scribner's, 1992). More recently, former CIA officers

have explained Polyakov's case in detail; see Grimes and Vertefeuille, *Circle of Treason*.

92. Murphy, Kondrashev, and Bailey, *Battleground Berlin*, 267–81, 311, 343–46.

93. Garthoff, "The KGB Reports to Gorbachev," 235.

94. In the United States District Court for the District of Maryland, *United States of America v. David Henry Barnett*, Rule 11 Statement of Facts, quoted in Rafalko, *A Counterintelligence Reader*, 3:173–76.

95. National Security Council Report, NSC 5509, "Status of United States Programs for National Security as of December 31, 1954," March 2, 1955, part 7, in Department of State, *The Emergence of the Intelligence Establishment*, 613.

96. Andrew, *Defend the Realm*, 438–41.

97. Grimes and Vertefeuille, *Circle of Treason*, 29, 64.

98. Robert Hathaway and Russell Jack Smith, *Richard Helms as Director of Central Intelligence, 1966–1973* (Washington, DC: Central Intelligence Agency, 1993), 105–13, 120.

99. Usdin, *Engineering Communism: How Two Americans Spied for Stalin*, 195. Grimes and Vertefeuille, *Circle of Treason*, 44.

100. Douglas Garthoff, *Directors of Central Intelligence as Leaders of the U.S. Intelligence Community* (Washington, DC: Central Intelligence Agency, 2005), 42–46.

101. Aldrich, *GCHQ*, 220.

102. Affidavit of R. D. Kovar in *General William C. Westmoreland v. CBS Inc. et al.*, US District Court (Southern District of New York), July 27, 1983, 7; accessed October 1, 2009, at www.vietnam.ttu.edu/star/images/025/0250147001.pdf.

103. Johnson, *American Cryptology during the Cold War, 1945–1989*, book II, 405–10.

104. Ibid., 361–68, 374.

105. Editorial note recounting the minutes of Nixon's discussion with the president's Foreign Intelligence Advisory Board on July 18, 1970, reprinted as Document 210 in Department of State, *Foreign Relations of the United States, 1969–1972*, vol. 2, *Organization and Management of US Foreign Policy* (Washington, DC: Government Printing Office, 2006), 446–47.

106. Memorandum from the president's assistant for national security affairs (Kissinger) to President Nixon, "NIE 11-8-69, 'Soviet Strategic Attack Forces,'" November 26, 1969, reprinted as Document 198 in Department of State, *Organization and Management of U.S. Foreign Policy*, 1969–72, 409–10.

107. Memorandum from the president's assistant for national security affairs (Kissinger) and the Director of the Office of Management and Budget (Shultz) to President Nixon, 'Review of the Intelligence Community,' undated [probably March 22, 1971]; reprinted with Document 229 in Department of State, *Organization and Management of U.S. Foreign Policy*, 1969–72,

494–98; accessed on May 4, 2008, at www.state.gov/documents/organiza tion/77856.pdf.

108. The Schlesinger Report's text and transmittal letters are reprinted as "A Review of the Intelligence Community," March 10, 1971, Document 229 in Ibid.

CHAPTER 5

Cold War: Ideology

It would be unthinkable and unforgivable for us to refuse help to the working class of any country in its struggle against the forces of capitalism.

—KHRUSHCHEV, ON THE 1956 HUNGARIAN UPRISING, IN
KHRUSHCHEV REMEMBERS

The Cold War between communism and liberalism that had recessed in 1941 resumed again at the close of World War II. The power relations between the sides, however, had changed. Both soon had atomic weapons, making them strong enough to resist a direct military challenge even though neither had rebuilt from the war. But the age of Western imperialism had reached its end. No one could foretell when and how the many colonies would attain independence—or how these newly self-governing peoples would organize and align themselves in the world order. The intelligence systems of the liberal and Communist nations confronted one another on the plane of ideas in Europe, and then militarily in those colonies, which collectively constituted what soon would be called the developing world. The confrontations between the Europeans and the colonized peoples were now more equal than ever as modern arms and ways of handling them had spread across the earth as a result of two world wars. The unfolding of these conflicts would influence the intelligence systems of the democracies and the progressive world as much as did the technological imperatives reviewed in the last chapter.

Before 1975, intelligence had been, for the public, a field for scandals or a staple of fiction, both of the literary and cinematic varieties. Very little was reliably known about it, at least outside of national security circles. As a result of the confrontation in the developing world, by 1980 (at least in the United States and Britain, and soon in other democracies as well) intelligence issues could be debated in public for the first time by people who had real knowledge of analysis and operations—including by some of those responsible for approving, conducting, or funding such activities. This new openness itself would mark something of a revolution in intelligence.

Hearts and Minds in Europe

World War II ended in Europe in May 1945 with the victorious Allies already arguing over the shape of the peace to come. Stalin kept the Soviet Army in the lands it had taken from Hitler—the word "liberation" hardly seemed apt for peoples who exchanged one tyrant for another. The Americans left Europe as fast as they could, shifting forces to the Pacific and, when Japan capitulated that September, demobilizing their huge military establishment with all possible haste. By 1946, the Americans had left behind on the continent light constabulary forces, but hardly any combat formations. In Eastern Europe, local Communist parties and the organs of Soviet state security set about remaking the countries that Stalin had promised his allies at Yalta would be granted self-determination. The fate of Western Europe, meanwhile, swung in the balance.

Political stability and the very future of liberal democracy in Europe required economic stability—and vice versa. Neither seemed likely. The continent had been exhausted by war, with whole societies roiled by the Nazi occupation. Germany was physically devastated; recovering France and Italy had constantly shifting coalition governments, as well as strong (and armed) leftist movements that had recently fought the Germans and commanded the loyalty of sizable voting blocs. For a time, Communists in the West cooperated with the "bourgeois" governments and pleaded for one Europe, undivided by ideological cleavages, while working to take control of labor unions and their parliamentary clout. Opposition to the Communists seemed weak and divided. Britain's ambassador in Paris noted in 1946, "It looks as though the Communists are having everything their own way. They have the great advantage of knowing what they want."[1]

Washington's announcement of the Truman Doctrine to confront Communist agitation against Greece and Turkey in early 1947, followed quickly by the Marshall Plan to spread America's purchasing power and rebuild the continent's economies, forced the issue. President Truman invited the USSR to accept Marshall Plan aid, but Stalin rejected the plan and what he judged its onerous conditions. At the time, Stalin commanded obeisance from every Communist party in the world, and in response to the Marshall Plan he assembled the key parties in a new Communist

Information Bureau (better known as the Cominform). At the Cominform's inaugural meeting in Poland that September, his delegates reversed the wartime notion of "national roads to socialism," vowed to suppress the vestiges of pluralism in Eastern Europe, and ordered the parties in the West to do what they could, short of armed insurrection, to oppose the consolidation of American "hegemony" in their countries.[2]

By year's end, waves of strikes threatened to paralyze France and Italy before Marshall Plan aid could arrive. The Cominform also mounted a "peace offensive" in October 1947, reaching out via party operatives and fellow travelers to unions, peace organizations, veterans groups, youth and student assemblies, and other organizations, and urging them to adapt a common message: the United States was seeking to divide Europe and precipitate a third world war. Meanwhile, Stalin consolidated his domination of Eastern Europe through coups in Hungary (1947) and Czechoslovakia (1948), and he blockaded access to the Western allies' sectors of West Berlin in an attempt to halt the creation of a Federal Republic of Germany out of the French, British, and American occupation zones.

The Second World War's ending had thus initiated a struggle for hearts and minds in Europe, which seemed destined for a new global conflict. This crisis on the continent would help to cause significant changes in the intelligence systems on both sides of the Iron Curtain. In the East, as we have seen, Moscow had created an intelligence alliance of sorts by building up fraternal Communist security services to cooperate against Western intelligence collection. That same coalition would also spend at least as much of its collective effort working to counter the subversive influences of Western media and culture. In the West, the United States, from 1947 on, took the lead in creating a covert capability to oppose Communist influence in Western Europe and to encourage discontent and resistance to Soviet domination.

Countering the Cominform forced a dilemma on European leaders. They could not ignore pressure tactics exerted from within their societies by a united dissident movement obedient to Moscow; yet, they feared to suppress the parties or the unions and the groups they controlled for fear of sparking an uprising, or at least lending support to Communist charges of an armed American hegemony. Many in the West appreciated the Marshall Plan and eventually NATO; Western governments argued over the particulars of these measures in public, submitting them to democratic processes.

At the same time, however, French labor leaders and any number of private groups and politicians on the continent did not want open subsidies, especially from America, as these opened them to rhetorical assaults from the Left.[3] The riposte to Moscow's "vicious psychological efforts" (as America's new National Security Council described them in 1947) thus came via a Western psychological offensive against the Communists on both sides of the Iron Curtain. The main effort of the counteroffensive was always overt and conducted by the Voice of America, the BBC, the US Information Agency, the British Council, and various official programs for cultural and educational exchanges. Former Assistant Secretary of State for Public Affairs Edward Barrett made the point in the title of his 1953 book on these efforts: *Truth Is Our Weapon*. From the outset, however, a significant share of the work was covert in nature, seeking to produce public effects by secret means.

Britain and America, the two Western countries with global intelligence programs, took different approaches to covert psychological warfare. In Britain, the Labour government of Clement Attlee used a couple of bureaus in the Foreign Office for this purpose. The Cultural Relations Department, with tips from MI5 and SIS, quietly helped British students and youth leaders to understand Communist co-optation of international youth groups and establish independent alternatives between 1945 and 1949. Attlee's government also created an Information Research Department (IRD) under Foreign Office control in January 1948. IRD operated until 1977 as a secret government think tank, drafting comments and observations on world events and feeding them to selected journalists and NATO partners. Eventually its list of trusted contacts reached around the world, and its mission was to place factual stories about the Soviet Union and communism in venues where they might have more effect if they were not obviously sourced to the British government.[4]

In the United States, diplomats were even more concerned to minimize the risk of being caught running covert operations. Hence the infant CIA received its psychological warfare mission in December 1947, just weeks after the agency's statutory authorization by Congress.[5] By the following spring the CIA had scored its first covert action success: some "last-minute, frantic assistance" that helped Italy's Christian Democrats win a thumping parliamentary majority that they in turn used to secure Italian membership in NATO.[6] Nevertheless, the State Department's guru of "Containing"

Soviet ambitions, George Kennan, soon had second thoughts about an independent arm to perform psychological warfare. Hence the creation in 1948 of another new CIA staff, the Office of Policy Coordination (OPC), which served three masters (counting the White House through the staff of the National Security Council) without fully answering to any. Kennan ensured that State held a tight rein over covert action, although his brief oversight of the CIA's new office raised corresponding concerns in the Department of Defense, which sought to ensure that military requirements also received attention in CIA planning.

OPC operations expanded dramatically in the Korean War emergency, though its smaller covert projects often proceeded with little efficacy or relevance to larger policy goals.[7] Many of these operations failed—especially OPC's brief efforts to mobilize émigrés from the "satellites" into guerrilla movements behind the Iron Curtain.[8] Nonetheless, even failed covert actions like those the CIA attempted in Europe and Asia, Thomas Powers has argued, had at least one salutary effect: they probably helped convince Moscow and Beijing that the West was serious about defending its vital interests.[9]

The CIA learned the covert influence business by subsidizing non-Communist unions and parties and then creating new organizations to oppose (with mixed success) the Soviets in specific fields. These operations comprised OPC's "Mighty Wurlitzer," the main pipes of which were the National Committee for Free Europe (NCFE) and its better-known affiliates, Radio Free Europe (RFE) and Radio Liberty.[10] "The Radios" differed from the Voice of America in being ostensibly privately funded organizations legally chartered in the United States, but with no visible ties to the US government.[11] In reality they were, until 1971, CIA operations run with State Department oversight, in which the agency's covert action subsidies passed through boards of prominent private citizens who were nominally in charge. George Kennan at State had proposed the idea for NCFE in hopes of giving Eastern European émigrés in the United States an outlet for their energies (and diverting them from pressuring State Department officials).[12] They did so in part by seeking, in the words of an early RFE policy handbook, to "remind listeners constantly that they are governed by agents of a foreign power whose purpose is not to further the national interest, but to carry out the imperialistic aims of the rulers of Soviet Russia."[13] By 1952, an NSC working group judged Radio Free Europe and the Voice of

America to be "the only significant remaining programs which effectively reach the people of either or both the USSR and the Satellites."[14] Indeed, Communist leaders hated and feared the Western radios in general and RFE in particular.[15]

The CIA's psychological warfare campaign had sizable effects on the young agency's development and on the future course of American intelligence. Officials in Washington suspected the Soviets were spending lavishly on party-led efforts to consolidate Communist rule beyond the Iron Curtain and to sway opinion in Western Europe. Indeed, State's Edward Barrett mentioned to CIA officials in 1951 the fantastic sum of $2 billion in rubles being spent annually on "propaganda and directly related activities."[16] The Office of Policy Coordination tried to keep pace with the inflated estimates of Soviet spending, though its own efforts seemed dwarfed in comparison; OPC had forty-seven overseas stations and spent $82 million in 1952, seventeen times more than in 1949. Even discounting for Korean War programs, however, those figures represented a major institutional commitment for a single office in a single intelligence agency (by comparison, the much larger Office of Strategic Services had spent only about $135 million over four years during World War II).[17] DCI Walter B. Smith fretted to his lieutenants in 1951 that operations had grown so large "in comparison with our intelligence function that we have almost arrived at a stage where it is necessary to decide whether CIA will remain an intelligence agency or becomes a 'cold war department.'"[18] What OPC built became the basis of a large and permanent CIA operational presence, both around the world and in councils in Washington.

Ironically, all this money hardly bought Washington control over its client groups. The more public and effective they were, the less they needed covert funding and direction. Labor leader and CIA partner Jay Lovestone dubbed his agency contacts the "Fizz-Kids" and sometimes refused to follow their lead.[19] The CIA's Tom Braden, head of OPC's International Operations Division, recalled that although "Lovestone wanted our money, he didn't want to tell us precisely how he spent it." The agency eventually cut Lovestone's subsidy for French and Italian unions and gave the savings to other labor organizations, with the result that within two years "the free labor movement, still holding its own in France and Italy, was going even better elsewhere."[20] Though contentious, that was part of the attraction for CIA officials—groups that did not toe an American policy line had more credibility overseas. It "took a fairly sophisticated point of view to understand that the public exhibition of unorthodox views was a potent weapon against monolithic Communist uniformity of action," noted a CIA internal history in the 1970s.[21] The line between freedom and license with covert funds, however, could be difficult to draw with consistency. An outside review of CIA covert action programs, drafted for President Eisenhower in 1956, depicted the situation in starker terms. An NSC staffer, summarizing the review's findings, explained that the operations directorate of the CIA was "operating for the most part on an autonomous and free-wheeling basis in highly critical areas involving the conduct of foreign relations"—and that frequently the State Department knew "little or nothing" of what the CIA was doing.[22]

In 1956, the West gained two lasting victories in the war for European opinion. A secret speech by Soviet premier Nikita Khrushchev at the 20th Party Congress in Moscow that February denounced Stalin and his "cult of personality," which in Khrushchev's reckoning caused over a million arrests and hundreds of thousands of executions in the 1930s. The purges, of course, had marked but the tip of the proverbial iceberg—Khrushchev spoke of the damage Stalin had done to the party rather than the nation, and he did not mention Stalin's forced collectivization and other horrors, nor did he apologize for the miseries since the revolution—but he had conceded the basic truth of countless charges made against the Soviet Union over the decades. Rumors of his speech reached the Western press within two weeks. Israeli intelligence got the full text from a Polish Jew in April and passed it to the CIA, which in turn gave it to the *New York Times* and Radio Free Europe. By late June, Khrushchev's entire speech had been broadcast to listeners behind the Iron Curtain, to the consternation of Communist leaders throughout the Warsaw Pact.[23]

The speech "started the process of purifying the Party of Stalinism," Khrushchev recalled, but it also sent shock waves of discontent with Communist rule that crested in Hungary that fall.[24] Hungarians had watched protests and reforms in Poland over the summer (or rather, they heard about them from RFE and other Western broadcasters), and hoped for even more. When the government of Imre Nagy asked the Soviet Army to leave Hungary in October, the leaders in the Kremlin complied, and suddenly the party seemed on the verge of losing its hold on power. Khrushchev was appalled: "Active Party members and especially Chekists were being hunted down in the streets. Party committees and Chekist organizations were crushed."[25] RFE's rebroadcast of calls from low-power Hungarian stations for resistance to the Soviets and a withdrawal of Hungary from the Warsaw Pact increased the alarm in Moscow, which soon ordered the tanks to fight their way back in.[26] In a few days, the uprising was over, with hundreds killed on both sides.

"The help we gave the Hungarian people in crushing the counterrevolution was approved unanimously by the working people in the Socialist countries, by all progressives throughout the world," Khrushchev explained in his memoir.[27] Perhaps, but 1956 was a public relations disaster for Moscow that marked a turn in the ideological conflict in Europe. The Cold War struggle would continue for decades longer, of course, but the events in Hungary dramatized the increasingly obvious fact that life was better in the West than in the East. Western Europe had recovered from the war by 1956 and had begun its economic takeoff; thereafter, growth and social welfare policies improved the lot of working class families, while the political, intellectual, and cultural spheres were tolerant and diverse in comparison with the USSR and its satellites. The erection of the Berlin Wall five years later symbolized this divide. Even the workers in socialist East Berlin preferred life in the Western zone—and now the East had to erect barriers to keep its people from leaving. Henceforth, the greatest threat to East Germany would be West Germany—not for its military might, but because it showed East Germans another way for Germans to live.

The intelligence services of the Warsaw Pact never conceded defeat in the ideological contest, but instead worked even harder to smear opponents as hypocrites who ignored their own ideals. This was stock in trade for Soviet press organs, of course; a typical insinuation was one like *Izvestia*'s "scoop" in 1961, which blamed the CIA for the recent, abortive generals' putsch against President Charles de Gaulle of France.[28] The KGB was integral to this campaign, though East Germany's Stasi also helped. The latter preferred to expose targets as former Nazis, or as Nazi collaborators, or at least as persons who had done too little to oppose the Nazis.[29] The KGB, on the other hand, libeled the persons of its main opponents; forgeries depicted FBI Director J. Edgar Hoover alternatively as a right-wing extremist or a closeted homosexual, while KGB spy Kim Philby (writing from exile in Moscow) depicted his CIA counterparts (at least one of whom, James Angleton, was still in service) as drunks and incompetents.[30] And, the KGB

5.1 FBI Director J. Edgar Hoover, 1961. *Library of Congress*

insinuated through books and articles that the CIA had ties to the assassination of President Kennedy.[31] This charge took wings when a crusading New Orleans prosecutor heard a version from the KGB's favorite Italian newspaper, *Paese Sera*. The paper's allegation—that an American businessman (and sometime CIA contact) in Rome, Clay Shaw, had hired Lee Harvey Oswald to shoot the president—indirectly inspired a major motion picture two decades later and thus entered popular culture as one of the most successful lies in history.[32]

The Hungarian uprising also helped change the way the Western services, or at least the Americans, viewed the ideological struggle. Even as the crisis unfolded, Moscow began accusing various Western leaders and institutions of cynically fomenting bloody revolution in Hungary.[33] CIA leaders discounted such charges by the Soviets as *de rigueur*.[34] What really stung was the simultaneous accusation by Hungarian revolutionaries that

America, through RFE, had incited their revolt only to abandon them when the Soviets invaded.[35] The Radios and their Washington overseers learned to be more dispassionate and objective in their broadcasting; indeed, there would be no hint of incitement when the Soviets similarly suppressed Czechoslovakia's Prague Spring in 1968.

By then, early misgivings about covert action had revived. As the head of the Voice of America had privately argued in 1951, America did not need *covert* propaganda in Eastern Europe because "the Russians are doing our work for us."[36] While Stalin lived, that logic could not convince officials in the CIA, the State Department, or the Pentagon. It became compelling, however, as Western Europe grew increasingly prosperous and less vulnerable to subversion. Indeed, Washington gradually lost interest in supporting political parties and front groups against the Communists in Europe, even though such support had come to be expected by its recipients. In 1967, a meeting of Johnson administration, State Department, and CIA officials to review the subsidies for Italy noted, "The wind-down of covert political support to Italian parties ahead of schedule was enthusiastically welcomed by the committee." Participants agreed with the conclusions of a paper prepared for their session; to wit, that the socialist and Christian Democratic parties could now succeed without American funds—and that Washington had higher priorities elsewhere. Indeed, "the amount of covert assistance the United States is prepared to offer" would no longer have more than "peripheral impact on the Italian political scene."[37] Even the crown jewels of CIA's covert action enterprise—Radio Free Europe and Radio Liberty—were moved off the agency's books by the International Broadcasting Act of 1973, transferring to a quasipublic (and completely overt) organization called the Board for International Broadcasting.

What ultimately won the ideological conflict in Europe was truth. The effects of Western covert psychological and political action, in the short term, were mostly trivial. In the long run, however, the economic disparity between East and West was more than communism could bear. Moscow's exile of the writer Alexander Solzhenitsyn in 1974 surely ended any idea that art flourished under Marxism, so the West won the cultural struggle as well. At the same time, the candid treatment of President Richard Nixon's denouement in the Watergate scandal by RFE and Radio Liberty helped convince Eastern listeners that the Radios were credible sources of news, not mere propaganda organs.[38] Blue jeans and rock music would thenceforth be the West's most powerful persuasive tools. For these, no covert subsidies were needed.

Revolutions

Since you are such good soldiers, why do you fight for the colonialists? Why don't you fight for yourselves and get yourselves a country of your own?

—QUESTION POSED TO ALGERIAN SOLDIERS OF THE FRENCH ARMY
TAKEN AT DIEN BIEN PHU BY THEIR VIETNAMESE CAPTORS.
QUOTED IN HORNE, *A SAVAGE WAR OF PEACE*

World War II had blasted and bankrupted Europe, and the resulting political and ideological reverberations lasted for decades. The war's effects in the rest of the world, moreover, would be at least equally profound. Europeans had ruled much of the globe in 1939. In India and Algeria and elsewhere, no one could remember a time without European dominance. For other lands, like Palestine, the Western presence was still novel. But the Europeans had neither the means nor the will to hold their empires. In some places, after 1945, decolonization happened without revolutions; in others it was hastened forward by token revolts. In a few spots, it sparked full-fledged war. Even where voluntary, European departures and cessions of power to local leaders were bound to cause contention, if not conflict and dislocation, as power struggles decided who would replace the old elites.

The Cold War's battle of ideas inevitably colored these disputes. In many of them, the "developing world" made a rich field for intrigues. Modern weapons had spread worldwide during World War II, becoming increasingly available to various groups fighting for (or against) independence. Now modern intelligence methods also touched those lands and others, and altered their histories. What historian Martin Thomas has called Britain's and France's "empires of intelligence" had been disrupted by the war. Local leaders had learned the trades of espionage, sabotage, and security in classes taught by the Western services in wartime, whether in regular formations to fight the Nazis or Japanese directly, or as guerrillas to resist their occupiers in places like Vietnam, China, Yugoslavia, and Burma. Some learned their lessons very well.

The ideological struggle in the developing world also scrambled the alliances that had held up roughly through the Korean War. Unity could not be long maintained on either side of the Iron Curtain, especially when it came to colonial policies (and intelligence support for the same). American leaders, of course, felt themselves to be descended from ex-colonists and revolutionaries. Their own empire in the western Pacific and the Caribbean had fallen to them almost by default in 1898, and weighed on their consciences. By 1946, with the independence of the Philippines, the American empire was no more, and thereafter the United States had little patience for colonialism anywhere. As early as 1950, a British psychological warfare officer posted to Washington privately reminded colleagues at home that, with regard to troubles in Malaya and elsewhere, the United States seemed to care about the spread of communism but not the maintenance of order in the colonies: "It seems very dangerous to pretend that the troubles in Malaya are not caused by Communists but only by a kind of local banditry. . . . This is especially so in a colony; and instead of receiving sympathy and support from American public opinion in our praiseworthy struggle to combat the well-known international Communist menace, we shall merely be regarded as a bad colonial power coping with rebellions."[39]

The Western alliance did not fracture over decolonization, but the foreign policies of its major actors diverged, which meant that alliances formed by Western intelligence services in contesting the Soviets and Chinese did not fully extend to the developing world. The Europeans would return Washington's indifference, of course, with regard to later American interventions in Latin America and Vietnam. But Western disagreements over the developing world paled in significance and hostility when compared with the divides in the progressive camp. Marxism was a mode of thought, not an organized force. Indeed, Soviet communism was but one manifestation of it. Its other main current after 1936 flowed through China. Sino-Soviet rivalry for the allegiance of revolutionary movements had turned to antagonism by 1960, and indeed, when Chinese and Soviet troops skirmished in 1969 the two sides nearly came to war. Until Mao's death and even beyond, the socialist world was bitterly divided. Much of the intelligence struggle in the developing world thereafter had some relation to the clash of the Communist giants.

For two-fifths of the world's population, European power ended with dramatic suddenness just after the end of World War II in 1945. Britain gave up India without a struggle in 1947, though the subcontinent's subsequent massacres and upheaval would leave it a perennial source of instability. Most of the history made there was consumed locally—unlike in the Balkans, to steal a famous phrase—which is why the great human drama on the subcontinent produced little that was of international import for the intelligence field. But if the Indians learned their intelligence lessons from British colonial methods, the Chinese learned the business of intelligence from protracted warfare in the countryside, and from Stalin. Both of these factors would make China's upheaval and the overthrow of the Nationalist regime (with its liberal Western allies and investors) globally significant.

The new Chinese regime in Beijing had not yet developed much in the way of a foreign intelligence service, but it efficiently curtailed Western efforts to collect from operatives inside China.[40] Mao's favorite Kang Sheng faded into the background of Chinese intelligence after the war, with his place as head of party political and military intelligence assumed by Li Kenong, one of the agents who for a time had burrowed inside the Guomintang. With the internal security and military aspects of intelligence work being split off to the new Ministry of Public Security and the People's Liberation Army, Li stayed in uniform, rising to colonel general and joining the CCP's Central Committee in 1956. For a time the Chinese and Soviet intelligence systems cooperated; the Soviets on Khrushchev's orders revealed their unilateral network of agents in China, and the Chinese Ministry of Public Security helped Soviet illegals of Asian ethnicity build background legends before their postings abroad.[41] By the early 1960s, however, Li had died, and Mao brought back his henchman Kang Sheng to begin a fresh purge of the party. From his post in the party secretariat, Kang took charge of intimidating and neutering, on Mao's behalf, the various party bureaus and offices whose main business by 1965 had come to be investigating one another. When the Cultural Revolution broke with full force on the party and then the country at large in 1966, Kang Sheng stood with Mao at every turn of the tragedy.[42] Stalinist intelligence methods in China thus reached the equivalent force and violence they had exercised in Stalin's Great Terror; the sword and shield of the party turned on itself to uphold yet another cult of personality.

China's Communist revolution nevertheless exerted a powerful intellectual influence on anticolonial movements. The confluence of decolonization at the point of maximum East-West tension was to cause the spread of Maoist methods of revolutionary practice and internal security to nations in Latin America, the Middle East, and East Asia. The ethnically Chinese

Malayan Communist Party (MCP) rose in 1948 against British rule, and in the Philippines, the Marxist Hukbalahap rebellion gathered momentum against the newly independent government in Manila (a government famously advised by Col. Edward Lansdale, a US Air Force officer detailed to CIA).[43] Both uprisings, however, had their centers of gravity in minority ethnic groups and were isolated on virtual or geographic islands, which allowed traditional colonial counterinsurgency methods to overcome them (eventually), employing mostly measured uses of force and lots of human intelligence. Britain ran its intelligence campaign from the Special Branch of the Malayan colonial police, which ultimately specialized in penetrating the MCP with informers, each providing tips to operations and additional recruitments, not to mention demoralizing and intimidating party cadres by convincing them that the police had spies everywhere. "Secret penetration was achieved at the highest Party level," recalled one senior intelligence official, "and much disruption was caused in Party ranks. The leaders were quite pathological in their suspicions and many loyal comrades were ruthlessly purged on the slimmest of evidence."[44]

The Communist-led revolution in Indochina, however, made for another story. Vietnamese Marxist Ho Chi Minh had been hardened by years of covert work against the French and Japanese, and several of his lieutenants had been trained in intelligence by the Chinese Communists and by OSS, SIS, and even by US Navy cryptologists during World War II.[45] His Viet Minh also received a windfall as World War II ended, when French Sûreté authorities decamped from Hanoi in haste and abandoned their archive. Officers of the Viet Minh's new Ministry of Public Security pored over the files, marveling at the numbers of French-run agents and learning how a modern European service ran colonial intelligence. A few of the French-trained Vietnamese civil servants of the Sûreté even found new jobs with the new regime's intelligence organs; "I once again realized that they were an invaluable resource which the revolution had to know how to use," wrote one Viet Minh official later. The Viet Minh combined these skills and insights with ruthless sabotage and assassination operations (including suicide bombings) against the French and their local allies.[46] They also learned the hard way at French hands, suffering from a well-run French deception that had them torturing their own officials in quest of a mythical spy, "H122," high in their ranks.[47] Ironically, indigenous revolution subsequently failed in South Vietnam in the 1950s, as that new nation began coalescing under Ngo Dinh Diem in Saigon and Hanoi sat out the struggle, allowing local Viet Minh cadres to contest the countryside alone against the forces of the South, which were improving under American tutelage. Indeed, without the CIA's covert help in Saigon, there might not have been a South Vietnam to fight over. From 1954, the United States had an embassy there, an aid mission, and a growing military advisory mission, but for two decades the local CIA station played a quiet but key role in facilitating bilateral relations.[48] Diem survived a shaky start and consolidated his power in Saigon, and—while feeding resentments that would ultimately imperil his rule—he almost vanquished the Communist political struggle against him in the countryside.[49] Indeed, by 1957 Diem briefly looked, to Washington, like a miracle worker who had all but ended the conflict in South Vietnam.[50]

Another sort of revolt against European rule brewed in Palestine. This would be a war of ideas of a different sort, pitting Muslim Arabs against British authorities and Jewish settlers. With Jewish help, the British military and police had put down an Arab revolt in the late 1930s, but the Anglo-Jewish intelligence alliance in Palestine did not survive the early days of World War II.[51] Radical Jewish groups like Irgun and its breakaway faction Lohami Harut Israel (abbreviated Lehi and known as the Stern Gang) turned against Britain when London reversed course to oppose Jewish emigration to Palestine on the eve of World War II. Thereafter, both Arab and Jewish extremists worked separately against any possibility of a negotiated peace. The exiled Grand Mufti of Jerusalem, Hajj Muhammad Amin al-Husayni, spent the war in Germany, meeting Hitler and recruiting Bosnian Muslims for the SS. He promised the Führer that the Arabs stood ready to fight the English, the Jews, and the Communists with "acts of sabotage and the instigation of revolutions," and after the war he incited Palestinian resistance to an independent Israel from his new home in Egypt.[52] Irgun and Lehi (one of history's last organizations to call itself a terrorist group) were equally anti-British; they launched a campaign of bombings and shootings as the war ended. Both killed Arabs and British officials and soldiers. Lehi mailed letter bombs to leaders in Britain, and even planted dynamite in Whitehall. The bomb was a dud, as was fitting for a terror campaign that accomplished little besides hardening British opinion against an independent Israel. Both MI5 and SIS devoted considerable energy to the ensuing campaign to restore order; MI5 had charge of internal security in Palestine, and SIS futilely sought to sabotage ships carrying new Jewish immigrants.[53]

But though Zionist extremists squabbled with the Jewish agency—which in turn shared tips with MI5 to hunt their leaders—they readily cooperated with it in the 1948 war to create an independent state of Israel.[54] Indeed, that victory convinced all the Israeli factions to let bygones be bygones. Out of the war came a ban on Irgun and Lehi by the new government of Israel, followed by an amnesty of their members and leaders, two of whom (Menachem Begin and Yitzhak Shamir) would go on to serve as Israeli prime ministers.

The notion that winning matters above all was not lost on Muslim opponents of the French government and *colons* (European settlers), in Algeria. Their revolution combined the horrors of Palestine and Vietnam, and by no coincidence burst open shortly after the Viet Minh's final victory and capture of 11,000 French troops at Dien Bien Phu in 1954. During the following year an Algerian *Front de Libération Nationale* (FLN) regional commander turned the war against the French *colons* feral, declaring, "To colonialism's policy of collective repression we must reply with collective reprisals against the Europeans, military and civil, who are all united behind the crimes committed upon our people. For them, no pity, no quarter!"[55] French intelligence could not cope; it had never recovered from an abortive Muslim rebellion at the end of World War II, and thus had shifted from subtlety to repression.[56] Massacre followed massacre after 1954, with both sides taking revenge and perpetrating fresh outrages. Algerian-born Albert Camus raged against the horror, but particularly against the idea that all French citizens and the substantial number of not-yet-radicalized Arabs were legitimate targets:

> we ought to condemn with equal force and in the bluntest of terms the terrorism practiced by the FLN against French civilians and, even more frequently, Arab civilians. This terrorism is a crime, which can be neither excused nor allowed to develop. In the form in which it is currently practiced, no revolutionary movement has ever tolerated it, and the Russian terrorists of 1905 would sooner have died (as they proved) than stoop to such tactics. It is wrong to transform the injustices endured by the Arab people into a systematic indulgence of those who indiscriminately murder Arab and French civilians without regard to age or sex.[57]

The French won for a time when they adopted totalitarian methods of their own against a rash FLN attempt to fight in Algiers in early 1957.

Clue by clue, French military intelligence built up a picture of the FLN's operatives, bombmakers, and commanders in the city. Paratroop officers leading the intelligence effort, many of them veterans of Indochina, seized police records and rounded up FLN suspects, instituted tight surveillance by loyal Muslims, and practiced the intense questioning of suspects that degenerated into what liberal France soon dubbed *La Torture*. Paratroop commander Major General Jacques Massu claimed he tried the *gégène* (an army signals magneto equipped with electrode clips) on himself with no ill effects, but recalcitrant suspects passed to special interrogation centers could expect rougher treatment. "All day, through the floorboards, we heard their hoarse cries, like those of animals being slowly put to death," wrote one paratrooper. Local official Paul Teitgen, himself a survivor of Dachau, "recognized on certain detainees profound traces of the cruelties and tortures that I had personally suffered fourteen years ago in the Gestapo cellars." Liberal French and world opinion recoiled. Quipped Teitgen: "All right, Massu won the Battle of Algiers; but that meant losing the war." The FLN's loss in Algiers forced it to a sanctuary in Tunisia, from where, in 1959, it devised a new strategy and soon new military leadership as well, that would ultimately force a negotiated and hasty French withdrawal in spring 1962.[58] By then, however, all possibility of a multiethnic Algeria had been erased by *colon* and FLN atrocities, President Charles de Gaulle had narrowly escaped assassination, and Algeria's non-Muslims were fleeing en masse.

The United States could not watch complacently as its European allies lost their colonies. Americans had never liked the empires, but Washington liked even less the idea of Moscow gaining new friends in the exchange— as happened in North Vietnam. The American CIA won two early rounds against elected but poorly organized opponents in Iran and Guatemala when their leaders veered leftward, but in both cases US diplomats and the agency's representatives did so by inciting army coups. The CIA pressured the Guatemalan army with a comic opera invasion (Operation PBSUCCESS), while in Iran, Near East division chief Kermit Roosevelt badgered the Shah to turn his generals on his prime minister, Mohammed Mossadeq (Operation TPAJAX).[59] The fact that the CIA had officers on the ground in these countries spoke to the expansiveness of its intelligence gathering and its covert action authorities. Before World War II, the United States had no career intelligence officers to post overseas, and what intelligence it collected was gleaned more or less overtly by diplomats and attaches. By the early 1950s, however, CIA stations worked in dozens of countries with the intelligence and in some cases the leaders of host governments.[60] Those dealings often, but not always, facilitated bilateral relations with the United States. The ability to carry on such quiet diplomacy—albeit usually on less-momentous matters—was a mainstay of the Central Intelligence Agency's business.

The CIA's mechanisms, however, soon failed spectacularly in Cuba. Ironically, they did so partly for reasons that emerged half a world away, when the early unity of purpose of the Communist bloc fragmented. Growing tensions between the Soviets and Chinese flared openly in 1960, after Mao's Great Leap Forward with its "samovar blast furnaces" (Khrushchev's term) had wrecked China's economy and squandered Soviet aid. According to Khrushchev, Mao "was following in Stalin's footsteps" with his own personality cult, and Mao called peaceful coexistence with the West a "bourgeois pacifist notion." China demanded territorial concessions in Siberia, although what Mao really wanted remained a mystery to Moscow: "It's impossible to pin these Chinese down," Khrushchev later complained.[61] The Chinese gave as good as they got. "Your credentials are much more shallow than mine!" Mao's lieutenant Kang Sheng told Khrushchev to his face in early 1960, when the Soviet premier took umbrage at Kang's criticism of Soviet policy.[62] All this played out as Fidel Castro consolidated his own revolution after seizing power in Cuba. Whereas Moscow previously knew little about Latin America, now the Soviets assiduously exerted their influence to assist Castro—and to keep the Chinese from seizing the leadership of progressive forces for themselves.[63]

Castro proved a nightmare come true for the United States, just ninety miles from Key West. Moscow had both the motivation and the means to help Fidel. Soviet assistance ensured the Cuban revolution could stand against American anger, and against CIA covert action. Khrushchev boasted in 1960 that Soviet artillerymen could support Cuba with rocket fire, but it was the KGB that (at Castro's behest) gave practical advice and aid—far more than came from Moscow's Foreign Ministry. CIA did all in its power to derail the revolution and then to destroy Fidel, but its power was limited. The agency's ill-conceived effort to repeat the Guatemala coup operation failed at the Bay of Pigs in April 1961. There was no CIA station chief left in Havana to persuade Cuban generals to rebel; the US Embassy and station had closed months earlier as the diplomatic rift widened. Castro, moreover, had already placed the military and intelligence services under his brother, Raul, and purged them of potential coup leaders. The CIA's ensuing invasion—1,500 Cuban émigrés to secure a 40-mile wide beachhead—collapsed under Castro's counterassault in just three days.[64] Castro then cited the Bay of Pigs to implement Soviet-coached internal security measures. Indeed, the public fact of a CIA plot against him gave Castro an excuse to declare that Cuba was now a socialist state and to announce, on May Day, 1961, that the Cuban people voted for socialism every day and therefore needed no more elections.[65]

Vietnam

The United States tried much harder in Vietnam to stop the spread of Maoist methods. The ensuing war showcased both sides' abilities to bring intelligence to bear on the battlefield, and beyond that to the political struggle for allies and the benefit of world opinion. The Democratic Republic of Vietnam (DRV) committed to armed struggle in the South in 1959, but Hanoi would not yet risk an outright invasion as had Kim Il-sung in Korea. Instead, while the FLN learned to fight the Algerian War from its base to Tunisia, the North Vietnamese assisted local militias in the South (the Viet Cong) in their campaign to demonstrate the Saigon regime's inability to secure the countryside. As South Vietnam reeled toward collapse, Hanoi upped the stakes in 1964 by committing its People's Army of Vietnam (PAVN) to the fight. That in turn pulled in substantial American ground and air forces, seeking to prevent a Communist conquest of the South while avoiding a larger war with the North—or with Mao's China (another lesson of the Korean War). In the end, the world's most sophisticated system for collecting secrets lost to a local regime that was unsurpassed at keeping them.

Both sides in the struggle needed to understand the intentions and capabilities of both their allies and opponents among the Vietnamese. Washington and Moscow alike found Hanoi inscrutable. The CIA and the US military could not penetrate either Ho Chi Minh's inner circle or the North Vietnamese countryside with human agents, and NSA never read Hanoi's high-level communications.[66] For their part, the Soviets and Chinese provided the DRV with vital weapons and tools, ranging from bullets and trucks to surface-to-air missiles and MiG jet fighters. Indeed, without the Sino-Soviet split, North Vietnam could not have prosecuted the struggle as it did; as Khrushchev noted, the rockets fired at US bases "weren't manufactured in the jungles of Vietnam. They came from factories in the Soviet Union."[67] Hanoi skillfully played the Chinese and the Soviets to gain aid from both. Nonetheless, the KGB gained little insight into the DRV's councils, and it ran operations there as it did in Western countries—under tight local surveillance.[68] The CIA did far better in the South, with contacts and assets of all sorts for reporting intelligence and exerting influence over senior officials in Saigon.[69] While this arrangement helped keep the bilateral relationship alive, especially during periods when the two sides were barely talking, the question of whether it presented Washington's policies and wishes clearly and effectively to Saigon may never be answered.[70] In short, Hanoi held a clear advantage in the intelligence struggle. The DRV guarded its plans and secrets from allies and foes alike. American analysts were left arguing over scraps of hard information on Hanoi's intentions.[71] In South Vietnam, furthermore, the North Vietnamese received information from, and exerted influence by means of, recruits in the countryside and key assets in the South Vietnamese capital. These included an aide to South Vietnamese President Nguyen Van Thieu, a prominent South Vietnamese army officer (Pham Ngoc Thao), and the journalist Pham Xuan An—who seemingly knew everyone of importance in Saigon.[72]

Both sides likewise ran operations aimed at contesting the loyalties of the South Vietnamese population. For Hanoi, this meant picking off the government's smaller garrisons, creating a shadow government in the South, and silencing those who opposed the Communists through bombings and assassinations.[73] The CIA partnered with the South's internal security forces to contest this Maoist-inspired strategy by rooting out Hanoi's networks of local officials and operatives. In 1966, the agency began coordinating South Vietnamese district- and province-level security and intelligence files and activities against the Viet Cong. Thus began the Phung Hoang or "Phoenix" program, with its affiliated Provincial Reconnaissance Units (PRUs) for apprehending VC suspects. With CIA support and guidance, and often with US military advisers, the PRUs were as effective (if sometimes brutal) a method of rooting out Viet Cong leaders as was ever devised, partly because many PRU team members were locals who hated the VC.[74] Phoenix probably only delayed the deluge. As the CIA's internal history judged, "by 1965 it was already too late for the [government of

South Vietnam] to engage its own population in successful opposition to the Communists."[75] By about 1970, moreover, Phoenix had given rise to the enduring allegation that the apprehension of Viet Cong officials had caused roughly 20,000 deaths—many of them of innocents swept up to meet local quotas.[76] Official US historians and veterans concede that Viet Cong suspects not infrequently died resisting arrest, but though they dispute the charge that Phoenix was an "assassination program," the stigma attached itself to the campaign and helped to undermine support for the war effort in America and abroad.

Considerations of national and international opinion also governed much of America's military effort, especially as support for it eroded. On and over the battlefield, the combatants played a deadly game of cat and mouse. Hanoi sought to keep enough PAVN formations in the south to maintain control of the countryside and exhaust the Americans, but had to keep them out of the way of US firepower. Signals intelligence aided the DRV; aided by American radio chatter, the Viet Cong and PAVN usually decided when and where to engage US troops. Indeed, after American troops overran a PAVN intercept unit in late 1969, NSA confirmed the enemy was collecting copious information on US units and operations, including locations, order of battle, morale, and sometimes intentions as well.[77] By 1967, it was also clear that the North Vietnamese had reliable indicators of incoming bombing raids—especially those by B-52s, which needed prodigious (and stereotyped) support from tankers and other aircraft to complete their missions.[78]

The Americans aimed to fix and finish PAVN troop concentrations so as to give the South Vietnamese breathing space to root out Viet Cong cadres. The Americans brought every intelligence discipline in the toolkit to the war, from human agents to electronic sensors to airborne reconnaissance. The crucial direction-finding (DF) mission went airborne in Vietnam, for instance, with the US Army honing the use of DF sets in aircraft, and forcing the PAVN and the Viet Cong to be more careful with their radios.[79] Processing time from interception of jungle transmissions to dissemination of their locations to American field commanders was cut from twenty-four hours to six minutes by the end of 1966.[80] SIGINT integration also advanced, led initially by marines and their innovative 1st Radio Battalion in northern South Vietnam.[81] From the United States, the National Security Agency supported army and marine efforts in the field to chart Communist radio nets and read their messages; NSA was eventually able to decrypt some PAVN communications (an internal history suggests these were limited to regimental level or below), and could do so at its headquarters near Washington in as little as four hours from collection to passage of plaintext to American commanders in Vietnam.[82] US Army Vice Chief of Staff General Bruce Palmer attested to fellow officers that "field commanders in Vietnam, continue to say that [signals intelligence] is the backbone of their intelligence effort. They can't live or fight without it. I want to stress to everyone in this room just how important this effort is. . . . I can't think of anything more important because they are just blind over there without this effort."[83] This testimony notwithstanding, not all commanders would act on intercepts, perhaps because SIGINT was still segregated from other intelligence sources (at least up to the division level); it was a security rule that sometimes forced field commanders to act as their own analysts in evaluating its reports in light of other information.[84]

The air war over North Vietnam would inevitably be a US victory, given the comparative strengths of the opponents. The Americans had too many of the best aircraft and pilots in the world, and they could operate in almost all weather conditions. The question was how costly Hanoi would make it for the Americans, bound as they were by strict rules of engagement forbidding strikes on DRV combat airfields or leadership facilities. US Air Force and Navy signals intelligence increased in 1965 as rising aircraft losses forced efforts to monitor the signals and radar emissions from the DRV's sophisticated air defenses. As in Korea the previous decade, the problem for American air power was tightening the integration of operations and intelligence in order to speed warnings to pilots of approaching MiG fighters and surface-to-air missiles.[85] Computers greatly assisted this effort, allowing American pilots to be warned of threats, though the necessary innovation and integration proved painful chores for the balkanized US military.[86] Not until autumn 1972 did air force and navy signals intelligence and operations staffs coordinate their efforts in earnest. Improved warnings from signals intelligence and an improved command and control system (TEABALL) made the subsequent "Christmas bombing" missions in December 1972 safer for the B-52s, and encouraged the Americans to plan new ways of controlling air missions in future campaigns. In addition, the integrated circuit made computers smaller, cheaper, and durable enough to build into weapons systems and even into the munitions themselves.

Precision-guided bombs saw their first combat use in 1972, when a handful of US aircraft used them to drop North Vietnam's Thanh Hoa bridge—a span ringed with guns and missiles, which had survived determined airstrikes since 1965. For the US Air Force jets that wrecked the bridge, the mission was a milk run; they flew high above the defenses and guided their bombs to the target using laser beams. They did so, moreover, without loss to themselves, and thereby demonstrated that the bombing campaign had swung decisively in America's favor.

The Vietnam War provided another footnote that would hold growing importance later. For the Americans, covert action in Indochina came closest to success where the North Vietnamese overextended themselves in the neighboring kingdom of Laos. There the United States and its local allies between 1960 and 1974 turned the tables and kept the Communist Pathet Lao and the PAVN from controlling the country outright. The campaign on both sides was covert from start to finish, as both Washington and Hanoi had violated international agreements by installing forces in Laos. Thus the American side of it—in contrast with the looser command relationships in Saigon—was tightly controlled by successive US ambassadors in Vientiane, who guided and directed all the US agencies and forces in-country more like generals than diplomats.[87] The Americans had two objectives. In the southern Laotian "panhandle," they worked with the US Air Force and ineffectually sought to constrict Communist supply lines running into South Vietnam.[88] In the northern part of the country, Hanoi's troops were the outsiders using conventional military formations to quiet an ethnically diverse populace, and they faced Vang Pao's agile CIA-sponsored guerrillas, backed again by the air force.[89] Guerrillas and modern air power made for an odd combination of symmetric and asymmetric means, but according to the CIA's internal history of the campaign, the effort diverted at least two regular army divisions that Hanoi could have sent (and did send, after 1973) to the fighting in South Vietnam.[90] It was also comparatively cheap; the CIA's annual budget in Laos amounted to about a day's spending on the US military effort in South Vietnam, noted one US Senator to DCI Richard Helms in 1967.[91]

The ultimate futility of American intervention in Vietnam would prove to be a catalyst for change in the US military, and that in turn would have far-ranging implications for the nation's intelligence system. American intelligence in Vietnam was much better at the end of the conflict than it had been at the outset, though the ebbing of US combat power meant that the new capabilities merely slowed the Communist tide long enough for Washington to extricate itself from Indochina. Ultimately, the CIA's contacts with President Nguyen Van Thieu in Saigon helped to exert direct and indirect pressure on him to accept the Paris peace accords that he had had little role in negotiating—and which provided diplomatic cover for a formal end to America's military role in the conflict in 1973.[92] After the Accords, Hanoi took two years to gather its strength, and then poured resources into a World War II–style blitzkrieg of tanks and guns. With no US air power to stop them, they conquered the South in the spring of 1975, and ensured that compliant regimes ruled in neighboring Laos and Cambodia by 1979.

Two lessons emerged from Vietnam. The Pentagon concluded that new (and increasingly computerized) systems of surveillance, targeting, and controlling forces on the battlefield could vastly increase the combat power of the world's most sophisticated military. Observers of Vietnamese strategy and tactics, however, drew the lesson that the US military could be beaten, provided sufficient manpower, weapons, and time to wear down the patience of America's civilian leadership. Both lessons would help guide the course of intelligence for the next generation.

The Rise of Terror

One, two, many Vietnams!

—Che Guevara, in his last public speech, Algiers, 1965

The Vietnam War looked grim for the Americans as early as 1965, but Cuban revolutionary Che Guevara's optimism proved fatally misplaced. Fidel had asked the Soviets and the KGB for help in spreading aid to "Communist parties and progressive movements" across Latin America, promising "an uncontrollable revolutionary storm" in three years. Moscow sent conventional arms and nuclear missiles to Cuba instead.[93] Despite Fidel's boast, the success of such revolutions outside of Indochina was by no means guaranteed, before or after their victories in Cuba and Algeria. The closest Fidel came to a satellite was far-away Chile, which did not fall to a Maoist peasant revolution but instead elected as president the Socialist Party's Salvador Allende in 1970. Chile ironically proved to be the outer limit for the clandestine efforts of both sides in the Cold War. The CIA had given $3 million

5.2 Maoism for the Americas; Che Guevara, Cuba, 1958. *Museo Che Guevara*

to Allende's centrist opponents in the 1964 presidential election, but decision makers in Washington had tried to extricate themselves from covert election operations after that.[94] President Nixon ordered the agency to intervene in the 1970 contest too late to accomplish much, and the agency's hasty dealings with Chilean officers resulted in a bungled and fatal attempt to kidnap the army chief of staff (who fellow officers saw as an obstacle to their desire to bar Allende from power).

Once in power, however, Allende proved a poor leader and an indifferent student of history. The Chilean currency collapsed, and opposition to him remained strong, subsidized by $7 million more from the CIA between 1970 and 1973.[95] As the Americans found in Vietnam, now it was Moscow's turn to learn how little covert means could help local allies. Allende's Soviet advisers pleaded with him to purge his most dangerous opponents, according to a file the KGB kept on its dealings with him: "In a cautious way Allende was made to understand the necessity of reorganizing Chile's army and intelligence services, and of setting up a relationship between Chile's and the USSR's intelligence services. Allende reacted to this positively."[96] But he did not do enough. Provoked by mounting political and economic turmoil, the Chilean army grew restive. CIA officers had heard of various coup plots—as had their KGB counterparts. Finally, one succeeded under the army's new chief of staff, General Augusto Pinochet, whom Allende had appointed to his post just three weeks earlier, and who now reversed the socialist victory and gave Chile two decades of another sort of autocracy.[97]

The result in Chile merely underlined the fact that revolution seldom worked. Even an election was no guarantee, and armed methods were not promising. Liberation insurgencies succeeded in China and Cuba and Vietnam, but could cost enormously in lives, resources, and time. Despite the fears of Western statesmen and developing world autocrats, Maoist doctrine did not export well; even little Nicaragua could and did frustrate its own insurgency for over a decade, more than once coming close to annihilating it.[98] Indeed, Fidel's attempt to export revolution to South America failed in the 1960s (costing his lieutenant Che Guevara his life at the hands of CIA-advised troops in Bolivia), though it managed to foment a permanent insurrection led by an offshoot of the Colombian Communist Party, the Revolutionary Armed Forces of Colombia (FARC).[99] Western intervention made the odds even steeper; the North Vietnamese suffered more than a million battlefield dead over two decades to win control of the South, most of them in fighting the Americans. Against Israeli control of the West Bank and Gaza and the Golan Heights, moreover, revolution from within seemed hopeless.

Thus was born in the Middle East a new tactic—what the West now calls terrorism, but which does not quite have a name that wholly fits. The idea was to weaken a strong adversary politically and create conditions for a guerrilla campaign. Where the guerrillas could not pick off isolated garrisons and liberate the countryside, they could attack the target regime's citizens in other countries. In June 1967, Israel's military had responded to a growing crisis by preemptively attacking the mobilizing forces of Syria, Egypt, and Jordan. The result was a swift victory—the Six-Day War ended with battlefield humiliation for the Arab coalition. Israel now held on to territory from its Arab neighbors in the hope of compelling their regimes to trade peace for land. But there was no peace. Soon Arabs seeking vengeance began copying the North Vietnamese rhetorically, depicting Israel as the occupier of the Palestinian homeland. Yasir Arafat's Fatah, the largest faction of the new Palestine Liberation Organization (PLO), mounted commando raids into Israel from Jordan. George Habash and his PLO faction, the Popular Front for the Liberation of Palestine (PFLP), devised another twist on this strategy, hitting Israeli targets in Western Europe and hijacking airliners bound for Israel, beginning with an El Al flight in 1968 and soon seizing trans-Atlantic flights as well. PFLP operatives spectacularly grabbed four flights almost simultaneously in September 1970 and diverted three to a remote field in Jordan, where for the benefit of the world's news media they publicized their cause before trading away their hostages and blowing up the planes.

Two strands had come together in this new Palestinian insurgency. First and oldest was the nineteenth-century anarchist tradition of dynamite terrorism, exported to the Middle East a generation earlier by Zionist and Palestinian radicals. As Camus had observed in Algeria, the earlier anarchists and socialists had shot and bombed leaders of government and industry to spread "the Propaganda of the Deed." The Maoists had bombed many more targets and used clandestine methods to harass and weary the ruling power and terrify its allies—and to carve out liberated areas from which to mount military assaults. The PLO and its rivals infused these tactics with new revolutionary theory coming out of places like Algeria, bolstered by secular pan-Arabism and the general stirrings of anticolonialism in the 1960s. The object of violence now was to polarize the population, forcing everyone to take sides for or against the revolution. Ultimately there could be only two sides—oppressed and oppressor—according to Frantz Fanon's *The Wretched of the Earth* (published in French in 1961). The oppressed were justified in resorting to violence against their oppressors, who had had to use violence to conquer them in the first place and to keep them subjugated. "The colonized world is a world divided in two," wrote Fanon; indeed, it is "inhabited by different species." The colonized feel from birth "that their cramped world, riddled with taboos, can only be challenged by out and out violence," the object of which is to "destroy the colonial world . . . burying it deep within the earth or banishing it from the territory."[100]

National liberation movements in Vietnam and Algeria had shown that the way to do so was to attack the legitimacy of the colonial administration, demonstrating that it could not defend its supporters. But something different was needed when the regime was not a colonial power but a class enemy firmly in command of the levers of power and social control.

For this, the revolution moved from the countryside back to the streets, perhaps inspired by the public relations defeat that the Vietcong inflicted on the Johnson administration by launching their Tet offensive assaults in South Vietnamese cities in early 1968. Brazilian radical Carlos Marighella, shortly before being killed by security forces in 1969, wrote a "Mini Manual for Urban Guerrillas" that explained how the strategy of polarization now applied. The guerrillas aimed to make the regime take them seriously— and for it to feel that it has "no alternative except to intensify its repression." Standard police methods can only make "life in the city unbearable," ushering in a military dictatorship, political repression, and a deployment of the armed forces to keep order. Soon the people "refuse to collaborate with the government, and the general sentiment is that this government is unjust, incapable of solving problems, and that it resorts simply to the physical liquidation of its opponents. The political situation in the country is transformed into a military situation in which the 'gorillas' appear more and more to be the ones responsible for violence, while the lives of the people grow worse."[101]

The targets of this new revolutionary impulse, by contrast, were not in the countryside but in the cities, in the heart of the regime's power; they were "the entire complex of national maintenance." Marighella listed such targets in suggesting that the regime should have to guard "all the banks, industries, armories, military barracks, prisons, public offices, radio and television stations, North American firms, gas storage tanks, oil refineries, ships, airplanes, ports, airports, hospitals, health centers, blood banks, stores, garages, embassies, residences of high-ranking members of the regime such as ministers and generals, police stations, official organizations, etc." His implication was clear: civilians caught in the crossfire were collateral damage, and their deaths resulted from the inability of the regime to keep order, or from its bumbling and vengeful reactions to the revolutionaries' assaults. By "heightening the disastrous situation" the guerrillas would eventually be able to "open rural warfare in the middle of uncontrollable urban rebellion."[102] Terrorism in the cities thus paved the way to Maoist insurgency in the countryside.

The Palestinian cause presented itself in this vein as a national liberation movement fighting an imperialist Israel. This justified not only fresh violence against civilian targets but also membership in a world struggle against imperialism. "We have formed very strong ties with the liberation movements all over the world—in Cuba, in China, in Algeria and in Vietnam," explained Arafat in 1969. "We must not forget that in a war of liberation we should make use of every source and means that will help us reach our ultimate goal—that is the liberation of our homeland."[103] The biggest group under the PLO, Arafat's Fatah, waged guerrilla war along Israel's borders, first from Jordan and later from Lebanon. The smaller groups used other tactics. The most important of these, George Habash's PFLP, took its inspiration more directly from Marxism and Che Guevara, criticizing their fellow insurgents (and implicitly Fatah) for lacking a "clear class affiliation" and a revolutionary ideology. After all, "the liberation struggle is mainly a class struggle"—and tactical alliances with reactionary states and the Arab bourgeoisie only delayed the liberation of the workers and peasants across the Middle East.[104]

No sooner had this wave of violent resistance to Israel begun than it was under assault from within and without. The anarchic tendency to quarrel over ideology dogged the Palestinian movement and gave rise to factions intent on ever more violent demonstrations of their daring and zeal. The PFLP's hijacking of airliners to Jordan in September 1970 provoked the Jordanian government to unleash its army on the Palestinians; indeed, the PFLP's continued resistance to Jordanian authority egged King Husayn to expel the PLO in a bloody, months-long campaign (many *fedayeen* went to Lebanon, where they formed another state-within-a-state and destabilized that country's fragile multiethnic society). Various splinter groups castigated Fatah and even the PFLP for their relative moderation and mounted still more attacks, like "Black September's" massacre of Israeli athletes at the Munich Olympic Games in 1972. Breakaway PFLP members worked with German self-styled urban guerrillas of the Revolutionary Cells. PFLP pupil Ilich Ramírez Sánchez—"Carlos the Jackal"—nabbed Arab oil ministers as they met in Vienna in 1975. Polarization made more enemies of the revolution than friends, but it also established the stateless bands *a la Marighella* as credible threats to the security of Westerners bound for the Middle East, of many traditional Arab regimes, and of every citizen of Israel.

Western Europe and the United States also got various doses of urban revolution. Britain suffered perhaps the worst after the Troubles arose in Northern Ireland in 1969. The old Irish Republican Army split over the strategy of whether to emphasize a political or military struggle. Its breakaway militants in the new Provisional IRA mounted a campaign of shootings and bombings in Northern Ireland beginning in 1971, indeed almost crippling the electrical power grid there before moving on to targets in England itself three years later.[105] Nations on the continent suffered as well. The Red Brigades in Italy, and in Germany the Red Army Faction and other groups, bombed and kidnapped to publicize their respective views on the revolution. The Japanese Red Army teamed with the PFLP to massacre passengers at Tel Aviv's airport in 1972. America had its Weather Underground. Though historians may debate why the years after 1968 produced so many such campaigns, the global wave of violent radicalism had two important connections to the spread of intelligence methods and expertise.

These guerrilla campaigns aimed to polarize populations and opponents ("heightening the disastrous situation"—Marighella), but rarely to kill for sake of killing. If operatives sometimes demonstrated suicidal courage, they usually did not specifically undertake suicide missions. They also needed some degree of organization, however decentralized, and they needed organic intelligence capabilities. These capabilities emphasized operational targeting and especially counterintelligence. "There is a technique of obtaining information, and the urban guerrilla must master it," Carlos Marighella explained. "Information, which is only a small segment of popular support, represents an extraordinary potential in the hands of the urban guerrilla. The creation of an intelligence service, with an organized structure, is a basic need for us. The urban guerrilla has to have vital information about the plans and movements of the enemy; where they are, how they move, the resources of their banking network, their means of communication, and the secret activities they carry out." As Lenin had found, however, a regime had its potent intelligence organs with which to counter. The danger of penetration was always present, for "the enemy encourages betrayal and infiltrates spies into the guerrilla organization." Such miscreants must be "properly punished"; indeed, "the urban guerrilla must not evade the duty—once he knows who the spy or informer is—of physically wiping him out."[106] The PIRA's in-house manual, *The Green Book*, made much the same point: "Volunteers who engage in loose talk shall be dismissed. Volunteers found guilty of treason face the death penalty."[107]

The revolutionaries also needed a quotient of arms and training from outside. The PIRA sought weapons in Libya; Scotland Yard helped to foil one such five-ton shipment in 1972, passing a tip to the Irish navy.[108] Various

Palestinian groups obtained stocks from a Soviet Union worried about losing the revolutionary mantle to Mao's China. Leaks from the KGB's archives later showed that the service provided assistance but rarely managed events or operations. For most of the 1970s, for instance, two KGB assets secretly reported from the PFLP's leadership, and more than once the Soviets provided small arms to the Front. Soviet arms also reached the Official IRA in 1972, though they probably were used mostly in clashes with the PIRA rather than in attacks on the British. The intelligence services of Moscow's Warsaw Pact allies were more openhanded. East Germany provided training, arms, and sanctuary, becoming a veritable "El Eldorado for terrorists," according to that state's last (non-Communist) interior minister in 1990.[109] Between 1970 and 1989, the Stasi trained almost 1,900 guerrillas and security officials hailing from fifteen countries (with many of the security officers doubtless former guerrillas themselves).[110] Communist material and rhetorical support to the campaigns of the IRA, the PLO, and other revolutionaries did not, however, translate into direction and control. As even their leaders would attest, once set in motion, such movements were notoriously factious and chaotic; they could act with great discipline operationally, but ideologically and organizationally they could rarely form more than passing coalitions of cells and individuals.

Responding to Terror

The nations afflicted by these campaigns counterattacked, using their intelligence services for protection and revenge. The Cold War ideological standoff ruled out a universal condemnation of terror and concerted global action against the revolutionaries. Indeed, one man's terrorist was another man's freedom fighter, ran a grim quip borrowed from Gerald Seymour's spy thriller *Harry's Game* (1975). Many member states of the United Nations General Assembly, moreover, had recently been colonies, and thus shared a certain sympathy for liberation struggles. They feted Yasir Arafat and condemned Zionism as racism in 1974, and gave Ugandan tyrant Idi Amin's call for genocide in Palestine a standing ovation the following year. The Western states did not have to fight terror all on their own—they shared plenty of leads on revolutionary groups and members—but those directly targeted by terror campaigns hesitated to lend legitimacy to their instigators by treating them as enemy combatants rather than violent criminals. This was not problematic for authoritarian regimes; Yugoslavia, for instance, dealt with troublesome exiles (many of them willing to use violence themselves) through assassinations and cunning intelligence provocations worthy of the Czar's Okhrana.[111] Western nations, however, could hardly be seen doing so. By declaring their counterterror efforts to be matters of law enforcement, moreover, they obligated themselves to apply visible standards of criminal procedure and to honor the civil liberties of even their citizens who might aid the revolutionaries. These obligations forged constraints on intelligence practices that the Western services spent years working to resolve.

Early responses to political violence and hijackings probably caused more problems than they solved. Indeed, they were likely as dangerous for hostages and bystanders as the initial incidents. This was no accident. The revolutionaries aimed to provoke overreaction: to compel the Israeli Defense Force (or the German police at the 1972 Munich Olympics) to mount hasty and bloody rescue missions, or to lash out in anger, bombing refugee camps and killing Palestinian civilians. Israel's intelligence service, the Mossad, launched Operation Wrath of God to comb Europe and the Middle East for the planners of the Olympics massacre. "I am not saying that those who were involved in Munich were not marked for death. They definitely deserved to die. But we were not dealing with the past; we concentrated on the future," explained former service chief Zvi Zamir in 2006.[112] Mossad got to several PLO operatives, but it also murdered a Moroccan waiter in Norway in a horrible case of mistaken identity; the subsequent investigation and trial crippled the service's operations in Europe. Popular demonstrations and even riots could have the same polarizing results if they ended in bloodshed. British paratroopers' shootings of unarmed Catholics during disturbances in Londonderry on Bloody Sunday, 1972—though they came after months of bombings and PIRA sniper attacks on soldiers—enhanced the PIRA's appeal and led to the suspension of local control and direct rule of Northern Ireland from London.[113] This was a militarization of the political situation practically straight from Marighella's manual. Mass internments of PIRA suspects without trial, and the intense questioning of fourteen suspects in 1971, caused a predicable outcry and prompted a European Commission on Human Rights finding that the interrogation techniques employed, while not torture per se, nonetheless amounted to "inhuman and degrading treatment."[114] An official British investigation of the interrogations conceded that any such official misconduct "defers the day of the return of peace in the community. It strengthens the propaganda campaign and provides ammunition for the enemies of society who are adept and experienced in inventing allegations against the police, even without any justification. We have seen evidence which establishes that this is their declared purpose."[115]

The militarization of intelligence was not a full response—it needed strategic and civilian intelligence support. The national intelligence agencies built for the Cold War, however, were slow to react. Intelligence in Northern Ireland was the province of the Royal Ulster Constabulary (RUC) and then the British Army. The RUC, of course, had little credibility among local Catholics who feared it favored their loyalist and Protestant neighbors—some of whom were quite capable of their own brand of terrorism.[116] For a time MI5 had but two harried desk officers following the Troubles, one of them being Stella Rimington (who would become the service's first female chief). She later noted that visitors to their nook in the head office were "faced with two disheveled-looking women, one chattering like a parrot and the other [herself] peering squirrel-like from behind a tottering pile of paper."[117] Military intelligence officers in the Irish Republic, moreover, knew little about what was happening in Northern Ireland besides what they read in the press; Irish historian Eunan O'Halpin notes the place "might as well have been North Korea, so sparse was the reliable information available."[118] His comparison was apt on more than one level. The countries behind the Iron Curtain observed a certain etiquette regarding adversarial intelligence operations; they rarely tortured or killed foreign case officers caught *in flagrante*. Police and army methods of intelligence gathering against terrorist targets, by contrast, could be fatal. For example, the Four Square Laundry, a legitimate (and cheap) cleaning service in Catholic neighborhoods that was secretly operated by the British Army for months to test the washing for traces of weapons, had its delivery truck ambushed by the PIRA soon after the Provos wrung a confession from an informer in their ranks.[119] The unwritten niceties of espionage carried even less weight for the PFLP and other offshoots of the PLO.

Once engaged, however, national services provided vital collection and organizational assistance to police and military intelligence work.[120] By 1977, the PIRA's insurgency had passed its peak and London felt confident enough to relinquish army control of the Northern Ireland security situation to the Royal Ulster Constabulary's Special Branch. SIS and the Security

Service together established and manned an Irish Joint Section in the early 1970s with offices in Belfast and London, and MI5 also concluded (again) that liaison with foreign intelligence services on terrorism was essential to tracking such highly mobile suspects and operations.[121] The army and RUC pooled intelligence and leads at a central point and jointly decided how to act on them, and the appointment of retired SIS chief Maurice Oldfield to coordinate information improved matters as well. Greater surveillance of the borders, public places, and suspects also helped.[122] The key aspect of this surveillance, however, was the running of informants inside the PIRA and other radical organizations. Much speculation has ensued, particularly around the alleged confession of one Freddie Scappaticci to having been both an internal security officer for the PIRA and a longtime informant that the British Army called "Stakeknife." The Security Service's official historian in 2009 would say only that because of "the guarantee given to Security Service and SIS agents that their identities will be kept secret indefinitely, all information about them remains classified."[123]

The Israelis, having pioneered special operations against terrorists, made rapid improvement. The secret lay in dedicated units, drilling relentlessly in commando tactics. The Israeli army's Sayeret Matkal pulled off perhaps the most spectacular rescue mission in 1976, after a breakaway faction of the PFLP together with a team from the (West German) Revolutionary Cells hijacked an Air France flight to Idi Amin's Uganda. A hundred Israeli commandos flew 2,500 miles, fought a pitched battle with the hijackers and Ugandan soldiers, and rescued almost all the passengers—while losing only one man of their own. West Germany had made similar arrangements after the Munich disaster, forming a special unit of their federal police, GSG 9. The outfit succeeded spectacularly in Mogadishu in 1977, rescuing all eighty-six passengers from a Lufthansa flight hijacked by the PFLP. Britain's Special Air Service stormed the Iranian embassy in London three years later, freeing all but one of the hostages still held by Arab separatists. Such operations were as much intelligence as military successes, for they reflected well on the abilities of the Israeli, German, and British services to amass and speedily provide the quantities of tactical details essential for mission planning and execution.[124] They also made it clear that Western special forces were more than a match for hostage takers, prompting a change in terrorist tactics toward an even greater emphasis on shootings and bombings.

Americans had felt this new wave of terror less directly, though they were not completely safe. The United States had its own Marighella-inspired urban guerrillas in the Weather Underground, which was penetrated early by the FBI, and which killed mostly its own members in premature explosions. A bureau informant attended a living room seminar for the Weathermen's Detroit cell in February 1970, and recalled one of the leaders of the movement, Bill Ayers, "conducting a session to reiterate what we should and shouldn't do now that we were an underground organization. Much of the material he was covering came from the *Mini-manual of the Urban Guerrilla* and from [Regis Debray's] *Revolution in the Revolution*. As we walked in, Ayers was giving tips for survival. He was covering the major danger facing all of us, pig spies. Their only punishment should be death. This would discourage others from trying to infiltrate our groups. Statements like that never helped my nervous system."[125] Washington for a time could deal with terrorism abroad through its CIA station chiefs and their foreign hosts. The agency's man in Jordan, with his ties to the Jordanian throne and army, came close to being assassinated by PLO hotheads in 1970. Ironically, his colleague in Beirut was simultaneously in contact with Yasir Arafat's intelligence chief; the CIA worked assiduously to gather information from all sides, and to interpret American policy to them as well.[126] As in Vietnam, whether the foreign contacts heard the messages Washington wished to transmit was an open question.

Agency officers were sometimes targets; Greece's Revolutionary Organization 17 November terrorist group murdered the CIA station chief in Athens in 1975. President Nixon had ordered his intelligence agencies, stovepiped as they were in foreign and domestic channels since the National Security Act of 1947, to share information and coordinate action on terror, but the agencies showed little innovation in response. When the Americans became directly involved, however, such methods did not suffice, and new ones had to be improvised from European and Israeli models, resulting in a humiliating failure in the Iranian desert in 1980, when special forces tried to rescue hostages from the occupied American embassy in Tehran.

Terror proved a two-edged sword for its practitioners, who adopted intelligence methods devised by states to fight the originators of terror. Their tactics alienated many in the West, and they stirred up rebellious apprentices—it is likely more terrorists were killed by other terrorists than by law enforcement or commandos. In response, nations of the West were forced to learn new intelligence methods. But if the Jordanian monarchy was at risk from a PLO coup in 1970, no Western state was seriously endangered by terror. Inside the West there was somewhat more cooperation between intelligence and law enforcement in response—and with it the potential for great controversy, as it risked criminalizing Western citizens for their thoughts, or their ethnicity. This forced back on the West the dilemma of violence and legitimacy, and made accurate *and* ethical intelligence all the more valuable.

Intelligence and Liberal Ideals

The dilemmas of fighting insurgencies and terrorism nearly toppled the French republic in the early 1960s and began roiling the domestic politics of the United States a few years later. Soon such controversies would precipitate events that transformed the governance of America's intelligence community and establish precedents for every other democracy running a substantial intelligence establishment. One event in particular illustrated the sea change. In 1974 a new government in Lisbon decided it could no longer hold onto Portugal's African colonies of Guinea, Mozambique, and Angola, where the Portuguese had had a presence for three centuries. Lisbon's attempts to broker a power-sharing deal for Angola's rival factions failed, and by independence in November 1975, a civil war was well under way. Washington feared a Soviet-inspired coup. Moscow feared the Americans, the South Africans, or even the Chinese would capitalize on the situation, and Havana saw its opportunity. The Americans that summer had launched a CIA-run covert action to arm and assist the non-Communist factions, seeking to mount an insurgency of its own like the one it ran against the North Vietnamese in Laos. When events seemed to be running against the Marxists, however, Fidel Castro pulled the Soviets along in his wake and hurried in thousands of Cuban troops (on Soviet aircraft) to turn the tide of battle. The CIA's program, moreover, had been thoroughly briefed to Congress, thanks to a new legal requirement for covert action funding passed just months earlier. Congress refused to provide more funds, and its refusal leaked to the press. In June 1976, they formalized Congress's ban by passing a law prohibiting covert aid to the Angolan rebels.[127]

Thus for perhaps the first time a legislature had not only intervened to stop an intelligence operation but actively banned it to boot. Congress's action stemmed from the difficulty of building consensus around secret operations to oppose the spread of revolution in the developing world. After a decade of war in Southeast Asia and 58,000 American dead, even the United States' most ardent anti-Communists had little desire for another intervention in a revolutionary insurgency. The foreign policy consensus that had lasted for a generation had thus cracked over how to fight the Cold War. Some policymakers and experts still endorsed the "domino theory" espoused by President Eisenhower in the 1950s; he had argued that American tolerance of Communist North Vietnam's aggression would allow all of Indochina to fall to the Reds, and thus endanger neighboring lands like Malaya, Thailand, and Indonesia. Critics countered in the 1960s that preventing a North Vietnamese victory was not worth the possibility of overextending America's limited strategic power—which was better focused on Europe and Latin America—and that the budding "detente" with Moscow proved that world communism was no longer on the march. On the Left, though the United States had no revolutionary movement of its own, it did have precincts that combined traditional isolationism with progressivism to argue that the country should promote social justice and civil rights at home instead of venturing overseas in quest of foreign monsters (and markets). The arguments between and among these factions, moreover, took on added volume and drama over the issue of conscription, as the draft pulled in hundreds of thousands of young American men for the war in Southeast Asia.

Even before this point, arguments over foreign policies had begun to constrain intelligence activities on both sides of the Atlantic. Protests by the nongovernmental watchdog Amnesty International over British army-led interrogations in Aden prompted an inquiry and restrictions on the questioning of detainees; when those procedures were ignored in Northern Ireland in 1971, the *Sunday Times* soon exposed the abuses and sparked an international outcry.[128] Debates over Cold War policies had similar effects in the United States. Director J. Edgar Hoover's public spat with former Attorney General Robert Kennedy over the authorization of wiretaps during the term of the late President Kennedy had led him to scale back some of the bureau's more aggressive collection efforts.[129] Even the CIA felt the winds of change. A long-running covert action blew up in the agency's face in 1967 when antiwar American college students whom the agency had long asked to pass money to their foreign counterparts loudly repudiated the CIA. Media coverage of the resulting *Ramparts* flap (after the New Left magazine that broke the story) not only exposed the covert action funding network that CIA had built up in the United States, but it also led the agency to impose sharp limits on its use of Americans in operations abroad. "We are now in a different ballgame," the CIA's operations director cabled his stations. "Some of the basic ground rules have changed. When in doubt, ask [headquarters]."[130] In these and other ways the legislators, the media, and the public pushed back against policy assumptions and security restrictions that had been in place almost since the war emergency in 1940.

A wave of revelations by intelligence insiders added facts and rumors to the growing curiosity and controversy over intelligence. Apart from a sensational (and long-unsolved) burglary of the FBI's office in Media, Pennsylvania in 1971, these revelations came from two directions: disgruntled and sometimes radicalized former employees, and World War II veterans hoping to tell their stories at last. Though their motivations were poles apart, the results were equally appalling to intelligence and security services on both sides of the Atlantic. Kim Philby's memoir *My Silent War* (1968) was the prototype; Philby wrote it during his Moscow exile, and he slyly caricatured both British and American intelligence efforts. A former CIA officer, Victor Marchetti, though not a traitor like Philby, published an unsanctioned account of the agency and saw his royalties garnished by the federal government.[131] Another, Philip Agee, linked up with Cuban intelligence (after the KGB turned him away as a *provocation*) and from London published his own memoir, which named 250 reputed CIA officers working in Latin America.[132] He also lent his new-found fame to a scandal sheet titled *Covert Action Information Bulletin,* which speculated about the CIA affiliations of US officials posted in Europe and Africa.[133]

By coincidence, these and other accounts emerged alongside pathbreaking books published by British authors. Intelligence revelations from World War II had a long past; the fact that the United States had broken Japanese diplomatic codes came out in Congress's Pearl Harbor hearings just weeks after Japan surrendered, for instance, and photointerpreter Constance Babington-Smith had explained in detail the workings of wartime British imagery intelligence in 1957.[134] But she and other authors had steered clear of Ultra, which London indeed worked assiduously for decades to keep secret.[135] F. W. Winterbotham's 1974 book *The Ultra Secret* changed that forever. Winterbotham had delivered the precious wartime intercepts to Churchill, and his account could not be denied or hushed.[136] Along with

J. C. Masterman's first-hand account of the Double Cross system (published two years earlier in the United States to stay beyond the reach of the Official Secrets Act), *The Ultra Secret* caused a wholesale rewriting of the military history of the Second World War.[137] In Britain, that rewriting ultimately led to a magisterial, official history of British intelligence in the conflict.[138]

When the Watergate scandal caused President Nixon's resignation in 1974, Congress and the media were thus primed for new revelations about government corruption and intelligence operations. Indeed, the season of scandals prepared the public for Congress to assert its influence over presidential war powers—and over intelligence. Congress's power of the purse had always given some degree of oversight of the Intelligence Community in the House and Senate appropriations committees, but that had been exercised quietly and leniently, and proposals to create public oversight had been rebuffed by Republican and Democratic presidents for two decades. This began changing with an amendment to foreign aid legislation in late 1974. Revelations of the 1970 covert action in Chile prompted bills to ban such operations altogether, but cooler heads prevailed on Capitol Hill and compromise legislation passed instead at the end of the year. Informally dubbed the Hughes-Ryan Amendment, this adjustment required the president, as a condition for receiving funds for a proposed covert action, to "find" that the operation comported with the national interest, and to have his finding briefed (in camera, of course) to no fewer than six congressional committees.[139] President Gerald Ford complained, but as Richard Nixon's unelected successor, facing a Democratic Congress recently energized by gains in midterm elections, he had no political clout to sustain a veto. Arguments over how to fight the Cold War had thus reached the CIA itself, as Hughes-Ryan had the effect of adding not only congressional but also partisan scrutiny of a favorite presidential tool of Cold War diplomacy. Within months that scrutiny, empowered by Hughes-Ryan, had ended the covert action in Angola.

President Ford by then had bigger problems on the intelligence front. News about CIA spying on the anti–Vietnam war movement and about Kennedy-era attempts to assassinate developing world leaders like Fidel Castro exploded in early 1975. Members of Congress demanded access to executive branch officials and documents, and though Ford tried to forestall such probes by appointing his own blue-ribbon panel of inquiry, he soon acceded to congressional and media pressure. The quick result was not one but two special investigating committees, operating simultaneously with separate staffs and marching orders. The House's inquiry was poorly managed and staffed, and proved inconsequential (though its draft report leaked to the press in 1976).[140] The Senate's probe, by contrast, would have real influence. Chairman Senator Frank Church (a Democrat from Idaho) came across as a hanging judge with his early quip that the CIA "may have been behaving like a rogue elephant on the rampage."[141] Despite such missteps, the committee hired a top-flight staff and persuaded officials like DCI William Colby (who feared "cheap TV theatrics at the expense of the CIA's secrets") to testify in open session.[142] Church Committee staffers also had access to still-classified historical documentation, including sensitive FBI files left by the late J. Edgar Hoover, in-house histories of the CIA, and the "Family Jewels," a 693-page compendium of real and suspected CIA wrongdoing that Colby had compiled at the first dam break in the Watergate scandal two years earlier.

The Church Committee's findings supercharged the debate over intelligence in the United States. They covered over thirty years of Cold War intelligence activities at the FBI, CIA, NSA, and the US Army. Compressed into a single report, their cumulative effect proved shocking. "Too many people have been spied upon by too many Government agencies," concluded the report's authors. Various misdeeds that the Church Committee and simultaneous investigations unveiled retain their power to appall even today, like the CIA's ad hoc testing of LSD on anonymous and unsuspecting American citizens (Project MKULTRA), and Director Hoover's retailing of salacious rumors about civil rights martyr Martin Luther King in the early 1960s.[143] Ironically, Hoover at the very same time had been using FBI informants to smash the thuggish Ku Klux Klan in the Deep South—his vendetta against King was not racist but personal.[144] A few of the Intelligence Community's misdeeds perhaps made sense when they began. The warrantless reading of telegrams and mail between the United States and the Soviet Union at the outset of the Cold War, for instance, seemed logical but had morphed into long-running but marginal programs with no statutory basis or oversight.[145] Some just looked foolish, like proposals to kill a scuba-diving Fidel Castro with an exploding seashell—or at least to make his beard fall out.

Notwithstanding the revelations, however, the actual effect of the Church Committee proved more moderate, and lasting. Its report repudiated its own chairman's quip that the CIA had become a "rogue elephant"—"The

CIA, in broad terms, is not 'out of control.'" His committee instead commended the overall efforts of the Intelligence Community, and tacitly endorsed even covert action as a regrettable necessity.[146] Divided government had thus led to united control of intelligence, a paradox instantiated by the new resolve in both houses of Congress to establish standing committees to oversee intelligence matters. By virtue of the centripetal force of funding authorizations, moreover, these committees would gradually exert a reforming and centralizing influence on the Intelligence Community. Indeed, the Church Committee implicitly endorsed the main findings of the then-classified Schlesinger Report (1971), and though it stopped short of recommending a Director of National Intelligence, the committee helped turn the debates over intelligence toward stronger central management and direction of programs and funding.[147] The scandalous revelations of domestic misconduct also prompted the FBI to shutter its intelligence division and return (via a new set of guidelines from Attorney General Edward Levi) to its 1924 mandate to investigate federal crimes, and not mere hunches or suggestions from the bureau's political masters. Congress furthermore passed a statute—the Foreign Intelligence Surveillance Act—to finally give rigor and regularity to the use of wiretaps for intelligence in the United States.

The "Time of Troubles" for the Intelligence Community also had a subtle but powerful effect on intelligence scholarship in the English-speaking world. As an academic field, intelligence studies dates from this time. There had been serious work done earlier; a few scholars like Sherman Kent, Harry Howe Ransom, and Roberta Wohlstetter had written on intelligence analysis and organization, and historians like David Kahn and Barbara Tuchman had preserved the intelligence revolution of World War I before living memory faded forever. The real flowering of scholarship, however, came with the escape of the Ultra secret in 1974 and the publication of the Church Committee's eight-volume report two years later. These provided a reliable timeline for the US intelligence system, and they alerted researchers to the importance of the Allies' overall intelligence dominance in World War II. Service on the Church Committee staff, moreover, equipped several scholars (such as Richard Betts, Gregory Treverton, and Loch Johnson, some of them in a loose "Consortium for the Study of Intelligence" formed in 1979) to lead the burgeoning intelligence studies field. As the field expanded on both sides of the Atlantic in the 1980s, academics in America, Canada, and Britain realized they had findings to share. Thus began a fruitful collaboration and cross-national comparison of intelligence experiences that continues to this day.

Openness had one distinct drawback for intelligence, at least in the United States. Fearful forecasts about a premature end to America's ability to collect and keep secrets did not materialize, but the fact that intelligence judgments could be discussed more easily in public nonetheless had already created powerful incentives for lawmakers to cite assessments in order to criticize White House policies. In 1969, for instance, Senator J. William Fulbright complained that what DCI Richard Helms had recently told him in closed session about new Soviet missiles "sure didn't sound like what the Secretary of Defense [Melvin Laird] has been saying." Fulbright and allied senators a few weeks later publicly grilled the secretary and other administration witnesses on the differences between their views and a recent national intelligence estimate. Laird did his best to defend administration policies, but Fulbright's charge could not be refuted in open session without declassifying the estimate in question—and thereby exposing sensitive sources and methods.[148] This confrontation offered a foretaste of things to come. Debates over arms control intelligence indeed highlighted the argument in the United States (and by extension in NATO) over how to deal with the Soviets. Data from missile dimensions and telemetry could not speak for themselves. Any interpretation of their significance could have policy implications, as it could be portrayed as supporting (or undermining) mutually exclusive perceptions of Soviet motivations and behavior. This dilemma perhaps inevitably affected the Intelligence Community analysts themselves in time. The stakes in this policy argument in Washington seemed to be no less than the life and death of the planet, which made the debate a bitter one, complete with insinuations of bad faith by analysts, policymakers, and observers in Congress and the media.

Even the Ford administration's attempt to surmount such controversies through an exercise in competitive analysis fell victim to the mutual suspicions stirred by the public use of intelligence to defend (or critique) arms control and nuclear modernization policies. DCI George H. W. Bush in 1976 established two teams of analysts to review the intelligence on Soviet strategic intentions and capabilities—over which the Intelligence Community's analysts themselves were arguing. One, dubbed "Team A," comprised community officers drafting and coordinating the latest national intelligence estimate on Soviet strategic objectives (soon to be issued as NIE 11-3/8-76), who completed their assignment according to standard estimative practices.[149] Team B, on the other hand, drew from universities and think tanks and took a divergent view of the problem itself, arguing that Moscow's revolutionary motivations were not mere rhetoric and thus had to factor into any assessment of Soviet strategic policy. Views of the Team A-Team B exercise then and now have tended to vary widely. Some observers have seen it as a salutary experiment that improved the quality of the community's analysis, or at least did no harm.[150] Others complained that the very idea behind the exercise demonstrated a partisan desire to bend intelligence to support more aggressive policies toward the Soviets, and contended its implementation subtly adulterated the community's objectivity by signaling to analysts what their political masters wished to hear.[151]

In a crucial respect, the changes in American intelligence in the 1970s did not improve it. The Intelligence Community received no gift of prescience, and thus in 1978 its analysts missed a momentous change in faraway Iran, which since 1953 had been a usually helpful partner for US collection efforts against the Soviets. The Shah, whose throne the CIA had saved a generation earlier, abdicated in the face of growing protests, and into the vacuum stepped the Ayatollah Ruhollah Khomeini, fresh from his Paris exile and determined to transform utterly Iran's society and relations with its neighbors. This was not supposed to happen—the Middle Ages were long over, vanquished by Enlightenment thinkers like Locke and Rousseau, and religion was not a driving ideology of social change. Such assumptions proved mistaken. Analysis had failed, but before the Iranian revolution no one was listening anyway. "We could not give away intelligence on Iran before the crisis," quipped one CIA analyst.[152] Indeed, events in Iran surprised observers in Moscow and the world over as much they did analysts and policymakers in Washington.[153] Responses to the shock would drive events on both sides of the Iron Curtain, and across the Islamic lands, transforming intelligence and the world.

Conclusion

The character and methods of Josef Stalin overshadowed the development of intelligence around the world for a generation after his death in 1953. In Europe, the fear that Soviet armies or subversion would march westward prompted the Western powers to counter the Soviet prowess at "psychological warfare." For the new Intelligence Community in America, this meant establishing a permanent covert action infrastructure that could also be employed in the developing world. In Asia, Mao Zedong admired and imitated Stalin, and bitterly contested the leadership of the world progressive movement after Stalin's heirs criticized the master's legacy. That Sino-Soviet struggle over the revolutionary mantle would cause massive collateral damage in the developing world, spreading modern arms and intelligence methods to autocrats of all sorts, and enabling new forms of terror that sought not only to kill reactionary elites but to polarize societies through atrocities against civilians. Western intelligence responses to these incidents and trends caused plenty of damage themselves—not least to liberal ideals at home, and to the security consensus that had briefly marked Western politics and diplomacy at the start of the Cold War. Intelligence in the West would thus be scrutinized as never before.

The resulting revolution in intelligence governance for a few years remained a mostly American story; events in Washington would be watched with fascination and horror by other intelligence services around the world. Soon those events would indirectly influence those services as well. They came at a moment of doubt and indecision on both sides of the Iron Curtain. The tide of history, at least in the developing world, seemed to be running Moscow's way, with victories in Indochina, Africa, and soon even Latin America. Mao had died in 1976, and China had once again turned inward as the party debated its legacy and chose his heirs. The liberal West looked beset economically by inflation and slow growth, and politically by Eurocommunism at the ballot box and terrorists in the streets. And yet appearances can and did deceive. The West was stronger than it looked, while the Communist world was weaker. In ten years the long argument between progressive and liberal ideals would seem decisively settled in the latter's favor. Western intelligence systems would share in and assist this victory, turning new technological innovations from ideas into reality in ways that the East could not match. At the same time, however, the diffusion of modern intelligence methods to smaller states and stateless revolutionaries, which accelerated during the Cold War, would spread to the Islamic world as well, creating a challenge to every intelligence service.

Notes

1. Quoted in Ted Morgan, *A Covert Life: Jay Lovestone—Communist, Anti-Communist, and Spymaster* (New York: Random House, 1999), 178.
2. Vojtech Mastny, *The Cold War and Soviet Insecurity: The Stalin Years* (New York: Oxford University Press, 1996), 30, 32–34.
3. Morgan, *A Covert Life*, 179.
4. Richard J. Aldrich, *The Hidden Hand: Britain, America, and Cold War Secret Intelligence* (London: John Murray, 2001), 122–41, 443–63. See also Linda Risso, "A Difficult Compromise: British and American Plans for a Common Anti-Communist Propaganda Response in Western Europe, 1948–1958," *Intelligence and National Security* 26:2–3 (April–June 2011): 331, 336, 353.
5. National Security Council, "Psychological Operations," NSC 4–A, December 17, 1947, reprinted in Department of State, *Foreign Relations of the United States, 1945–1950, Emergence of the Intelligence Establishment* (Washington, DC: Government Printing Office, 1996), 644.
6. William Colby, who served as a case officer in Italy in the mid-1950s and rose to become Director of Central Intelligence, says the operations continued for over a decade; William Colby and Peter Forbath, *Honorable Men: My Life in the CIA* (New York: Simon & Schuster, 1978), 109, 114–20.
7. Michael Warner, "The CIA's Office of Policy Coordination: From NSC 10/2 to NSC 68," *International Journal of Intelligence and Counterintelligence* 11 (Summer 1998): 212–15.
8. Peter Grose, *Operation Rollback: America's Secret War behind the Iron Curtain* (Boston: Houghton Mifflin, 2000), 171–85.
9. Thomas Powers, *Intelligence Wars: American Secret History from Hitler to al-Qaeda* (New York: New York Review of Books expanded edition, 2004), 306.
10. The sobriquet "Mighty Wurlitzer" came from the head of OPC, Frank Wisner, who compared its projects to a big theater organ capable of playing a great variety of sounds and tunes; see Hugh Wilford, *The Mighty Wurlitzer: How the CIA Played America* (Cambridge, MA: Harvard University Press, 2008), 7.
11. A. Ross Johnson, *Radio Free Europe and Radio Liberty: The CIA Years and Beyond* (Palo Alto: Stanford University Press, 2010). Colby and Forbath, *Honorable Men*, 301, 468.
12. Office of Policy Coordination [probably drafted by Tom Braden], "Meeting at Mr. Barrett's Home on Tuesday Evening, November 20, 1951 to discuss USIE and OPC Relationships," November 23, 1951, reprinted in Department of State, *Foreign Relations of the United States, 1950–1955, The Intelligence Community* (Washington, DC: Government Printing Office, 2007), Document 94.
13. The quote comes from RFE's 1951 policy handbook; Johanna Granville, "'Caught with Jam on Our Fingers': Radio Free Europe and the Hungarian Revolution in 1956," *Diplomatic History* 29:5 (2005): 822.
14. Psychological Strategy Board, "Status Report on the National Psychological Effort and First Progress Report of the Psychological Strategy Board," PSB

D-30, August 1, 1952, reprinted in Department of State, *The Intelligence Community*, Document 125.

15. Granville, "Caught with Jam on Our Fingers," 819–22.

16. "Meeting at Mr. Barrett's Home on Tuesday Evening, November 20, 1951 to discuss USIE and OPC Relationships." Barrett later reduced the figure to $1.5 billion in public; see his *Truth Is Our Weapon* (Funk & Wagnalls, 1953), 188.

17. Anne Karalekas cited these figures in a history of the CIA that she prepared for the US Senate's Select Committee to Study Governmental Operations with Respect to Intelligence Activities (often called simply the "Church Committee," 94th Congress, 1st Session, 1976); her 1976 history is Book IV, *Supplementary Detailed Staff Reports on Foreign and Military Intelligence*, 31–32; accessed March 26, 2012, at www.aarclibrary.org/publib/contents/church/contents _church_reports_book4.htm. For the OSS comparison, see Michael Warner, *The Office of Strategic Services: America's First Intelligence Agency* (Washington, DC: Central Intelligence Agency, 2000), 9.

18. [no author], "Staff Conference" [Minutes of the DCI's staff meeting], October 22, 1951, reprinted in Michael Warner, ed., *The CIA under Harry Truman* (Washington, DC: Central Intelligence Agency, 1994), 436.

19. Morgan, *A Covert Life*, 219–23.

20. Thomas W. Braden, "I'm Glad the CIA Is 'Immoral,'" *Saturday Evening Post*, May 20, 1967, 14.

21. Cited in Michael Warner, "Sophisticated Spies: CIA's Links to Liberal Anti-Communists, 1949–1967," *International Journal of Intelligence and Counterintelligence* 9 (Winter 1996/97): 428.

22. J. Patrick Coyne to McGeorge Bundy, Special Assistant for National Security Affairs, May 1961, John F. Kennedy Library, President's Office Files, Series 7, Department and Agencies, Foreign Intelligence Advisory Board, Box 94, Briefing Material 5/61, 13. This document contains the "Bruce-Lovett Report" to President Eisenhower; it was accessed March 26, 2012, at www.foia.cia.gov/ helms.asp.

23. Granville, "Caught with Jam on Our Fingers," 821.

24. Khrushchev, *Khrushchev Remembers*, 351.

25. Ibid., 416.

26. Granville, "Caught with Jam on Our Fingers," 833.

27. Khrushchev, *Khrushchev Remembers*, 429.

28. Alistair Horne, *A Savage War of Peace: Algeria, 1954–1962* (New York: Viking, 1977), 446; *Izvestia* ran its piece on April 25, 1961.

29. The Stasi kept an archive of Nazi-era files for this purpose; see Christopher Andrew and Vasili Mitrokhin, *The Mitrokhin Archive: The KGB in Europe and the West* (London: Penguin, 1999), 573–74.

30. Andrew and Mitrokhin, *The Mitrokhin Archive*, 306–7. Kim Philby, *My Silent War* (London: Granada, 1980 [1969]), 139–40, 164.

31. Ibid., 295–97; Andrew and Mitrokhin argue that KGB files attribute the insinuation to the efforts of KGB agent Carl Marzani, a former OSS employee who was once convicted of lying to investigators about his party membership.

32. Max Holland, "The Lie That Linked CIA to the Kennedy Assassination," *Studies in Intelligence* (Fall/Winter 2001); accessed January 8, 2012, at www.cia.gov/library/center-for-the-study-of-intelligence/kent-csi/vol45no5/html/v45i5a02p.htm#rft0. *Paese Sera* was founded by the Italian Communist Party and subsidized by the KGB as late as the 1980s; Andrew and Mitrokhin, *The Mitrokhin Archive*, 390.

33. William J. Holden, "Soviet Says West Incited Hungary: Approval of Rebel Plans by 'High U.S. Circles' Alleged," *New York Times*, November 9, 1956, 14.

34. Granville, "Caught with Jam on Our Fingers," 839.

35. "Radio Free Europe Accused by Rebels," *New York Times*, November 20, 1956, 29. For the effect on CIA's Frank Wisner, see Evan Thomas, *The Very Best Men: Four Who Dared—Early Years of the CIA* (New York: Simon & Schuster, 1995), 146–48.

36. The remark by Foy Kohler was paraphrased in "Meeting at Mr. Barrett's Home on Tuesday Evening, November 20, 1951 to discuss USIE and OPC Relationships," Department of State, *The Intelligence Community*, 217.

37. "Minutes of the Meeting of the 303 Committee, 22 August 1967," Memorandum for the Record, August 22, 1967; along with this minute is a relevant extract from the background paper noted above, and both are quoted in Department of State, *Foreign Relations of the United States, 1964–1967*, vol. 12, *Western Europe* (Washington, DC: Government Printing Office, 2001), Document 133.

38. Hoover Institution, "Cold War Broadcasting Impact: Report on a Conference Organized by the Hoover Institution and the Cold War International History Project of the Woodrow Wilson International Center for Scholars at Stanford University, October 13–16, 2004"; accessed January 7, 2012, at media.hoover.org/documents/broadcast_conf_rpt.pdf.

39. Adam Watson was Britain's psychological warfare liaison in Washington in 1950; he is quoted in Aldrich, *The Hidden Hand*, 513.

40. Keith Jeffery, *The Secret History of MI6: 1909–1949* (New York: Penguin, 2010), 698–702; Nicholas Dujmovic, "Extraordinary Fidelity: Two CIA Prisoners in China, 1952–73," *Studies in Intelligence* 50:4 (2006): 21–36; accessed March 26, 2012, at www.cia.gov/library/center-for-the-study-of-intelligence/csi-publications/csi-studies/studies/vol50no4/two-cia-prisoners-in-china-1952201373.html.

41. Christopher Andrew and Vasili Mitrokhin, *The World Was Going Our Way: The KGB and the Battle for the Third World* (New York: Basic Books, 2005), 271.

42. Central Intelligence Agency, Special Research Staff, "Communist China: The Political Security Apparatus," part II, "Destruction and Reconstruction, 1965–1969," published as part of the "Polo" series, November 28, 1969; accessed February 10, 2012, at www.foia.cia.gov/CPE/POLO/.

43. Thomas L. Ahern Jr., *CIA and the House of Ngo: Covert Action in South Vietnam, 1954–63* (Washington, DC: Central Intelligence Agency, 2000), 15; accessed February 12, 2012, at www.foia.cia.gov/vietnam.asp.

44. Matthew Jones, "Intelligence and Counterinsurgency: The Malayan Experience," in Robert Dover and Michael S. Goodman, eds., *Learning from the Secret Past: Cases in British Intelligence History* (Washington, DC: Georgetown University Press, 2011), 135–54; the quote is from John P. Morton, p. 149.

45. Christopher E. Goscha, "Intelligence in a Time of Decolonization: The Case of the Democratic Republic of Vietnam at War (1945–50)," *Intelligence and National Security* 22:1 (February 2007): 106–7. Robert J. Hanyok, *Spartans in Darkness: American SIGINT and the Indochina War, 1945–1975* (Ft. Meade, MD: National Security Agency, 2002), 371; accessed March 26, 2012, at www .fas.org/irp/nsa/spartans/index.html.

46. Merle L. Pribbenow, "The Man in the Snow White Cell," *Studies in Intelligence* 48:1 (2004): 60.

47. Goscha, "Intelligence in a Time of Decolonization," 104–5, 126–27.

48. Thomas L. Ahern Jr., *CIA and Rural Pacification* (Washington, DC: Central Intelligence Agency, 2001), 404; Ahern argues Diem retained his independence but the agency was never far away with advice in Saigon. Accessed September 6, 2009, at www.foia.cia.gov/vietnam.asp.

49. Ahern, *CIA and Rural Pacification*, 404.

50. Ahern, *CIA and the House of Ngo*, 115.

51. Martin Thomas, *Empires of Intelligence: Security Services and Colonial Disorder after 1914* (Berkeley: University of California Press, 2007), 244–56.

52. "German Chancellor Adolf Hitler and Grand Mufti Haj Amin al-Husseini: Zionism and the Arab Cause (November 28, 1941)," in Walter Laqueur and Barry Rubin, eds., *The Arab-Israeli Reader: A Documentary History of the Middle East Conflict*, 6th ed., 52 (New York: Penguin, 2001).

53. Jeffery, *The Secret History of MI6*, 692.

54. Christopher Andrew, *Defend the Realm: The Authorized History of MI5* (New York: Alfred A. Knopf, 2009), 353–57.

55. Horne, *A Savage War of Peace*, 78, 119.

56. Khrushchev, *Khrushchev Remembers,* 470–74.

57. Albert Camus, *Algerian Chronicles* (Cambridge, MA: Harvard University Press, 2013 [1958]), 27.

58. Horne, *A Savage War of Peace*, 190–207, 326–28, 412–13.

59. Donald Wilber, "Overthrow of Premier Mossadeq of Iran, November 1952-August 1953," CIA Clandestine Service History, March 1954; accessed April 27, 2013, at www.gwu.edu/~nsarchiv/NSAEBB/NSAEBB28/. Nicholas Cullather, *Secret History: The C.I.A.'s Classified Account of Its Operations in Guatemala, 1952–1954* (Palo Alto, CA: Stanford University Press, 1999).

60. Church Committee, Book IV, *Supplementary Detailed Staff Reports on Foreign and Military Intelligence*, 32, 49.

61. Khrushchev, *Khrushchev Remembers*, 470–74.

62. Byron and Pack, *The Claws of the Dragon*, 252; Andrew and Mitrokhin, *The World Was Going Our Way*, 272–75.

63. Aleksandr Fursenko and Timothy Naftali, *"One Hell of a Gamble": Khrushchev, Castro, Kennedy, and the Cuban Missile Crisis, 1958–1964* (New York: Norton, 1997), 49–52.

64. Michael Warner, "The CIA's Internal Probe of the Bay of Pigs Affair," *Studies in Intelligence* 42 (1998): 99.

65. Hugh Thomas, *The Cuban Revolution* (New York: Harper & Row, 1977), 593; Fursenko and Naftali, *"One Hell of a Gamble,"* 99.

66. Hanyok, *Spartans in Darkness*, 105, 465. See also Thomas L. Ahern Jr., *CIA and the Generals: Covert Support to Military Government in South Vietnam* (Washington, DC: Central Intelligence Agency, 1998), 231; accessed September 6, 2009, at www.foia.cia.gov/vietnam.asp.

67. Khrushchev, *Khrushchev Remembers*, 486.

68. Andrew and Mitrokhin, *The World Was Going Our Way*, 265–66.

69. Ahern, *CIA and the Generals*, 5–7.

70. For examples, Ahern, *CIA and the House of Ngo*, 17; Ahern, *CIA and the Generals*, 18–22.

71. Thomas L. Ahern Jr., *Good Questions, Wrong Answers: CIA's Estimates of Arms Traffic through Sihanoukville, Cambodia, during the Vietnam War* (Washington, DC: Central Intelligence Agency, 2004), 44–48; accessed November 10, 2012, at www.foia.cia.gov/vietnam/4_GOOD_QUESTIONS_WRONG_ANSWERS. pdf. See also Bruce Palmer Jr., "US Intelligence and Vietnam," *Studies in Intelligence* 28 (1984): 49–52, 76–78; accessed November 10, 2012, at www .foia.cia.gov/docs/DOC_0001433692/DOC_0001433692.pdf.

72. Trong seemed to be an agent of influence for Hanoi as well; Ahern, *CIA and the Generals*, 94–95; and Hanyok, *Spartans in Darkness*, 381–82. See also Larry Berman, *The Perfect Spy: The Incredible Double Life of Pham Xuan An, Time Magazine Reporter and Vietnamese Communist Agent* (Washington, DC: Smithsonian, 2008 [2007]), 3.

73. Pribbenow, "The Man in the Snow White Cell," 60.

74. Andrew R. Finlayson, *Marine Advisers with the Vietnamese Provincial Reconnaissance Units, 1966–1970* (Quantico, VA: US Marine Corps History Division, 2009), 8; Ahern, *CIA and Rural Pacification*, 297–300.

75. Ahern, *CIA and Rural Pacification*, 300–303, 413.

76. William Colby, DCI from 1973 to 1976, earlier had a prominent role in Phoenix and claimed the 20,000 killed figure came from a misreading of congressional testimony he had given in 1971; see Colby and Forbath, *Honorable Men*, 272.

77. John D. Bergen, *Military Communications: A Test for Technology* (Washington, DC: Center of Military History, 1988); Hanyok, *Spartans in Darkness*, 389–94.

78. Thomas R. Johnson, *American Cryptology during the Cold War, 1945–1989, Book II: Centralization Wins, 1960–1972* (Ft. Meade, MD: National Security

Agency 1995), 551–55; accessed March 26, 2012, at www.gwu.edu/~nsarchiv/NSAEBB/NSAEBB260/index.htm.

79. Ibid., 506–9, 530.

80. James L. Gilbert, *The Most Secret War: Army Signals Intelligence in Vietnam* (Fort Belvoir, VA: US Army Intelligence and Security Command, 2003), 36, 64.

81. Scott Laidig, *Al Gray, Marine: The Early Years, 1950–1967* (Arlington, VA: Potomac Institute Press, 2012), 348–58.

82. Johnson, *Centralization Wins*, 538; Hanyok, *Spartans in Darkness*, 149.

83. Quoted on the inside cover of Gilbert, *The Most Secret War.*

84. Julian J. Ewell and Ira A. Hunt Jr., "Sharpening the Combat Edge: The Use of Analysis to Reinforce Military Judgment," (Washington, DC: Department of the Army, 1995), 99; accessed November 26, 2008, www.army.mil/cmh-pg/books/Vietnam/Sharpen/. See also Hugh Shelton with Ronald Levinson and Malcolm McConnell, *Without Hesitation: The Odyssey of an American Warrior* (New York: St. Martin's, 2010), 86–87.

85. Thomas R. Johnson, *American Cryptology during the Cold War, 1945–1989,* Book I: *The Struggle for Centralization, 1946–1960* (Ft. Meade, MD: National Security Agency, 1995), 48–51, accessed March 26, 2012, at www.gwu.edu/~nsarchiv/NSAEBB/NSAEBB260/index.htm.

86. Hanyok, *Spartans in Darkness*, 296–98.

87. Thomas L. Ahern Jr., *Undercover Armies: CIA and Surrogate Warfare in Laos* (Washington, DC: Central Intelligence Agency, 2006); accessed September 6, 2009, at www.foia.cia.gov/vietnam.asp. See also Bernard C. Nalty, *The War against Trucks: Aerial Interdiction in Southern Laos, 1968–1972* (Washington, DC: Air Force History and Museums Program, 2005).

88. Nalty, *The War against Trucks,* 132.

89. Victor B. Anthony and Richard R. Sexton, *The United States Air Force in Southeast Asia: The War in Northern Laos,* 1954–1973 (Washington, DC: Center for Air Force History, 1993). See also William Greenhalgh, "Tactical Reconnaissance," in *The United States Air Force in Southeast Asia,* 211–13.

90. Ahern, *Undercover Armies,* 522–28.

91. Richard Helms with William Hood, *A Look over My Shoulder: A Life in the Central Intelligence Agency* (New York: Random House, 2003), 261.

92. Ahern, *CIA and the Generals,* 7, 117.

93. Fursenko and Naftali, *"One Hell of a Gamble,"* 168–72.

94. Robert M. Hathaway and Russell Jack Smith, *Richard Helms as Director of Central Intelligence* (Washington, DC: Central Intelligence Agency, 1993), 83. See also National Security Council (Special Group), "Support for the Chilean Presidential Elections of 4 September 1964, Document 250 in Department of State, *Foreign Relations of the United States,* 1964–1968, vol. 31, *South and Central America; Mexico* (Washington, DC: Department of State, 2005).

95. Hathaway and Smith, *Richard Helms as Director of Central Intelligence,* 95–96.

96. Andrew and Mitrokhin, *The World Was Going Our Way,* 72, 82.

97. Hathaway and Smith, *Richard Helms as Director of Central Intelligence*, 98; Andrew and Mitrokhin, *The World Was Going Our Way*, 84–85; Kristian Gustafson, *Hostile Intent: U.S. Covert Operations in Chile, 1964–1974* (Dulles, VA: Potomac Books, 2007), 231.

98. Andrew and Mitrokhin, *The World Was Going Our Way*, 47–48.

99. John A. Gentry and David E. Spencer, "Colombia's FARC: A Portrait of Insurgent Intelligence," *Intelligence and National Security* 25:4 (2010): 453–78.

100. Frantz Fanon, *The Wretched of the Earth*, trans. Constance Farrington (New York: Grove Weidenfeld, 1963), 3–6.

101. Carlos Marighella, "Popular Support," in his *Mini-manual for the Urban Guerrilla*, June 1969; accessed February 26, 2012 at www.marxists.org/archive/marighella-carlos/1969/06/minimanual-urban-guerrilla/index.htm.

102. Carlos Marighella, "Objectives of the Guerrilla's Actions," in *Mini-manual for the Urban Guerrilla*.

103. "PLO Chairman Yasir Arafat (Abu Ammar): An Interview," August 1969, in Laqueur and Rubin, *The Arab-Israeli Reader*, 136.

104. John K. Cooley, *Green March, Black September: The Story of the Palestinian Arabs* (London: Frank Cass, 1973), 135. See also "Popular Front for the Liberation of Palestine: Platform," in Laqueur and Rubin, *The Arab-Israeli Reader*, 140–41.

105. Tony Craig, "Sabotage! The Origins, Development and Impact of the IRA's Infrastructural Bombing Campaigns, 1937–1997," *Intelligence and National Security* 25:3 (June 2010): 320.

106. Carlos Marighella, "Information," in *Mini-manual for the Urban Guerrilla*.

107. *The Green Book* is reprinted in an appendix in Martin Dillon, *The Dirty War: Covert Strategies and Tactics Used in Political Conflicts* (New York: Routledge, 1990), 452.

108. Andrew, *Defend the Realm*, 622–23.

109. Andrew and Mitrokhin, *The World Was Going Our Way*, 253–56; the remark by Interior Minister Peter-Michael Diestel appears on p. 144. Andrew and Mitrokhin, *The Mitrokhin Archive*, 502.

110. Jens Gieseke, "East German Espionage in the Era of Detente," *Journal of Strategic Studies* 31:3 (June 2008): 427.

111. John R. Schindler, "Defeating the 6th Column: Intelligence and Strategy in the War on Islamist Terrorism," *Orbis* 49 (Autumn 2005): 703–4.

112. Yossi Melman, "Preventive Measures," *BA*, February 17, 2006; accessed March 17, 2012, at www.ba.no/nyheter/urix/article1960706.ece.

113. Sir Mark Saville, William L. Hoyt, and John L. Toohey, *Report of the Bloody Sunday Inquiry* [the Saville Report], vol. 1, chapter 8, June 15, 2010, National Archives (UK); accessed March 17, 2012 at The Report of the Bloody Sunday Inquiry.

114. See sec. 167 in *Ireland v. the United Kingdom*, 5310/71 (1978) ECHR 1 (January 18, 1978); accessed March 18, 2012, at www.worldlii.org/eu/cases/ECHR/1978/1.html.

115. Secretary of State for Northern Ireland, "Report of the Committee of Inquiry into Police Interrogation Procedures in Northern Ireland" [the Bennett Report], March 1979, accessed March 18, 2012, at http://cain.ulst.ac.uk/hmso/bennett.htm.

116. Eunan O'Halpin, "The Value and Limits of Experience in the Early Years of the Northern Ireland Troubles, 1969–1972," in Dover and Goodman, eds., *Learning from the Secret Past*, 200.

117. Stella Rimington, *Open Secret: The Autobiography of the Former Director-General of MI5* (London: Hutchinson, 2001), 105.

118. Eunan O'Halpin, *Defending Ireland: The Irish State and Its Enemies since 1922* (New York: Oxford 2002, [1999]), 306.

119. Bradley M. Bamford, "The Role and Effectiveness of Intelligence in Northern Ireland," *Intelligence and National Security* 20:4 (Dec. 2005): 588–89.

120. See, for instance, David A. Charters, "'Have a Go': British Army/MI-5 Agent-running Operations in Northern Ireland, 1970–72," *Intelligence and National Security* 28:2 (April 2013): 206–16.

121. Andrew, *Defend the Realm*, 621, 649.

122. Bamford, "The Role and Effectiveness of Intelligence in Northern Ireland," 593–94.

123. Andrew, *Defend the Realm*, 651.

124. Ibid., 686.

125. Larry Grathwohl and Frank Reagan, *Bringing Down America: An FBI Informer with the Weathermen* (New Rochelle, NY: Arlington House, 1976), 145.

126. Jack O'Connell with Vernon Loeb, *King's Counsel: A Memoir of War, Espionage, and Diplomacy in the Middle East* (New York: W. W. Norton, 2011), 95–99.

127. Colby and Forbath, *Honorable Men*, 422–23; John Ranelagh, *The Agency: The Rise and Decline of the CIA* (New York: Simon & Schuster, 1987 [1986]), 608–9, 616; Andrew and Mitrokhin, *The World Was Going Our Way*, 451–53.

128. Richard J. Aldrich, "'A Skeleton in Our Cupboard': British Interrogation Procedures in Northern Ireland," in Dover and Goodman, eds., *Learning from the Secret Past*, 163.

129. United States Senate, Select Committee to Study Governmental Operations with Respect to Intelligence Activities [the Church Committee], Final Report of the Select Committee to Study Governmental Operations with Respect to Intelligence Activities, Book II, Intelligence Activities and the Rights of Americans, 94th Congress, Second Session, 1976, 105, 107, 272–74; accessed March 25, 2012, at www.aarclibrary.org/publib/contents/church/contents_church_reports_book2.htm.

130. Michael Warner, "Sophisticated Spies: CIA's Links to Liberal Anti-Communists, 1949–1967," 426. The quote from Desmond FitzGerald appears in United States Senate, Select Committee to Study Governmental Operations

with Respect to Intelligence Activities [the Church Committee], Final Report of the Select Committee to Study Governmental Operations with Respect to Intelligence Activities, book I, Foreign and Military Intelligence, 94th Congress, Second Session, 1976,187 accessed March 26, 2012, at www.aarclibrary.org/publib/church/reports/book1/html/ChurchB1_0098a.htm.

131. Ranelagh, *The Agency*, 537. See also Victor Marchetti and John D. Marks, *The CIA and the Cult of Intelligence* (New York: Knopf, 1974).

132. Andrew and Mitrokhin, *The World Was Going Our Way*, 104; Philip Agee, *Inside the Company: CIA Diary* (Bungay, Suffolk: Chaucer Press, 1975).

133. Congress in 1982 acted to protect the identities and lives of intelligence officers by passing the Intelligence Identities Protection Act.

134. Constance Babington-Smith, *Evidence in Camera: The Story of Photographic Intelligence in the Second World War* (London: Chatto and Windus, 1957).

135. Richard J. Aldrich, "Policing the Past: Official History, Secrecy and British Intelligence since 1945," *English Historical Review* 119 (2004).

136. F. W. Winterbotham, *The Ultra Secret* (London: Weidenfeld and Nicolson, 1974).

137. J. C. Masterman, *The Double-Cross System in the War of 1939-45* (New Haven, CT: Yale University Press, 1972).

138. F. H. Hinsley, et al., *British Intelligence in Second World War*, 5 vols. (New York: Cambridge University Press, 1984-1990).

139. L. Britt Snider, *The Agency and the Hill: CIA's Relationship with Congress, 1946-2004* (Washington, DC: Central Intelligence Agency, 2008), 272-74; accessed March 24, 2012, at www.cia.gov/library.

140. Gerald K. Haines, "The Pike Committee Investigations and the CIA," *Studies in Intelligence* (Winter 1998/99); accessed March 26, 2012, at www.cia.gov/library/center-for-the-study-of-intelligence/csi-publications/csi-studies/studies/winter98_99/art07.html.

141. Robert L. Jackson, "No Presidential Role Found in CIA Plots," *Los Angeles Times*, July 19, 1975.

142. Colby and Forbath, *Honorable Men*, 404, 441.

143. Church Committee, book II, Intelligence Activities and the Rights of Americans, 5, 219, 275-77.

144. Tim Wiener, *Enemies: A History of the FBI* (New York: Random House, 2012), 249-51.

145. L. Britt Snider, "Unlucky SHAMROCK: Recollections from the Church Committee's Investigation of NSA," *Studies in Intelligence* (Winter 1999-2000): 43-51; accessed March 25, 2012, at www.cia.gov/library/center-for-the-study-of-intelligence/csi-publications/csi-studies/studies/winter99-00/art4.html.

146. Church Committee, Book I, Foreign and Military Intelligence, 449.

147. Church Committee, Book II, Foreign and Military Intelligence, 423-24, 427, 437-39, 459.

148. Senator Fulbright quoted in Thomas Powers, *The Man Who Kept the Secrets: Richard Helms and the CIA* (New York: Alfred A. Knopf, 1979) 211–12. United States Senate, Committee on Foreign Relations, *Intelligence and the ABM*, 91st Congress, 1st Session, 1969. John W. Finney, "Pentagon Charged with Changing Data to Help Antimissile Plan," *New York Times*, May 15, 1969.

149. Raymond L. Garthoff, "Estimating Soviet Military Intentions and Capabilities," in Gerald K. Haines and Robert E. Leggett, eds., *Watching the Bear: Essays on CIA's Analysis of the Soviet Union* (Washington, DC: Central Intelligence Agency, 2001), 159–60.

150. Richard Pipes, "Team B: The Reality behind the Myth." *Commentary* 82 (October 1986), 25–40.

151. Melvin A. Goodman, *Failure of Intelligence: The Decline and Fall of the CIA* (Lanham, MD: Rowman & Littlefield, 2008), 122, 150.

152. Quoted in Robert Jervis, "Why Intelligence and Policymakers Clash," *Political Science Quarterly* 125:2 (Summer 2010).

153. Andrew and Mitrokhin, *The World Was Going Our Way*, 180.

CHAPTER 6

The Liberal Triumph?

These extraordinary tools of a police state's machinery of repression should give pause for thought. They reveal the ultimate powerlessness of repression when it seeks to impede the development of a historical necessity and to defend a regime that is against the needs of society. However powerfully equipped it might be, all it can achieve is to add to the suffering by gaining a little time.

—SERGE, *MEMOIRS OF A REVOLUTIONARY*

The 1980s saw something brief but unprecedented: a period in which the leader of one superpower and the vice president of the other were former chiefs of their respective nations' key intelligence services. Yuri Andropov had headed the KGB for longer than anyone before him, before becoming the General Secretary of the Communist Party of the Soviet Union in 1982. George H. W. Bush served briefly as director of central intelligence and then won election for vice president on the 1980 Republican ticket headed by Ronald Reagan. The time in which Bush and Andropov shared this distinction witnessed the opening scenes of some of the most hopeful, and yet dangerous, years in history. At several points between 1982 and 1991, catastrophic conflict loomed as a real possibility. Though Bush and Andropov had something unique in common, the intelligence systems that served them as national leaders performed very differently in the ensuing global transformation. Those performances would prove the ruin of one, but, ironically, the other's relative success would slip away almost before anyone noticed. And, as revolutionary ideology ceased to be a major motivation for some of the world's most powerful intelligence services, all the services were challenged on their own turf by threats they had not imagined twenty years earlier.

The New Cold War

The Cold War reignited in the late 1970s, this time with an ideological intensity not seen for a generation. As they had at the beginning of the Cold War, Washington and Moscow felt both confident and beleaguered—ostensibly assured of the correctness of their mutually exclusive readings of history's course, but beset by opposition to their efforts and doubts about their ability to keep history on track. To an extent not seen since the 1940s, this new Cold War marked a bald struggle between liberal and progressive ideals. A new American president, Jimmy Carter, sought to adjust the nation's foreign policy toward a liberal emphasis on human rights on both sides of the Iron Curtain, and away from the "Realism" of his predecessors that had allied the United States with anti-Communist dictators like those in South Vietnam— while also making overtures to the Communist regime in China. In theory, this meant overt American opposition to human rights violations wherever they occurred, and in practice it meant both a softening of US support to regimes like the shah's in Iran and overt sympathy for dissidents in Eastern Europe and the Soviet Union.

When physicist and Nobel Peace Prize recipient Andrei Sakharov wrote to Carter the day after the president's inauguration, Carter promptly replied, and emphasized America's commitment to promote human rights for all. Soviet General Secretary Leonid Brezhnev was not amused, and three weeks later he, of all people, lectured Carter on the principle of mutual "non-interference into the internal affairs of the other side." Only such restraint, Brezhnev insisted, could allow "a stable, progressive development of relations between the USSR and the USA."[1] While Soviet leaders hated Carter's indictment of communism's fitness to rule, they also saw new opportunities to support revolution abroad. Moscow stepped up intelligence operations in the developing world as its rivals seemed to be abandoning the field.

The US Congress had curtailed assistance to South Vietnam in 1975, and to anti-Communist guerrillas in Angola later that same year. China, still reeling from the Cultural Revolution, drew closer to the United States under Mao's successors; so much so that Fidel Castro told the Non-Aligned Movement Summit in 1979 that the "ruling Chinese clique" not only defended NATO but also joined "with the United States and the most reactionary forces in Europe and the world."[2] Under its rising new leader, the quintessential survivor Deng Xiaoping, China left off fomenting revolution, and by 1980 its intelligence services were secretly discussing mutual interests with their American counterparts.[3]

Soviet perceptions of challenge and opportunity gave encouragement to revolutions in Africa, Asia, and Latin America. Key to Moscow's strategy was a less-visible Soviet hand, and that meant roles for Cuban and East German proxies, who often had more revolutionary credibility in the developing world than did the USSR. The new strategy worked well on the ground in Angola, and soon afterward in Ethiopia. In 1977, Moscow had the luxury of choosing between two client regimes, and shifted its support from Somalia to the larger and strategically more important Ethiopia, sending Cuban troops on Soviet transport aircraft to turn the tide of battle (and supplementing them with Soviet military advisers and intelligence officers of East Germany's MfS to coach Ethiopia's security service).[4] The revolutionary regime of Mengistu Haile Mariam subsequently mounted a rolling purge of Ethiopian society; when an official in Moscow asked one of Mengistu's political advisers why the killings had gone on for years, he was told, "We are doing what Lenin did. You cannot build socialism without the Red Terror. We have too many enemies."[5]

The Soviet Bloc's military and intelligence aid had fueled internal struggles in the former colonies of Africa, but had not directly caused the turmoil that ensued as the European colonizers departed and left local powers to settle disputes dating back for decades. In Afghanistan, however, Soviet meddling precipitated that nation's descent into civil war in the 1970s. The nightmare began in April 1978, with a coup by the factious People's Democratic Party of Afghanistan (PDPA) that ousted the president (who himself had toppled his cousin the king five years earlier). Thereafter, the KGB was never far from Afghan leaders and events in Kabul, whether arming and training the new regime, or advising it not to purge party rivals while suppressing Muslim religious leaders.[6] After a second coup in fall 1979, KGB officials grew alarmed; the new head of the party and de facto ruler of Afghanistan, Hafizullah Amin, had no history of dealings with their service and was alleged by rivals to be an American spy. A note from the KGB (probably from service head Yuri Andropov himself) to General Secretary Brezhnev highlighted the danger: "There are increasingly frequent reports of an intended shift of the [Democratic Republic of Afghanistan]'s foreign policy to the right. H. Amin's men and representatives of the right-wing Muslim opposition are trying to find a way to solve the conflict. H. Amin himself has met the US chargé d'affaires a number of times, but he has given no indication of the subject of these talks in his meetings with Soviet representatives."[7]

Dissent and rebellion against the PDPA and the Soviets spread throughout the country. Soon Andropov began urging Soviet military intervention in order to forestall American intervention and set the revolution back on track. In the ensuing overthrow of Amin and invasion of Afghanistan by the Soviet army that December, the KGB performed in typical fashion, seeing spies and foreign agents everywhere (in fairness, China, Saudi Arabia, and Pakistan had apparently already talked to Washington about aiding the Afghan opposition by the summer of 1979). The KGB also exhibited operational daring (and suffered high casualties) in mounting the commando assault that finally killed Amin and his family. Ultimately, the service gave the Central Committee in Moscow a self-serving and over-optimistic assessment of the new regime—which was now headed by a long-time KGB contact, Babrak Karmal—and of its prospects for pacifying an increasingly restive Afghanistan.[8]

Half a world away, Fidel Castro's dream of revolutions in Latin America finally seemed within reach. The first upheaval came to Nicaragua, where the dictator Anastasio Somoza had, by 1978, alienated virtually all walks of society. Popular resistance to Somoza crystallized that August when guerrillas of the Sandinista National Liberation Front (FSLN), under the command of Eden Pastora, seized the entire National Congress and managed to bargain away their hostages for a planeload of political prisoners and safe passage to Cuba. Their astonishing feat—which Moscow Center files later showed to have been aided with KGB training and funds—sparked uprisings across Nicaragua.[9] Somoza kept a lid on the country until the following spring, when the rival Sandinista factions (at Castro's urging) forged a united front and mounted an invasion of Nicaragua from Costa Rica. Washington and Havana thereafter worked at cross purposes in ways that ensured Somoza's downfall. President Carter had cut off aid to the Somoza regime, while the Costa Ricans—in contravention to their assurances to the United States—quietly allowed Cuban advisers and fifteen tons of arms to reach the FSLN and the revolt it was now leading.[10] CIA analysts watching the situation in mid-June changed their minds and now predicted a Sandinista victory.[11] Hasty attempts by the American ambassador and CIA station to find a successor to Somoza failed in July, and his National Guard, out of ammunition and leaderless when he fled to Miami, surrendered to the advancing Sandinistas on July 19.[12] The irony was palpable. In 1954, the State Department and CIA had sponsored an invasion of Guatemala and a coup against that country's leftist president to prevent a Soviet bridgehead in Central America. In 1979, an American embargo and machinations in Managua facilitated the success of an invasion reminiscent of the Guatemala episode a quarter century earlier—only this time, the invaders were on the other side of history.

The Cubans and their Soviet patrons now had their bridgehead in Central America. The KGB's newly arrived representative in Managua reported to Moscow in October that the Sandinista leadership assured him they would not unduly provoke the United States but nevertheless knew where they wanted to go: "The FSLN leadership had firmly decided to carry out the transformation of the FSLN into a Marxist-Leninist Party, including within it other leftist parties and groups on an individual basis. The centrist and bourgeois mini-parties already existing in the country would be kept only because they presented no danger and served as a convenient facade for the outside world."[13] Losing no time, the Cubans and Sandinistas sought to replicate the Nicaraguan success in nearby El Salvador. They pushed the various Salvadoran radical groups into an alliance that ultimately announced itself as the Farabundo Marti National Liberation Front (FMLN) in October 1980. FMLN adherents trained in guerrilla warfare in Nicaragua, while the head of the Salvadoran Communist Party made a world tour of Communist states gathering promises of aid and arms—particularly from Vietnam, which provided three battalions' worth of captured US-made weapons.[14] As the new year turned, the hurriedly equipped and organized FMLN guerrillas mounted a "Final Offensive" to seize power.

The Salvadoran regime, however, had not wasted the interval. "Death squads" alleged to belong to the army suppressed real and imagined revolutionaries in the most brutal fashion, but at the same time the ruling junta had both broadened its support by adding new members and had implemented enough social reforms to blunt the Left's appeal.[15] There would be no popular uprising like that which the Sandinistas had ridden to victory in Nicaragua. The Salvadoran army won in hard fighting, though it owed its victory in part to the operational mistakes by the FMLN, which pulled cadres out of the cities in favor of guerrilla war in the countryside but spent its strength in piecemeal, uncoordinated attacks.[16] Decision making in Washington had improved since Somoza's downfall as well, partly because of a determined effort to improve intelligence collection. As a result, reports emerged of Cuban arms aid to the FMLN weeks before the offensive. Though the United States provided the bulk of its military and economic aid to El Salvador through overt channels, President Carter also authorized several covert actions (beginning in July 1979) in hopes of "helping the government deal with the insurgency" and of publicizing Soviet and Cuban support for violent revolution in Central America.[17] Thereafter, the FMLN settled in for a prolonged insurgency, mounting sabotage operations and unsuccessfully seeking to dampen participation in the 1982 national elections (and, when that failed, by attacking the newly elected government's reputation abroad).

Revolution could be stopped by more conventional military means as well. Yet the same law of unintended consequences also pertained in these cases, as the Israelis found in 1982 when they mounted a full-scale invasion of southern Lebanon to expel the quasi-state that the PLO had constructed there. The invasion marked a military win but at best a strategic draw for Tel Aviv. Under the gun barrels of the Israeli Defense Force (IDF), the defeated PLO fighters boarded ships for Tunisia in August 1982, but peace did not come to Lebanon. Israel's Christian allies took revenge on Palestinian refugees, killing hundreds, and the country slid back into civil war as the IDF withdrew to the south and various ethnic and sectarian rivals battled for power in the resulting political vacuum. The following year, American and French efforts to halt the bloodshed in Beirut ended after suicide bombings against their troops—a new tactic being employed by local Shia militias, acting in all probability with the assistance of Khomeini's Iran.[18] The US embassy was their first target; a van loaded with explosives destroyed the embassy and killed more than sixty in April 1983 (they included the CIA's chief Arab analyst, Robert Ames, and several other officers).[19] More bombings came before the year ended. In a single morning that October, two more bomb-laden vans killed almost 300 at the US Marine barracks beside Beirut's airport and at a barracks used by French paratroopers. That December, suicide bombers mounted an even more ambitious operation in Kuwait. In one day they struck the French and American embassies along with the airport and three industrial facilities; if the bombs had worked as intended, the loss of life would have been heavy.[20] The net effects—which had hardly been caused by the Lebanon War but were certainly heightened by it—were (1) a sense that Western forces and diplomats could not survive in parts of the Middle East, and (2) a vast increase in covert action and intrigue across the region.

Both the Sunni and Shia branches of the Muslim faith had their radical adherents, and fanatics on both sides were willing to wage covert war not only on Israeli and Western targets but also on secular Arab leaders, like Egypt's President Anwar Sadat, assassinated by members of the (Sunni) Islamic Jihad in October 1981. The Arab world would henceforth serve as not only a Cold War battleground but also as the arena for the next phase of the age-old struggle between Shi'ites and Sunnis, now to be carried on with modern military and intelligence methods that spread outward to smaller and smaller bands of men with grievances and a willingness to kill. Militancy on the Sunni side drew inspiration from many sources, prominent among them the writings of Sayyed Qutb (1906–66), the Egyptian novelist, critic, commentator on the Koran, and theorist of political and social Islam. Qutb had endured years imprisoned by the Nasser regime, which finally hanged him for his unrepentant opposition to the ideal of a secular Arab state. In the 1940s, he had also spent two years teaching and traveling in America, which he loathed for its hedonism, its brazen women, and its "primitive" music.[21]

These national-level jihads, however, met with fierce resistance in the established Arab regimes, both kingdoms and secular Ba'athist states. Indeed, the regimes reacted much in the manner of the European countries faced with anarchist and socialist violence a century earlier—with an important twist. The Arabs assiduously employed the tested methods of penetration and surveillance, but some added torture to their toolkit as well. These means, from the 1960s on, would allow the Arab secret services to crush localized Islamic ferment. Much as their forbears had in Europe, the services of those disparate and rival regimes also found common cause in sharing information on jihadists, who in turn responded with reflections echoing those from generations earlier. Explaining another disaster for jihadists in Syria in the early 1980s, Mustafa Setmariam Nasar (Abu Musab al-Suri) of the Syrian Muslim Brotherhood sounded like Lenin in his complaint: "The cooperation and coordination of security services between Jordan, Iraq, Syria, and other Muslim countries was evident, and by studying our organizations they were able to wage effective campaigns against similar Islamic organizations . . . in the neighboring countries." The need for security among the Sunni Muslim revolutionists would ultimately change their organizational and operational practices.

Counterrevolutionaries

The intelligence system of the United States by then had fully engaged in this global chess match, seeking new allies to block Soviet gains and also making trouble for Moscow in its own sphere of influence. In doing so, the Americans did their part to spread covert skills and methods worldwide. As former Director of Central Intelligence Robert Gates emphasized in his memoir, by the end of the Carter presidency, covert action was once again a preferred instrument of national policy in Washington. Carter overtly gave new resources to Radio Free Europe and Radio Liberty (now independent of CIA sponsorship), and he approved covert efforts to smuggle publications about democracy and regional cultures into the Soviet Union along with writings by leading dissidents, such as Solzhenitsyn's *Gulag Archipelago*. His successor, Ronald Reagan, made trouble for the Soviets in Poland after their client regime there declared martial law in 1981, supplementing the assistance that American labor unions were sending Polish workers with a CIA program for providing "printing materials, communications equipment, and other supplies for waging underground political warfare." Peaceful efforts to undermine Soviet rule behind the Iron Curtain were an easy sell to both Republican and Democratic members of Congress. Once the Soviets invaded Afghanistan, moreover, even lethal assistance in certain places became acceptable as well. In Angola, the Reagan administration approved covert arms to the rebels of the National Union for the Total Liberation for Angola (UNITA) fighting the Cuban regime in 1985—a step made possible by the recent congressional repeal of the Clark Amendment's ban on such aid. The covert action to aid Afghan *mujaheddin* against the Soviet occupation, however, was surely the biggest program of them all. The Carter administration had made tentative efforts to provide nonlethal aid even before the Soviet invasion, and had entertained offers of help from China, Pakistan, and Saudi Arabia. Within a year of the invasion, assistance totaled tens of millions worth in aid; by 1985 the effort was a multinational one, spending several hundred million dollars a year.[22]

Yet Congress was not ready to end the debates over foreign policy that had roiled Washington since the Vietnam War. President Reagan continued Carter's covert programs in Central America, but pushed beyond the bipartisan consensus in December 1981 by adding lethal assistance to the aid mix for the budding revolt against the Sandinistas in Nicaragua.[23] But Reagan found little allied support for this venture. America's new friends in

Angola and Afghanistan were no Boy Scouts, but the Nicaraguan "Contras" were closer to home and easily tarred as former Somoza regime diehards in cahoots with El Salvador's infamous death squads. All the same, some measure of support for denying the Soviets a Central American beachhead endured in Congress as the Sandinistas repeatedly hurt their own cause, in both Washington and Latin America, with what one historian has recently called their "incompetence, brutality, and missteps."[24]

The CIA's developing world rebels may have been scarcely better than the Soviet-backed regimes they fought, but America had attributes unthinkable behind the Iron Curtain: a free press to expose the misdeeds of American clients, and a Congress to investigate. Leaks to the papers about Contra aid, followed by Reagan's public embrace of it, provoked the Democratic majority in Congress to ban covert support to the Contras in late 1982. Thereafter, the program and the policy devolved into scandal and even farce. Director of Central Intelligence William Casey, a veteran of the wartime OSS, had found his CIA operations directorate timid and sloppy; "a blindered fraternity living on the legends and achievements of their fore-bears," in the words of his young chief of staff, Robert Gates. Hence Casey bypassed the directorate's formal machinery, treating it like he treated Congress—as an occasionally useful nuisance. He alienated Senate sup-porters by mining Nicaraguan harbors in 1983, and nearly brought down his own president three years later, when news broke that he and his fellow "zealots" (Gates's term) in the White House had been diverting profits from secret arms sales to Iran into accounts for the Contras.[25] The ensuing Iran-Contra scandal ended with strict new laws restricting the procedures for authorizing and conducting covert actions.

No such restrictions hampered Moscow, which assailed Reagan and his policies both rhetorically and covertly, abetting a wave of terrorist attacks at Western military sites and personnel in Europe. The leftist cells from the 1970s now got their second wind, aided by the fraternal social-ist states of the Warsaw Pact. Italy's Red Brigades kidnapped a US Army brigadier general in 1982 and held him for six weeks before his rescue by a commando unit of the Italian police. In Germany, the Red Army Faction ("Don't argue—destroy!") had almost assassinated NATO supreme com-mander Alexander Haig in 1979, and now launched a fresh wave of car bombings and sniper attacks on the US military in Germany. They almost killed US Seventh Army commander Frederick Kroesen in 1981 with an antitank grenade fired at his armored Mercedes. The RAF and other groups did not exactly take direction from Moscow, but they enjoyed support from the KGB's allies, particularly the Stasi—which trained RAF members to mount attacks like that on General Kroesen.[26]

Moscow did not have to direct terror from the Center. Soviet clients mounted their own campaigns for their own causes, and they shared resources and expertise with likeminded radicals who needed no Soviet help. The Abu Nidal Organization (ANO) long operated out of Saddam Hussein's Iraq, though it had moved to Syria shortly before trying to kill the Israeli ambassador in London. It thus precipitated Israel's invasion of Lebanon and the expulsion of the PLO—a disaster welcomed by Abu Nidal, who considered Arafat's Fatah too moderate. The ANO's 1982 attempt on the Israeli ambassador caught the British government flat-footed. It was mounted by Palestinian and Iraqi students holding visas to study in London; one MI5 official reflected that "nothing short of a blanket refusal to admit Arab students can prevent an assassination team in that guise entering the UK." Libya soon joined the sponsor list for ANO, and also increased its arms shipments to the Provisional Irish Republican Army's (PIRA) decade-old campaign against British targets.[27] Libyan agents based in East Berlin also bombed West Berlin's La Belle discotheque, filled with US serviceman, in April 1986—the attack killed three and wounded 229 others.[28] The PIRA by this point had assassinated Lord Louis Mountbatten (1979) on vacation in Ireland, and nearly killed Prime Minister Margaret Thatcher with a bomb in her Brighton hotel during the Conservative Party conference in October 1984. She and her husband were unhurt, though five people died. A PIRA statement swiftly placed the attack in context: "Today we were unlucky, but remember we only have to be lucky once. You will have to be lucky always."[29] The Western response to this campaign was a comprehensive one, blending law enforcement, intelligence, and military action. London put MI5 firmly in charge of counterterrorism efforts against Irish radicals and all other sources, and made the service capable of round-the-clock operations. In addition, MI5 increased cooperation with continental services and gradually won more cooperation from the FBI as the bureau realized the universality of the terrorism problem (though American juries could still balk at convicting on charges of running guns to the PIRA).[30] Congress passed the Omnibus Diplomatic Security and Antiterrorism Act of 1986, which empowered the FBI to arrest terrorists overseas—as the G-Men did to Fawaz Younis of Hezbollah after luring him to international waters off Lebanon the following year. President Reagan approved a "finding" authorizing worldwide covert action against terrorism in 1986, and in the mid-1980s the CIA created its Counterterrorist Center to coordinate intelligence operations and analysis.[31] And where he thought it prudent, Reagan ordered retaliatory raids on the state sponsors of terror; just days after the La Belle discotheque bombing, US aircraft struck military and political targets in Libya, narrowly missing the country's dictator, Muammar Gadaffi.

The Computer Age

President Reagan ordered those strikes on Libya confident that the US military could execute a complicated raid involving dozens of aircraft traveling long distances with split-second timing. The bombs and missiles they carried were marvels of the military art; compact yet powerful devices guided by laser beams to within inches of their targets. That precision had not come cheaply; it had cost millions of dollars and years of effort stretching back a generation. And it would have a lasting impact not only on military planning and operations but on intelligence as well. Whereas covert action by both sides in the Cold War had sought to change the shape of the strategic chessboard, the transformation in military technology on display in the 1980s gave the West a new queen.

This transformation came, ironically enough, from America's futile intervention in Vietnam. By the late 1970s, US Air Force and Navy air planners were forging the future of air combat; it combined intelligence and battle management to suppress sophisticated air defenses and to put munitions exactly on target. No enemy installation or weapon that could be seen from above was safe from American bombs or missiles, launched from ranges that kept aircrews largely immune from ground-based defenses. The Pentagon refined its conduct of air-to-air combat as well, ensuring with better sensors and tactical intelligence that American pilots and aircraft would be vectored toward adversaries with the best possible odds of downing them. The strategic implications for the defense of Europe—where NATO forces were outnumbered by the Warsaw Pact—were immense. As the Americans shared these innovations with their allies, NATO could now even the odds and nullify Moscow's offensive strength without early resort to nuclear weapons (Q: "What is a *tactical* nuclear weapon?" A: "One that lands in Germany," ran a grim joke among analysts at the time).

The Vietnam War also convinced leaders in the US military to recommit their services to the principles of the military art—in short, to develop new doctrines and an offensive mindset that could employ the new sensors and weapons to maximum capability. Junior officers like Colin Powell feared that the warrior mentality had lapsed in Vietnam; "[a] corrosive careerism had infected the Army. And I was part of it," he recalled a generation later.[32] That conflict had demonstrated that the US military was less than the sum of its parts, fighting a series of individual service-dominated campaigns instead of truly integrating its capabilities. The result in the 1970s was intense reflection and revision that gave rise (through stages) to the AirLand Battle concept in 1981. This change in joint army and air force doctrine was enabled by the new weapons, communications, and computers; by now they were cheap enough to deploy widely across the military and the Intelligence Community to perform all manner of tasks, from the mundane to the highly sensitive and specialized—and to do so, moreover, in the field as well as in Washington.

The new systems also made what was now being called the "Revolution in Military Affairs" cheap enough to export. Integrated circuits put processing power in spaces as small as guidance modules for missiles and bombs—in effect, they condensed military targeting and intelligence analysis into "smart" weapons. Western militaries quickly observed the US innovations and began deploying both American-made and locally produced variants, improving their control of forces and weaponry for maximum impact on the battlefield. British pilots showed the superiority of advanced conventional warfare in the quick and violent campaign to retake the Falkland Islands from Argentina in 1982. The availability of the latest US-made air-to-air missiles ensured air superiority to protect the Royal Navy and the assault troops, and the navy pilots' superior training and skill gave them the victory over Argentinean defenders who fought bravely—and in many cases with French, British, and American-made weapons—but lacked the winning coherence of a modern Western force. The skies over Lebanon witnessed an even more convincing demonstration of the new warfare at almost the same time. As the Israeli invasion of Lebanon opened and Syrian forces there braced to meet the IDF on the ground, the Israeli Air Force (IAF) sprang an electronic trap. Israeli unmanned aircraft mimicked incoming bombers, alerting Syria's local surface-to-air missile batteries. When the SAMs prepared to fire at the drones, IAF bombers fired radar beam-riding missiles at their tracking radars and launchers. Syrian jets scrambled to defend the missile batteries, and IAF fighters ambushed them in turn, downing dozens (a quarter of Damascus's air force) in a single day—and depriving the Syrian army and its PLO allies of air cover. The IAF lost not one pilot.[33]

Such results convinced Western militaries and their intelligence agencies to increase the connectivity of all levels of the intelligence system. At least two directors of the National Security Agency (Lincoln Faurer and William Odom) made it their priority to provide signals intelligence to tactical and operational-level commanders.[34] The British, German, and French militaries joined in similar efforts; Britain had found in the Falklands that tactical units were collecting intelligence of national import while national collectors back at GCHQ had vital clues to what was happening on the battlefield.[35] The question was how to integrate what everyone saw. Such efforts in Western militaries depended on innovations in communications technology to increase the bandwidth to the field while ensuring the security of the traffic it carried.[36] They also required vast new computer and database resources, like those encompassed in the US Navy's Operational Intelligence (OPINTEL) program for tracking the Soviet Navy.[37]

The message to Moscow in these conflicts and programs was clear: Western tactics and weapons had advanced to a point where their qualitative advantage in conventional conflict might be insurmountable. British and Israeli forces had bested brave and well-armed opponents with relatively minimal losses. As the United States deployed its new systems on a crash basis in the early Reagan administration, NATO promised to raise conventional war to levels of ferocity that even the Soviets could not match. The US military's swift subduing of Cuban advisers and local forces on the island of Grenada in 1983 showed that Washington was willing to roll back socialist gains when it could. Yet even that military performance did not satisfy Congress. The invasion of Grenada had been hastily mounted (in spite of and not in conjunction with London, as Grenada was a member of the Commonwealth despite its Marxist government), and it had unfolded clumsily. Congress noted the growing gap between the sophisticated new weapons and the allegedly hide-bound institutions that employed them, and, as a consequence, moved to modernize the Pentagon's command structures in the Goldwater-Nichols Act of 1986. In particular, that act pushed the authority to run campaigns forward to regional combatant commands, thereby ensuring that the military services would no longer wage parallel instead of "joint" campaigns (as they had in the skies over North Vietnam), and also ensuring that the new commands' headquarters themselves would soon develop an insatiable appetite for intelligence collection and analysis.

Was the new Western military advantage a growing sophistication of command and control, or intelligence? It was both and more—a fact that tested even the Pentagon's champion acronym writers. They rose to the challenge with new coinages like "ISR" (Intelligence, Surveillance, and Reconnaissance) and "C3I" (a somewhat older term for Command, Control, Communications, and Intelligence). Still later they devised "C4I" (Command, Control, Communications, *Computers*, and Intelligence), and the ultimate, "C4ISR" (C4I plus Surveillance and Reconnaissance).

While the "operational-level" reforms advanced, the strategic implications of the military revolution manifested themselves in a shift of American nuclear doctrine. New ballistic missiles and cruise missiles coming into the arsenal in the late 1970s promised startling increases in accuracy, opening up a wide range of targets to American planners—and forcing the need to prioritize targets that would have the most "mission impact." Target selection in turn rested not only on computing power but also on the collection improvements since the 1960s, and on industrial-scale analysis of highly technical data on Soviet systems and deployments. President Carter's new nuclear targeting doctrine implicitly recognized the dilemma and the imperative that "improvements should be made to our forces, their supporting C3 and intelligence, and their employment plans and planning apparatus, to achieve a high degree of flexibility, enduring survivability, and adequate performance in the face of enemy actions."[38] The incoming Reagan administration took this warfighting doctrine a step farther, according to the historian Lawrence Freedman, who noted that C3I was central to turning war-winning theories into practice and also to "claims that it was becoming possible to design and execute subtle nuclear tactics during a prolonged conflict."[39]

Whether or not such doctrines would have worked in a nuclear exchange with the Soviet Union, they did help drive the evolution of military intelligence in the United States. A new sophistication fused intelligence and planning at the strategic level, for example, in helping the US Navy change its role in containment strategy. Various collection breakthroughs, "predominantly SIGINT" but with "some very significant HUMINT penetration [sic]" helped shed light on Moscow's own nuclear doctrine, particularly for the Soviet navy—in home waters as well as the open ocean.[40] This, combined with patient analysis of the patterns of Soviet naval deployments, prompted a flash of insight for American planners: the Soviets had no wish to refight the U-boat war in the North Atlantic. Moscow instead had staked its naval strategy on defending Soviet nuclear ballistic missile submarines like an underwater battery of field artillery, in their Arctic bastions. "My God, these flag officers are Army marshals in Navy uniforms!" exclaimed an American admiral as he grasped what the Soviets were doing. The US Navy responded with its Maritime Strategy in 1985, seeking to demonstrate its own ability and willingness to fight in the Arctic as well—and implicitly holding Soviet missile boats at risk in a conflict.[41] These and other efforts—particularly the Defense Intelligence Agency's analysis of Soviet command and control—led the Reagan administration in July 1985 to emphasize the targeting of Moscow's most dangerous nuclear capability—its land-mobile ICBMs. Though the ability to hit such targets was always problematic, the bunkers for Soviet leaders in a crisis were not deemed as difficult. Early in the term of Reagan's successor George H. W. Bush, Washington took advantage of the new collection and analysis to revise its nuclear war plans in an effort to hold "at risk" the Soviet leadership and its ability to maintain control over the Soviet Union.[42]

The new capabilities came together in ways that prompted organizational as well as doctrinal innovation for intelligence. The US Army changed its divisional structure to give these formations organic intelligence support with "combat electronic warfare and intelligence" components (instead of attaching the support on an ad hoc basis).[43] Key changes came about via mainframes and minicomputers dispersed in computer centers, and then as terminals and even "personal computers" on desktops, using more and more networked information. The advances by 1983 enabled a DIA experiment, the Central America Joint Intelligence Team (CAJIT), a "fusion center" to support US and El Salvadoran officials combating the FMLN-led insurgency. Based near Washington and comprising analysts from several Intelligence Community agencies, CAJIT "used powerful databases and improved communications technology to quickly analyze and disseminate intelligence used in U.S. support of the Salvadoran military as a way to improve its operations against the insurgents." A recent DIA history claims CAJIT "was extremely effective, and enabled the Salvadorans to beat back the insurgents that threatened to defeat [that nation] early in the decade."[44]

6.1 A US marine radioman relays the direction of an approaching plane to another marine preparing to fire a Stinger missile during a training exercise in 1984. *Department of Defense*

CAJIT would be the prototype for US military joint intelligence centers—a reversion of sorts to the joint, all-source intelligence centers that had served British and American commanders in World War II, but this time with "reachback" to the United States for analytical support.

As the Reagan administration increased aid to rebel groups fighting Moscow's allies in the developing world, the temptation to share smart weapons with them too became irresistible. Guided battlefield missiles for defense against tanks and aircraft had been exported in quantities by Washington and Moscow since the 1960s, but the new generation of US-designed devices had greatly improved accuracy and robustness. They were simple enough for Angolan and Afghan tribesmen to use effectively, light enough for one or two men to carry, and they functioned reliably in harsh conditions. Besides, the technology employed in at least some of these weapons had already been purchased by Soviet intelligence in Europe, according to a CIA source.[45] In 1986, the National Security Council approved covert provision of guided antitank missiles (TOWs) and Stinger antiaircraft missiles to Jonas Savimbi's UNITA. According to Robert Gates, by then the CIA's deputy director for intelligence, "we were dumbfounded by the relative effectiveness of the missiles and the soldiers using them in Angola. Indeed, until we began getting video pictures and other evidence, the US Army was quite skeptical of the kill rates being reported." That success helped convince the NSC to send Stingers to the *mujaheddin* in Afghanistan, where they changed the war by forcing Soviet jets and helicopters to fly too high to provide effective support to Soviet and Afghan regime troops. "We began to hear stories from the field about how those who had the Stingers had become even bolder in combat," Gates recounted; "many of the fighters regarded the Stinger as a kind of 'magic amulet' that would protect them against the Soviets."[46]

Computers for All

The same integrated circuits then revolutionizing Western militaries had even larger effects on industrial processes and soon on consumer electronics as well. By the early 1980s, a hundred thousand transistors could be packed on a single silicon chip. Computers not only did office payrolls but controlled machinery in factories as well as engines and myriad other products. And they made radios, televisions, audio and video recorders, photocopiers, and a host of other devices smaller and cheaper, so much so that they could spread beyond the West to the developing world and even behind the Iron Curtain. A consumer market for home computers opened up in the late 1970s and took off with the 1981 introduction of the IBM PC, an inexpensive microcomputer using an operating system from a company called Microsoft. Home computer builder Apple Corporation's products soon featured graphical interfaces to ease the user experience—an innovation quickly copied by IBM and Microsoft in a system dubbed Windows. By then an entire industry had developed around "cloned" IBM machines, making the consumer market for computer hardware, software, and peripherals grow exponentially across the West, and driving innovation in all phases of the intelligence production cycle. The clones also brought the PC culture to Western intelligence agencies, beginning with NSA's purchase of 21,000 IBM XTs in 1984.[47]

Comparatively few home users in the early 1980s paid the fees to connect to corporate, government, and research networks, but enough did, or at least found their way "online" by other means, to create a subculture of "hackers" interested in exploring this new virtual world—often without permission from the creators of the networks they visited. Not a few devoted considerable ingenuity to duping the telecommunications carriers to gain free connections, and tested their skills against the security of private and (especially) government networks. "Some hackers spend 12 hours a day trying to break into computers at the CIA or the Pentagon," an FBI special agent told the *New York Times* in 1983: "They have a keen interest in the systems of the US military."[48] Indeed, warnings of "Trojan horses" and other such malicious threats to data "even in environments where security appears to be of urgent importance" had been coming to DoD for at least a decade, and the department by this point was losing confidence in the security of its more than 8,000 ever-more-networked computers.[49] An assistant secretary of defense for C3I predicted in 1983 "[t]here'll be more of these hackers, and we're going to have to deal with their increasing sophistication."[50]

The Reagan administration responded with a then top-secret order to secure federal data. National Security Decision Directive (NSDD)-145 noted that "traditional distinctions between telecommunications and automated information systems" were blurring, and explained that computerized databases and telecommunications networks were growing "highly susceptible to interception, unauthorized electronic access, and related forms of technical exploitation, as well as other dimensions of the hostile intelligence threat. The technology to exploit these electronic systems is widespread and is used extensively by foreign nations and can be employed, as well, by terrorist groups and criminal elements. Government systems as well as those which process the private or proprietary information of US persons and businesses can become targets for foreign exploitation." NSDD-145 secretly made the National Security Agency (because of its traditional communications security mission) responsible for setting standards and guidance, conducting research, and doing some monitoring of the security of all "*government* telecommunications systems and automated information systems*" (emphasis added).[51] Congress soon reversed NSDD-145, however, declining to put an intelligence agency (NSA) in overall charge of the security of federal information systems—though it did leave NSA responsible for the safety of data in "national security" systems.[52]

Computers and Intelligence

The connection between computers and intelligence agencies merits a look back. Computers had been targets for spies since at least 1968, when West Germany's police caught a mole for the HVA's Markus Wolf in IBM's

German subsidiary.[53] Computer security experts, moreover, sensed that computers were not only targets but tools for intelligence collection. One US Air Force officer publicly listed dozens of tricks for gaining access from afar in a 1979 article citing his work on "tiger teams" testing the security of military networks. If anything, he noted, the ease with which these teams penetrated real computers holding sensitive data masked the depth of the problem, as they largely missed the possibility of intentional compromise of the systems in question:

> Most tiger teams concentrate on accidental flaws that anyone might happen to find, but the deliberate flaws are dormant until activated by an attacker. These errors can be placed virtually anywhere and are carefully designed to escape detection. Yet most military systems include programs not developed in a secure environment, and some are even developed abroad. In fact some systems can be subverted by an anonymous remote technician with no legitimate role in the system development. These errors can be activated by essentially any external interface—from an unclassified telegram to a unique situation set up for detection by a surveillance system.[54]

This lesson in vulnerability had already been driven home to the Intelligence Community. The revelation came in 1972, with a test of a database that would pool data from several agencies to allow the sharing of reports across agency lines. An NSA historian later recounted what happened when DIA, the system's creator, challenged NSA and other members of the Intelligence Community to probe it for security flaws: "By the time the attacks terminated, the penetration was so thorough that a penetrator at a distant remote terminal had actually seized control of the system. DIA never got its accreditation, and the results of the exercise made many at NSA skeptical that multilevel security could ever be achieved."[55]

As if to prove the point, a system administrator at Lawrence Berkeley Lab in 1986 stumbled upon a group of West German intruders, paid in money and drugs by the KGB, roaming inside Defense Department and contractor networks. These "Hannover hackers" seem to have accomplished little for Moscow beyond alerting US defense and intelligence agencies to the fact that remote network penetration was no longer a merely theoretical possibility. "We've had a real problem convincing various entities that computer security is a problem," noted a senior NSA officer to the astronomer from California whose logbook had tracked the Hannover hackers' exploits; "this is the first documented case."[56] CIA analysts cited the case as well when computer networking opportunities between East and West began expanding late in the decade. "The idea of conducting intelligence collection via electronic mail might seem ludicrous," noted one study in 1990, but the information in databases might help case officers spot targets for traditional espionage, and "computer networking represents a new communications medium with global reach and a quick response time."[57]

The Hannover hackers also illustrated a dilemma for the Soviets. Their spies could steal computers and data, but the East could not use computers as the West could. Worse yet, Moscow was every year falling farther behind the accelerating pace of innovation; the Soviets could no longer apply even the inventions they stole in ways to match the West's lengthening lead in computers and advanced technologies. CIA analysts in 1989 estimated that Soviet computer technology was five to fifteen years behind the West's, and had progressed in no small measure through the illegal diversion of new Western systems and the purchase of used computers in Europe (which, though obsolete, were still better than what the Soviets could build). "US reexport relicensing agreements are virtually ignored by European second-hand computer sellers," explained the CIA, and some evidence suggested that "falsification of end users in export licenses is so common that listing a destination in Austria or Switzerland for a used computer is almost assumed by them to be a diversion."[58]

Keeping Up?

The Soviets would have to spy harder, and they certainly tried. In traditional terms, the spy war was probably a draw in the 1980s; each side had real successes against the other. Britain, France, and the United States pulled in key defectors from Soviet intelligence after working them in place for significant lengths of time. SIS helped spirit senior KGB officer Oleg Gordievsky out of the USSR in 1985, after he served for several years in the Soviet embassy in London. He represented one of the most important agents of the Cold War, and the SIS-MI5 operation that ran him in London stands as a model of the genre.[59] The CIA and FBI cooperated as never before.[60] The CIA ran a Polish colonel, Ryszard Kuklinski, who provided hints at Soviet war plans, and a Russian radar engineer named Adolf Tolkachev, whose information saved the United States years of research and development in countering new Soviet systems.[61] The French netted KGB officer Vladimir Vetrov ("Farewell"), whose reporting "caused my worst nightmares to come true," recalled National Security Council staffer Gus Weiss; "it appeared that the Soviet military and civil sectors [in the 1980s] were in large measure running their research on that of the West."[62] The revelations of Soviet espionage against Western technology helped prod NATO into toughening security and export restrictions—and, the KGB alleged, to sabotaging equipment illicitly bound for the USSR.[63] SIS and other services worked hard to enforce the technology embargo, and arrests of spies in the West did have an effect.[64]

All such diligence, of course, could still be wiped out by penetrations of the Western services themselves. The Americans suffered particularly from this. In 1987, for instance, a defecting Cuban intelligence officer, Florentino Aspillago Lombard, told the CIA that virtually all its agents there for at least the preceding decade—more than four dozen—had in fact been controlled by Cuban intelligence. What would not be clear until another decade had passed was that two Cuban spies were even then launched on careers that would land them senior analytical jobs at DIA (Ana Montes) and the State Department's Bureau of Intelligence and Research (Kendall Myers).[65] Robert Hanssen (FBI) and Aldrich Ames (CIA) separately but concurrently devastated US intelligence operations behind the Iron Curtain; the Justice Department's affidavit against Ames alleged that his 1985 compromise of at least ten "penetrations of the Soviet military and intelligence services deprived the United States of extremely valuable intelligence material for years to come."[66] One stalwart of CIA's Soviet operations remained convinced almost two decades later that the activities of Hanssen and Ames and a third CIA defector (Edward Lee Howard) still did not account for all the American and British assets lost to Moscow's counterintelligence in the "Year of the Spy" (1985). "The conclusion is almost inescapable," wrote Milt Bearden, "that there was a fourth man—an as yet unidentified traitor who may have left Langley or simply stopped spying by 1986."[67]

But while the Soviets could blunt Western intelligence collection, they could do little to halt Western analysis of the reams of data that necessarily escaped the USSR. For Moscow this remorselessly shifting reality caused no little anxiety. The traditionally poor analytical capabilities of the East credulously accepted crude partisan charges from President Reagan's critics and judged him an unstable warmonger. The result was a "war scare" for the

Soviet leadership in 1983, and though that alarm was false, what the United States was actually doing was worrisome enough.[68] The American economy was growing again, and the Soviet Union's was not, which meant the West had ever more resources for refining and deploying the new technology. Reagan's Strategic Defense Initiative (SDI), though derided as "Star Wars" and not yet technologically feasible, threatened to change the strategic balance by neutralizing much of Moscow's nuclear arsenal. Leaders in the Kremlin might regard SDI as a ruse, but they could not be certain, and they knew they could not match it. Only fundamental reform in the East could enable the Soviets to compete once again on even terms.

The End of History

> Now why should a good society fear that its people are going to run away? If you are so good, people will try to get in, not out, for heaven's sake! This is very simple logic.
>
> —CHINESE SCIENTIST FANG LIZHI, DESCRIBING HIS TRIP TO
> EAST BERLIN TO AN AUDIENCE IN SHANGHAI, 1986

Moscow's response to the growing gap between East and West precipitated one of the most tumultuous periods in modern history. Enormous changes wracked the Soviet empire and its satellites, culminating in a dizzying transfer of power and relatively open elections. In the beginning of 1989, every Eastern European nation was Communist; at year's end only Yugoslavia and Albania still had party governance (neither was a Soviet client). Within two years, the Soviet Union itself—the world home of Marxism-Leninism— would be dissolved, to be replaced by fifteen independent and nominally non-Communist nations. All these events took place with relatively little bloodshed, though the potential for tragedy loomed throughout. Space does not allow a full timeline of events, which defy hyperbole and indeed almost belief. They are still being chronicled and interpreted in a voluminous and growing literature that improves every year as new sources come to light. The key for our purpose is the ways in which events shaped the intelligence services of the two sides, and the vital roles that the services themselves played in shaping those events. This was the third and final world crisis of the twentieth century, and as in the first two, intelligence was important on both sides. The crisis, however, was not one that the intelligence services of the two Cold War sides had expected or been built to encounter. Thus, it strained the services on both sides of the Iron Curtain, and their ability to understand events. Eastern and Western services alike fell short, though in significantly different ways.

Both sides misunderstood the Soviet economy when the Soviet Union's new general secretary, Mikhail Gorbachev, began to reform it in 1985. Gorbachev, like his predecessors, determined that the East was falling farther behind the West. Khrushchev had glimpsed the rot in the late 1960s: "Of course, there are still people of principle among Communists, but there are also many people without principle, lickspittle functionaries and petty careerists."[69] The problem was not only political—it had material implications as well. "Economic growth had virtually stopped by the beginning of the 1980s and with it the improvement of the rather low living standard," Gorbachev remembered. "We were faced with the prospect of social economic decline."[70] He (again like his predecessors) sought to impose greater efficiency on the society and the economy. Unlike them, however, Gorbachev recognized the party as part of the problem, and he showed both a radical willingness to experiment with forms and rules of governance (*perestroika*) and a flexibility in foreign affairs calculated to ensure that new international tensions did not spur even faster rearmament and modernization in the West. Doing so, in both cases, implied a requirement for accurate knowledge of conditions both abroad and at home.

Here is where the East failed grievously. Soviet policymakers themselves had to rely on scanty economic data and would not share the data even with Politburo members; whole areas of government expenditure, like defense and intelligence spending, were closed books for all but two or three of the nation's highest leaders.[71] In the early 1980s, Gorbachev, then a member of the Politburo, went with one of his allies to General Secretary Yuri Andropov seeking access to the state budget. "Nothing doing! You are asking too much," responded Andropov. "The budget is off limits to you."[72] Indeed, some of the best economic data on the USSR available in Moscow had been produced in the West.[73] Sometimes the numbers came from CIA analysis—which was growing increasingly pessimistic about the Soviet economy. The agency in July 1984 judged that overall growth had stagnated at less than 2 percent per annum, but saw little chance that the downturn would prompt political liberalization or popular unrest—or that it would "bring to power a leadership with significantly different foreign policy aims."[74]

Indeed, CIA analysts felt confident in their knowledge of the USSR's economy and its burden of military spending. Not everyone at the agency shared this confidence. Director of Central Intelligence James Schlesinger claimed later to have told the analysts in 1973 that their estimates of Soviet military spending seemed low; in his words, the CIA's "major bureaucratic investment in that particular interpretation" made it slow to adjust its assessments.[75] Robert Gates spent time as the agency's deputy director for intelligence (and thus chief of the analytical section) on his way to becoming DCI himself, and he admitted in his memoir, "I was never comfortable with our estimates of Soviet military spending." Gates declined to quibble with the analysts' methodology, but worried that the "lack of communication between the economists and the military experts seemed hopeless."[76] Yet he could not effect a fundamental change in the analysis: "Despite my supposed intimidation of the Soviet office, I was remarkably unable to alter at all their approach to the Soviet economy—even to persuade them to acknowledge uncertainty, or to take seriously other points of view."[77] A decade after the dissolution of the Soviet Union the argument still boiled. Gorbachev himself had claimed in 1996 that military expenditures comprised 40 percent of state spending and 20 percent of the Soviet gross national product (GNP).[78] But how big was that economy? At a conference in 2001 to assess the CIA's analytical record, a senior agency economist conceded Soviet GNP was indeed smaller than CIA judged it in the 1980s, perhaps only 40 percent as large as the GNP of the United States (as opposed to the 49 percent figure used in the 1991 edition of CIA's publicly available *Handbook of Economic Statistics*). At that same conference, RAND Corporation economist Charles Wolf Jr., insisted that actual Soviet GNP was 30 percent of the United States', and thus Soviet defense spending was 25 percent of GNP, not the roughly 15 percent that the CIA had claimed.[79]

The correct numbers might never be known, but in the mid-1980s it seemed clear that military spending represented a huge burden on a Soviet economy that itself had largely ceased to grow. What this meant for national policies was fiercely debated in Washington. Indeed, here was a crucial divide between Western and Eastern intelligence systems. Leaders in Congress and the White House knew enough about the intelligence to debate its meaning, thus forcing some flexibility and alertness on the intelligence collectors and analysts. Gates might have doubted his own analysts' assessments, but he carried them downtown even after the agency's 1983 conclusion that military spending had plateaued: "I was treated to repeated lectures at Defense and the White House on the problems we were creating with this analysis. We never backed off one iota." All the same, Gates felt "frustrated both because of my own skepticism over our estimates of Soviet military spending, and because I saw members of Congress as well as senior administration officials misusing—and abusing—our analysis, citing it out of context to support their particular agenda."[80] Democratic members of Congress wondered if the Republican administration was overspending on defense against a decaying Soviet threat, and by 1986 some key Senators (despite overall praise for the quality of the Intelligence Community's analysis) publicly and privately suggested that CIA analysts could be missing big changes in the USSR.[81] Though partisan debates in Washington caused late nights and bruised feelings at the agency, the give and take in relative terms forced greater objectivity in the Intelligence Community and thus on balance probably represented a source of strength for the American intelligence system.

Communist nations saw no such debates over intelligence analysis. No leader likes information that seems counter to the official line, but in the West those policies were set by elected representatives and parties that competed for votes; under communism there was but one truth and its one legitimate party. If the Eastern economies were stagnating, that must be the result of malignant outside forces. One KGB leader in 1983 secretly warned Warsaw Pact partners that a "significant change had taken place in the political-operational situation" in recent years and thus "the securing of the people's economies" had assumed high importance. Economic warfare through "spying, sabotage and diversion" now occupied "a particular place in the 'anti-Communist crusade' of the imperialists against Socialism."[82] Even where Eastern services were highly proficient—the Stasi and its HVA, for instance, had ample penetrations of the West German government and society—they mostly passed on what their Western sources wrote, and they carefully phrased reports on economic developments to ensure they comported with Marxist ideology. Even still, East Germany's leadership not infrequently rejected analyses that discomfited them.[83] Stasi chief Erich Mielke, himself a member of the Politburo and thus both a consumer and producer of intelligence, directed the service in 1982 to help secure the economy against "all subversive attacks" and to support "state and economic management organs in guaranteeing considerable internal stability in all economic branches."[84] There were exceptions to this dogmatism. In late 1985, Gorbachev wrote to KGB chairman Victor M. Cherbikov "on the impermissibility of distortions of the factual state of affairs in messages and informational reports sent to the Central Committee of the CPSU and other ruling bodies." Cherbikov used the opportunity to remind his subordinates of the Chekist duty to fulfill "the Leninist requirements that we need only the whole truth."[85]

Here lay the paradox of the party-based intelligence model. Viewing the world in terms of class struggle meant the party intelligence systems had to struggle against enemies within the homeland as well as abroad. By the 1980s, the Communist regimes had intelligence and security services that were incredibly good at surveillance, having laced entire societies with microphones and informants on the theory that every mote of dissent was dangerous. "We simply do not have the right to permit even the smallest miscalculation" that could lead ultimately to an underground, a "transition to terrorism," or even "create the conditions for the overthrow of socialism," then–KGB Chairman Yuri Andropov told his officers in 1979.[86] East Germany's Stasi stood unmatched as the most meticulous of all the internal security organs. Officially titled the Ministry for State Security, the Stasi's motto—"Sword and Shield of the Party"—expressed its official focus on building socialism. In 1989, the Stasi boasted 91,000 employees and kept in contact with 189,000 informers (about 1 percent of the country's population).[87] Such resources enabled the organization to monitor all facets of life in East Germany, and, since the Stasi cowed the judicial system, it could ensure maximum efficiency in disposing of the cases that came its way.[88]

French philosopher Michel Foucault could hardly have imagined such a system of oppression in his discussion of *surveillance* as a mechanism for self-generated social control. Such fearsome internal security services (the KGB and Stasi differed from their Eastern Bloc partners only in degree, not in kind) had the intended effect of teaching the citizenry that any stray remark could find its way to the authorities. But while these systems inevitably corrupted and cowed most people, they also made heroes of a few. Men and women like Karol Wojtyla, Lech Walesa, Vaclav Havel, Andrei Sakharov, and Yelena Bonner learned to live under the microscope. In response, the regimes sought to surround them with spies and to weave webs of lies about their characters. Any bit of compromising information could serve, such as the allegation that Walesa, while an electrician at the Lenin Shipyard in the 1970s, had himself given reports on coworkers to Poland's secret police, the *Służba Bezpieczeństwa* (SB). Confronted by his former SB case officer while detained after the imposition of martial law, Walesa refused to be intimidated. By then, of course, he was a world figure and soon to be the recipient of the Nobel Peace Prize. His courage immunized him to whatever the regime might throw at him, and though Walesa has always denied the charge, it speaks to the distrust that the surveillance system injected into Polish society that the controversy continues over real or fabricated evidence of his dealings with the SB.

Communist societies might have looked stable to outsiders, but underneath the surface of events strong crosscurrents threatened the regimes' very existence. Popular cynicism about Marxist dogma and discontent over declining living standards prevailed across the socialist world. Party leaders and officials, however, feared to lose their privileges and only reluctantly went along with Gorbachev's economic restructuring (*perestroika*). Frustrated by the stagnation, the general secretary in 1988 accelerated the pace of change with radical steps to force the party to reform its outlook and practices. His openness campaign or *glasnost* opened the party leadership to unaccustomed criticism. His new law on cooperatives, passed in May, allowed local co-ops to set their own prices and make deals overseas.[89] In June, the Council for Mutual Economic Assistance (Comecon) countries decided they could directly negotiate their own national trade deals with the European Community. Gorbachev also sought to build an independent political power base outside the party.

The KGB tried to follow Gorbachev's shifting line. The service sent fewer agents abroad, and assured the Central Committee of the Communist Party of the Soviet Union that it was learning "to work in a new way" along "the path to forming a state based on law." The new "socio-political situation in the country" in 1988 prompted the KGB leadership to seek "the flexible utilization of the whole arsenal of chekist means in the struggle with the activity of antisocialist elements." But those means were tempered. By 1989, the KGB was taking fewer "prophylactic measures" against Soviet citizens (only 338 that year, as compared to 15,000-plus in 1985), and it assisted in the mostly posthumous rehabilitation of 838,630 citizens. Perhaps most telling, the KGB's report to Gorbachev for 1989 (completed in early 1990) came addressed to him in his post as chairman of the Supreme Soviet of the USSR, instead of as previously in his capacity as general secretary of the Central Committee.[90]

The first non-Communist-controlled elections in the USSR came in early 1989, followed by elections in Poland and then Hungary that spring that had seriously weakened the party's grip on power. Gorbachev had told Warsaw Pact leaders in March 1985 that he favored "all parties taking full responsibility for the situation in their own countries."[91] The USSR would not interfere in their internal affairs—the Soviet army would stay in its barracks if local regimes faced popular unrest.[92] He promised the United Nations in December that half a million Soviet troops would soon leave Eastern Europe, and the last Soviet formations departed Afghanistan in February 1989. The parties ruling Moscow's allies were truly on their own by the summer of that momentous year. In the autumn they fell like dominoes.

Citizens of Poland, Hungary, East Germany, Czechoslovakia, Bulgaria, and finally Romania filled the streets that fall, showing that the people desired to take charge of the peoples' republics. Their numbers overwhelmed the ability of the security services to respond, and with the Soviet and Warsaw Pact troops sitting in their garrisons, the local party governments had to negotiate power sharing deals and ultimately elections that swept the Communists from power. Only Romania briefly saw bloodshed; its *Securitate* fought back futilely, and dictator Nicolae Ceaucescu and his wife were soon captured and shot. The groundswell of popular revulsion to the regimes of the peoples' republics stemmed directly from the stifling of dissent that the party-dominated security services had maintained so well. In lands where all criticism was effectively anti-party, all blame thus attached to the party, meaning its rule could not last when challenged from below. The breaching of the Berlin Wall on November 9, 1989, marked the revolution's joyous consummation.

A bizarre scene in Berlin on November 13 captured the essence of the revolution. The country's Marxist leadership had abdicated a week earlier, but the new members of the *Volkskammer* (parliament) soon called former ministers to render accounts on national television. When his turn came, Erich Mielke of the Ministry of State Security, dressed in a suit instead of his white uniform, summarized the Stasi's mission as maintaining peace, strengthening the national economy, and ensuring that "the working people can communicate their troubles and problems." Mielke's insinuation that the Stasi's "extraordinarily high contact with the working people" amounted

to some sort of national grievance process, plus his insistence on addressing his audience as "Comrades," struck the delegates as ridiculous. When a
non-Communist delegate interrupted and demanded not to be called comrade, Mielke groveled (over mounting laughter) "My apologies, this is only
. . . this is only natural love for humankind . . . this is just a formality . . . I
love . . . but I love all . . . all human beings." The Sword and Shield of the
Party had shrunk to a tired old man, powerless to harm anyone.[93]

The loss of the Soviet empire hastened reform in the USSR and
strengthened nationalist desires that soon threatened to tear that country
apart as well. As the crisis unfolded, the American Intelligence Community
gave national leaders generally good situational awareness. In late 1989, the
agency summarized the possibilities for President Bush before his summit
with Gorbachev at Malta. Bush received a raft of briefs: "I found the CIA
experts particularly helpful, if pessimistic. One analysis paper concluded
that Gorbachev's economic reforms were doomed to failure, and that his
political changes were beginning to cause problems he might not be able to
control. It argued that the reforms were strong enough to disrupt the Soviet
system, but not strong enough to give the Soviet people the benefits of a
market economy."[94]

Over the next couple of years, CIA analysts sent ever-gloomier assessments on the worsening situation in the USSR. Many such reports went to
a special and secret team that had been created by the NSC's Robert Gates
in September 1989 to plan US options, "because the situation in the Soviet
Union could go bad in a hurry."[95] The sustained analytic effort enabled the
agency to help policymakers understand a fast-moving and complex situation, with wide-ranging opinions in Washington and the West, and one
furthermore fraught with the danger of bloodshed and civil war (as happened in Yugoslavia in 1991). In the summer of 1991, the agency's analysts performed one of their best services. Their daily brief to President
Bush on August 17, 1991, warned of a possible coup attempt by "conservatives" against Gorbachev at any time, as the new Union treaty scheduled
to be signed in three days would further devolve power from Moscow and
make the odds of a "restoration" even longer.[96] The blow fell in Moscow
on August 19.

That final desperate act to impede the onrush of history was cospon-
sored by KGB Chairman Vladimir Kryuchkov, who for months had been
trying to alert fellow Communist leaders, and indeed the Soviet populace,

of the growing danger to socialism. Not a few of the coup's plotters hated their growing dependency on the West's good will. In December 1990, Kryuchkov publicly noted that "extremely radical political tendencies" had been set loose, some of them receiving "lavish moral and material support from abroad," and he warned that subversive elements were combining to "undermine our society and our state, and to liquidate Soviet power." He told a closed session of the Supreme Soviet in June 1991 that outside forces—namely "agents of influence" run by Western intelligence—were wrecking the USSR.[97]

Western intelligence had no tactical warning of the August 1991 coup (Gates noted the CIA "never recruited a spy who gave us unique political information from inside the Kremlin"), but then, Gorbachev himself, with far better sources in the Kremlin, was surprised as well.[98] Here one of his greatest mistakes possibly saved his life, even if it wrecked the USSR. He had allowed the creation of independent power centers outside the party, thus transitioning the formerly monolithic Soviet Union into a confederacy. The coup plotters, among them Kryuchkov, struck too late in the transition process. Success would have required them to isolate Moscow from the outside world long enough to complete the reversal of Gorbachev's political reforms and liquidate their rivals. By August 1991, the new president of Russia, Boris Yeltsin, had amassed enough power to mobilize popular opposition to the coup, and a global news media was so ubiquitous even in Moscow that Yeltsin could rally international support from Western capitals. Satellite news feeds showed the world what was happening, while fast CIA analysis explained its nuances to policymakers in Washington. What they and other Western leaders saw, with CIA help, was that the coup was timid and inept. Western leaders coordinated their responses within hours, betting that the putsch could be reversed.[99] The coup thus failed because the KGB had failed—it was a great sword and shield, but lacked brains to understand the changing world. The plotters neglected to cut the phone lines for the surrounded Russian Supreme Soviet, allowing President Bush to speak with Yeltsin directly. The Soviet Army refused to obey the junta and attack Yeltsin; a tank served as his podium for addressing the swelling crowds. The plotters soon lost their nerve and submitted, allowing a weakened Gorbachev to resume his post as president of the USSR. The following day, a jubilant crowd assembled before the Lubyanka, the KGB's famous headquarters, and used a crane to topple the immense statue of the first

Chekist, Felix Dzerzhinsky. Gorbachev assented to the Soviet Union's dissolution on Christmas Day, 1991, and the Cold War was over.

The West Triumphant

Just weeks before the fall of the Berlin Wall, an official at the US Department of State asked aloud if the world had reached "the End of History." In his soon-famous article, Francis Fukuyama surveyed recent events in China, the Soviet Union, and Eastern Europe and tallied an "unabashed victory of economic and political liberalism," with "the total exhaustion of viable systematic alternatives to Western liberalism" everywhere except in a few backwaters like Nicaragua.[100] Fukuyama was soon proved wrong on a minor point; a coalition of Nicaraguan opposition parties from across the political spectrum trounced the ruling Sandinistas in a February 1990 election, effectively ending the civil war there (peace talks to end the conflict in El Salvador as well soon followed). Whether or not his grand thesis about the End of History holds validity, Fukuyama's insight about the importance of ideology in shaping events was soon to be amply verified by the changed trajectory in the development of intelligence structures and practices.

The 1990s began with the Anglo-American intelligence superpower seemingly supreme. Though a few party-based systems remained, most notably in China and North Korea, they were nationalist in their aspirations, and in places where they might have thought in universalist terms, such as in Cuba, they were isolated and bankrupt. The collapse of the party regimes and associated services in Eastern Europe also offered a windfall for the Western services. Robert Gates, now the deputy head of the National Security Council, recalled that the "CIA moved quickly in late 1989 and early 1990 to establish contact with the security services of the new, democratic governments in Eastern Europe. The object was partly to obtain information on Soviet espionage operations run in concert with the spy organizations of the old Warsaw Pact organizations, partly to provide assistance as the new services tried to establish their independence of the KGB, partly to gain access to military and KGB communications equipment, and partly to lay the foundations for future cooperation."[101] Such cooperation in some cases began very quickly. A CIA officer witnessed the official transfer of custody of KGB property to Lithuanian authorities in August 1991, two days after treating his new liaison contacts to dinner in a Vilnius restaurant. He was doubly pleased to find "an artificial exchange rate for US currency allowed me to host the entire leadership of the Lithuanian intelligence service for about nine US dollars."[102]

Disaffected and suddenly impoverished Warsaw Pact intelligence officers seeking their way in the new world offered up copious files from their old agencies. One gave the CIA a trunk load of 17,000 file cards recording West German telephone numbers, in effect providing "a road map to the Stasi's operations" there, and a boon to West German counterintelligence. Another brought "thousands of pages of documents from inside the Stasi, including organization charts and rosters of MfS and HVA officers"—which enabled more recruitments from the dying service. In Czechoslovakia the intelligence service itself, now under new management, detailed officers who "worked with the Americans and British to clear their books of old sleeper agents burrowed deep into Western society."[103] The allies almost competed over the windfalls. When local CIA officers failed to recognize an opportunity, Britain's SIS netted a former KGB archivist, Vasili Mitrokhin, who told a British diplomat in the Baltics that he had an amazing story to tell: Over the course of 1992 he managed to bring out thousands of pages of notes he had compiled for twenty years on KGB operations dating back to the 1920s.[104] Another archive—the microfilmed agents list of Markus Wolf's HVA—apparently ended up at the CIA after the Stasi gave it to the KGB for safekeeping.[105] Finally, if CIA veteran Milt Bearden is correct, the disarray in Moscow might also have induced a "Russian agent" to provide vital clues that eventually steered the agency toward the most damaging spy to date in its midst—Aldrich Ames.[106]

A Unipolar World

The dominance of Western-style power, projected against dictators who resisted with conventional military formations, soon showed to dramatic effect in the Persian Gulf War. Iraq's Saddam Hussein surprised Kuwait and the world when he invaded his small but wealthy neighbor in August 1990, but he had picked the wrong historical moment for this enormity. Like many dictators, Saddam prided himself on his analytical acumen and assured his secret services that he would divine America's response: "I forbade the intelligence outfits from deducing from press [reports] and political analysis. I told them this was not their specialty. . . . I said I don't want either intelligence organization to give me analysis; that is my specialty."[107] But the United States at that moment had troops to spare, with heavy formations departing the soon-to-be-reunited Germany, while both China and the Soviet Union had reasons of their own not to veto action against Iraq in the UN Security Council. A coalition of national contingents led by American forces assembled in Saudi Arabia and launched a bombing campaign to paralyze Iraqi resistance in January 1991, followed by a blitzkrieg into Kuwait and southern Iraq five weeks later. Saddam had the fourth-largest army in the world, though his strength in armor and aircraft availed him little given the battlefield superiority of Western forces using precision-guided munitions and aided by superb tactical intelligence. Coalition forces could fight at night as well as during the day, and the speed and ferocity of their advance overwhelmed Iraqi defenders.

The fighting over Kuwait saw the largest tank battles since the Second World War, but ironically much of the intelligence drama happened in Washington. Two decades of hard work had ensured that analysts at CIA and DIA, with help from satellite sensors and digital networks, could formulate timely and granular insights on battlefield conditions, and could share them with policymakers and commanders. That in turn allowed members of Congress, on both sides of the debate over expelling Saddam from Kuwait, to cite intelligence judgments; indeed, opponents of the war policy criticized its proponents in the White House and Congress for allegedly politicizing the analysis to support an invasion.[108] At almost the same time, the CIA's assessments of Saddam's capacity to repel a counteroffensive seemingly differed from those of the theater commander, General H. Norman Schwarzkopf, and the dispute reached the White House almost on the eve of the coalition's ground assault.[109] President Bush rightly deferred to Schwarzkopf's judgment of battlefield conditions, and days later the war ended in a rout of the Iraqi forces. Schwarzkopf showed little magnanimity, however, soon complaining in his bestselling memoir, "If we had waited to convince the CIA, we'd still be in Saudi Arabia."[110] Such disagreements echoed disputes during the Vietnam War, but in that case the positions had taken years to harden; with the increased connectivity of Washington to the battlefield and the higher velocity of analysis, now analysts, commanders, and policymakers could clash in weeks or days.

The end of the Cold War and the dominance demonstrated in Kuwait convinced legislatures across the West that military and intelligence budgets could safely be trimmed. The existential threat posed by the Soviet Union was no more, but defenders of the agencies' budgets at least tried to argue that the lack of such a peril had actually increased the need for better capabilities for dealing with new threats. "Yes, we have slain a large dragon," conceded President Bill Clinton's first nominee for director of central intelligence, R. James Woolsey, in his 1993 confirmation hearing. "But we live now in a jungle filled with a bewildering variety of poisonous snakes. And in many ways, the dragon was easier to keep track of."[111] The Lord Chancellor (then Lord Mackay of Clashfern) introduced Britain's Intelligence Services Bill in December 1993 with a similar argument: "Superpower rivalry may have created its own grim version of stability, but the collapse of communism, while reducing the scale of one particular threat, has brought new dangers: the rising tide of nationalism and fanaticism, untried alliances, untested groupings, new rivalries and new ambitions. The end of communism marked the lifting of a shadow, but it has provided the opportunity, not the achievement, of a new and more stable world order."[112]

Legislators might have wanted to cut more, but cut they did all the same. US intelligence budgets took their largest absolute reductions in four decades in fiscal year 1993, and remained flat for several more years. Personnel totals at CIA and some other Intelligence Community agencies dropped by a sixth in the mid-1990s.[113] NSA's budget and manpower fell by about a third.[114] SIS, GCHQ, and the Security Service saw lower budgets and consequently imposed their first personnel layoffs since World War II.[115] Even ministers proved deaf to arguments from agency chiefs. Stella Rimington, the Security Service's first female director general (itself another indicator of change), could not convince her customers that a few thousand pounds was a cheap price to pay for preventing an IRA bombing in London, and came away "wondering ruefully why I had put so much effort into stopping them all getting blown up."[116] Guidance for the agencies in spreading those declining resources across increasing requirements was not always forthcoming, at least in Washington. DCI Woolsey had little direction from above. Referring to the sad case of a man who dove his Cessna at the executive mansion, Woolsey quipped after his brief tenure that he had little access to his boss: "Remember the guy who in 1994 crashed his plane onto the White House lawn? That was me trying to get an appointment to see President Clinton."

The dispute between the analysts and General Schwarzkopf over the timing of the ground offensive to liberate Kuwait imposed yet another reform on the suddenly cash-strapped US Intelligence Community. The

Pentagon, despite losing hunks of its budget to a post–Cold War "peace dividend," continued its emphasis on getting national-level intelligence to the battlefield. "No combatant commander has ever had as full and complete a view of his adversary as did our field commander [General Schwarzkopf]" in the Persian Gulf, wrote Colin Powell, chairman of the Joint Chiefs of Staff, in the Pentagon's war report to Congress.[117] Ironically, that remarkable performance by intelligence automatically came to be the minimum expected of it in future conflicts—and the military's leaders did not shrink from demanding the resources of the CIA and other agencies to sustain it. Robert Gates, now director of central intelligence, complained to Congress in 1992 that cuts in the defense budget were already forcing the military to trim tactical intelligence programs and pass their work on to the national intelligence services.[118] President Clinton supported the Pentagon in this campaign, issuing in 1995 (shortly after DCI Woolsey's departure) a Presidential Decision Directive (PDD-35) setting new priorities for the Intelligence Community. As Clinton explained to CIA employees that summer, since commanders needed "prompt, thorough intelligence to fully inform their decisions and maximize the security of our troops," the first priority of the community was now to support "the intelligence needs of our military during an operation."[119]

Shrinking budgets also had to stretch to cover a wholesale recapitalization of the intelligence agencies' computer systems. NSA had bought a $25 million supercomputer it called FROSTBURG in 1991; the "massively parallel processing" machine could perform 65 billion computations per second, but was pulled from service for obsolescence in 1997.[120] At the consumer end of the spectrum, the Pentagon relinquished governance of the internet in 1990, the same year as the new world wide web simplified access to global networks and helped spark a surge of computer innovation for businesses and home users. Developments such as these swiftly rendered obsolete the remaining government-built networks deployed in American intelligence agencies, and hastened the deployment of commercially designed devices running the now-ubiquitous Microsoft operating systems and hooked together in internal "local area networks" (or LANs), many of which in turn were linked in 1994 by an Intelligence Community-wide network called Intelink.[121] All of that meant that much more information was available to many more people—information that could be easily copied and purloined. Spies like Ana Montes and Robert Hanssen soon took advantage of this new access and the ease of moving data to the wrong hands.[122] [Aldrich Ames explained to investigators that the computer systems to which he had access in CIA offices before 1991 "were 'really no more than bona fide [sic] electric typewriters,'" but that changed when he logged on to the Counternarcotics Center's LAN. Its terminals not only carried operational message traffic but had their A:/ drives left open for pocket-sized storage disks that could hold an enormous (for the time) 1.44 megabytes worth of documents apiece: "Ames clearly viewed his access to the CNC LAN as a very significant event in his ability to conduct espionage. The broadened access, combined with the compactness of disks, greatly enhanced the volume of data he could carry out of Agency facilities with significantly reduced risk. Fortunately, he was arrested before he could take full advantage of this system vulnerability."[123]]

The scandal resulting from Ames's espionage helped spur reforms in the Intelligence Community. Access to networks and files tightened considerably. Congress demanded accountability at CIA, and Woolsey essentially wrecked his credibility on Capitol Hill by declining to impose harsh sanctions on the Soviet-area operations officers who had long managed Ames.[124] Members from both political parties also insisted that the US intelligence budget be spent more wisely, and gave Woolsey's successors as DCI (John Deutch, 1995–1997, and George Tenet, 1997–2004) more deputies but only marginally more power to manage expenditures across the entire community.[125] In the end, concluded staff members on a congressionally chartered study of the community in the mid-1990s, the secretary of defense was "an 800-pound gorilla" for US intelligence, as most of the community's agencies, spending a combined four-fifths of intelligence dollars, still reported to him. The DCI, by contrast, "more resemble[d] the organ-grinder's monkey."[126]

Public arguments over the governance of intelligence agencies were possible in part because governments on both sides of the Atlantic greeted the new era with gestures toward greater openness. The secrecy that had always cloaked British intelligence had already worn thin by 1986, when Oxford historian Sir Michael Howard explained to American readers, "So far as official Government policy is concerned, the British security and intelligence services, MI5 and MI6, do not exist. Enemy agents are found under gooseberry bushes and intelligence is brought by the storks."[127] London slowly acknowledged the inevitable, publicly avowing the existence of the Security Service in 1988 and of SIS in 1992, and even naming their chiefs as well. Two years later, SIS moved into its modern headquarters building, a Sumerian Revival edifice on the Thames that quickly became one of London's landmarks, if not exactly a destination for tourists. Also in 1992, the Department of Defense and CIA jointly declassified the existence of the National Reconnaissance Office, which had built and flown America's spy satellites for four decades. Openness took on a scholarly cast in several countries. DCI Robert Gates revived a CIA office, the Center for the Study of Intelligence, to encourage scholarship in the field through publishing and declassification. Though the center focused on CIA materials, it also worked with NSA, FBI, and GCHQ in 1995 to release materials on Venona, the Anglo-American exploitation of KGB messages in the 1940s.[128] SIS had already paired Cambridge historian Christopher Andrew with defector Oleg Gordievsky in the late 1980s to write a history of the KGB; now it teamed him with another prize, Vasili Mitrokhin, to produce two dense volumes presenting Mitrokhin's "archive" on Soviet operations worldwide.[129] Finally, in the new Russia, the remnants of the KGB themselves earned some much-needed cash by striking deals with Western publishing houses to allow historians brokered access to the files on old spy cases, operations in Berlin, and the Cuban Missile Crisis. These and parallel efforts in the 1990s collectively boosted intelligence studies across the West.[130]

Another form of openness drove reforms in the nations of the European Community, especially the United Kingdom. Cases in the European Court of Human Rights (ECHR) in the mid-1980s had prompted London to take preemptive action against the possibility that its intelligence activities might be declared in violation of British treaty obligations. The specific issue in question was the ECHR's insistence that suspects could be subjected to legal sanctions only in accordance with the provisions of law. Since Britain had never avowed its national intelligence organizations, let alone enshrined them in statute, intelligence collection methods and the Security Service that conducted them were technically extralegal and unlikely to withstand ECHR scrutiny should new espionage cases involving them come before the court. In response, Parliament passed the Interception of Communications Act in 1985, and then the Security Service Act in 1989. The latter not only acknowledged the existence of MI5 but also hallowed the principle that the service (unlike SIS and GCHQ) would set its investigative priorities independently of political tasking and according to its own assessment of threats to the realm.[131] After the end of the Cold War, the government of Prime Minister John Major decided to follow the Act's precedent with an analogous bill to put SIS and GCHQ on a firm legal footing. The resulting Intelligence Services Act, passed in 1994, defined the functions of those two agencies and also provided for quasi-parliamentary oversight of both (and MI5 as well) in the form of an Intelligence and Security Committee (ISC) comprising members drawn from the House of Commons and House of Lords in consultation with the Opposition. The ISC would report on the "expenditure, administration and policy" of the services annually to the prime minister, who would then lay the report before Parliament.[132] That in effect authorized the publication of Britain's intelligence budget, at least in aggregate terms. Despite public misgivings about its independence from the prime minister, the ISC set out in earnest to provide oversight to the services.[133] Members of Parliament serving on the committee did not always have much knowledge of the business, however, and at least one seemed relieved to tell MI5 staffers "You are obviously sane and ordinary people."[134]

Eastern intelligence services emerging from the ruins of the Warsaw Pact had much bigger problems. They had been in effect the eyes and ears of their local parties, though built to work as adjuncts to the KGB (the major exception being Romania's *Securitate*). Needless to say, these services proved to be of limited utility and no little concern to the more or less democratic governments that took power in 1989. Germany solved its Stasi problem outright by liquidating it; the Federal Republic extended its security and intelligence functions over the newly reunited country in October 1990. Other states did not have this luxury. In effect they had to reconstruct the authorities, personnel, and practices of their intelligence arms while still employing them, and they had to do so, moreover, while their blighted economies sputtered to life and their legislatures, governments, and judicial systems painfully learned how to act according to democratic norms. Results naturally varied according to local conditions. As a rule, the Communist-era services were immediately shrunk through layoffs, and their personnel accepted for continued employment only after vetting, which differed in quality from country to country. Czechoslovakia dissolved its State Security (StB) in 1990 and tried to start again from scratch; reportedly SIS provided field training, and CIA gave them new communications.[135] When that nation in turn split amicably into Slovakia and the Czech Republic in 1992, the Czechs held to this long-term strategy while the Slovaks rehired StB veterans who then dominated their new service for another decade. Western nations hesitated to give direct aid to the legacy services that had suppressed human rights, though some assistance could be given under the table. As the decade proceeded, the promise of NATO membership proved the needed carrot and stick in several Eastern Europe capitals, providing deadlines for compliance with NATO's security standards as well as resources and expertise to help local services attain them.[136]

Russia's experience with intelligence reform hardly paralleled that of its Eastern European neighbors. There was no inducement of NATO membership to prompt changes, and the initial flirtation with democracy soon gave way to oligarchy. In late 1991, just before the USSR's end, the KGB was split into its domestic and foreign functions—respectively the Federal Counter-Intelligence Service (FSK) and the Foreign Intelligence Service (SVR). As indicated above, by this point both had serious problems with discipline, morale, and security, though Soviet military intelligence (the GRU), with its capable foreign intelligence apparatus, apparently weathered the storm with little or no damage to its workforce and operations. By the mid-1990s the SVR, the ultimate heir to the KGB's overseas stations and assets, had seemingly regained its footing. Domestic security work, on the other hand, also suffered during the crisis of Russia's state and society, as reformers and the old guard struggled over the nation's future course. FSK in turn took on its current identity as the Federal Security Service of the Russian Federation (FSB) three years later, and in 1998 gained a new chief with KGB experience. His name was Vladimir Putin.

The World Online

Washington at this time began to grow alarmed about threats in a novel venue. Not entirely by coincidence, when the Cold War ended in 1990, the world wide web was invented, making computer networks so much easier to navigate that the average citizen could do so with the right interfaces. This web soon reached homes and businesses via cheap connections and Internet browsers, and thus what had been a technical security problem for network administrators would now be everyone's problem. President Bill Clinton in 1996 had appointed a commission to examine the risk of attacks on critical infrastructure. His panel expressed itself publicly in a dramatic fashion: "A satchel of dynamite and a truckload of fertilizer and diesel fuel are known terrorist tools. Today, the right command sent over a network to a power generating station's control computer could be just as devastating as a backpack full of explosives, and the perpetrator would be more difficult to identify and apprehend. The rapid growth of a computer-literate population ensures that increasing millions of people around the world possess the skills necessary to conduct such an attack."[137]

American military thinkers had already formulated similar ideas about using "information warfare" techniques against nation-state adversaries, and foreign militaries also took notice. Both China and Russia had had no choice but to acquire Western (often American) computer hardware and software if they wanted to join the global information revolution. This did not sit well. The KGB had reported finding sabotaged Western computers coming into the USSR in 1988.[138] Now a few years later the internet made such problems even worse. A former Russian general told *Pravda* in 1996: "Many people are happy that they got access to the Internet Web, but the owners are American, not us. Now in Russia lots of American servers have been set up, and they supply their equipment for low prices. . . . We must remember about the 'logical bombs' . . . inlaid in their programs. Can you imagine what would happen if one day on a special command all the equipment was to be rendered useless? The system of state government will be paralyzed."[139] Matching sentiments arose in China, where military experts in 1995 discussed the American enthusiasm for information warfare. One noted that "computer viruses were used to destroy the computer systems of Iraq's air defense system" in the Gulf War, and argued China "must not fall behind the times."[140]

At least one Chinese military thinker saw opportunity in this situation. China and the United States had recently sparred diplomatically over Beijing's test-firing of missiles to influence a Taiwanese election; once again the two giants were at odds, and China felt its naval inferiority to American forces in the Western Pacific. An article in *Liberation Army Daily* in the summer of 1996 noted that a million personal computers had been sold in China the previous year, and that sales might soon triple. These computers and their networks could be "not only instruments, but also weapons. A people's war under such conditions would be complicated, broad-spectrum, and changeable, with higher degrees of uncertainty and probability, which requires full preparation and circumspect organization. An information war is inexpensive, as the enemy country can receive a paralyzing blow through the Internet, and the party on the receiving end will not be able to tell whether it is a child's prank or an attack from its enemy."[141] An exercise run the previous year by the RAND Corporation had helped convince US policymakers that such a possibility was indeed realistic. The scenario involved a new conflict with Saddam's Iraq, only this time the Iraqis were not held to conventional means for striking the Americans. The vulnerability of "interconnected network control systems for such necessities as oil and gas pipelines, electric grids, etc." in the United States ensured that Iraqi cyber attackers had plenty of targets. "In sum," concluded RAND's report, "the U.S. homeland may no longer provide a sanctuary from outside attack."[142]

Public confirmations that such concerns were justified came rapidly. In early 1998, "intrusions" in unclassified Pentagon networks seemed to originate in the Middle East, prompting fears of an Iraqi cyber attack before the American teenagers behind the break-ins were caught. NSA Director Kenneth Minihan told Congress that summer that "tactical-level attacks occur every day" on the department's information systems.[143] For the Pentagon, moreover, a more serious intruder was already inside the wire. James Adams reported in 2001 that a group of unidentified but possibly Russian hackers had, since early 1998, been conducting "a still ongoing operation that American investigators have code-named Moonlight Maze." The intruders had already "stolen thousands of files containing technical research, contracts, encryption techniques, and unclassified but essential data relating to the Pentagon's war-planning systems."[144] Fears of attacks on critical infrastructure seemed another step closer to reality in the spring of 2001. California's electrical power distribution authority spotted a series of intrusions aimed at the network's controls and suspected Chinese cyber actors (the attempts were routed via China Telecom). Although the intrusions happened in the midst of a statewide power crisis, California officials insisted that the intrusions had not affected electrical supplies, let alone caused any outages. Legislators in Sacramento, nonetheless, complained that such an intrusion had not only occurred but had gone unnoticed for weeks.[145]

Conclusion

What is socialism? The most difficult and tortuous way to progress from capitalism to capitalism.

—OVERHEARD AT A MEETING OF COMMUNIST BLOC INTELLIGENCE
SERVICES IN EAST BERLIN, 1988

In 1980, the world had two intelligence superpowers. A decade later only one was left. The Anglo-American intelligence alliance, with help from Western allies and non-Western partners of convenience, showed itself increasingly dominant and ultimately victorious in its ability to contain, understand, and influence adversarial states that were motivated by a materialist ideology. Yet that dominance proved fleeting in crucial areas.

Intelligence found it difficult to deal with familiar threats in the 1990s. Several national intelligence systems, not to mention the United Nations, sought to monitor Saddam Hussein's interest in acquiring weapons of mass destruction. After the Persian Gulf War, UN inspectors discovered that Iraq had pulled far closer than imagined to the ability to build an atomic bomb.[146] Intelligence collection and analysis thus underperformed even when focused on the correct adversary at the right time; when their attention was elsewhere, they did even worse. In 1998, for example, elections in India brought to power the Bharatiya Janata Party, which had publicly vowed to test a nuclear weapon. When that test duly occurred ten weeks later, however, the world learned of it from an Indian government press release. DCI George Tenet told Congress "we didn't have a clue" about what was coming.[147] Apparently no intelligence service did.

Even the good news was mixed. Led by the United States, Western military powers became superb at providing intelligence to operational planners and battlefield commanders. When NATO forces cooperated in a massive coalition effort against Serbia in defense of Kosovo at the end of the decade, the intelligence support that was considered remarkable during the Persian War had been far surpassed. Intelligence sharing flowed laterally across the alliance, between alliance members, and between analysts in national capitals and commanders in the field through innovations like video teleconferences.[148] In the Bosnian (1996) and Kosovo (1999) campaigns, former DCI George Tenet recalled, "we decentralized access to intelligence by pushing its analysis and exploitation as close as possible to the war fighter—whether in the foxhole or in the cockpit. Not only did we convey this data to the field in nanoseconds, but we also allowed our deployed forces to reach back into giant databases to pull the data they believed they needed to do their jobs. Military men and women far away from Washington actually know best what they need most, and today they have the ability to reach in and get it."[149] Such intelligence was not flawless, of course. With weapons so powerful and accurate, the information to targeters had to be triple checked, as demonstrated by the errant bombing of the Chinese embassy in Belgrade after the CIA offered mistaken coordinates, supposedly for a Yugoslav intelligence facility, to strike planners.[150] A single slip could cause a diplomatic disaster.

At the turn of the new century, American policymakers feared that rogue states or terrorists might penetrate the United States' virtually unguarded information networks and critical infrastructure to steal files, corrupt data, and even damage vital public functions. The Joint Chiefs of Staff in 1997 ran an exercise dubbed ELIGIBLE RECEIVER to test the military's ability to work with other departments in responding to a cyber attack on critical infrastructure. NSA Director Minihan told Congress that the exercise showed how "a moderately sophisticated adversary can cause considerable damage with fewer than thirty people and a nominal amount of money if the systems they are attacking are not adequately protected and defended."[151] Deputy Secretary of Defense John J. Hamre concluded "[t]his country is wide open to attack electronically." The "red team" playing the adversary in ELIGIBLE RECEIVER was restricted to using store-bought computers and hacking tools downloaded from the internet, but that did not seem to hamper its work. "We didn't really let them take down the power system," Hamre told an audience of business leaders, "but we made them prove they knew how to do it."[152]

The intelligence alliance that emerged from the Cold War by the end of the century was finding itself overwhelmed by technological change. Its members had competed well against the Soviet Union, explained NSA Director Michael Hayden in 2002, but now they had to "keep pace with a global telecommunications revolution, probably the most dramatic revolution in human communications since Gutenberg's invention of movable type."[153] In addition, the threat of a paralyzing sneak attack against critical infrastructure that ninety years earlier apparently came from state adversaries now seemed capable of coming from anywhere. Closed societies, moreover, began viewing the internet as not only an avenue of sabotage but as a carrier of ideological subversion that could undermine a regime's control of its citizens. The very content on the web, and not just the malicious tools it could carry, posed a danger.[154] If societies themselves were now vulnerable to digital attacks, individuals had no sanctuary either. The new forms of surveillance were creating "a transparent society of record" (in the words of sociologist Gary T. Marx), in which documentation of everyone's behavior seemed a real possibility.[155] Indeed, by 2000 the technological challenge to Western intelligence would be matched by an ideological one as well.

NOTES

1. Brezhnev's February 25, 1977 letter to President Carter can be read at http://astro.temple.edu/~rimmerma/Carter_Brezhnev_letters.htm; accessed April 16, 2012.

2. Fidel Castro, "Sixth Summit Conference of the Nonaligned Countries," Havana Domestic TV, Foreign Broadcast Information Service, report date September 4, 1979; accessed April 15, 2012, at http://lanic.utexas.edu/project/castro/db/1979/19790903.html.

3. Robert M. Gates, *From the Shadows: The Ultimate Insider's Story of Five Presidents and How They Won the Cold War* (New York: Simon & Schuster, 2006 [1996]), 123.

4. John C. Schmeidel, *Stasi: Shield and Sword of the Party* (New York: Routledge, 2008), 118, 153.

5. Dmitrii Antonovich Volkogonov, *The Rise and Fall of the Soviet Empire: Political Leaders from Lenin to Gorbachev,* Harold Shukman, trans. (London: HarperCollins, 1998), 417.

6. Vasili Mitrokhin, *The KGB in Afghanistan*, intro. and ed. Christian F. Ostermann and Odd Arne Westad, Cold War International History Project, Working Paper No. 40, 28, 37; accessed April 21, 2012, at www.wilsoncenter.org/publication/the-kgb-afghanistan.

7. Ibid., 30, 86.

8. Christopher Andrew and Vasili Mitrokhin, *The World Was Going Our Way: The KGB and the Battle for the Third World* (New York: Basic Books, 2005), 394, 397, 401–5; Mitrokhin, *The KGB in Afghanistan*, 97–98, 104; Gates, *From the Shadows*, 144–47.

9. Andrew and Mitrokhin, *The World Was Going Our Way*, 117.

10. Robert A. Pastor, *Condemned to Repetition: The United States and Nicaragua* (Princeton, NJ: Princeton University Press, 1987), 318; Gates, *From the Shadows*, 127.

11. Gates, *From the Shadows*, 126.

12. Anthony Lake, *Somoza Falling* (Boston: Houghton Mifflin, 1989), 252–57.

13. Andrew and Mitrokhin, *The World Was Going Our Way*, 120–21.

14. Ibid., 122–24.

15. Hal Brands, *Latin America's Cold War* (Cambridge, MA: Harvard University Press, 2010), 6.

16. Jose Angel Moroni Bracamonte and David E. Spencer, *Strategy and Tactics of the Salvadoran FMLN Guerrillas: Last Battle of the Cold War, Blueprint for Future Conflicts* (Westport, CT: Praeger, 1995), 19, 26, 31, 34, 50, 120, 125.

17. Gates, *From the Shadows*, 127, 150–53.

18. Office of Global Issues, CIA Directorate of Intelligence, "The Islamic Jihad," September 25, 1984, reprinted in John Hollister Hedley, ed., *The Directorate of Intelligence: Fifty Years of Informing Policy, 1952–2002* (Washington, DC: Central Intelligence Agency, 2002), 252.

19. Robert Baer, *See No Evil: The True Story of a Ground Soldier in the CIA's War on Terrorism* (New York: Random House, 2003 [2002]), 67.

20. Robin Wright, *Sacred Rage: The Wrath of Militant Islam* (New York: Simon & Schuster, 2001 [1985]), 112. The CIA station chief in Beirut was kidnapped in 1984, apparently by the same Shiite group, Islamic Jihad, that bombed the US and French barracks. He died in captivity the following year.

21. Daniel Burns, trans., "Said Qutb on the Arts in America," Hudson Institute, *Current Trends in Islamist Ideology* 9 (November 18, 2009); accessed June 10, 2012, at www.currenttrends.org/research/detail/said-qutb-on-the-arts-in-america.

22. Gates, *From the Shadows*, 144–47, 164, 174–77, 237, 251, 347–48. See also Milt Bearden and James Risen, *The Main Enemy: The Inside Story of the CIA's Final Showdown with the KGB* (New York: Ballantine, 2004 [2003]), 381.

23. Gates, *From the Shadows*, 242.

24. Brands, *Latin America's Cold War*, 6.

25. Gates, *From the Shadows*, 209, 212, 222, 295, 306–8.

26. Schmeidel, *Stasi*, viii, 157–58. See also Markus Wolf, *Man without a Face: The Autobiography of Communism's Greatest Spymaster* (New York: PublicAffairs, 1997), 310.

27. Christopher Andrew, *Defend the Realm: The Authorized History of MI5* (New York: Knopf, 2009), 691.

28. Wolf, *Man without a Face*, 307. See also John Schmeidel, "My enemy's enemy: Twenty Years of Co-operation between West Germany's Red Army Faction and the GDR Ministry for State Security," *Intelligence and National Security* 8:4 (October 1993): 63–64.

29. Andrew, *Defend the Realm*, 705.

30. Ibid., 698–702.

31. National Commission on Terrorist Attacks upon the United States, *The 9/11 Commission Report* (New York: Norton, 2004), 92, 113.

32. Colin Powell with Joseph E. Persico, *My American Journey: An Autobiography* (New York: Ballantine, 1996 [1995]), 142.

33. Kenneth M. Pollack, *Arabs at War: Military Effectiveness, 1948–1991* (Lincoln: University of Nebraska Press, 2002), 533–34.

34. Thomas R. Johnson, *American Cryptology during the Cold War, 1945–1989*: Book IV: *Cryptologic Rebirth, 1981–1989* (National Security Agency: Center for Cryptologic History, 1999), 266–69; cited hereinafter as *Cryptologic Rebirth*, and accessed June 10, 2012, at www.nsa.gov/public_info/_files/cryptologic_histories/cold_war_iv.pdf.

35. Richard J. Aldrich, *GCHQ: The Uncensored Story of Britain's Most Secret Intelligence Agency* (London: Harper, 2010), 411, 413, 450, 452, 454.

36. Johnson, *Cryptologic Rebirth*, 290, 296–98.

37. Christopher A. Ford and David A. Rosenberg, *The Admirals' Advantage: US Navy Operational Intelligence in World War II and the Cold War* (Annapolis, MD: US Naval Institute Press, 2005), 100–102.

38. Jimmy Carter, Presidential Directive 59, "Nuclear Weapons Employment Policy," July 25, 1980; accessed May 5, 2012, at http://en.wikisource.org/wiki/Index:Carter_Presidential_Directive_59,_Nuclear_Weapons_Employment_Policy.djvu.

39. Lawrence Freedman, *The Evolution of Nuclear Strategy* (New York: Palgrave MacMillan, 2003 [1981]), 386, 389.

40. Ford and Rosenberg, *The Admirals' Advantage*, 80–82, 99.

41. Ibid., 80–82, 93–96.

42. Johnson, *Cryptologic Rebirth*, 339; Desmond Ball and Robert C. Toth, "Revising the SIOP: Taking War-Fighting to Dangerous Extremes," *International Security* 15:4 (Spring 1990): 70–75, 89.

43. John Patrick Finnegan and Ramona Danysh, *Military Intelligence* (Washington, DC: Center of Military History, 1998), 179, 181.

44. Defense Intelligence Agency, "History: 50 Years of Excellence in Defense of the Nation"; accessed April 30, 2012, at www.dia.mil/history. See also Max G. Manwaring and Court Prisk, eds., *El Salvador at War: An Oral History of Conflict from the 1979 Insurrection to the Present* (Washington, DC: National Defense University Press, 1988), 310–12.

45. Bearden and Risen, *The Main Enemy*, 29.

46. Gates, *From the Shadows*, 347, 350. See also Bearden and Risen, *The Main Enemy*, 245–48.

47. Johnson, *Cryptologic Rebirth*, 291.

48. William. J. Broad, "Computer Security Worries Military Experts," *New York Times*, September 25, 1983.

49. James P. Anderson and Co., "Computer Security Technology Planning Study," ESD-TR-73–51, vol. 2, October 1972, 62–63; accessed November 11, 2012, at csrc.nist.gov/publications/history/ande72.pdf.

50. Broad, "Computer Security Worries Military Experts."

51. National Security Decision Directive 145, "National Policy on Telecommunications and Automated Information Systems Security," September 17, 1984; accessed April 30, 2012, at www.fas.org/irp/offdocs/nsdd145.htm. See also Johnson, *Cryptologic Rebirth*, 295–96.

52. Linda Greenhouse, "Computer Security Shift Is Approved by Senate," *New York Times*, December 24, 1987. Congress did so via the Computer Security Act of 1987, which was implemented by President George H. W. Bush by means of his National Security Directive 42, "National Policy for the Security of National Security Telecommunications and Information Systems," July 5, 1990; accessed April 30, 2012, at www.fas.org/irp/offdocs/nsd/nsd42.pdf.

53. "EDV abgezapft," *Der Spiegel*, April 14, 1969; accessed June 10, 2011, at www .spiegel.de/spiegel/print/d-45702341.html. See also Wolf, *Man without a Face*, 201.

54. Roger R. Schell, "Computer Security: The Achilles' Heel of the Electronic Air Force?," *Air University Review*, January-February 1979; accessed June 10, 2012, at www.airpower.maxwell.af.mil/airchronicles/aureview/1979/jan-feb/schell .html#schell.

55. Johnson, *Cryptologic Rebirth*, 293.

56. Cliff Stoll, *The Cuckoo's Egg: Tracking a Spy through the Maze of Computer Espionage* (New York: Doubleday, 1989), 246–47, 251, 272, 307–13.

57. Office of Scientific and Weapons Research, Directorate of Intelligence, "Soviet and East European Computer Networking: Prospects for Global Connectivity," SW 90-10054X, September 1990, 11–12; accessed June 8, 2012, at www.foia .cia.gov.

58. Office of Scientific and Weapons Analysis, Directorate of Intelligence, "Soviet Bloc Computers: Direct Descendants of Western Technology," SW 89-10023X, June 1989, 30–31; accessed June 8, 2012, at www.foia.cia.gov. Soviet scientists independently reached similar conclusions about the backwardness of their computers; see Roald Z. Sagdeev, *The Making of a Soviet Scientist* (New York: John Wiley and Sons, 1994), 297–300.

59. Oleg Gordievsky, *Next Stop Execution* (London: Macmillan, 1995), 16–24; Andrew, *Defend the Realm*, 724–27.

60. Sandra Grimes and Jeanne Vertefeuille, *Circle of Treason: A CIA Account of Aldrich Ames and the Men He Betrayed* (Annapolis: US Naval Institute Press, 2012), 87, 190.

61. Benjamin Weiser, *A Secret Life: The Polish Officer, His Covert Mission, and the Price He Paid to Save His Country* (New York, PublicAffairs, 2004), 185; Barry G. Royden, "Tolkachev, A Worthy Successor to Penkovsky," *Studies in Intelligence* 47:3 (2003), accessed May 6, 2012 at www.cia.gov/library/center-for-the-study-of-intelligence/kent-csi/vol47no3/html/v47i3a02p.htm.

62. Gus W. Weiss, "The Farewell Dossier," *Studies in Intelligence* 39:5 (1996): 124–25.

63. Sergei Kostin, Eric Raynaud, and Catherine Cauvin-Higgins, *Farewell: The Greatest Spy Story of the Twentieth Century* (Las Vegas: Amazon Crossing, 2011), v–viii. See also Gates, *From the Shadows*, 359. Documents on the Soviet and Bulgarian collaboration in the scientific intelligence in the 1980s, for instance, have recently become available; see Jordan Baev, "Spying on the West:

Soviet-Bulgarian Scientific Intelligence Cooperation," January 2011; accessed May 19, 2012, at www.php.isn.ethz.ch/collections/coll_KGBBulg/intro_baev .cfm?navinfo=126115#_edn28. Raymond Garthoff, "The KGB Reports to Gorbachev," *Intelligence and National Security* 11:2 (April 1996): 237.

64. Paul Maddrell, "British Intelligence through the Eyes of the Stasi: What the Stasi's Records Show about the Operations of British Intelligence in Cold War Germany," *Intelligence and National Security* 27:1 (February 2012): 72.

65. L. Britt Snider, *The Agency and the Hill: CIA's Relationship with Congress, 1946– 2004* (Washington, DC: Central Intelligence Agency, 2008), 241; Brian Latell, *Castro's Secrets: The CIA and Cuba's Intelligence Machine* (New York: Palgrave Macmillan, 2012), 3, 10.

66. David A. Vise, *The Bureau and the Mole: The Unmasking of Robert Philip Hanssen, the Most Dangerous Double Agent in FBI History* (New York: Grove, 2002), 47, 70, 88; *United States of America v. Aldrich Hazen Ames: Statement of Facts*, United States District Court for the Eastern District of Virginia, Criminal no. 94–64–A; this is reprinted in Frank J. Rafalko, ed. *A Counterintelligence Reader*, vol. 3 (Washington, DC: National Counterintelligence Center, 1999), 310, accessed May 6, 2012, at www.fas.org/irp/ops/ci/docs/ci3/ch4.pdf. See also Grimes and Vertefeuille, *Circle of Treason*, 170–78.

67. Bearden and Risen, *The Main Enemy*, 515–17.

68. While there is no doubt that leaders in Moscow had heightened concerns about American war preparations in 1983, historians debate the degree to which Soviet commanders had alerted their forces to the danger of hostilities. Len Scott provides a good overview in "Intelligence and the Risk of Nuclear War: Able Archer-83 Revisited," *Intelligence and National Security* 26:6 (December 2011).

69. Quoted in Nikita Khrushchev, *Khrushchev Remembers*, Edward Crankshaw, ed., and Strobe Talbott, trans. (Boston: Little, Brown, 1970), 17.

70. Mikhail Gorbachev, *Memoirs* (New York: Doubleday, 1996), 216.

71. Ibid., 203–4, 215.

72. Ibid., 147, 204.

73. Vladimir G. Treml, "Western Analysis and the Soviet Policymaking Process," in Gerald K. Haines and Robert E. Leggett, eds., *Watching the Bear: Essays on CIA's Analysis of the Soviet Union* (Washington, DC: Central Intelligence Agency, 2001), 196–97, 202–5.

74. James Noren, "CIA's Analysis of the Soviet Economy," in Haines and Leggett, *Watching the Bear*, 32. Reflecting on that assessment, Noren, one of the CIA's senior economists, conceded "In most respects, the paper's predictions were off the mark."

75. See Schlesinger's comments in Haines and Leggett, *Watching the Bear*, 258.

76. Gates, *From the Shadows*, 318–19, 386.

77. Ibid., 388.

78. Gorbachev, *Memoirs*, 215.

79. Noren, "CIA's Analysis of the Soviet Economy," 51, 56.

80. Gates, *From the Shadows*, 319.
81. Ibid., 386; Snider, *The Agency and the Hill*, 205–6.
82. Remarks of KGB Lieutenant-General Fyodor Shcherbak at the multilateral conference of the organs responsible for the security of the economy, cited in Paul Maddrell and Matthias Uhl, "A KGB View of CIA and other Western Espionage against the Soviet Bloc, 1983," in R. Gerald Hughes, Peter Jackson, and Len Scott, *Exploring Intelligence Archives: Inquiries into the Secret State* (London: Routledge, 2008), 246.
83. Paul Maddrell, "The Stasi's View of the Federal Republic of Germany," paper presented at the International Studies Association conference, Montreal, 2011, 13, 14, 22–23.
84. Maddrell and Uhl, "A KGB View of CIA and other Western Espionage against the Soviet Bloc," 251.
85. Garthoff, "The KGB Reports to Gorbachev," 226.
86. Andrew and Mitrokhin, *The Mitrokhin Archive*, 431.
87. Kristie Macrakis, Thomas Wegener Friis, and Helmut Müller-Enbergs, eds., *East German Foreign Intelligence: Myth, Reality and Controversy* (London: Routledge, 2010), 3.
88. Schmeidel, *Stasi*, 24, 40.
89. Robert Service, *A History of Twentieth-Century Russia* (Cambridge, MA: Harvard University Press, 1997), 460–61.
90. Garthoff, "The KGB Reports to Gorbachev," 224, 235–41.
91. Gorbachev, *Memoirs*, 465.
92. Service, *A History of Twentieth-Century Russia*, 463–64.
93. Andreas Glaeser, *Political Epistemics: The Secret Police, the Opposition, and the End of East German Socialism* (Chicago: University of Chicago Press, 2011), 5–7. Mielke's address can be viewed at www.goethe.de/wis/med/rtv/mpg/en4430294.htm.
94. George Bush and Brent Scowcroft, *A World Transformed* (New York: Alfred A. Knopf, 1998), 154.
95. Gates, *From the Shadows*, 526.
96. Ibid., 521. See also Bush and Scowcroft, *A World Transformed*, 519.
97. Martin Ebon, *KGB: Death and Rebirth* (Westport, CT: Praeger, 1994), 17, 20. See also Julie Fedor, "Chekists Look Back on the Cold War: The Polemical Literature," *Intelligence and National Security* 26:6 (December 2011): 851.
98. Gates, *From the Shadows*, 560.
99. Bush and Scowcroft, *A World Transformed*, 520–28; Gates, *From the Shadows*, 522–24.
100. Francis Fukuyama, "The End of History?," *The National Interest,* Summer 1989. Fukuyama served as deputy director of the State Department's policy planning staff.
101. Gates, *From the Shadows*, 469.
102. Michael J. Sulick, "As the USSR Collapsed: A CIA Officer in Lithuania," *Studies in Intelligence* 50:2 (2006): 5–10.

103. Bearden and Risen, *The Main Enemy*, 385, 416, 427.

104. Andrew and Mitrokhin, *The Mitrokhin Archive*, 17–19. See the transcript of "Panel III: Espionage and Counterintelligence," recorded at a conference sponsored by CIA's Center for the Study of Intelligence at Texas A&M University in 1999, 50; accessed June 8, 2012, at www.foia.cia.gov/docs/DOC_0001445139/DOC_0001445139.pdf.

105. Robert Gerald Livingston, "An Operation Called 'Rosenholz': How the CIA Bought the Stasi Files for $75,000," *Atlantic Times*, March 2006; accessed June 3, 2012, at www.atlantic-times.com/archive_detail.php?recordID=451. See also Bearden and Risen, *The Main Enemy*, 428; Jens Gieseke, "East German Espionage in the Era of Detente," *Journal of Strategic Studies* 31:3 (June 2008): 397–98.

106. Bearden and Risen, *The Main Enemy*, 514–15.

107. Kevin M. Wood, David D. Palkki, and Mark E. Stout, *The Saddam Tapes: The Inner Workings of a Tyrant's Regime, 1978–2001* (New York: Cambridge University Press, 2011), 36.

108. Snider, *The Agency and the Hill*, 207–9.

109. Richard L. Russell, "CIA's Strategic Intelligence in Iraq," *Political Science Quarterly* 117:2 (2002): 199, 202–3.

110. H. Norman Schwarzkopf with Peter Petre, *It Doesn't Take a Hero* (New York: Bantam, 1993 [1992]), 501.

111. Douglas Jehl, "CIA Nominee Wary of Budget Cuts," *New York Times*, February 3, 1993.

112. HL Deb 09, December 1993 vol. 550 cc1024; accessed June 2, 2012, at http://hansard.millbanksystems.com/lords/1993/dec/09/intelligence-services-bill-hl.

113. Snider, *The Agency and the Hill*, 185.

114. Michael V. Hayden, director, National Security Agency, statement for the record to the Joint Inquiry of the Senate Select Committee on Intelligence and the House Permanent Select Committee on Intelligence, October 17, 2002; accessed November 4, 2012, at www.gwu.edu/~nsarchiv/NSAEBB/NSAEBB24/nsa27.pdf.

115. Andrew, *Defend the Realm*, 780.

116. Stella Rimington, *Open Secret: The Autobiography of the Former Director-General of MI5* (London: Hutchinson, 2001), 226.

117. Department of Defense, *The Conduct of the Persian Gulf War: Final Report to Congress* (Washington, DC: Department of Defense, 1992), 333.

118. Testimony of Robert Gates on April 1, 1992, at the Joint Hearing, Senate Select Committee on Intelligence and House Permanent Select Committee on Intelligence, "S. 2198 and S. 421 to Reorganize the United States Intelligence Community," 102nd Congress, 2nd Session, 1992, 108.

119. President William J. Clinton, address to the US Intelligence Community, delivered at the Central Intelligence Agency's headquarters, July 14, 1995; accessed June 10, 2012, at www.presidency.ucsb.edu/ws/index.php?pid=51616&st=langley&st1=#axzz1xP49QrgH.

120. FROSTBURG literally became an artifact; its caption in the National Cryptologic Museum can be read here: http://en.wikipedia.org/wiki/File:Frostburg-nsa-description.jpg. For a narrative of supercomputer deployments at NSA, see James Bamford, *Body of Secrets: Anatomy of the Ultra-Secret National Security Agency* (New York: Anchor, 2002 [2001]), 589–607. See also Johnson, *Cryptologic Rebirth,* 292.

121. Hedley, *Fifty Years of Informing Policy,* 15–16.

122. Scott W. Carmichael, *True Believer: Inside the Investigation and Capture of Ana Montes, Cuba's Master Spy* (Annapolis: UN Naval Institute Press, 2009), 139–40; Bob Wallace and H. Keith Melton, with Henry R. Schlesinger, *Spycraft: The Secret History of the CIA's Spytechs, from Communism to Al-Qaeda* (New York: Plume, 2009), 451–52. Hanssen used diskettes from 1988 to convey his takings to the Soviets; David Wise, *Spy: The Inside Story of How the FBI's Robert Hanssen Betrayed America* (New York: Random House, 2002), 79–80. See also Vise, *The Bureau and the Mole,* 88, 92–93.

123. Director of Central Intelligence to Heads of Agency Offices, "Distribution of Unclassified Abstract IG Report of Ames Investigation," October 21, 1994; accessed May 27, 2012, at www.loyola.edu/departments/academics/political-science/strategic-intelligence/intel/hitzrept.html.

124. Snider, *The Agency and the Hill,* 322–26.

125. Michael Warner, ed., *Central Intelligence: Origin and Evolution* (Washington, DC: Central Intelligence Agency, 2001), 12–15.

126. Loch K. Johnson and Kevin J. Scheid, "Spending for Spies: Intelligence Budgeting in the Aftermath of the Cold War," *Public Budgeting & Finance* 17:4 (December 1997): 12.

127. Michael Howard, "Cowboys, Playboys and Other Spies," *New York Times,* February 16, 1986.

128. Robert Louis Benson and Michael Warner, eds., *Venona: Soviet Espionage and the American Response, 1939–1957* (Washington, DC: Central Intelligence Agency, 2001), v.

129. The two volumes were Christopher Andrew and Vasili Mitrokhin, *The Mitrokhin Archive: The KGB in Europe and the West* (London: Penguin, 1999); and Christopher Andrew and Vasili Mitrokhin, *The World Was Going Our Way: The KGB and the Battle for the Third World* (New York: Basic Books, 2005). Chapter 1 of the former work narrates Mitrokhin's career and defection.

130. Four histories emerged from these deals: Aleksandr Fursenko and Timothy Naftali, *"One Hell of a Gamble": Khrushchev, Castro, Kennedy, and the Cuban Missile Crisis, 1958–1964* (New York: Norton, 1997); David E. Murphy, Sergei A. Kondrashev, and George Bailey, *Battleground Berlin: CIA vs KGB in the Cold War* (New Haven, CT: Yale University Press, 1996); Alexander Vassiliev and Allen Weinstein, *The Haunted Wood: Soviet Espionage in America—The Stalin Era* (New York: Random House, 1997); and John Costello and Oleg Tsarev, *Deadly Illusions* (New York: Crown, 1993).

131. Andrew, *Defend the Realm*, 767.

132. Intelligence Services Act 1994; accessed June 3, 2012, at www.legislation.gov .uk/ukpga/1994/13/contents.

133. Peter Gill, "'A Formidable Power to Cause Trouble for the Government'?: Intelligence Oversight and the Creation of the UK Intelligence and Security Committee," in Robert Dover and Michael S. Goodman, eds., *Learning from the Secret Past: Cases in British Intelligence History* (Washington, DC: Georgetown University Press, 2011), 45–48.

134. Andrew, *Defend the Realm*, 778.

135. Bearden and Risen, *The Main Enemy*, 416.

136. Larry L. Watts, "Intelligence Reform in Europe's Emerging Democracies," *Studies in Intelligence* 48 (2004): 19–22; accessed May 27, 2012, at www.cia .gov/library/center-for-the-study-of-intelligence/csi-publications/csi-stud ies/studies/vol48no1/article02.html.

137. President's Commission on Critical Infrastructure Protection, Final Report, *Critical Foundations Protecting America's Infrastructures*, October 1997, x; accessed on June 10, 2012, at www.fas.org/sgp/library/pccip.pdf.

138. Garthoff, "The KGB Reports to Gorbachev," 237.

139. Quoted in James Adams, *The Next World War: Computers Are the Weapons and the Front Line Is Everywhere* (New York: Simon & Schuster, 1998), 238–39, 244.

140. Wang Pufeng, "The Challenge of Information Warfare," *China Military Science*, Spring 1995; accessed June 10, 2012, at www.fas.org/irp/world/china/ docs/iw_mg_wang.htm.

141. Wei Jincheng, "Information War: A New Form of People's War," *Liberation Army Daily*, June 25, 1996; accessed June 10, 2012, at www.fas.org/irp/world/ china/docs/iw_wei.htm.

142. Roger C. Molander, Andrew S. Riddile, and Peter A. Wilson, *Strategic Information Warfare: A New Face of War* (Santa Monica, CA: RAND, 1996), xvii; accessed May 27, 2012, at www.rand.org/pubs/monograph_reports/MR661 .html.

143. Kenneth A. Minihan, director, National Security Agency, "Cyber Attack: Is Our Nation at Risk?," testimony before the Senate Governmental Affairs Committee, June 24, 1998; accessed on June 10, 2011, at www.defense.gov/ speeches/speech.aspx?speechid=704.

144. James Adams, "Virtual Defense," *Foreign Affairs* 80:3 (May/June 2001): 99.

145. "Hackers Victimize Cal-ISO," *Los Angeles Times*, June 9, 2001.

146. Commission on the Intelligence Capabilities of the United States regarding Weapons of Mass Destruction, *Report to the President of the United States* (the WMD Commission Report) (Washington, DC: Government Printing Office, 2005), 53; accessed June 9, 2012, at www.gpoaccess.gov/wmd/index .html.

147. Tenet and Harlow, *At the Center of the Storm*, 44–45; see also the WMD Commission Report, 355.

148. John W., "Supporting Military Operations," in Hedley, *The Directorate of Intelligence*, 299.
149. Tenet and Harlow, *At the Center of the Storm*, 503.
150. Ibid., 46–47.
151. Minihan, "Cyber Attack: Is Our Nation at Risk?"
152. John J. Hamre, deputy secretary of defense, speech to the Fortune 500 CIO Forum, Aspen, Colorado, July 21, 1998; accessed on June 10, 2012, at www.fas.org/irp/congress/1998_hr/98-06-11hamre.htm.
153. Hayden, statement to the Joint Inquiry, 5.
154. Geoffry Taubman, "A Not-So World Wide Web: The Internet, China, and the Challenges to Nondemocratic Rule," *Political Communication* 15:2 (April–June 1998): 261–68.
155. Gary T. Marx, "Ethics for the New Surveillance," *The Information Society* 14:3 (1998): 171.

CHAPTER 7

The Shadow War

There are two kinds of combat: one with laws, the other with force.

—MACHIAVELLI, *THE PRINCE*

The world changed on a clear American morning in September 2001. Operatives dispatched by a Saudi expatriate named Osama bin Ladin mounted simultaneous attacks in New York, Virginia, and Pennsylvania, showing that a handful of extremists with audacity and a modest budget could kill thousands in what was purportedly the best-defended country on earth. Those sudden attacks, however, had a long prelude. While Western intelligence services came late to understanding and penetrating the growing threat from Sunni jihadists, after 1997 they made up for the neglect and relentlessly pursued bin Ladin and his men. Even then, however, the CIA missed a score of operatives entering the United States. Once inside, they were free enough from the attentions of the FBI to plan and mount a complicated series of simultaneous attacks. By summer 2001, as DCI George Tenet said later, "the system was blinking red."[1] The US Intelligence Community knew something bad was afoot, but did not know what, or when, or where. Thus the West could no longer protect its cities against mass casualty attacks. Intelligence for the first time in decades was once again a competitive endeavor for all, with many actors possessing the capability to cause an earthquake.

The comparatively huge intelligence budgets of the United States had not protected its citizens from the elemental horrors of 9/11—a fact that altered the risk calculus of leaders in Washington, London, and other capitals. Only months later, the analyses produced by the British and American intelligence communities did not tell their political leadership that Iraqi strongman Saddam Hussein had no appreciable weapons of mass destruction, and that he represented far less a danger to regional peace than thought. Nor did the intelligence systems of any Western power predict or prevent a wave of cyber espionage that by mid-decade victimized governments and private enterprises around the world. Finally, all governments felt awash in a tide of leaks, as it were, that embarrassed political leaders in the West and undermined regimes in the Arab world and beyond. With all this said, however, intelligence capabilities still improved dramatically in the years after 9/11. The threats of terrorism and cyber operations forced reorganization, higher proficiency, and innovative techniques in many intelligence systems. Indeed, so extensive were those new techniques that, by 2013, many of them had spread well beyond the intelligence agencies, creating unprecedented threats to privacy.

The New Terror

East or West, by the mid-1990s, all the intelligence systems began turning scarce resources toward a resurgent terrorist threat. Terrorism as a phenomenon of the revolutionary Left had faded with the collapse of its state sponsors in Eastern Europe and the USSR. While the tide ebbed, however, it never receded for good. The Ayatollahs in Iran, and Saddam Hussein in Iraq, continued their encouragement of terrorist acts (indeed, Iraqi proxies plotted to kill former President George H. W. Bush when he visited Kuwait in 1993). In Ireland, the PIRA also kept mounting sporadic attacks in England. The Provos had taken some support from militant regimes like Libya but had also bought black market arms in the United States and elsewhere; and since their radicalism was at base more nationalist than Marxist, the end of the Cold War had little direct effect on them. The PIRA launched a daring mortar attack in the heart of London in February 1991, narrowly missing Prime Minister Major and his War Cabinet meeting at 10 Downing Street to discuss the campaign in Iraq. More bombs followed more ceasefires in later years, with the biggest bombings in London and Manchester in early 1996.

The PIRA also tried to revive a tactic from its past that others were considering as well—attacks on the infrastructure of a modern society. In the 1930s and again in the 1970s, IRA bombers had targeted electrical power grids. After the bombings in Manchester and London's Canary Wharf killed two and caused over 500 million pounds in damage, an elite team of PIRA operatives began reconnoitering electrical power substations across the capital and assembling thirty-seven bombs in order to destroy them. If not for MI5's disruption of the plot (Operation AIRLINES), the attack might have darkened London for days and caused outages for a month—a result that would surely have been fatal to scores if not hundreds of innocents. "You will find no mercy here!" the trial judge told the PIRA defendants standing before him for sentencing.[2] Other groups preferred more novel weapons. A cult calling itself *Aum Shinrikyo* (Supreme Truth) released nerve gas on five Tokyo subway trains during the morning rush in March 1995, killing a dozen people and injuring a thousand more. That same year, Chechen separatists pulled a potentially deadly publicity stunt when they pointed a Moscow television station toward a bomb they had hidden in a local park; the small device could have spread enough radioactive cesium-137 to poison a whole neighborhood.[3]

The most deadly terror campaigns were offshoots of the previous decade's conflicts in Palestine and Afghanistan. The new attackers, however, were distinctly Islamist in motivation. The latter conflict had created a generation of Arab adventurers and holy warriors, and more importantly, an expectation among them that with one infidel superpower vanquished the other should be confronted as well. America felt their wrath in early 1993, when a young Pakistani, Mir Aimal Kasi, angered by violence in the Middle East but acting on his own, gunned down CIA employees waiting in their cars at a traffic light in front of the agency's Virginia headquarters. Weeks later a team of homegrown jihadists living around New York parked a truck bomb under the World Trade Center in Manhattan. Though news reports described the attack as inept, it was anything but. The explosion and fire killed six and injured a thousand, and authorities determined that many more deaths could have resulted had the bomb been parked a few feet from its final location. Accomplices of the World Trade Center bombers tried again the same year, planning to hit several New York landmarks, though this time an FBI informant tipped the bureau in time to disrupt the plot.[4] Such tactics had been used for decades by revolutionary "urban guerrillas," but hitherto they had not found their way to American soil. France endured a wave of bombings perpetrated by the Algerian Groupe Islamique Armé, which in 1994 had also hijacked an airliner with the idea of crashing into downtown Paris (French commandos stormed the plane in Marseilles). Israel soon suffered from another innovation—individual attackers willing to blend into Israeli crowds and then blow themselves to bits in order to kill the Israelis around them. These terrorists often served a relatively new Palestinian group called Hamas, an offshoot of Egypt's Muslim Brotherhood.

Some of this jihadist terror differed in kind, not degree, from the revolutionary campaigns of previous decades. The late Sayyed Qutb's writings and activism (he had been a member of the Muslim Brotherhood) guided Sheikh Omar Abdel Rahman, whose preaching in turn had inspired the Sadat assassination and later, from a mosque in Brooklyn, the 1993 World Trade Center bombing.[5] The most famous intellectual heir of Qutb, however, would prove to be a wealthy Saudi named Osama bin Ladin, who had organized support (dubbed "the base" or *al-Qaeda*) for the Afghan *mujaheddin*. Bin Ladin and the CIA had the same enemy in Afghanistan, but that did not make them friends. In later years al-Qaeda and the US government agreed wholeheartedly on one thing: al-Qaeda had not been aided by the CIA's operation to assist the *mujaheddin*.[6] After the war Osama bin Ladin turned his attention westward, and conceived of an essentially Leninist strategy of provoking Washington to a global overreaction that would galvanize and unite the Muslim world. He adopted Qutb's notion that all those not living according to God's law (Sharia) were apostates or infidels; democracy by definition compromised Sharia, and had to make way for a Caliphate of all the Believers.[7] Bin Ladin found several reasons for concentrating on attacking the "far enemy" in America rather than the apostate regimes in the Middle East, but foremost among them seems to have been the brutal efficiency of the Arab secret services. The pluralistic societies of the West—despite the technological prowess of their internal security functions—provided his followers better operating conditions.[8]

By 1995 bin Ladin was gathering planners and operatives intending to deliver the biggest possible blows to the United States. These men wanted to cause civilian casualties in the most spectacular manner they could manage. One of bin Ladin's lieutenants, Khalid Sheikh Mohammed, teamed with his nephew Ramzi Yousef (a fugitive World Trade Center bomber) to plot a simultaneous hijacking of twelve airliners over the Pacific. While that plan failed when a bomb-making accident in Manila attracted Filipino authorities, al-Qaeda succeeded in bombing two US embassies in Africa on the same day in August 1998. Indeed, earlier that year bin Ladin had pronounced a *fatwa* against the United States, in effect declaring war, and he insisted that no American should feel safe. From his new sanctuary in Afghanistan, now ruled by his Islamic allies the Taliban, he told ABC News reporter John Miller in May 1998 "we do not differentiate between those in military uniforms and civilians; they are all targets in this *fatwa*."[9]

Campaigns against the jihadists varied. Western services had long seen terrorism as a left-wing or at least secularist phenomenon. Indeed, with regard to traditional terrorist threats, the West maintained a fairly high degree of effectiveness, as shown in the steady pressure exerted by MI5 and SIS on the PIRA (and back-channel diplomacy with the Provos seeking to build an exit from violence), which helped bring about the Good Friday Agreement to end Northern Ireland's Troubles in 1998.[10] Yet religious motivations seemed too subjective and ephemeral (unless the terrorists were Shiites affiliated with Iran, or Sikhs in India) to guide the deadliest terrorist movements. The day of the Tokyo sarin attacks, NSC staffer Richard Clarke found both FBI and CIA almost completely ignorant of this particular threat: "Except for press reports from the previous twelve hours, they had nothing in their files on the Aum."[11] Sunni Islamists hence surprised both British and American analysts. CIA regarded bin Ladin as a financier of terrorists rather than one of their leaders; according to George Tenet, the agency's head at the time, the CIA began paying more attention when an al-Qaeda defector, in 1996, reported that the group actively sought weapons of mass destruction.[12] But MI5 in late 1995 assured local police officials that media reports about jihadist terrorism were "greatly exaggerated"; indeed, links between Islamic extremists in the West appeared "largely opportunistic at present and . . . unlikely to result on the emergence of a potent trans-national force."[13]

Once engaged in earnest in the late 1990s, the Western services worked to track bin Ladin back to Afghanistan. Yet they did not entirely understand the threat and they did not follow every lead, at least in the United States. At the same time, America in the 1990s effactually revised its rules for the sharing of law enforcement and intelligence information to provide some of the highest protections for individual privacy against state power in any industrialized nation in history. The new rules, dubbed "the Wall," kept vital clues from being shared by CIA and FBI officers who might have understood their broader significance.[14] The Wall even hamstrung cooperation in FBI field offices. In the summer of 2001, special agents in New York squabbled over access to information needed for the investigation of al-Qaeda's recent suicide bombing of the destroyer USS *Cole* in Aden. One agent wrote in frustration: "Whatever has happened to this—someday someone will die—and wall or not—the public will not understand why we were not more effective and throwing every resource we had at certain 'problems.'"[15]

9/11 and Its Aftermath

I would have preferred that we get the information another way. But the choice between security and values was real.

—GEORGE W. BUSH, *DECISION POINTS*

In late 1999, the US government mounted a hasty but comprehensive campaign to prevent attacks by al-Qaeda operatives that the Intelligence Community anticipated around the New Year. Departments and agencies across the government went to battle stations; the Central Intelligence Agency alone spoke quietly to dozens of liaison services, giving them data and motivation to disrupt al-Qaeda wherever it touched ground. This international teamwork succeeded in foiling several plots (by Western estimates), and at least prevented any significant incidents around the millennium.[16] The following summer, the CIA even caught sight of al-Qaeda leader Osama bin Ladin at a camp in Afghanistan. Agency officers watched the tall Saudi on live video taken by an unarmed Predator drone and streamed via satellite back to the agency on the other side of the globe. The CIA called for a missile strike, but nothing could be done fast enough to satisfy the White House that the strike would succeed, and bin Laden went to bed that night unaware of the crosshairs that had brushed his head.[17]

A year later, a new president, George W. Bush, would be warned by his Intelligence Community that bin Ladin was working to mount attacks on American soil. The CIA's warning in the President's Daily Brief for August 6, 2001, however, named no specific target, date, or attack method—in short, it offered nothing for US military, intelligence, or law enforcement officers to act on.[18] Washington thus had no tactical warning of the attacks that came on 9/11. Al-Qaeda's suicide teams simultaneously hijacked four airliners, flying three of them into the Pentagon and the towers of the World Trade Center. Almost 3,000 people died in these crashes and in a fourth in the Pennsylvania countryside. For decades, airline hijackings had been rare in the United States. Al-Qaeda operatives managed four hijackings in one morning, finalizing their plot figuratively under the noses of the FBI and within a bicycle ride from NSA's Ft. Meade headquarters.[19] The plotters had had a single security lapse when one of their number got himself arrested on immigration charges while attending flight school in Minnesota, but otherwise their operation proceeded according to plan. Nineteen hijackers had entered the United States and completed their preparations while receiving directives and funds from overseas, assured of operational security by their relative anonymity and the banality of their phone calls and e-mails in the midst of millions of personal communications flowing into and out of the United States every day.[20]

Countries around the world responded swiftly to the 9/11 attacks, implementing new surveillance measures and banding together against al-Qaeda suspects and sympathizers. Within days, the United Nations passed Security Council Resolution 1373, calling for international cooperation against terrorism, including the sharing of intelligence; states were to "[f]ind ways of intensifying and accelerating the exchange of operational information, especially regarding actions or movements of terrorist persons or networks." In the United States, Congress poured money into the intelligence agencies (CIA's analysts dedicated to terrorism increased manyfold, and overall the Counterterrorist Center grew by a factor of ten in the weeks after the attack), and passed the PATRIOT Act to remove the "Wall" that had hampered the sharing of clues between intelligence and law enforcement.[21] The White House and Congress the following year assembled several agencies into a new Department of Homeland Security to coordinate federal, state, and local prevention and recovery measures (the department was soon both a producer and consumer of intelligence on these topics). President Bush created a national "fusion" cell, the Terrorist Threat Integration Center, colocated with the CIA and charged with linking Intelligence Community reporting with federal law enforcement leads (the organization soon became the National Counterterrorism Center).[22] Britain followed a similar course in fusing terrorism information, forming its Joint Terrorism Analysis Centre (JTAC) in 2003. Though housed with MI5, JTAC had an interagency information sharing mission similar to TTIC's but with a broader representation of departments and agencies to include police liaison.[23]

Key to these and related measures was the blending of intelligence and evidence. The two streams of data were collected for divergent purposes by agencies operating under different statutes, and integrating them at first could only be effected by quartering personnel from the various organizations at adjacent desks. Previously, legacy agency databases and networks had been built in virtual silos that barely connected, but the urgency of preventing another attack ("our working assumption had always been that the attacks of 9/11 were simply the first wave," remembered George Tenet) fostered a feeling that even half measures were better than none.[24] In the urgency of the moment, President Bush also determined that his constitutional powers as commander-in-chief authorized him to take all necessary steps to protect the nation against new plots. These included "the interception of the content of communications into and out of the United States where there was a reasonable basis to conclude that one party to the communication was a member of al-Qa'ida or related terrorist organizations."[25] Such traffic would ordinarily have been monitored under court orders obtained in accordance with the 1978 Foreign Intelligence Surveillance Act (FISA), but the White House, the DCI, and NSA deemed that process obsolete and uncertain in the new technological context, and informed a handful of congressional leaders that the president's "Terrorist Surveillance Program" was proceeding with or without an amendment to FISA.[26] Lt. Gen. Michael Hayden, who as director of NSA implemented the program, probably captured the mood best with a football metaphor, later telling a gathering of human rights groups that the administration and the Intelligence Community intended to operate right up to the bounds of legality: "My spikes will have chalk on them. . . . We're pretty aggressive within the law. As a professional, I'm troubled if I'm not using the full authority allowed by law."[27]

The United States also gathered a coalition of allies to attack al-Qaeda in its Afghan bastion, then ruled by the Islamic fundamentalist Taliban. The resulting success in Operation ENDURING FREEDOM looked miraculous. Two vital components made possible the victory over al-Qaeda troops and their Taliban hosts. First, the CIA convinced rival Afghans to attack the Taliban, and second, US and coalition aircraft were able to hit Taliban and al-Qaeda centers of resistance, ensuring that the offensive by America's Afghan allies did not lose momentum. The latter advantage had been presaged in recent conflicts in the Persian Gulf and the Balkans, and it rested on absolute control of the skies over the battlefield. Air supremacy allowed surveillance drones and coalition bombers to loiter above the reach of antiaircraft defenses while awaiting targets of opportunity. Many of the bombs and missiles they carried could now be guided precisely by laser spotting devices operated by Special Forces and CIA teams on the ground, with friendly Afghan forces eager to end the fanatical reign of the Taliban and expel the foreigners fighting with al-Qaeda. Blending the nineteenth century with the twenty-first, at one point Special Forces spotters orchestrated a devastating bombing run in support of an Afghan cavalry charge.[28] When American B-52 bombers began hitting front-line positions, noted one CIA veteran of the campaign, "Taliban radio communications in the aftermath of the bombing were full of panic and fear as the full extent of the damage and the casualties became known."[29] In this crucible of war, several CIA experiments rapidly became realities, like Predator drones armed with guided missiles, and a "Global Information System" that depicted CIA and Special Forces teams along with friendly and enemy positions on a three-dimensional virtual map.[30] This combination of forces routed the Taliban and al-Qaeda from Afghanistan's cities and chased them into some of the roughest terrain on earth, along the border with Pakistan. There, however, Osama bin Ladin and his cadres went to ground, dispersing into the smallest possible fighting units and working to lure American soldiers to places where they either had to fight on foot or destroy houses and mosques to get at the militants hiding among the terrorized local population.

Operation ENDURING FREEDOM proved to be both an intelligence windfall and a diplomatic problem. When the final offensive began in November 2001, coalition forces bagged thousands of Taliban and al-Qaeda prisoners, along with bystanders caught up in the rout. Several hundred of them found their way to a prison at the US military base at Guantanamo Bay, Cuba. The Bush administration deemed Guantanamo the "least worst choice" for al-Qaeda captives who could not be safely held in Afghanistan but who also had to be questioned for clues to future terrorist attacks—something that could not be done in detail if the prisoners gained the constitutional rights accorded to inmates in American jails.[31] Desperate times called for extraordinary measures in the Intelligence Community as well. The feeling among CIA officers at headquarters, according to one of their leaders, was "[m]aybe if I stay just one more hour, pore over a few more documents, listen to a handful more transcripts, I can find the key that will prevent another attack."[32]

The hard work began paying off early in 2002, when CIA officers and Pakistani authorities, cued by a massive technical collection and analytical effort, nabbed Abu Zubaydah, the first in what would be a string of al-Qaeda leaders. Bush had recently signed an executive order establishing military tribunals for terror detainees, and Secretary of Defense Donald Rumsfeld would broaden the range of permissible techniques for interrogations at

Guantanamo.[33] Abu Zubaydah, with his knowledge of al-Qaeda plans, however, seemed a special case. When he defied his CIA and FBI questioners that summer, the agency won authorization from the president and the Justice Department to employ "enhanced interrogation techniques" to elicit his cooperation.[34] Bush recalled that the CIA wanted "total control over his environment"—something presumably unavailable at Guantanamo.[35] The agency built special sites on foreign soil to hold Zubaydah and others, and hastily found case officers with the right languages and contractors to improvise techniques above and beyond those that had served CIA and US military interrogators since the 1960s.[36] Once again, congressional leaders were informed, not consulted.[37] CIA officials insisted the measures were harmless but effective. Abu Zubaydah "became part of our team" after being waterboarded, related a CIA interrogator to CTC chief Jose Rodriguez.[38] Partly from these techniques, used on him and subsequently on others, most notably on 9/11 planner Khalid Sheik Mohammed, the CIA learned how the 9/11 operation had unfolded and finally gained insight into the workings of al-Qaeda. Nonetheless, the interrogation techniques from their inception struck some in the CIA and the Congress as torture.[39] British SIS and Security Service officers had access to some American-held detainees in Afghanistan and Guantanamo and watched US interrogation methods warily, as their government was bound by treaty claims enforceable under the European Convention on Human Rights. They had no access to the CIA's black sites, but nonetheless shared in at least some of the take, for which they had a high regard. The services assured members of the Intelligence and Security Committee in early 2005 that they had "received intelligence of the highest value from detainees, to whom we have not had access and whose location is unknown to us, some of which has led to the frustration of terrorist attacks in the UK or against UK interests." [40]

The attacks on 9/11 changed outlooks in Washington and other capitals; "conventional risk assessments no longer applied," remembered DCI George Tenet.[41] Al-Qaeda constituted a threat that gave no warning of its attacks, sought to inflict mass casualties, and could not be deterred by the threat of death or any strategic concessions that civilized nations could offer. Terror attacks by Islamist groups sympathetic to al-Qaeda caused horror in Bali (more than 200 killed in October 2002) and in the siege of a Moscow theater a few days later (Russian forces pumped poison gas into the building in an effort to subdue the Chechen terrorists, but almost 130 of their hostages died in the rescue attempt). Indeed, "increased intelligence-collection capabilities produced a continuing flood of threat information," recalled Rodriquez. "Many of the threats were cataclysmic in nature. We knew that most of them were bogus; we just didn't know which ones."[42] In June 2002, bin Ladin's son-in-law and spokesman posted an online justification for al-Qaeda's "right to kill four million Americans, including one million children."[43] Captured laptops and evidence from sites in Afghanistan only heightened the certainty at CIA and elsewhere that al-Qaeda intended to use chemical, biological, or radiological weapons in Western cities.[44] Indeed, in 2007 Khalid Sheik Mohammed proudly told his captors "I was directly in charge ... of managing and following up on the cell for the production of biological weapons, such as anthrax and others, and following up on dirty bomb operations on American soil."[45] "For those who regard this type of plotting as more in the realm of science fiction than fact," recalled CIA senior analyst Philip Mudd, "what we saw would have convinced any skeptic that Al-Qaeda, had it maintained the room to experiment in an Afghan safehaven, would have moved inexorably toward WMD capability.[46]

Where could al-Qaeda get such weapons? The White House worried they might come from Saddam Hussein's Iraq. The fact that Saddam had or could easily acquire these weapons seemed beyond dispute. In February 2001, months before 9/11 and just days after President Bush took office, DCI Tenet told Congress in public session:

> Our most serious concern with Saddam Hussein must be the likelihood that he will seek a renewed WMD capability both for credibility and because every other strong regime in the region either has it or is pursuing it. For example, the Iraqis have rebuilt key portions of their chemical production infrastructure for industrial and commercial use. The plants he is rebuilding were used to make chemical weapons precursors before the Gulf War and their capacity exceeds Iraq's needs to satisfy its civilian requirements. We have similar concerns about other dual-use research, development, and production in the biological weapons and ballistic missile fields; indeed, Saddam has rebuilt several critical missile production complexes.[47]

Nothing the Intelligence Community learned in the next couple of years diminished confidence in its judgment about Saddam's desire and ability to possess weapons of mass destruction. By early 2002, President Bush had

7.1 On September 20, 2001, President George W. Bush greets British Prime Minister Tony Blair at the White House where they were convening to contemplate the dark days ahead in the War on Terror. *George W. Bush Library, National Archives*

resolved to treat Iraq as an imminent threat to the United States, and his administration began recruiting allies and planning the steps to either force Saddam to comply with United Nations disarmament resolutions or to remove him from power. Prime Minister Tony Blair proved Bush's staunchest ally, in no small part because British intelligence assessments matched those of the Americans. The prime minister explained the judgment of his analysts in an unprecedented public dossier released in September 2002 to support the government's case for disarming Saddam: "What I believe the assessed intelligence has established beyond doubt is that Saddam has continued to produce chemical and biological weapons, that he continues in his efforts to develop nuclear weapons, and that he has been able to extend the range of his ballistic missile programme. I also believe that, as stated in the document, Saddam will now do his utmost to try to conceal his weapons from UN inspectors."[48]

Opponents of intervention in Iraq largely conceded the intelligence that Saddam had such weapons and could well use them, but nonetheless doubted intervention's chance of success and dreaded its likely consequences for stability in the Middle East. Indeed, both the British and American governments based their public arguments for intervention on the certainty of Saddam's weapons programs. As shown by Blair's September 2002 dossier (and a parallel white paper released by the DCI's National Intelligence Council the following month), the phrasing of the intelligence they cited in support of their joint policy became ever less nuanced as war loomed.[49]

Few in Washington or London noticed, however, that the underlying hypothesis that Saddam possessed weapons of mass destruction had hardened into a nonfalsifiable certainty. CIA analysts, for example, had not yet discovered "just how broken and ineffective the Iraqi regime was," and "did not spend adequate time examining the premise that the Iraqis had undergone a change in their behavior," concluded an agency postmortem.[50] When United Nations inspectors finally set to work again in Iraq in late 2002, the fact that they discovered little or nothing became not a basis for reconsidering the intelligence but, ironically, proof of Saddam's cunning—and thus of his intent to protect Iraqi stockpiles. In a classic understatement, members of Lord Butler's commission, subsequently appointed to dissect the resulting intelligence failure, recorded their "surprise that policy-makers and the intelligence community did not, as the generally negative results of [United Nations] inspections became increasingly apparent, re-evaluate in early 2003 the quality of the intelligence."[51]

Iraq policy in Washington (and London) thus came together in haste under the twin assumptions that time was running out to stop Saddam's ambitions and that the US military and Intelligence Community had reinvented modern war in Afghanistan. The unprecedented achievements of Operation ENDURING FREEDOM became by default the baseline expectations for the new Operation IRAQI FREEDOM to remove Saddam and change the Iraqi regime. In reality, however, the IC was overstretched and its leaders exhausted after a year and a half of supporting the war in Afghanistan and the relentless worldwide pursuit of al-Qaeda. Fortunately for the coalition, when the invasion began in March 2003, Saddam's regime fought its last war rather badly. The Iraqi regular army was not a factor, and the Republican Guard divisions—the heart of Iraqi power before 1991— were brave but dilapidated. Instead, Saddam sent his most fanatical followers in armed civilian trucks to charge coalition tanks. American and British commanders and intelligence officers thus discovered that Saddam's regime wanted to fight in a different way than expected. His power depended less on the Republican Guard than on face-to-face intimidation of Iraqis. Accordingly, the coalition's "main effort"—the fast, armored spearheads of the US Army and Marines, with the British Army taking Basra in the south—turned out to be the supporting elements that enabled coalition forces to conduct the urban battles that they had hoped to avoid.

Within days of the invasion, coalition commanders resigned themselves to urban fighting, and were justly confident that their troops would ultimately win. Battlefield leadership was a vital factor in this result, and good intelligence was crucial to that leadership. The coalition that launched Operation IRAQI FREEDOM consumed intelligence inputs on a vast and unprecedented scale in order to know and to "shape" the battlefield. Combat intelligence had its flaws—most notably in misunderstanding Saddam's emphasis on irregular forces and urban combat. American commander General Tommy Franks had anticipated "there might be up to forty thousand of these Fedayeen-type irregulars," but complained afterward that "[o]ur lack of reliable HUMINT had given us a nasty surprise: We'd had no warning that Saddam had dispatched these paramilitary forces from Baghdad."[52] Nevertheless, intelligence collection, analyses, and operations gave coalition commanders the insights to adapt and vanquish the irregulars, then to push forces into places like Baghdad, Basra, and Nasiriyah to destroy Saddam's regime within four weeks of crossing the line of departure.[53]

The questioning began as soon as Saddam's chemical and biological stockpiles failed to materialize. In short order, such queries turned to the competence of the intelligence agencies that produced the mistaken prewar assessments—and of President Bush, Prime Minister Blair, and their lieutenants, who had built support for the war by citing the intelligence on the danger that Saddam posed. The shock of discovering that American and British intelligence had grossly overestimated Iraq's arsenal reverberated for years across the two nations' political and intelligence systems. In Britain, the political furor emboldened Labour Party critics of Blair's Iraq policy. While they hardly wanted to topple a government of their own party, they shaped public perception of the war and demanded probes (most notably by Lord Butler) and subsequent reforms to prevent intelligence from being used to support controversial policies. Debates in America followed a different course, given the constitutional separation of powers. Congress reacted angrily to the Intelligence Community's performance. Supporters of the Bush administration blamed the intelligence system, and especially the CIA; a postmortem by the Senate's Republican-led intelligence oversight committee, for example, observed how "a broken corporate culture and poor management" had undermined human-source reporting across the community, and found that the CIA at times had "abused its unique position in the Intelligence Community, particularly in terms of information sharing, to the detriment of the Intelligence Community's prewar analysis."[54] In contrast, some of the president's Democratic opponents alleged that administration officials had neglected their duty to scrutinize the intelligence they were receiving. Senator Richard Durbin, for example, dissented from the Senate's report by noting that the analysts' doubts about links between al-Qaeda and Iraq were questioned by the administration's war hawks while their Iraq weapons judgments were accepted on their face: "Undoubtedly, this was because the Administration had already decided to invade Iraq, and the WMD intelligence analysis supported that objective, while the terrorism analysis did not."[55]

A season of investigations followed, culminating with the release during the 2004 presidential election season of the blue-ribbon 9/11 Commission's report. Iraq had had no connection to 9/11, and a probe of the 2001 attacks might in ordinary times have had no tie to the controversy over the war, but these times were not ordinary. Just as it became clear that Anglo-American intelligence had failed in Iraq, the allied services scored a major success in Libya, cornering Libyan strongman Muammar Qaddafi with evidence of his weapons of mass destruction programs and persuading him to publicly renounce them in late 2003.[56] Hereinafter, however, the news was all bad for the intelligence agencies. The 9/11 Commission drafted its best-selling report as the acrimony over Iraq peaked, and its call for intelligence reform would have become an issue in the 2004 presidential campaign had President Bush and a bipartisan group of Senators not pressed for a statute creating a "Director of National Intelligence" to improve information sharing and community management. As senior officials in Washington noted, while the US Intelligence Community was being reformed in 2004, making such changes while fighting two wars was like undergoing surgery while galloping on a horse.[57] As a result, in 2005 a director of national Intelligence empowered to oversee both foreign and some domestic intelligence replaced the old director of central intelligence, and the CIA in effect

DNI replaced the DCI

lost its leadership position in the community.[58] Recriminations over Iraq continued through the end of Bush's tenure, however, shaping, for instance, the response in Congress and the administration to the community's 2007 estimate that Iran had paused in its quest for a nuclear weapon.[59]

Controversy over the beginnings of the Iraq War proceeded in tandem with the dilemma over how to manage the war once it became clear that a full-fledged insurgency confronted coalition efforts to build a new government on the social and economic rubble left by Saddam's dictatorship. The ensuing Iraq conflict was, in effect, a collection of insurgencies against the coalition forces and against rival ethnic and political groups—making for still more complexity for the intelligence collectors, analysts, and officers on the ground. After Bush proved willing to send marines into house-to-house combat in Fallujah to retake the city from Sunni insurgents in 2004, the war settled into a grinding counterinsurgency struggle. Coalition forces sought to disperse the insurgents, while the fledgling Iraqi government raised and trained its own police and troops to keep order. For their part, the insurgents worked to hit vulnerable coalition and Iraqi security forces wherever possible by sniping, rockets, ambushes, and bombs hidden alongside roadways or driven by suicide bombers. The conflict was also an intelligence struggle from the beginning, but one with a twenty-first-century twist. Insurgents sought to infiltrate the security forces and used observers, the internet, and other electronic tools to monitor coalition and Iraqi forces.[60]

The Americans countered with an advantage not present in previous counterinsurgencies: the ability to utilize national and battlefield sensors and databases in near-real time to plan operations. Major General Stanley McChrystal helped to build this fusion, adding a "joint interagency task force" (JIATF) to supply intelligence to his special operations Task Force 714 in Baghdad in 2004. The JIATF imported Washington-based analysts from the national intelligence agencies to work directly with operators in the field in Iraq (and later Afghanistan). They could reach back to their home agencies' databases, but would live much closer to the front line and to the raw intelligence take. "It was extraordinarily powerful," McChrystal recalled, "to share information, to brief operators on their assessments, to hear the rotors of an assault force launching on their information, and then to debrief together after the operation."[61] The CIA helped by shifting personnel forward; by mid-2004 its Baghdad station was the agency's biggest since Vietnam, and it was losing armored vehicles to hostile action at a rate

of approximately one a week.[62] This collection and analytical edge gradually helped to shape the struggle against the insurgents, who proved unable
to prevent national elections in 2005 and 2006, or to halt the formation
of Iraqi political parties and (for the Arab world) a generally representative political process. Coalition casualties, moreover, remained relatively
low given the size of the forces engaged. The total number of US military
deaths from 2003 through 2011 reached just over 4,400 killed—a grim total
comparable to the toll of American dead in the Philippine Insurrection (in
which 4,165 died, most from disease, between 1899 and 1902).

Iraq's insurgency had foreign repercussions as well. By now the nter-
net provided the insurgents and their allies with a cheap, global, and somewhat secure aid to recruiting, communicating, and fundraising.[63] Al-Qaeda
lieutenant Abu Musab al-Zarqawi hoped to drive out the coalition's partners, killing the United Nations' special representative to Baghdad with a car
bomb in August 2003 and prompting the UN to leave the country to the
coalition.[64] The ongoing war and al-Qaeda's resilience inspired jihadists in
Madrid to bomb four commuter trains, virtually simultaneously, during the
morning rush in March 2004, just days before Spain's general election. In
all, 191 died and 1,800 suffered injuries, and the incoming Spanish government swiftly kept its preelection promise to withdraw from the occupation
in Iraq. British intelligence had been hiring more officers and warning of
the possibility of attacks since 2003 and, with insights from analysis of more
than 4,000 telephone contacts associated with the conspirators, helped disrupt a scheme the following year (Operation CREVICE) in which plotters
contacted al-Qaeda in South Asia and hoped to buy a radiation bomb from
the Russian mob.[65] Nonetheless, London had no warning before a homegrown terror cell inspired by al-Qaeda replicated the Madrid attacks in the
Underground on July 7, 2005; indeed, the Joint Terrorism Analysis Centre,
just six weeks earlier, had lowered its overall threat level from "severe" to
"substantial."[66] Three suicide bombers wrecked trains within fifty seconds
of each other, and an hour later a fourth bomb destroyed a bus crowded
with commuters working their way home after the Underground was paralyzed. The bombs killed fifty-two and wounded 700. Another plot a year
later could have killed thousands; more British jihadists were disrupted in
the midst of fabricating bombs out of plastic drinking bottles filled with
peroxide, intended to be triggered by the flash mechanisms from dispos-
able cameras.[67] Had the plot succeeded, it would have destroyed up to ten

airliners over the Atlantic or even over American cities. British authorities drew a pointed contrast between the jihadist attacks and those of the PIRA in earlier years. Irish radicals had sought to avoid capture and had often telephoned warnings at least a few minutes ahead of explosions. Such measures, while cynical, had in relative terms lowered casualties and preserved the possibility of a political solution to the Troubles, explained Peter Clarke, chief of the (London) Metropolitan Police Counter Terrorism Command in 2007. Al-Qaeda-inspired jihadists shared no such inhibitions: "There are no warnings given and the evidence suggests that, on the contrary, the intention frequently is to kill as many people as possible."[68] The democracies and their intelligence systems, of course, were not the only societies stressed by jihadist terrorism. In Russia, Chechen rebels faced one of the world's toughest internal security systems, and still proved able to mount horrendous attacks—like the siege of a school in Beslan in which over 350 died (including more than 150 children) in September 2004. The Chechens could persevere in part because they had turned to new technology to aid their insurgency, learning to use the internet for publicity, fundraising, recruiting, planning, and communications.[69]

Still, most victims of al-Qaeda and other jihadists in the decade after 9/11 were Muslims. The death toll is staggering, and it helped to turned popular opinion against al-Qaeda and its tactics. Zarqawi had hoped to destroy Jordan's intelligence headquarters but instead coordinated simultaneous suicide bombings of Jordanian hotels—which he suspected of harboring intelligence liaison meetings—in November 2005; one bomb killed dozens of wedding-goers at Amman's Radisson Hotel and prompted popular demonstrations against al-Qaeda.[70] Undeterred, Zarqawi struck in another direction three months later, bombing a Shi'a shrine, the Golden Mosque in Samarra, in hopes of fomenting civil war between Iraq's Sunni and Shi'a sects. He almost succeeded, precipitating some of the bloodiest fighting in the entire Iraq conflict. An American precision-guided bomb killed Zarqawi in June 2006, but the car bombings continued, including a series of explosions in August 2007 that killed almost 800 in northern Iraq in a single day. By this time, however, al-Qaeda's Iraqi affiliates were themselves on the defensive. Growing distaste for their violent fanaticism had "awakened" Sunni tribes in western Anbar province in 2006, and with quiet American support that awakening grew into a counterinsurgency campaign to neutralize al-Qaeda in Iraq. That, and the new intelligence-led tactics championed by American commander General David Petraeus, by 2008 had stabilized Iraq and made a political solution to the conflict (and an orderly American exit from the country) a real possibility.[71]

By then, however, a revived insurgency in Afghanistan claimed increasing attention from American and NATO leaders. The intelligence available to commanders showed measurable improvements across the coalition. British troops in Afghanistan had the benefit of organic signals intelligence units, unmanned drones to collect on enemy emissions, and orbiting Nimrod aircraft to make sense of the electronic battlefield.[72] The Americans had even more intelligence resources at their command. By 2009 the director of intelligence for NATO forces in country, US Army Major General Michael Flynn (formerly the intelligence chief for Task Force 714 in Iraq), observed that national-level intelligence now flowed down to the brigade level: "Resources are abundant; there are broadband classified and unclassified networks and technicians to keep them running, printers and map plotters that actually work, hot chow and showers, and, at least at the brigade-level, scores of military intelligence analysts."[73]

Nevertheless, as insurgency tactics from Afghanistan had helped transform the Iraq war in 2004, now lessons about fighting a coalition in Iraq worked their way back to Taliban and al-Qaeda leaders in their sanctuary along the rugged border with Pakistan. President Bush watched with dismay as his intelligence maps showed the insurgency spreading back into Afghanistan month by month from 2006 on. In the summer of 2008, Bush authorized Predator strikes against insurgent and al-Qaeda leaders across the border in Pakistan itself.[74] The problem was not going away. Major General Flynn publicly complained that the brigade-level intelligence units lacked "what the battalions have in abundance—information about what is actually happening on the ground." Local observations by tactical commanders did not flow upward, and most of the intelligence that reached the battlefield discussed insurgent activities, but offered little insight into the society in which those insurgents lived. Thus, American operations emphasized killing enemies rather than making friends.[75] British and coalition troops in forward positions lacked even the inadequate intelligence possessed by the Americans; officers of the Welsh Guards in Helmand in 2009 noted the paucity of surveillance assets and the scarce knowledge of local Taliban forces, comparing their situation unfavorably with the intelligence on the foe available in Northern Ireland the previous decade.[76] Security worsened even as insurgents could rarely gather in forces larger than a few dozen to mount attacks (in Vietnam they had sometimes deployed in multiple battalions). Indeed, they could still find and reach even well-protected coalition targets. In a telling instance, a Jordanian doctor whom the CIA believed to be a penetration agent inside al-Qaeda turned himself into a suicide bomber and killed seven CIA officers at their base near Khost in December 2009.[77]

As a result of intelligence-led tactics in the West and in the war zones in the Middle East, South Asia, and East Africa, al-Qaeda and its imitators by the late 2000s were clearly on the defensive. As a rule, the operations they planned seemed to be simpler and, if anything, more crude, eschewing the multiple, simultaneous attacks that Osama bin Ladin had trademarked a decade earlier. Nonetheless, even cruder operations could prove deadly. The war on Israeli civilians, of course, never ended, whether conducted by Sunni or Shi'a groups.[78] India became a target of jihad, too. A Kashmiri group called Laskhar-e-Taiba set off pressure cooker bombs on seven trains in eleven minutes in Mumbai on June 11, 2006, and then shot up several targets in the city in November 2008 before barricading themselves in the Taj Mahal Hotel. Together, these attacks killed and injured more than a thousand people. Even a lone gunman in a crowded room could wreak havoc. A US Army psychologist, Major Nidal Malik Hasan, came to the attention of the FBI by soliciting advice from a US citizen and al-Qaeda affiliate, the cleric Anwar al-Aulaqi, in Yemen. Al-Aulaqi took little notice of Hasan's e-mails, but braced nonetheless by al-Aulaqi's online teachings, the major opened fire on his fellow soldiers at Fort Hood, Texas, in 2009, killing thirteen and wounding twenty-nine.[79] How many more such jihadists were there? In Britain by late 2007, MI5 had identified about 2,000 individuals with links to international terrorism, and was investigating thirty "active plots."[80] Bombs could have killed hundreds in London, New York, Glasgow, and Detroit between 2007 and 2009 if their triggers had worked as designed. Indeed, a scarcity of reliable devices seemed to have become the main factor limiting attacks; FBI agents between 2009 and 2012 arrested seven would-be lone bombers in the United States after posing as al-Qaeda operatives providing weapons and explosives.[81] But, finally, they missed a plot in April 2013, when brothers from Chechnya detonated bombs at the finish line of the Boston Marathon.

American eyes had last seen Osama bin Ladin in person through the lens of a Predator-mounted video camera over Afghanistan in the summer of 2000. They finally beheld him again through a night-vision gunsight in his house in neutral Pakistan almost eleven years later. This time he did not survive. The raid by a SEAL team loaned to the CIA culminated a long string of intelligence leads going back to the agency's early interrogations of al-Qaeda lieutenants and proceeding through painstaking collection and analysis of myriad small clues.[82] Essentially, over a decade of war, the West showed its ability to hunt down all jihadist opponents in time, and to make swift judgments at the highest levels to decide who lived and who died. Speaking in 2012 about the bin Ladin raid, CIA's in-house counsel called the operation "illustrative of the careful attention to the law" in America's most sensitive counterterrorism efforts: "I cannot say the operation was heavily lawyered, but I can tell you it was thoroughly lawyered."[83] By October 2012. according to press reports, the list of enemies had been routinized in a "disposition matrix" managed by the White House and the Intelligence Community, and the total of militants and bystanders killed by drone strikes over the last decade stood at just under 3,000 people.[84] President Barack Obama explained the effect of all this effort and international cooperation in May 2013: "Much of our best counterterrorism cooperation results in the gathering and sharing of intelligence, the arrest and prosecution of terrorists. And that's how a Somali terrorist apprehended off the coast of Yemen is now in a prison in New York. That's how we worked with European allies to disrupt plots from Denmark to Germany to the United Kingdom. That's how intelligence collected with Saudi Arabia helped us stop a cargo plane from being blown up over the Atlantic. These partnerships work."[85] John E. McLaughlin, who had served as acting director of central intelligence in 2004, gave a differenct perspective on the targeting of terrorist leaders to a *New York Times* reporter. "You can't underestimate the cultural change that comes with gaining lethal authority. When people say to me, 'It's not a big deal,' I say to them, 'Have you ever killed anyone?' It is a big deal. You start thinking about things differently."[86]

Such measures forced jihadists to mount smaller attacks with fewer and more amateurish operatives. Nevertheless, they in turn had forced a rough stalemate on the West. They could still recruit young men and women willing to blend in with crowds and die for the sake of killing Israelis, Americans, Britons, Iraqis, Kenyans, or citizens of any other nation they chose. Thus the large and expensive intelligence and security institutions built up since

9/11—and the restrictive and intrusive security measures they helped to enforce—could not be dismantled.

A New Domain

In the late 1990s, a senior CIA operations officer, Henry Crumpton, found himself in a training course on computer-assisted espionage. The agency had worked in this realm for some time already, he knew: "Using human sources, the CIA had been stealing computer data since foreign secrets first landed on a hard drive. The CIA had been filching foreign intelligence from cyberspace since its inception." Still, this institutional memory could not prepare Crumpton for what he found in the new course, despite the fact that it had been "designed for ops officers with little or any technical training. If technical ignorance was the prerequisite, I was the most qualified in the class." The course and the new operations it explained sought to exploit "the relationship between foreign intelligence in digital form and human nature." Crumpton later recorded his astonishment at the results:

> The advent of espionage in cyberspace was nearly instantaneous. Its rapid growth and impact on our operations was stunning, even revolutionary. The scope and rewards of my own technical operations exceeded any of my expectations; the amount of raw data stolen and exploited became hard to measure by conventional standards. Instead of pages, we were now talking about terabytes of intelligence booty. By the time I entered the Counterterrorism Center in 1999, most of our technical operations were based in cyberspace. Our traditional and digital operations grew more symbiotic as we tracked, harassed, captured, and killed terrorists all over the world.[87]

The CIA had company in exploring the potential of cyber-enabled intelligence in the new century. In an operation as ambitious as anything the bureau mounted in the Cold War, FBI special agents conducted a patient counterintelligence sting against Russian SVR "illegals" in New York and Washington. Russian operatives supplemented classic espionage with digital means, rendering obsolete the encrypted diskettes passed by earlier spies like Ana Montes and Robert Hanssen. The FBI foiled them with equally up-to-date surveillance techniques and convincing old-time double agentry. By 2005, the FBI had a formidable arsenal of cyber tools, which (along with methods that special agents had used for generations) included reading the

Russians' e-mails and imaging the hard drives of their computers—which led in turn to websites and encrypted communications with Moscow Center that hid in innocent-looking digital images. The bureau watched the illegals for years, and toward the end of the operation a special agent impersonating a Russian consular official met one of them, Anna Chapman, to take her SVR-issued laptop for "repair."[88] In June 2010, the FBI swooped, arresting Chapman and nine other illegals, who were in turn swapped two weeks later for four persons held on spying charges in Russia.

Traditional espionage had not ended, but it did seem in eclipse with the rise of new digital means of collection. The US Intelligence Community noticed a worldwide shift of wealth and secrets to digital formats and networked repositories. The "things" that people, enterprises, governments, and societies valued were increasingly not things at all, but rather arrangements of ones and zeroes for instructing machines how to perform. They in turn were created, stored, moved, and shared by digital means. Intelligence operations soon followed. In 2000, the CIA had told Congress in open session that states and even terrorists might soon be using the internet to harm the United States and its allies. What the agency did not mention was the possibility that cyber exploitation like that in the contemporary "Moonlight Maze" intrusions in US networks (which journalists would be reporting on a year later) might grow dramatically in volume and audacity. By mid-decade, however, alarmed American officials set aside their earlier reticence. James Gosler of Sandia Labs, who had designed the course that Henry Crumpton had taken a few years earlier, explained what was happening: "US adversaries have collected and exfiltrated several terabytes of data from key Department of Defense networks. The apparent inability to patch US systems in a timely manner provides opponents with ample opportunities for access to our information systems. While we are aware of these operations, we do not appear to have the technical ability to close the access holes or to clearly attribute these operations to the perpetrator(s)."[89]

Some European and American officials pointed fingers at cyber actors in China. Maj. Gen. William Lord, then head of the US Air Force's Office of Warfighting Integration, claimed in public in August 2006 that Chinese hackers had downloaded ten to twenty terabytes of data from the Department of Defense's Non-Classified IP Router Network (NIPRNet).[90] In late 2007, MI5's Director General Jonathan Evans sent a letter to 300 officers of British financial and legal firms warning them they were under electronic espionage attack by "Chinese state organisations."[91] Chancellor Angela Merkel personally confronted China's visiting premier Wen Jiabao that same year, just after *Der Spiegel* reported that German security services had for months been combating Chinese hackers in Germany's official government networks.[92]

The ways in which these penetrations worked would be studied in detail by private security firms and internet service providers as well as by intelligence agencies. The "ISPs" could do so because they moved or screened most of the world's digital traffic, and thus had endless data sets to analyze for patterns and malicious software. Security firms also helped; in 2011 the American antivirus company McAfee publicized its discovery of a command-and-control server used by cyber intruders since at least mid-2006, and recovered the server's activity logs, which indicated the intrusions had continued for years. "After painstaking analysis of the logs, even we were surprised by the enormous diversity of the victim organizations and were taken aback by the audacity of the perpetrators," wrote Dmitri Alperovitch, McAfee's vice president for threat research. The pattern of the data thefts from organizations like the International Olympic Committee and the World Anti-Doping Agency—data with seemingly no commercial value—"was particularly intriguing" to Alperovitch because it "potentially pointed a finger at a state actor behind the intrusions." The single server that McAfee had found, moreover, only hinted at the larger problem: "We know of many other successful targeted intrusions (not counting cyber-crime-related ones) that we are called in to investigate almost weekly, which impact other companies and industries. This is a problem of massive scale that affects nearly every industry and sector of the economies of numerous countries, and the only organizations that are exempt from this threat are those that don't have anything valuable or interesting worth stealing."[93]

Whatever the sources of the intrusions spotted in business and government networks across the advanced industrial nations, cyber espionage had taken an unexpected turn. State secrets were still being targeted—a fact that suggested state sponsorship of the intrusions—but the Office of the National Counterintelligence Executive in the United States insisted much of the cyber espionage was aimed at stealing secrets that imparted competitive advantage in the marketplace.[94] "I believe we are suffering what is probably the biggest transfer of wealth through theft and piracy in the history of mankind," said US Senator Sheldon Whitehouse in 2010 after examining classified evidence.[95] General

Keith Alexander, by 2012 serving a dual appointment as the director of the National Security Agency and commander of the new US Cyber Command, summarized the situation to Congress: "State-sponsored industrial espionage and theft of intellectual capital now occurs with stunning rapacity and brazenness, and some of that activity links back to foreign intelligence services. Companies and government agencies around the world are thus being looted of their intellectual property by national intelligence actors, and those victims understandably turn for help to their governments."[96] Evidence assembled by private researchers and published in 2012 and 2013 suggested that the campaign of cyber espionage against economic targets had not slowed in response to adverse publicity.[97] "We have no practical deterrents in place today" to stop cyber espionage, lamented Congressman Mike Rogers while chairing a public hearing of the House's select committee on intelligence oversight in February 2013.[98]

The techniques involved in such campaigns seemed to have grown rapidly in sophistication and power. In 2008, the United States learned that its most sensitive military networks—systems requiring high security clearances just to access—were suddenly hosting malware created by a "foreign intelligence agency." What Deputy Secretary of Defense William Lynn publicly called "the most significant breach of U.S. military computers ever" prompted an urgent and expensive containment effort called Operation BUCKSHOT YANKEE to neutralize the bug.[99] The capabilities of such cyber espionage tools became clearer with the 2012 discovery of one such program dubbed "Flame" by the researchers who analyzed it at the Russian software security firm Kaspersky. Once again, the malware under the proverbial microscope could have performed chores for cyber criminals; but it seemed built to such exacting standards for use against so many targets of little commercial interest that analysts judged it to have been produced by a state actor. Though such "remote access trojans" (RATs) had been spotted by the computer security community as early as 2002, the Flame malware dated to 2008 or earlier, and had multiple functions combined in ways that impressed even experienced observers.[100] Most of its functions seem to have involved collecting and exfiltrating data from personal computers and even from nearby office equipment and workplace chatter: "Once a system is infected, Flame begins a complex set of operations, including sniffing the network traffic, taking screenshots, recording audio conversations, intercepting the keyboard, and so on. All this data is available to the operators through the link to Flame's command-and-control servers. . . . Overall, we can say Flame is one of the most complex threats ever discovered."[101]

As Henry Crumpton had anticipated a decade earlier, even these most capable and stealthy of espionage tools gained access to their targets by the simplest of means. The "Shady RAT" bug investigated by McAfee installed itself in the computers of employees who opened attachments or links in e-mails purportedly coming from coworkers or trusted institutions like banks and government agencies. The infection found in classified US military networks in 2008 "began when an infected flash drive was inserted into a U.S. military laptop at a base in the Middle East," according to Deputy Secretary Lynn.[102] Witting sabotage or intentional compromises probably played a lesser part in these and thousands of other data breaches around the world over the last two decades. Though such violations of security by insiders were always a danger, of far greater concern to network administrators has been the risk of loyal employees hurriedly or unwittingly taking shortcuts around security protocols.

The vulnerabilities that such practices could introduce into critical government and private information systems went far beyond the very serious exploitation of state secrets and intellectual property. Malware that can penetrate a target network can also damage that network and even the equipment it controls. Intelligence officials the world over issued public warnings about the dangers of cyber sabotage and remote penetrations. America's national counterintelligence executive, Joel Brenner, explained this problem in a 2009 speech, noting that his colleagues were: "seeing counterfeit routers and chips, and some of those chips have made their way into US military fighter aircraft . . . you don't sneak counterfeit chips into another nation's aircraft to steal data. When it's done intentionally, it's done to degrade systems, or to have the ability to do so at a time of one's choosing. There is no longer a meaningful difference between data security and operational security. Our operations depend on our networks—the same networks on which we create, move, and store data."[103]

The US military in 2004 quietly declared cyberspace one of the "domains of the battlespace" like air, land, sea, and space, and insisted that America's armed forces have the ability "to ensure access to these domains to protect the Nation, forces in the field and US global interests."[104] Secretary of Defense Robert Gates in 2009 announced the nomination of NSA's Director, then-Lieutenant General Keith B. Alexander, to serve simultaneously as the first head of a new US Cyber Command. According to a press report at the time, the command would merge the Pentagon's defensive and offensive cyber warfare units, and "leverage the NSA's technical capabilities."[105] Others were moving in a parallel direction. Israel's chief of military intelligence, Major-General Amos Yadlin, noted that his nation already had an offensive and defensive cyberwar program, telling an audience in 2009 that "the cyberwarfare field fits well with the state of Israel's defense doctrine."[106] Britain's minister of state for the armed forces, Nick Harvey, suggested in 2011 that offensive cyber weapons had become "an integral part of the country's armoury."[107]

The possibility of employing force in cyberspace to compel or destroy, which had exercised authors since the early 1990s, suddenly seemed quite real. Al-Qaeda had sought to damage the US economy with its attacks on 9/11, but disrupting governmental functions, critical infrastructure, and industrial processes was possible and more likely through cyberspace. Two of Russia's neighbors, Estonia and Georgia, suffered targeted disruptions of their governments and financial sectors in 2007 and 2008, respectively. Moscow disclaimed responsibility, but independent researchers concluded that in Georgia "[t]he organizers of the cyber attacks had advance notice of Russian military intentions, and they were tipped off about the timing of the Russian military operations while these operations were being carried out."[108] In 2012, moreover, David Sanger of the *New York Times* alleged that the United States and Israel had attacked the Iranian nuclear program with a cyber weapon that independent researchers had discovered and dubbed "Stuxnet." Michael Hayden, a former director of NSA and more recently of CIA as well, declined to discuss Stuxnet but told Sanger, "Somebody has crossed the Rubicon" in attacking the Iranian enrichment infrastructure. "We've got a legion on the other side of the river now. I don't pretend it's the same effect, but in one sense at least, it's August 1945."[109] Rivers, of course, can be crossed in both directions. Secretary of Defense Leon Panetta in October 2012 cited recent attacks on a Saudi oil company's networks, mounted by means of the "Shamoon" virus, which had rendered 30,000 of Saudi Aramco's computers inoperable; press speculation about the perpetrators centered on Iran.[110]

The volumes of data that could be stolen or destroyed through cyber operations were astronomical—they could barely be comprehended, let alone utilized by traditional methods of information management and analysis. In short, the collection of digital information by digital means easily outstripped the ability of analysts to sort through the take. The advent of spy satellites and early computer processing had challenged analysts in the United States and its Commonwealth allies decades earlier, as noted in the 1971 Schlesinger Report. The digital revolution compounded the problem many times over. Analysts and managers seemed to prefer water-based metaphors in describing the situation; they were being fire hosed, drowned, swamped, and deluged in the torrents of data. For everyone, the digital revolution placed an even higher premium on "all-source" analysis. Seemingly mundane issues like storage for the data, and power to run the required servers, also took on enterprise-critical significance. This was especially so for NSA in its effort to "create a new Signals Intelligence enterprise to exploit the global network," which suffered a setback in 2005 with the cancellation of an ambitious program named TRAILBLAZER.[111] NSA also distributed its operations across five states in the late 2000s and built a new data center in a sixth state.[112] By 2012, the US Intelligence Community was working to pool its databases in a "cloud" architecture, in part to control rising costs for storage, maintenance, and security.[113]

Oddly, too much data could seemingly become too little data. In 2012, the government of Prime Minister David Cameron proposed a Communications Data Bill to modernize the requirement for internet service providers to aid police and intelligence work by obtaining and storing "some communications data which they may have no business reason to collect at present."[114] "Communications data" here meant "information created when a communication takes place"—not its content. As MI5's director general explained to the Intelligence and Security Committee, such data were vital to modern intelligence work; "there are no significant investigations that we undertake across the service that don't use communications data because of its ability to tell you the who and the when and the where of your target's activities." Yet data flows—while increasing geometrically in volume with the spread of mobile telephones, Voice over internet Protocol calling, and social media, were yielding ever less communications data for the agencies because the internet service providers saw no business need to retain so much data—creating what the ISC called a growing "capability gap" and an "erosion of the ability of public authorities to access" the data they required.[115] Hence the Cameron administration's draft bill to oblige internet service providers to retain data for a year. Some observers also proposed an expansion of the disciplines of intelligence to include "social media intelligence" to account for and regulate legitimate authorities' perusal of all the data accumulating around citizens' use of the new technologies.[116] This new dilemma affected not just the Cold War signals intelligence alliance, but all intelligence agencies seeking to exploit digital collection opportunities. It has not been resolved, and as of this writing the Communications Data bill has not been reintroduced after Deputy Prime Minister Nick Clegg withdrew his support for it in April 2013.

For those with the patience and skill to glean nuggets from mountains of data, the digital revolution offered a bonanza. This trend applied not only to governments; private firms and researchers began analyzing online activity by more or less intrusive means, in effect performing intelligence functions in the ways invented in the twentieth century. As noted above, the organizations involved were diverse, including corporations like internet service providers seeking to unclutter their networks, and software security companies hoping to reduce the threats roaming the internet (as well as to burnish their reputations and market shares). Academics and private think tanks also developed skills to analyze malware and malicious activity. University of Toronto researchers, for instance, revealed in 2009 an operation, apparently of Chinese origin, that they dubbed "GhostNet." Its administrators had infiltrated at least 1,295 computers in 103 countries, "including many belonging to embassies, foreign ministries and other government offices."[117] Two years later, a small think tank in Virginia, Project 2049, examined China's internet to produce a study of the Peoples Republic's cyber and signals intelligence community. In the 1960s, such an effort might have been issued as a National Intelligence Estimate (NIE)—if the intelligence agencies of the US government had been able to write it at all.[118] "The world has no secrets from China," Russian antivirus magnate Eugene Kaspersky told an audience in Washington in spring 2013.[119]

In the digital age, corporations learned to act like military and intelligence agencies with secrets to keep from active adversaries. As cyber crime and espionage encroached on private and government computers around the world, the makers and owners of those systems found ways to collaborate with officials to fight back. In 2011, for instance, software giant Microsoft and the FBI obtained court orders to seize command and control servers for "botnets" (which were zombie computers—sometimes hundreds of thousands of them—remotely controlled by criminals). Microsoft creatively enforced its license rights, while the FBI (with Microsoft's assistance) switched out servers and substituted new ones that took control of portions of a botnet called Coreflood, receiving in the process large help-ings of stolen data that the botnet's managers in a foreign country were exfiltrating for themselves.[120] Everyday computer users in homes and busi-nesses found themselves increasingly having to act as if under surveil-lance, with constant instructions about password hygiene and warnings about opening malicious e-mail attachments. GCHQ chief Iain Lobban explained to a business audience in 2012: "Your IT systems may have already been compromised, attackers could already have your new prod-uct plans, bidding positions or research, they may already be running your process control systems. Are you confident that this has not already hap-pened to your business?"[121] At least one major corporate source of infor-mation technology and advice recommended that corporations build what were in essence military-grade classification systems to segregate and guard their most important data.[122] In a way, the digital revolution was mak-ing intelligence officers of everyone.

An End to Secrets?

The exposure of Stuxnet, Flame, and GhostNet by German, Russian, and Canadian researchers, respectively, spoke volumes about the state of intelli-gence in the early twenty-first century. Intelligence systems were more trans-parent than ever and even private parties, often with only modest means, could glean their secrets from afar. Digital intelligence operations could be spotted by experts possessing the skills to capture and analyze the relevant computer logs. But even intelligence officers employing traditional means found themselves uncomfortably scrutinized in the decade after 9/11. The End of History might indeed have occurred with the collapse of the Soviet Empire a decade earlier, but the liberal states of the West held multitudes of opinions about how states should improve security against threats from al-Qaeda and cyber espionage. Antiterror policies that required copious intelligence inputs and a rapid operational tempo proved especially con-troversial and surprisingly visible to critics with political and even parti-san motives to expose them. Critics soon turned to the internet to aid their sleuthing and to publicize their findings.

The modern era of exposure dates to arguments over the Iraq war. As noted above, both the Bush and the Blair administrations declassified intel-ligence morsels to support their calls for intervention. Critics of the loom-ing war also cited intelligence estimates (or the lack thereof) to bolster their case. Democrats controlling the Senate in September 2002 demanded an NIE be prepared, in just three weeks, before Congress voted on whether to support Republican President Bush's intention to use force in Iraq.[123] Senators calling for the estimate sensed that policy was ahead of intelligence, and publicly complained that the Intelligence Community had not acted in concert to formulate its views.[124] Administration and intelligence officials "reluctantly agreed" to their demand, believing the data requested by the senators "were already available in other documents."[125] The resulting NIE was drafted in near-record time by cobbling together prose from previous community publications and coordinated by the agencies in a marathon session; hence it has become a byword for flawed analysis.[126] According to DCI George Tenet, "[b]ecause of the time pressures, analysts lifted chunks of other recently published papers and replicated them in the Estimate."[127] Though the analytic findings matched previous reporting dating back to the Clinton administration, it nonetheless gave Democratic senators an opening to argue that the White House's Iraq policy diverged from intelligence judgments, and to claim that the NIE and an accompanying white paper for public release portrayed no truly imminent Iraqi threat to the United States that would justify a preemptive war.[128] The implication was clear—the Bush administration was politicizing the intelligence it cited in order to whip up public support for intervention and increase the political pressure on opponents of the war policy. The charge was also, however, a subtle rhetorical sleight of hand. It made administration officials bear the burden of proving the negative (i.e., that they were *not* politicizing the analysis) while depriving them of the required evidence, unless they exposed sensitive intelligence sources and methods they needed to conserve for the upcoming conflict.

The conspicuous absence of weapons of mass destruction in Iraq soon played a role as well, prompting investigations in Britain and America. It gave officials and legislators in all parties reasons to demand public answers about prewar intelligence. The probes of the Iraq analysis proceeded alongside the inquiry into the 9/11 attacks in the United States, and the investigators held hearings and released documents that collectively revealed a great deal about analysis and operations in both countries over the preceding decade. Memoirs and journalistic accounts added details and color, allowing officials to trade charges about who was to blame for the intelligence failure. In London, critics blamed Prime Minister Blair, who allegedly oversaw the process that "fitted" the intelligence to the policy and served up a "dodgy dossier" misstating Iraqi capabilities. The debates in Britain seemed subdued, however, compared with those in America. Bush administration officials blamed each other and also DCI Tenet, anonymously claiming that Tenet had insisted the existence of weapons in Iraq was "a slam dunk"— a *prima facie* case.[129] Former National Security Council official Richard Clarke blamed the Bush administration for politicizing and exaggerating the argument for the war in a book he published in time for the 2004 presidential election.[130] Tenet himself, in retirement, criticized his own handling of the intelligence but hinted that zealots at the Defense Department had wanted the conflict no matter what, in any case, the intelligence said.[131] By the time Tenet had departed, the White House was convinced that CIA managers had worked to undermine the administration's policies; a new DCI, former Congressman Porter Goss, arrived at the agency in September 2004 determined to restore discipline.[132] In this charged political climate, serious leaks from inside the government were not long in coming.

A year after Operation IRAQI FREEDOM toppled Saddam Hussein's regime, gruesome digital images depicting the abuse of prisoners by their US Army guards at Abu Ghraib prison sickened viewers around the world. Secretary of Defense Donald Rumsfeld twice offered to resign over the scandal, but Bush, having no one in mind to replace him, declined his offers.[133] By coincidence, as the scandal reverberated, the CIA's inspector general completed a special review of the agency's "enhanced interrogation program."[134] Some of its findings swiftly found their way to James Risen and Eric Lichtblau of the *New York Times*, including the allegation that 9/11 planner Khalid Shaikh Mohammed had been subjected to "graduated levels of force, including a technique known as 'water boarding.'" Indeed, the methods employed by the CIA were "so severe that senior officials of the Federal Bureau of Investigation have directed its agents to stay out of many of the interviews of the high-level detainees," reported the *Times* story, which also noted that unnamed officials had defended the methods as stopping short of torture.[135] Not a few American officials believed the legal rationale for those techniques could not be defended.[136]

Outrage over the Abu Ghraib prisoner abuse and the torture allegations created an international cause for watching the watchers. New revelations came from reporters seeking scoops, from airplane buffs, and from an irritated prosecutor in Italy. The *Guardian* reported in March 2005 that two Egyptian refugees and suspected terror sympathizers had been picked up by Swedish authorities soon after 9/11, taken to an airfield at Bromma, and sent to Egypt by

an American aircrew who flew them out of Sweden on a private executive jet. . . . We were able to chart the toing and froing of the private
executive jet used at Bromma partly through the observations of plane-
spotters posted on the web and partly through a senior source in the
Pakistan Inter Services Intelligence agency (ISI). It was a Gulfstream V
Turbo, tailfin number N379P; its flight plans always began at an airstrip
in Smithfield, North Carolina, and ended in some of the world's hot
spots. It was owned by Premier Executive Transport Services, incorpo-
rated in Delaware, a brass plaque company with nonexistent directors,
hired by American agents.[137]

At the same time, officials in Milan were analyzing the movements of
American officials in Italy, apparently also profiting from the data cited
by the *Guardian*. They alleged that the CIA, in cooperation with Italian
military intelligence, had kidnapped a radical Islamic cleric, Abu Omar,
off a Milan street in 2003, and bundled him off to Egypt. This "rendition"
curtailed an investigation that was being conducted by local authorities, who paid back the Americans (and the government in Rome) by
digging to the bottom of the affair and handing their findings to the
courts, which then indicted twenty-three Americans in absentia.[138] The
case made headlines in June 2005, and once again the *Guardian* summarized the evidence:

By ploughing through hundreds of thousands of mobile phone records,
tracing hotel registrations and bugging phone conversations, the Italian
police have built up a picture of the CIA's operation that offers several surprises. . . . A Learjet allegedly took Abu Omar from the joint US base at
Aviano in Italy to another US base at Ramstein, Germany, then a chartered Gulfstream V whisked him to Cairo. Yet barely a dollar was spent on
making the team's communications secure. The secret agents used ordinary mobile phones. Italian investigators put names to the abductors by
matching their calls to the phone contracts they had signed. And they
could be sure of the team's movements because they could see when the
calls had been made and from which mobile phone.[139]

Ultimately an appeals court in Milan sentenced the former head and
another official of the Italian military intelligence service (along with three
American officials in absentia) to prison in early 2013, though their sentences as of this writing are suspended, pending final appeal.

In short, a great deal of information was available when reporters, officials, and nongovernmental organizations sought to know what was happening in the War on Terror. In November 2005, *Washington Post* reporter Dana Priest put these and other clues together and reported that the CIA had its own "enhanced interrogation" program for captured al-Qaeda chiefs like Khalid Shaikh Mohammed, which it conducted in custom-built "black sites" overseas.[140] This prompted another outcry and a raft of inquiries, culminating in a February 2007 report by the European Union's parliament alleging the CIA had flown 1,245 flights in European airspace between 9/11 and late 2005, many of them for the "extraordinary rendition" of terror suspects to countries where they could be interrogated by torture. Extraordinary rendition, the report argued, constituted "an illegal instrument used by the United States" that had furthermore been shown to be "counterproductive in the fight against terrorism" because it damaged and undermined "regular police and judicial procedures against terrorism suspects."[141]

Such extraordinary revelations heightened concerns in Muslim communities and other quarters that the campaign against al-Qaeda would lead to persecution of Muslims in the West. Some made exactly this argument. At the conclusion of the trial of seven Muslim men arrested in Operation Crevice in 2004 (during which British authorities found them hoarding 1,300 pounds of ammonium nitrate and other bomb-making materials), the defendants had a spokesman declare

> This was a prosecution driven by the security services, able to hide behind a cloak of secrecy, and eager to obtain ever greater resources and power to encroach on individual rights. There was no limit to the money, resources and underhand strategies that were used to secure convictions in this case. This case was brought in an atmosphere of hostility against Muslims, at home, and abroad. . . . Anyone looking impartially at the evidence would realise that there was no conspiracy to cause explosions in the UK, and that we did not pose any threat to the security of this country. It is not an offence to be young, Muslim and angry at the global injustices against Muslims.[142]

In late 2005, that worry about surveillance grew into concern that the War on Terror was potentially targeting everyone. The *New York Times*'s reporting team of Risen and Lichtblau revealed the existence of the aforementioned Terrorist Surveillance Program, run for the Bush administration by

NSA.[143] Six months later, Risen and Lichtblau also contributed to the revelation of another secret effort to identify terrorist funds, conducted with the cooperation of banks and financial firms in America and Europe.[144] Similar concerns fostered controversy over the Blair government's proposed (and withdrawn) Intercept Modernisation Programme in 2008.

The collective weight of revelations forced the Bush administration and the Intelligence Community to respond. The White House ended the Terrorist Surveillance Program in early 2007 and notified congressional leaders that new monitoring procedures now ensured the government would have "the necessary speed and agility while providing substantial advantages," and thus "[A]ny electronic surveillance that was occurring as part of the Terrorist Surveillance Program will now be conducted subject to the approval of the Foreign Intelligence Surveillance Court."[145] Ironically, subsequent congressional changes to the underlying act in 2008 made it even more permissive than the TSP had been—suggesting that powerful intelligence tools could indeed be affirmed by democratic processes.[146] The scrutiny forced other operational adjustments as well. Deputy Director for Operations Jose Rodriguez recalled that the CIA had had to keep moving its black sites after "the media started an all-out effort to uncover and expose where the detainees were being held." Typically only one or two captives would be moved at a time, but when closing one site and opening another "as many as fourteen detainees were moved on a single flight."[147] After two years of this, President Bush and CIA Director Michael Hayden in September 2006 admitted the existence of the sites and transferred custody of their prisoners to the US military's facility at Guantanamo. Hayden felt compelled to make a public defense of the rendition and interrogation programs in a speech in New York in September 2007. He insisted renditions had been "conducted lawfully, responsibly, and with a clear and simple purpose: to get terrorists off the streets and gain intelligence on those still at large." Hayden also disputed the European Parliament report, claiming "The actual number of rendition flights ever flown by CIA is a tiny fraction" of the 1,245 flights cited, and that "the suggestion that even a substantial number of those 1,245 flights were carrying detainees is absurd on its face."[148] The agencies also spent a great deal of effort looking for leakers.[149] Revelations about the programs nonetheless dribbled out in Britain as well. The Intelligence and Security Committee, with an eye to the British nation's obligations under the European Convention on Human Rights, reported on the knowledge

THE SHADOW WAR   315

that its security services had gained about US rendition efforts in July 2007; Committee members regretted in at least one instance what they called "a lack of regard, on the part of the US, for UK concerns."[150]

Repercussions continued for years. Both the British and Canadian governments eventually paid settlements to their nationals (Binyam Mohamed and Maher Arar, respectively) who had been rendered to Middle Eastern states and allegedly tortured with the tacit complicity of the United States and their own countries. The incoming Obama administration's new Director of National Intelligence, Dennis Blair, revised the community's *National Intelligence Strategy* (2009) to state that the American intelligence system should "exemplify America's values: operating under the rule of law, consistent with Americans' expectations for protection of privacy and civil liberties, respectful of human rights, and in a manner that retains the trust of the American people."[151] The White House and Justice Department also released the CIA inspector general's report from five years earlier on the enhanced interrogation program, along with contemporary Bush administration debates over whether its methods constituted torture.[152] Public arguments between former CIA and FBI veterans over the effectiveness of the agency's interrogations continue to this day, reignited in late 2012 by *Zero Dark Thirty*, a Hollywood thriller based on the bin Ladin raid. Even a pair of US senators weighed in on the issue.[153]

The stakes seemed so high that it was probably only a matter of time before someone decided to leak official secrets by digital means. The European Union parliament was an independent actor in the war on terror, with no military or law enforcement responsibilities, and though many of its legislators hailed from countries allied to the United States in NATO, they felt bound to a higher calling and thus not only free but obliged to pursue intelligence abuses by using the copious information available on the web. More than a few private individuals felt a similar call, and Australia's Julian Assange advocated new ways for dissenting officials to expose secrets to a larger public. Where "leaking is easy," he explained, "secretive or unjust systems are nonlinearly hit relative to open, just systems. Since unjust systems, by their nature induce opponents, and in many places barely have the upper hand, mass leaking leaves them exquisitely vulnerable to those who seek to replace them with more open forms of governance."[154] In October 2006, Assange registered a domain name and soon established a website— wikileaks.org—to put his theory into practice. WikiLeaks started slowly, but by 2010 it was making headlines, releasing hundreds of thousands of official documents, many of them classified and copied from US State Department and military databases by US Army private Bradley Manning.[155] A similar idea motivated the private information security firm Mandiant in early 2013 to publicize what it described as clear evidence of Chinese online espionage, performed in this case by the Peoples Liberation Army's "Unit 61398." Mandiant conceded that its exposure of the unit's tools and practices would surely prompt that organization to adjust its procedures and thus "force us to work harder to continue tracking them with such accuracy. It is our sincere hope, however, that [our] report can temporarily increase the costs of Unit 61398's operations and impede their progress in a meaningful way."[156]

Such revelations proved capable of forcing change on US and allied intelligence services, but they had even larger consequences elsewhere. In combination with internet-based social media like Facebook and Twitter, they made an impact where almost no one expected—in the Arab despotisms that had spent decades fending off Leninist and then Islamist terror. The watchers were now the watched. Purloined and publicized US diplomatic cables detailing the corruption of the regime in Tunisia helped fuel popular unrest that toppled strongman Ben Ali in early 2011. Disturbances spread to Egypt, Libya, and other lands in the resulting Arab Spring. Both the Egyptian and Libyan regimes fell that year, the former with relatively little bloodshed, and the latter after a months-long civil war that eventually drew in NATO airpower in support of the rebels fighting the dictator Muammar Qaddafi. In all these struggles, both those that succeeded and those that were suppressed, the internet and social media proved an equalizing factor, giving protesters and rebels means for spreading news and propaganda, for concerting their efforts, and most significantly for gathering intelligence on the regimes they confronted.[157] The overall effect of the new media was to enable anyone to report news and information from anywhere. One such ad hoc intelligence actor was Rida Benfayed, a surgeon in Denver who returned to his Libyan hometown and created a veritable intelligence clearing house after he "got hold of the city's only two-way satellite internet connection and started accepting hundreds of requests to connect on Skype. He organized his contacts into six categories: English media, Arabic media, medical, ground information, politicians, and intelligence." He was soon in contact with experts and sources around the world volunteering information about the Qaddafi regime and its weapons.[158]

7.2 General Michael Hayden as director of the CIA, 2006. *Central Intelligence Agency*

Regimes anxious about internet-enabled dissent did not sit on their hands. Indeed, the Arab Spring saw furious skirmishing in cyberspace. Some of the programs these regimes used were commercially available espionage tools.[159] The civil war in Syria, for example, witnessed pro- and antigovernment forces fighting a protracted campaign on the internet. The Syrian regime blocked and filtered accesses to the web, helped by a shadowy group calling itself the Syrian Electronic Army that harassed opponents.[160] The Syrian opposition also found help from outside. A hacker collective calling themselves Anonymous struck back at Damascus in early 2012 by revealing millions of the Bashir al-Assad regime's e-mails.[161] Digital intelligence was no longer a tool only of criminality and surveillance but a weapon against oppression—although which side would prevail, and how much oppression would retreat, remained an open question.

And just what oppression entailed could be debated as well, as events in 2013 showed. A new wave of revelations in the United States and United

Kingdom resulted when an NSA contractor, Edward Snowden, left for Hong Kong and ultimately Moscow with a digital trove of classified files. He arranged with media outlets on several continents to publish selected documents on US an allied intelligence programs, and the resulting uproar featured widespread arguments over the proper limits on governmental surveillance in the internet age. Debates spread abroad as well, with commentators noting that the intelligence collection of US persons' communications looked comparatively measured and restrained beside the analogous efforts of some European states.[162] Even President Obama felt compelled to defend and adjust the collection programs.[163] As of this writing, the prospect of significant regulatory reforms to the surveillance appears likely if not certain. What does appear certain is that every intelligence service is now at serious risk of losing files to another "insider threat."

Conclusion

The intelligence agencies used the terrorism fight and the digital revolution to get better in the 2000s. A decade after 9/11, many were bigger and many were more capable. Still, that growth had been painful. Organizational turmoil followed 9/11 as intelligence systems built for one threat shifted to others. By 2013, moreover, the state intelligence systems were under siege from each other and from private actors with new powers of collection and analysis. A general lowering of what economists call the "barriers-to-entry" for intelligence trends made offensive intelligence cheaper; small states and nonstate actors now practiced espionage and even covert action against their larger neighbors, with modest investments and often with low risk to themselves. Technological innovations blurred the lines between states and nonstates in the intelligence field, putting powerful and stealthy weapons in private or nonstate hands. Digital technology gave virtually all nations—and even angry and determined groups and individuals—suites of intelligence capabilities that for a century had been almost the sole province of the richer and more advanced states. The intelligence monopoly had ended by 2001; the years afterward witnessed the spreading implications of this development.

But the story after 9/11 was not a wholly technological one. If the means of intelligence had spread to many more actors, its ends remained constant—to secure and possibly enrich those who employed it, and to hamper their adversaries. Those actors now came in a bewildering variety of forms. The dominant ones continued to be states, despite the European flirtation with union, and the most prosperous and free of those states more or less adhered to liberal traditions of representative government and freedom of conscience. Meanwhile, al-Qaeda lived on, a stateless menace, battling most regimes in the Muslim world and challenging the liberal societies to fashion security arrangements that would frustrate terrorist plots by the least intrusive means. What those means could be, however, remained a topic of fierce debate in the West, and intelligence activities came under even greater scrutiny as a consequence of that public controversy. Public and legal pressure on the Bush administration increased steadily after 2003 as a result of European demands that uses of force against terrorists (including their surveillance, detention, and interrogation) be kept accountable to independent oversight working by transparent procedures. That pressure extended to states cooperating with US intelligence in the War on Terror, and ultimately to their intelligence services as well. Within three years these pressures grew irresistible, compelling operational and policy changes in the US Intelligence Community. Thus new rules ultimately affected all the Western services.

In important respects, however, the most significant changes in the intelligence field occurred on the cultural, legal, and economic boundaries between the liberal West and the authoritarian regimes, whether tribal monarchies, dictatorships, or one-party socialist republics. Prosperous societies and enterprises came under cyber siege from those wanting to emulate their material success. At the same time, however, liberal values posed an implicit threat to traditional and authoritarian norms, and indeed, not a few citizens of the Western states took to commercially available means to challenge repression. Authoritarian regimes found themselves pressed from thousands of voices of conscience, such as the groups using satellite images to distinguish prison camps from the rest of North Korea.[164] The intelligence monopoly might be over, but the intelligence struggle has never been more rife.

NOTES

1. National Commission on Terrorist Attacks upon the United States, *The 9/11 Commission Report* (New York: W. W. Norton, 2004), 277.
2. Tony Craig, "Sabotage! The Origins, Development and Impact of the IRA's Infrastructural Bombing Campaigns, 1939–1997," *Intelligence and National*

Security 25:3 (June 2010): 323–25. See also Christopher Andrew, *Defend the Realm: The Authorized History of MI5*, (New York: Knopf, 2009) 795–97, 845.

3. International Atomic Energy Agency, "Inadequate Control of World's Radioactive Sources," IAEA Press Release 2002/09, 24 June 2002, accessed May 27, 2012, at www.iaea.org/newscenter/pressreleases/2002/prn0209.shtml.

4. *The 9/11 Commission Report*, 71–72.

5. Ibid., 56.

6. Ibid., 56, 467n23. Bin Ladin's deputy Ayman al Zawahiri insisted "the United States did not give one penny in aid" to the "Arab Afghans" assisted by bin Ladin during the struggle against the Soviet occupation; Jessica M. Huckaby and Mark E. Stout, "Al Qaida's Views of Authoritarian Intelligence Services," *Intelligence and National Security* 25:3 (June 2010): 346.

7. Mary R. Habeck, "Blessed September: Al-Qaeda's Grand Strategic Vision on 9/11," in Lorry Fenner, Mark E. Stout, and Jessica L. Goldings, eds., *Ten Years Later: Insights on al-Qaida's Past and Future through Captured Records* (Washington, DC: Johns Hopkins University Press 2012), 52–54.

8. Huckaby and Stout, "Al Qaida's Views of Authoritarian Intelligence Services," 330, 333.

9. *The 9/11 Commission Report*, 69.

10. Andrew, *Defend the Realm*, 783, 797; Len Scott, "Secret Intelligence, Covert Action, and Clandestine Diplomacy," in L. V. Scott and P. D. Jackson, *Understanding Intelligence in the Twenty-First Century: Journeys in Shadows* (London: Routledge, 2004), 173–74.

11. Richard Clarke, *Against All Enemies: Inside America's War on Terror* (New York: Simon & Schuster, 2004), 156.

12. George Tenet with Bill Harlow, *At the Center of the Storm: The CIA during America's Time of Crisis* (New York: Harper, 2008 [2007]), 102–3.

13. Andrew, *Defend the Realm*, 801.

14. Diane Carraway Piette and Jesselyn Radack, "Piercing the Historical Mists of FISA: The People and Events behind the Passage of FISA and the Creation of the 'Wall,'" *Stanford Law and Policy Review*: 17:2 (2006): 483.

15. *The 9/11 Commission Report*, 271.

16. Henry A. Crumpton, *The Art of Intelligence: Lessons from a Life in the CIA's Clandestine Service* (New York: Penguin, 2012), 139–41.

17. Ibid., 153–55.

18. The report is reprinted in *The 9/11 Commission Report*, 261.

19. Ibid., 252.

20. Ibid., 169–72.

21. Jose Rodriguez with Bill Harlow, *Hard Measures: How Aggressive CIA Actions after 9/11 Saved American Lives* (New York: Threshold, 2012), 34; Philip Mudd, *Takedown: Inside the Hunt for Al-Qaeda* (Philadelphia: University of Pennsylvania Press, 2013), 30, 37.

22. Tenet and Harlow, *At the Center of the Storm*, 452.

23. David Omand, *Securing the State* (New York: Columbia University Press, 2010), 41.

24. Tenet, *At the Center of the Storm*, 239.

25. Inspectors General of the Department of Defense et al., "Unclassified Report on the President's Surveillance Program," 2009–0013-AS, July 10, 2009, 1–2, 15; accessed August 20, 2012, at www.dni.gov/files/documents/Newsroom/Reports%20and%20Pubs/report_071309.pdf.

26. Bush, *Decision Points*, 163–64; Tenet, *At the Center of the Storm*, 238. See also the Inspectors General, "Report on the President's Surveillance Program," 5.

27. Dana Priest, "Covert CIA Program Withstands New Furor: Anti-Terror Effort Continues to Grow," *Washington Post*, December 30, 2005.

28. Doug Stanton, *Horse Soldiers: The Extraordinary Story of a Band of US Soldiers Who Rode to Victory in Afghanistan* (New York: Scribners, 2009), 222–23.

29. Gary C. Schroen, *First In: An Insider's Account of How the CIA Spearheaded the War Terror in Afghanistan* (New York: Ballantine, 2007 [2005]), 328, 356–60.

30. Crumpton, *The Art of Intelligence*, 148–59.

31. Bush, *Decision Points*, 166. The quote was from a remark by Secretary of Defense Donald Rumsfeld.

32. Rodriguez, *Hard Measures*, 77.

33. Philippe Sands, *Torture Team: Rumsfeld's Memo and the Betrayal of American Values* (New York: Palgrave Macmillan, 2008), 3–6.

34. CIA Inspector General, Special Report, "Counterterrorism and Interrogation Activities (September 2001–October 2003), 2003–7123.IG, May 7, 2004; see the memorandum by Jay S. Bybee, Assistant Attorney General to CIA's Acting General Counsel, August 1, 2002, in Appendix C; accessed August 12, 2012 at http://documents.nytimes.com/c-i-a-reports-on-interrogation-methods#p=1.

35. Bush, *Decision Points*, 167–71.

36. Rodriquez, *Hard Measures*, 51–55; Glenn L. Carle, *The Interrogator: An Education* (New York: Nation Books, 2011), 20, 64, 78, 84–85. See also M. Gregg Bloche, "Torture Is Wrong—But It Might Work," *Washington Post*, May 29, 2011. Also Steven M. Kleinman, "KUBARK Counterintelligence Interrogation Review: Observations of an Interrogator Lessons Learned and Avenues for Further Research," in Intelligence Science Board, *Educing Information: Interrogation Science and Art* (Washington, DC: National Defense Intelligence College, 2006), xiii; accessed August 20, 2012, at www.fas.org/irp/dni/educing.pdf.

37. Bush, *Decision Points*, 167–71; Rodriquez, *Hard Measures*, 51–55.

38. Rodriguez, *Hard Measures*, 81.

39. Ibid., 188.

40. Intelligence and Security Committee, *The Handling of Detainees by UK Intelligence Personnel in Afghanistan, Guantanamo Bay and Iraq* (London: Her Majesty's Stationery Office, March 2005), 15, 20; accessed August 21, 2012, at http://webarchive.nationalarchives.gov.uk/+/http://www.cabinetoffice.gov.uk/intelligence/special_reports.aspx.

41. Tenet, *At the Center of the Storm*, 265.
42. Rodriguez, *Hard Measures*, 76–77.
43. Tenet, *At the Center of the Storm*, 269.
44. Ibid., 259–63.
45. "Verbatim Transcript of Combatant Status Review Tribunal Hearing for ISN 10024 (Khalid Sheikh Muhammad)," March 10, 2007, U.S. Naval Base Guantanamo Bay, Cuba; accessed July 4, 2012, at http://en.wikisource.org/wiki/Verbatim_Transcript_of_Combatant_Status_Review_Tribunal_Hearing_for_ISN_10024.
46. Mudd, *Takedown*, 64.
47. Statement by Director of Central Intelligence George J. Tenet before the Senate Select Committee on Intelligence on the "Worldwide Threat 2001: National Security in a Changing World," February 7, 2001; accessed July 10, 2012, at www.cia.gov/news-information/speeches-testimony/2001/UNCLAS WWT_02072001.html.
48. See the foreword by Prime Minister Blair in "Iraq's Weapons of Mass Destruction: The Assessment of the British Government," September 24, 2002, 3; accessed July 17, 2012, at http://news.bbc.co.uk/nol/shared/spl/hi/middle_east/02/uk_dossier_on_iraq/pdf/iraqdossier.pdf.
49. Commission on the Intelligence Capabilities of the United States regarding Weapons of Mass Destruction, *Final Report of Commission on the Intelligence Capabilities of the United States regarding Weapons of Mass Destruction* [the WMD Commission], March 2005, 186; accessed July 17, 2012, at www.gpoaccess.gov/wmd/index.html.
50. Central Intelligence Agency, Directorate of Intelligence, "Misreading Intentions: Iraq's Reaction to Inspections Created Picture of Deception," January 5, 2006, 14–16; accessed November 2, 2012, at www.gwu.edu/~nsarchiv/news/20120905/CIA-Iraq.pdf.
51. Sir Robin Butler, et al., *Review of Intelligence on Weapons of Mass Destruction: Report of a Committee of Privy Counsellors* [the Butler Report], (London: The Stationery Office, 2004), 155; see Annex B for a digest of the major prewar intelligence reports on Iraq WMD; accessed July 17, 2012, at www.archive2.official-documents.co.uk/document/deps/hc/hc898/898.pdf.
52. Tommy Franks, *American Soldier* (New York: HarperCollins, 2004), 486–87.
53. Michael R. Gordon and Bernard E. Trainor, *Cobra II: The Inside Story of the Invasion and Occupation of Iraq* (New York: Random House, 2007 [2006]), 461; Richard J. Aldrich, *GCHQ: The Uncensored Story of Britain's Most Secret Intelligence Agency* (London: Harper, 2011 [2010]), 524–26.
54. Senate Select Committee on Intelligence, "US Intelligence Community's Prewar Intelligence Assessments on Iraq" [henceforth SSCI Report], S. Report 108–301, 108th Congress, 2d Session, 2004, 24, 27.
55. Ibid., 499.
56. WMD Commission Report, March 2005, 251–52; accessed July 17, 2012, at www.gpoaccess.gov/wmd/index.html.

57. Laurie West Van Hook, *Reforming Intelligence: The Passage of the Intelligence Reform and Terrorism Prevention Act* (Washington, DC: Office of the Director of National Intelligence, 2009), 7; accessed August 19, 2012, at www.fas.org/irp/dni/index.html.

58. For a detailed look at this process, see Michael Allen, *Blinking Red: Crisis and Compromise in American Intelligence after 9/11* (Arlington, VA: Potomac Institute Press, 2013).

59. David Crist, *The Twilight War: The Secret History of America's Thirty-Year Conflict with Iran* (New York: Penguin, 2012), 508; David Sanger, *Confront and Conceal: Obama's Secret Wars and Surprising Use of American Power* (New York: Crown, 2012), 175. National Intelligence Council, "Iran: Nuclear Intentions and Capabilities," November 2007; accessed April 6, 2013, at www.dni.gov/index.php/newsroom/reports-and-publications/167-reports-publications-2007/643-iran-nuclear-intentions-and-capabilities.

60. Anthony H. Cordesman and Emma R. Davies, *Iraq's Insurgency and the Road to Civil Conflict* (Washington, DC: Center for Strategic and International Studies, 2008), 2:657–58, 692, 714.

61. Stanley A. McChrystal, *My Share of the Task: A Memoir* (New York: Penguin, 2013), 117, 154–56.

62. James L. Pavitt, deputy director of operations, Central Intelligence Agency, remarks to the Foreign Policy Association, June 21, 2004; accessed September 28, 2013, at www.cia.gov/news-information/speeches-testimony/2004/ddo_speech_06242004.html.

63. Todd Hinnen, "The Cyber-Front in the War on Terrorism: Curbing Terrorist Use of the internet," *Columbia Science and Technology Law Review* 5 (2003).

64. Pam Benson, "CIA: Zarqawi Tape 'Probably Authentic,'" CNN, April 7, 2004; accessed July 18, 2012, at http://articles.cnn.com/2004–04–07/world/zarqawi.tape_1_al-zarqawi-zarqawi-organization-abu-musab-zarqawi?_s=PM:WORLD.

65. Andrew, *Defend the Realm*, 820; Rosie Cowan, "British Suspects Considered Blowing Up London Club, Court Told," *The Guardian*, March 22, 2006; accessed July 15, 2012, at www.guardian.co.uk/uk/2006/mar/23/terrorism.world. See also "MI5 Expands to Meet Terror Threat," *BBC News Online*, February 22, 2004; accessed August 20, 2012, at news.bbc.co.uk/2/hi/uk_news/3510611.stm. Intelligence and Security Committee, *Access to Communications Data by the Intelligence and Security Agencies*, presented to Parliament by the prime minister, February 2010, 8; accessed April 6, 2012, at www.scribd.com/doc/124152726/UK-ISC-Report-Access-to-Communications-Data-By-the-Intelligence-and-Security-Agencies.

66. Intelligence and Security Committee, *Report into the London Terrorist Attacks on 7 July 2005*, May 2006, 13, 20; accessed on July 15, 2012, at www.mi5.gov.uk/output/intelligence-and-security-committee-special-reports.html. See also Intelligence and Security Committee, *Could 7/7 Have Been Prevented?:*

Review of the Intelligence on the London Terrorist Attacks on 7 July 2005, May 2009, p. 54; accessed November 11, 2012, at www.fas.org/irp/world/uk/july7 review.pdf.

67. Rodriquez, *Hard Measures,* 6–10.

68. Peter Clarke, *Learning from Experience: Counter-terrorism in the UK since 9/11* (London: Policy Exchange, 2007), 19–20; accessed November 11, 2012, at www.policyexchange.org.uk/images/publications/learning%20from%20expe-rience%20-%20jun%2007.pdf.

69. Brian S. Petit, "Chechen Use of the Internet in the Russo-Chechen Conflict," unpublished masters thesis, US Army Command and General Staff College, 2003, 63–65; accessed September 28, 2013, at www.dtic.mil/dtic/fulltext/u2/a416403.pdf.

70. Huckaby and Stout, "Al Qaida's Views of Authoritarian Intelligence Services," 335; see also "Jordan 'Not Afraid' after Bombs," BBC, November 10, 2005; accessed July 19, 2012, at http://news.bbc.co.uk/2/hi/middle_east/4426458.stm.

71. Matthew M. Aid, *The Secret Sentry: The Untold History of the National Security Agency* (New York: Bloomsbury, 2009), 276–81; Fred Kaplan, *The Insurgents: David Petraeus and the Plot to Change the American Way of War* (New York: Simon & Schuster, 2013), 304. See also Shane Harris, "The Cyberwar Plan," *National Journal,* November 14, 2009; accessed on January 1, 2010, at www.nationaljournal.com/njmagazine/cs_20091114_3145.php.

72. Richard Aldrich, *GCHQ: The Uncensored Story of Britain's Most Secret Intelligence Agency* (London: Harper, 2010), 533–36. See also *UK AOC Newsletter,* "Outstanding NATO Unit 2008: Y Squadron, Royal Marines," January 2009; accessed July 20, 2012, at www.ukaoc.org/newsletters/jan09.htm.

73. Michael T. Flynn, Matt Pottinger, and Paul D. Batchelor, "Fixing Intel: A Blueprint for Making Intelligence Relevant in Afghanistan," Center for a New American Security, January 2010, 16; accessed July 15, 2012, at www.cnas.org/node/3924. McChrystal, *My Share of the Task,* 155.

74. Bush, *Decision Points,* 210, 217.

75. Flynn, Pottinger, and Batchelor, "Fixing Intel," 8–9, 16.

76. Toby Harnden, *Dead Men Risen: The Welsh Guards and the Defining Story of Britain's War in Afghanistan* (London: 2011), 531–33.

77. Rodriguez, *Hard Measures,* 50; Joby Warrick, *Triple Agent: The Al-Qaeda Mole Who Infiltrated the CIA* (New York: Vintage, 2012 [2011]), 1–6.

78. Matthew Levitt, *Hizbollah and the Qods Force in Iran's Shadow War on the West* (Washington, DC: Institute for Near East Policy, 2013), 6; accessed April 6, 2013, at www.washingtoninstitute.org/uploads/Documents/pubs/PolicyFocus123.pdf.

79. Senate Committee on Homeland Security and Governmental Affairs (Special Report by Sens. Lieberman and Collins), "A Ticking Time Bomb:

Counterterrorism Lessons from the US Government's Failure to Prevent the Fort Hood Attack," February 3, 2011, 35; accessed July 15, 2012, at www .washingtonpost.com/wp-srv/politics/documents/fthoodsenatere port.html?hpid=topnews. See also Federal Bureau of Investigation, *Final Report of the William H. Webster Commission on the Federal Bureau of Investigation, Counterterrorism Intelligence, and the Events at Fort Hood, Texas, on November 5, 2009,* July 12, 2012, 34, 48; accessed July 23, 2012, at www.fbi.gov/news/ pressrel/press-releases/judge-webster-delivers-webster-commission-report-on-fort-hood.

80. Andrew, *Defend the Realm*, 826.

81. Those arrested in these cases included Michael Finton (2009), Mohamed Osman Mohamud (2010), Rezwan Fardaus (2011), Sami Osmakac (2012), Farooqe Ahmed (2012), Amine El Khalifi (2012), and Quazi Mohammad Rezwanul Ahsan Nafis (2012). See also the *Final Report of the William H. Webster Commission*, 11–12.

82. Central Intelligence Agency (Center for the Study of Intelligence), "The Final Chapter in the Hunt for Bin Ladin," CIA Museum website gallery, July 2012; accessed August 19, 2012, at www.cia.gov/about-cia/cia-museum/experience-the-collection/index.html#!/story/13. See also Greg Sargent, "Private Letter from CIA Chief Undercuts Claim Torture Was Key to Killing Bin Laden," *Washington Post*, May 16, 2011.

83. Stephen W. Preston, general counsel, Central Intelligence Agency, "CIA and the Rule of Law," speech at Harvard Law School, April 10, 2012; accessed April 6, 2012, at www.lawfareblog.com/2012/04/remarks-of-cia-general-counsel-stephen-preston-at-harvard-law-school/.

84. Jo Becker and Scott Shane, "Secret 'Kill List' Proves a Test of Obama's Principles and Will," *New York Times*, May 29, 2012; accessed November 12, 2012, at www.nytimes.com/2012/05/29/world/obamas-leadership-in-war-on-al-qaeda .html?pagewanted=all&_r=0. Greg Miller, "Plan for Hunting Terrorists Signals U.S. Intends to Keep Adding Names to Kill Lists," *Washington Post*, October 23, 2012; accessed November 11, 2012, at www.washington post.com/world/national-security/plan-for-hunting-terrorists-signals-us-intends-to-keep-adding-names-to-kill-lists/2012/10/23/4789b2ae-18b 3-11e2-a55c-39408fbe6a4b_story.html. Greg Miller, Ellen Nakashima, and Karen DeYoung, "CIA Drone Strikes in Pakistan to Get Pass in 'Playbook,'" *Washington Post*, January 20, 2013.

85. Barack Obama, "Remarks by the President at the National Defense University," National Defense University, Washington, May 23, 2013; accessed May 26, 2013, at www.whitehouse.gov/the-press-office/2013/05/23/remarks-president-national-defense-university.

86. Mark Mazzetti, "A Secret Deal on Drones, Sealed in Blood," *New York Times*, April 6, 2013.

87. Crumpton, *The Art of Intelligence*, 79–81.

88. *United States v. "Christopher R. Metsos," et al.*, Sealed Complaint before Hon. James L. Cott, Southern District of New York, granted June 25, 2010, 7–10. *United States v. Anna Chapman and Mikhail Semenko*, Sealed Complaint before Hon. Ronald L. Ellis, Southern District of New York, granted June 27, 2010, 8–11. Both documents are posted at the FBI's website under "Operation Ghost Stories: Inside the Russian Spy Case," October 31, 2011; accessed July 25, 2012, at www.fbi.gov/news/stories/2011/october/russian_103111/russian_103111.

89. James Gosler, "Counterintelligence: Too Narrowly Practiced," in Jennifer E. Sims and Burton Gerber, eds., *Vaults, Mirrors, and Masks: Rediscovering US Counterintelligence* (Washington, DC: Georgetown University Press, 2008), 181–82. See also Crumpton, *The Art of Intelligence*, 80.

90. Dawn S. Onley, "Red Storm Rising," *Government Computer News*, August 17, 2009.

91. James Rossiter, Jonathan Richards, Rhys Blakely, and Richard Beeston, "MI5 Alert on China's Cyberspace Spy Threat," *Times* (London), December 1, 2007.

92. John Blau, "German Gov't PCs Hacked, China Offers to Investigate," *Washington Post*, August 27, 2007; accessed July 31, 2012, at www.washing tonpost.com/wp-dyn/content/article/2007/08/27/AR2007082700595.html.

93. Dmitri Alperovitch, vice president, Threat Research (McAfee), *Revealed: Operation Shady RAT*, August 3, 2011, 3, 6, 14; accessed July 24, 2012, at www. mcafee.com/us/resources/white-papers/wp-operation-shady-rat.pdf.

94. Office of the National Counterintelligence Executive, *Foreign Spies Stealing US Economic Secrets in Cyberspace: Report to Congress on Foreign Economic Collection and Industrial Espionage*, October 2011; accessed August 20, 2012, at www.ncix.gov/publications/reports/fecie_all/Foreign_Economic_Collection_2011.pdf.

95. Sen. Sheldon Whitehouse, "Cybersecurity," *Congressional Record* (Senate), July 27, 2010, S6265–S6266; accessed August 1, 2012, at www.fas.org/irp/con gress/2010_cr/cyber.html.

96. Keith B. Alexander, Command Posture Statement, US Cyber Command, House Committee on Armed Services, March 20, 2012, 5; accessed August 1, 2012, at www.au.af.mil/au/awc/awcgate/postures/posture_cybercom_20mar2012.pdf.

97. Michael Riley and Dune Lawrence, "Hackers Linked to China's Army Seen from EU to D.C.," *Bloomberg* online, July 26, 2012; accessed August 2, 2012, at www.bloomberg.com/news/print/2012–07–26/china-hackers-hit-eu-point-man-and-d-c-with-byzantine-candor.html.

98. Eric Engleman, "China, Iran Boost Cyber Attacks on U.S., Lawmaker Says," Bloomberg News online, February 14, 2013; accessed September 29, 2013, at www.bloomberg.com/news/2013-02-14/china-iran-boost-cyber-attacks-on-u-s-lawmaker-says.html.

99. William S. Lynn, "Defending a New Domain," *Foreign Affairs* (September-October 2010): 97; Ellen Nakashima, "Cyber-Intruder Sparks Massive Federal Response—and Debate over Dealing with Threats," *Washington Post*, December 8, 2011.

100. Roger A. Grimes, "Danger: Remote Access Trojans," Microsoft *TechNet* (reprinted from *Security Administrator*, September 2002); accessed August 17, 2012, at http://technet.microsoft.com/en-us/library/dd632947.aspx.

101. Alexander Gostev, Kaspersky Labs, "Back to Stuxnet: The Missing Link," *Securelist*, June 11, 2012; accessed July 24, at www.securelist.com/en/blog?weblogid=208193568; Ellen Nakashima, Greg Miller, and Julie Tate, "U.S., Israel Developed Flame Computer Virus to Slow Iranian Nuclear Efforts, Officials Say," *Washington Post*, June 19, 2012; Alexander Gostev, Kaspersky Labs, "The Flame: Questions and Answers," *Securelist*, May 28, 2012; accessed July 24, at www.securelist.com/en/blog/208193522/The_Flame_Questions_and_Answers.

102. Lynn, "Defending a New Domain," 97.

103. Remarks by National Counterintelligence Executive Joel F. Brenner at the Applied Research Laboratories, University of Texas at Austin, conference on business strategies in cyber security and counterintelligence, April 3, 2009; accessed on January 3, 2010, at www.dni.gov/speeches/20090403_speech.pdf.

104. Joint Chiefs of Staff, *The National Military Strategy of the United States of America*, 2004; accessed July 31, 2012, at www.defenselink.mil/news/Mar 2005/d2005031nms.pdf.

105. Ellen Nakashima, "Pentagon Computer-Network Defense Command Delayed by Congressional Concerns," *Washington Post*, January 3, 2010.

106. Dan Williams, "Spymaster Sees Israel as World Cyberwar Leader," *Reuters*, December 15, 2009.

107. Nick Hopkins, "UK Developing Cyber-Weapons Programme to Counter Cyber War Threat," *Guardian*, May 30, 2011; accessed November 11, 2012, at www.guardian.co.uk/uk/2011/may/30/military-cyberwar-offensive.

108. US Cyber Consequences Unit, "Overview by the US-CCU of the Cyber Campaign against Georgia in August 2008," August 2006, 3; accessed August 20, 2012, at www.registan.net/wp-content/uploads/2009/08/US-CCU-Georgia-Cyber-Campaign-Overview.pdf.

109. Sanger, *Confront and Conceal*, 188–93, 200.

110. "Remarks by Secretary Panetta on Cybersecurity to the Business Executives for National Security, New York City," October 11, 2012; accessed October 30, 2012, at www.defense.gov/transcripts/transcript.aspx?transcriptid=5136; Nicole Perlroth, "Cyber Attack on Saudi Firm Disquiets US," *New York Times*, October 24, 2012.

111. DoD Inspector General, Audit Report, "Requirements for the TRAIL-BLAZER and THINTHREAD SYSTEMS," December 15, 2004, 28; accessed http://en.wikipedia.org/w/index.php?title=File%3ARedacted-dod-oig-audit-requirements-for-the.pdf&page=1.

112. National Security Agency, "Military Construction, Defense-Wide FY 2008 Budget Estimates," February 2007; accessed August 4, 2012, at http://comptroller.defense.gov/defbudget/fy2008/budget_justification/

pdfs/07_Military_Construction/11_NSA.pdf. See also "Press Conference with Deputy Director of National Intelligence for Collection Mr. Glenn A. Gaffney, Camp Williams Data Center," Salt Lake City, October 23, 2009; accessed January 1, 2010, at www.dni.gov/index.php/newsroom/speeches-and-interviews.

113. Senate Report 112–173, *National Defense Authorization Act for Fiscal Year 2013—Report to Accompany S. 3254*, June 4, 2012, 170–72; accessed August 19, 2012, at www.govtrack.us/congress/bills/112/s3254/text.

114. Home Office, "Draft Communications Data Bill," Command Paper 8359, June 2012; accessed August 19, 2012, at www.official-documents.gov.uk/menu/cmd2012.htm.

115. Intelligence and Security Committee, *Access to Communications Data*, 4–5, 9, 11.

116. David Omand, Jamie Bartlett, and Carl Miller, "Introducing Social Media Intelligence (SOCMINT)," *Intelligence and National Security* 27:6 (December 2012): 801–2.

117. John Markoff, "Vast Spy System Loots Computers in 103 Countries," *New York Times*, March 29, 2009.

118. Mark A. Stokes, Jenny Lin, and L. C. Russell Hsiao, *The Chinese People's Liberation Army Signals Intelligence and Cyber Reconnaissance Infrastructure*, Project 2049, November 11, 2011; accessed August 2012, at http://proj ect2049.net/documents/pla_third_department_sigint_cyber_stokes_lin_ hsiao.pdf.

119. Kaspersky spoke on April 10, 2013, at the Georgetown University Institute for Law, Science and Global Security's third annual "International Engagement on Cyber" conference; accessed April 27, 2013, at http://lsgs.georgetown .edu/events/InternationalEngagementonCyber2013.

120. Richard Boscovich, Microsoft Digital Crimes Unit, "FBI and DOJ Take on the Coreflood Botnet," Microsoft online blogs, April 13, 2011; accessed August 4, 2012, at http://blogs.technet.com/b/microsoft_on_the_issues/ archive/2011/04/13/fbi-and-doj-take-on-the-coreflood-botnet.aspx; see also FBI press release, "Botnet Operation Disabled: FBI Seizes Servers to Stop Cyber Fraud," April 14, 2011; accessed August 4, 2012, at www.fbi.gov/news/ stories/2011/april/botnet_041411.

121. Tom Whitehead, "Hackers Could Be Running Company Computers, GCHQ Chief Warns," *Telegraph*, September 9, 2012; accessed November 2, 2012, at www.telegraph.co.uk/news/uknews/law-and-order/9522969/ Hackers-could-be-running-company-computers-GCHQ-chief-warns.html.

122. Cisco, *2011 Annual Security Report*, December 14, 2011, 17; accessed August 4, 2012, at www.cisco.com/en/US/prod/vpndevc/annual_security_report .html?CAMPAIGN=annual+security+report&COUNTRY_SITE=us&POSI TION=social+media&REFERRING_SITE=blog&CREATIVE=link.

123. WMD Commission, 186.

124. SSCI Report, 298–99.

125. Tenet, *At the Center of the Storm*, 322. See also SSCI Report, 215.

126. SSCI Report, 301.

127. Tenet, *At the Center of the Storm*, 324. See also SSCI Report, 300.

128. Ibid., 335–36. See also SSCI Report, 506.

129. Tenet, *At the Center of the Storm*, 362.

130. Clarke, *Against All Enemies*, 264.

131. Tenet, *At the Center of the Storm*, 302, 306–7, 345, 347.

132. Rodriguez, *Hard Measures*, 136, 140, 171. Tenet was approached in private by more than one of his lieutenants who criticized the looming war in Iraq, but he insisted they perform their duties despite their misgivings; *At the Center of the Storm*, 323.

133. Bush, *Decision Points*, 89.

134. CIA Inspector General, Special Report, "Counterterrorism and Interrogation Activities (September 2001–October 2003), 2003-7123.IG, May 7, 2004; accessed August 12, 2012, at http://documents.nytimes.com/c-i-a-reports-on-interrogation-methods#p=1.

135. James Risen, David Johnston, and Neil A. Lewis, "The Struggle for Iraq: Detainees; Harsh C.I.A. Methods Cited in Top Qaeda Interrogations," *New York Times*, May 13, 2004; accessed August 12, 2012, at www.nytimes.com/2004/05/13/world/struggle-for-iraq-detainees-harsh-cia-methods-cited-top-qaeda-interrogations.html.

136. Jack Goldsmith, *The Terror Presidency: Law and Judgment inside the Bush Administration* (New York: W. W. Norton, 2007), 146–54, 159–60.

137. Adrian Levy and Cathy Scott-Clark, "One Huge US Jail," *Guardian,* March 18, 2005; accessed August 11, 2012, at www.guardian.co.uk/world/2005/mar/19/terrorism.afghanistan.

138. Stephen Grey and Don Van Natta Jr., "In Italy, Anger at US Tactics Colors Spy Case," *New York Times*, June 26, 2005; accessed August 11, 2012, at www.nytimes.com/2005/06/26/international/europe/26milan.html?_r=1&pagewanted=all . Steve Hendricks, *A Kidnapping in Milan: The CIA on Trial* (New York: W. W. Norton, 2010), 172–92.

139. John Hooper, "CIA Methods Exposed by Kidnap Inquiry," *Guardian*, July 1, 2005; accessed August 11, 2012, at www.guardian.co.uk/world/2005/jul/02/usa.italy.

140. Dana Priest, "CIA Holds Terror Suspects in Secret Prisons: Debate Is Growing within Agency about Legality and Morality of Overseas System Set Up after 9/11," *Washington Post*, November 2, 2005. See also Dana Priest, "Covert CIA Program Withstands New Furor: Anti-Terror Effort Continues to Grow," *Washington Post*, December 30, 2005.

141. European Union report P6_TA(2007)0032, "Transportation and Illegal Detention of Prisoners: European Parliament Resolution on the Alleged Use of European Countries by the CIA for the Transportation and Illegal Detention

of Prisoners," February 14, 2007; accessed August 11, 2012, at www.europarl
.europa.eu/sides/getDoc.do?type=TA&reference=P6-TA-2007-0032&langu
age=EN&ring=A6-2007-0020.

142. Statement of the defendants read to the media by Imran Khan at the Old
Bailey on April 30, 2007; accessed August 12, 2012, at www.julyseventh
.co.uk/crevice/crevice-imran-khan-statement-for-defendants.html.

143. James Risen and Eric Lichtblau, "Spying Program Snared U.S. Calls," *New
York Times*, December 21, 2005; accessed August 12, 2012, at www.nytimes
.com/2005/12/21/politics/21nsa.html?_r=1&ex=1292821200&en=91d43431
1b0a7ddc&ei=5088&partner=rssnyt&emc=rss.

144. Eric Lichtblau and James Risen, "Bank Data Is Sifted by U.S. in Secret to Block
Terror," *New York Times*, June 23, 2006; accessed August 12, 2012, at www
.nytimes.com/2006/06/23/washington/23intel.html?ei=5088&en=168d69d26
685c26c&ex=1308715200&partner=rssnyt&emc=rss&pagewanted=all.

145. Attorney General Alberto Gonzales to Senators Patrick Leahy and Arlen
Specter, January 17, 2007; accessed August 12, 2012, at www.fas.org/irp/
agency/doj/fisa/ag011707.pdf.

146. Inspectors General, "Report on the President's Surveillance Program," 2009–
0013–AS, July 10, 2009, p. 31; accessed August 20, 2012, at www.dni.gov/
files/documents/Newsroom/Reports%20and%20Pubs/report_071309.pdf.

147. Rodriguez, *Hard Measures*, 114, 116.

148. Adam Goldman, "Hayden: CIA Had Fewer Than 100 Prisoners," Associated
Press online, September 7, 2007; accessed August 11, 2012, at www.usatoday
.com/news/nation/2007–09–07–502409224_x.htm.

149. CIA operations chief Jose Rodriquez grew convinced that someone in the
agency's Office of Inspector General was leaking to *Washington Post* reporter
Dana Priest; Rodriguez, *Hard Measures*, 172.

150. Intelligence and Security Committee, *Rendition* (London: Her Majesty's
Stationery Office, July 2007), 67; accessed August 22, 2012, at www.fas.org/
irp/world/uk/rendition.pdf.

151. Director of National Intelligence, *National Intelligence Strategy of the United
States of America*, August 2009, 2; accessed August 23, 2012, at www.dni.gov/
index.php/newsroom/reports-and-publications/165-reports-publica-
tions-2009.

152. Mark Mazzetti and Scott Shane, "C.I.A. Abuse Cases Detailed in Report
on Detainees," *New York Times*, August 24, 2009; see also *New York
Times* website, "CIA Reports on Interrogation Methods," April 14, 2009;
accessed August 11, 2012, at http://documents.nytimes.com/c-i-a-reports
-on-interrogation-methods#p=1.

153. See, for instance, Rodriguez, *Hard Measures*, 58–60, as well as the rejoinder by
former Special Agent Ali Soufan, "Will a CIA Veteran's Book Save a Terrorist?,"
Bloomberg News, May 8, 2012; accessed August 11, 2012, at www.bloom-
berg.com/news/2012–05–08/will-a-cia-veteran-s-book-save-a-terrorist-

.html. Press release by Senator Dianne Feinstein, "Feinstein, Levin Statement on CIA's Coercive Interrogation Techniques," April 30, 2012; accessed August 11, 2012, at www.feinstein.senate.gov/public/index.cfm/ press-releases?ID=f3271910-3fad-40a5-9d98-93450e0090aa.

154. Julian Assange, "The Nonlinear Effects of Leaks on Unjust Systems of Governance," Interesting Question [weblog], December 31, 2006; accessed August 12, 2012, at http://web.archive.org/web/20071020051936/http://iq.org/.

155. US Army, "*US v Bradley Manning* —New Charges Including Aiding the Enemy," March 1, 2011; accessed August 13, 2012, at www.scribd.com/doc/ 49908578/US-v-Bradley-Manning-New-Charges-Including-Aiding-the-Enemy.

156. Mandiant, *APT1: Exposing One of China's Cyber Espionage Units*, February 2013, 6; accessed April 6, 2013, at www.mandiant.com/blog/mandiant-exposes-apt1-chinas-cyber-espionage-units-releases-3000-indicators/.

157. Philip N. Howard and Muzammil M. Hussain, "Egypt and Tunisia: The Role of Digital Media," in Larry Diamond and Marc F. Plattner, *Liberation Technology: Social Media and the Struggle for Democracy* (Baltimore: Johns Hopkins University Press, 2012), 111–12, 121; Thomas Omestad, "USIP Conference Assesses Social Media's Role in Conflict," conference proceedings, US Institute of Peace, September 22, 2011; accessed August 14, 2012, at www.usip.org/ publications/usip-conference-assesses-social-media-s-role-in-conflict.

158. John Pollock, "People Power 2.0: How Civilians Helped Win the Libyan Information War," *Technology Review*, May-June 2012; accessed August 14, 2012, at www.technologyreview.com/featured-story/427640/people -power-20/.

159. Dennis Fisher, "DarkComet RAT Used in New Attack on Syrian Activists," *ThreatPost* (Kaspersky Labs), August 16, 2012; accessed August 18, 2012, at http://threatpost.com/en_us/blogs/darkcomet-rat-used-new-attack-syrian -activists-081612.

160. Ole Reissmann and Marcel Rosenbach, "A Geek Role in the Arab Spring: European Group Helps Tackle Regime Censorship," November 22, 2011; accessed August 15, 2012, at www.spiegel.de/international/world/a-geek-role-in-the-arab-spring-european-group-helps-tackle-regime-censor ship-a-791370-2.html ; see also Jillian C. York, "Syria's Electronic Army: Syrian Computer Hackers Put Their Own Spin on Democracy Protests in Syria," al Jazeera, August 15, 2011; accessed August 15, 2012, at www .aljazeera.com/indepth/opinion/2011/08/201181191530456997.html.

161. Barak Ravid, "Bashar Assad Emails Leaked, Tips for ABC Interview Revealed," *Haaretz*, February 8, 2012; accessed August 15, 2012, at www.haaretz .com/print-edition/news/bashar-assad-emails-leaked-tips-for-abc-inter view-revealed-1.411445; Don Goodin, "Anonymous Takes Credit for Hack That Exposes 2.4 Million Syrian E-mails," *Ars Technica*, July 9, 2012; accessed August 15, 2012, at http://arstechnica.com/security/2012/07/ anonymous-takes-credit-for-syrian-emails-hack/.

162. See the testimony of Stewart Baker, a former NSA general counsel, before a hearing on the administration's use of FISA authorities, Committee on the Judiciary, US House of Representatives. July 17, 2013, 9; accessed September 28, 2013, at www.skating onstilts.com/files/pdf-of-baker-testimony-to-house judiciary-committee-on-fisa-.pdf.

163. Barack Obama, "Signals Intelligence Activities," Presidential Policy Directive 28, January 17, 2014; accessed January 18, 2014, at www.whitehouse.gov/sites/default/files/docs/2014sigint_mem_ppd_rel.pdf.

164. David Hawk, *The Hidden Gulag, Second Edition: The Lives and Voices of "Those Who Are Sent to the Mountains"* (Washington, DC: Committee for Human Rights in North Korea, 2012), 48; accessed August 19, 2012, at www.hrnk.org/publications/hrnk-publications.php.

Intelligence All around Us

American case officers came to believe that it was no longer possible to break free of the KGB in order to conduct operations. They began to mutter about the mysterious, almost mystical capabilities of the KGB to follow their every movement. . . . You could never see this new surveillance, so there was no way to prove it didn't exist. Case officers began to second-guess their instincts on the streets of Moscow, aborting missions at the slightest sign of casual Soviet interest.

—BEARDEN AND RISEN, *THE MAIN ENEMY*

C IA officers in Moscow in the 1980s knew their every move could be watched. They also knew that the consequences of being caught in an operation could be arrest and scandal; for the assets they met, moreover, it could mean death. In the second decade of the twenty-first century, only the threat of certain death for espionage had changed (in some places). Today an average person at home or work can be watched just as closely from the moment she powers up her personal computer, tablet, or smart phone. Almost every room she enters has a networked device, or someone who is carrying one. Indeed, it seems that almost anyone can be monitored from virtually anywhere. Today we can all live like case officers in Moscow. Yet scrutiny now flows in all directions. The intelligence services of both the liberal and the self-proclaimed progressive societies have fallen under more public and private observation than ever before. This can be a salutary development, but it could also have the effect of inhibiting primarily the intelligence services that confront liars, thieves, and murderers—while leaving such actors undeterred.

The rise and fall of intelligence in the twentieth century accounts for this new and global situation. Intelligence as it arose after 1914 helped to win two world wars and to entrench communism from the Bering Strait to Havana. It briefly gave the superpowers and their allies a monopoly on the latest and many of the most effective collection techniques, together with the analytic wherewithal to evaluate the take. That monopoly, however, contained the logic of its own dissolution. The most intrusive collection techniques are now being mastered by people with few incentives to restrain themselves in their use. Intelligence still assists both the spread and the resistance to oppression, but now that assistance occurs in homes and board rooms as well as in government agencies. That might be seen as progress, but it implies consequences that we can barely begin to appreciate.

What Happened?

For most of history, the ways in which sovereign powers created, exploited, and protected secret advantages against their adversaries remained relatively simple and unchanging. Those means began to evolve rapidly in nineteenth-century Europe, impelled by the twin forces of industrialization and ideology. The metaphorical argument between Locke and Rousseau transformed Western societies, and by 1900 it had spread across the world with the diffusion of Western arms, goods, and ideals. These forces worked their influence indirectly but powerfully on the craft of spying, accelerating the evolution of espionage into the institutionalized activity we began to call intelligence in World War I. Driven by the necessity of total war, the Western powers yoked corporate-grade information processing methods to industrial-scale collection capabilities, and then in turn to the ancient arts of spying. As a result, they gained powers to understand and influence people and events that hitherto had been glimpsed only in the writings of visionaries like Sunzi and Kautilya. The most powerful industrialized states, whether liberal or progressive, built weapons of unimagined destructiveness, and some of their regimes came under the sway of ideologues who would not shrink from using such weapons on class or racial enemies.

Concerns over the ideological control of weapons of mass destruction drove intelligence evolution for generations afterward. By the end of World War II, technological and ideological factors had created a world in which only the two superpowers and their close allies could compete at the business of doing intelligence outside their national borders. The power of allied production and forces had first blunted the offensives of Hitler and Imperial Japan, and then rolled back their gains, finally destroying both regimes root and branch. Superb counterintelligence by the Allies helped create the conditions for victory, and the Anglo-American breaking of

German and Japanese ciphers helped ensure that victory would be won. The resulting Anglo-American intelligence alliance had the wherewithal to extend these advantages over the Soviet Union as the Cold War began, but the Soviets under Stalin possessed advantages of their own. His murderous but seemingly airtight internal security organs, combined with espionage in the West, blunted the Anglo-American technological edge, not only in the 1940s but again and again over the course of the Cold War. Intelligence agencies in Communist lands did not merely uphold the law; as the eyes and ears of the Communist Party, they were the law. These services helped the Warsaw Pact regimes to survive as long as they did in their defiance of human nature.

The Cold War competition caused a global diffusion of intelligence methods and, ironically, the first sustained and public campaigns for intelligence oversight. Both sides in the Cold War felt compelled to teach intelligence to their proxies. These methods, together with the arms that the superpowers supplied, occasionally made developing world guerrillas the equals of westernized armies on local battlefields. They also made terrorists a threat anywhere on Earth, and made revolutionary dictatorships seemingly invincible in their control of their own peoples. For a time, Cold War tensions threatened to spark a global conflagration, though Western monitoring of the growing Soviet arsenal helped ensure the conflict never resulted in a direct nuclear clash—a catastrophe that now seems even more narrowly averted in hindsight than it appeared at the time.[1] Ultimately, democratic ideals married to modern intelligence in the West helped undermine Communist Party regimes. Intelligence means had helped keep resistance to communism alive in the Eastern bloc, and aided Western leaders in understanding the fracturing of the Soviet empire—and in keeping events from precipitating civil or general war there.

At the end of the Cold War, only one intelligence superpower remained. Its superiority would be brief. As a result of events and outside forces, the latest intelligence techniques had developed rapidly and concentrated in a handful of sovereignties during the Cold War, but as a result of the further evolution of those forces, they diffused again to sovereignties, enterprises, and even individuals. Over the last generation we have seen yet another domain of conflict—cyberspace—the necessities of which are steadily forcing changes in statecraft and military operations in all the other domains, as well as transforming intelligence capabilities.

Competition from news media, as well as corporate and academic analysts, now makes intelligence-style databases and skills widely available. Thousands of actors, and many states, feel motivated to do deep analysis of data acquired by more or less sensitive means. Some of these actors also acquired (relatively cheaply) capabilities to observe rivals and victims in detail. Intelligence and operations that facilitate such surveillance are almost identical for all manner of actors on the internet, who can now do online what once had to be performed with spies, hidden cameras, and agents of influence.

Intelligence also drove the factors that drove it. Leninism, for example, forced every security service to change after World War I, but Leninism itself was partly a result of changes in police surveillance in the late 1800s—which in turn had grown up because of anarchist and socialist terrorism. Signals intelligence needs drove major advances in computers, which in turn had evolved in World War II and the early Cold War to break machine encipherment, itself a by-product of codebreaking in World War I. Computers, networks, and expertise built for SIGINT and C3I in the Cold War interacted with civilian developments; the two efforts together helped create the internet, opening broad new avenues for intelligence collection and analysis, and operations. While the Cold War intelligence duopoly is gone for good, a democratized form of intelligence is here to stay, at least for as far ahead as we can foresee digitally networked storage and communications. The fragile and provocative means that states once virtually monopolized are now available to many, and they are being used every hour of every day. The irreversible global spread of the internet seems destined to pervade every conceivable global scenario. Thus the future will be one of rivalry—if not open conflict—assuring the demand for intelligence as far into the future as we can envision.

What Does It Mean?

For much of history most people had little privacy but also little worth stealing. For a few decades some of them enjoyed comparative wealth and privacy. Now people have more wealth than ever, but thanks to the means and methods of intelligence, their privacy can be erased. This juxtaposition is something new in human existence. The shadowy and marginal realm called intelligence now affects our daily lives. We must study it to see how it is changing, and how it is forcing changes in other areas. This study can progress even absent additional declassification. There is much in the publicly available record today, and scholars need to address what already sits in the archives. Much more, of course, remains behind the official veil of secrecy. Decades might pass before crucial facts emerge to fill gaps in our knowledge, and some facts will never be released. Though those gaps will remain significant, enough is known to create real insight, and only by grasping that insight and understanding intelligence can we hope to increase public control over its effects.

Much has not been proven, which is why any normative conclusions must be tentative. Nonetheless, some warnings can be issued. Two trends, for instance, seem to imperil the uneven but salutary public oversight of intelligence, established since 1975, that has raised the Western intelligence agencies' probity, efficacy, and accountability. First, the digital revolution in some places has undermined democratic control by creating collection capabilities that outstripped the rules of governance written for earlier technologies (indeed, that mismatch between rules and capabilities has spurred many of the debates over intelligence since September 11, 2001). International institutions that have tried to fill the oversight breach have no track record in controlling intelligence capabilities; in addition, their democratic accountability remains incomplete. International controls over intelligence might improve its effectiveness and help control its growing digital surveillance capabilities. But there seem to be few grounds for confidence as of this writing, and any mistakes that international institutions make in their governance of intelligence might be very difficult to correct.

Second, a still greater concern looms. Online connections to people everywhere might finally make of us one truly global village. Yet human freedom takes a net loss when everyone has to live like a case officer in Moscow, constantly guarding a modicum of privacy. And people can be the watchers as well as the watched. Michel Foucault explained *surveillance* in the 1970s, but he could not foresee a world in which we are all potentially under observation while so many of us are also observers. Today we can live like case officers not only in shunning *surveillance* but in mounting it ourselves. Will citizens and their enterprises handle their new intelligence capabilities better than the intelligence agencies have done, at least in the West? The raging debates over internet privacy in national and international venues speak to growing concern on this point. In part because of their checkered pasts, Western intelligence agencies now have a modicum of oversight and accountability. So many intelligence actors, however, have no such scruples or curbs. Today the resources of criminal enterprises and even states are turned against private individuals and institutions, making a mockery of local and international privacy protections. This situation does not seem likely to improve any time soon.

One Last Word

Over the ages, espionage has mostly been used to trick or oppress. The rise of intelligence in the last century, however, has illustrated the possibility that secret means could also help defeat oppression. That experience has even shown us a path to democratic control of intelligence. We can see the growing urgency of taking that path. Now that intelligence has "fallen," and its powers are vast and ubiquitous, can it continue to be a force for good as well as ill?

Alexander Solzhenitsyn, accepting his Nobel Prize for Literature in 1970, spoke movingly of fellow writers lost in the prison camps administered by the Soviet intelligence system. Communism had created a cocoon of ideological oppression, stopping information from getting in and out, and leaving a "stunned silence" ruled by men who were hardly human beings at all but rather "a Martian expeditionary force, knowing nothing whatever about the rest of the Earth and ready to trample it flat in the holy conviction that they are 'liberating' it." Halting that oppression, Solzhenitsyn said, required the courageous refutation of lies, for they comprised the social oxygen of violence: "Let us not forget that violence does not and cannot flourish by itself; it is inevitably intertwined with lying. Between them there is the closest, the most profound and natural bond: nothing screens violence except lies, and the only way lies can hold out is by violence."[2]

Solzhenitsyn unwittingly offered us a scale for weighing intelligence in the years ahead. In his day, an ideological night encompassing the consciences of so many souls covered much of humanity. It has lightened somewhat in the East, but it has not passed; indeed, it could come again. Forgetting the past of espionage and intelligence is a way of making room for both old and new lies and for violence. Intelligence in the future should always have to pass this test: Does it try to deal in truth, or does it serve lies? That is a question for everyone engaged in the daily business of conducting or regulating intelligence activities. Each of them, and each of us, bears responsibility for the answer. The fall of "intelligence" is not yet bad, or good. It will be what we make it.

Notes

1. Gordon S. Barrass, *The Great Cold War: A Journey through the Hall of Mirrors* (Stanford, CA: Stanford University Press, 2009), 399.
2. Alexander Solzhenitsyn, Nobel Prize for Literature Lecture (1970), trans. from the Russian by F. D. Reeve; accessed July 10, 2012, at www.columbia .edu/cu/augustine/arch/solzhenitsyn/nobel-lit1970.htm.

WORKS CITED

Adams, James. *The Next World War: Computers Are the Weapons and the Front Line Is Everywhere.* New York: Simon & Schuster, 1998.

———. "Virtual Defense." *Foreign Affairs* 80:3 (May/June 2001).

Agee, Philip. *Inside the Company: CIA Diary.* Bungay, Suffolk: Chaucer Press, 1975.

Ahern Jr., Thomas L. *CIA and Rural Pacification.* Washington, DC: Central Intelligence Agency, 2001.

———. *CIA and the Generals: Covert Support to Military Government in South Vietnam.* Washington, DC: Central Intelligence Agency, 1998.

———. *CIA and the House of Ngo: Covert Action in South Vietnam, 1954–63.* Washington, DC: Central Intelligence Agency, 2000.

———. *Good Questions, Wrong Answers: CIA's Estimates of Arms Traffic through Sihanoukville, Cambodia, during the Vietnam War.* Washington, DC: Central Intelligence Agency, 2004.

———. *Undercover Armies: CIA and Surrogate Warfare in Laos.* Washington, DC: Central Intelligence Agency, 2006.

Aid, Matthew M. *The Secret Sentry: The Untold History of the National Security Agency.* New York: Bloomsbury, 2009.

Aldrich, Richard J. *GCHQ: The Uncensored Story of Britain's Most Secret Intelligence Agency.* London: HarperPress, 2010.

———. *The Hidden Hand: Britain, America, and Cold War Secret Intelligence.* London: John Murray, 2001.

———. "Policing the Past: Official History, Secrecy and British Intelligence since 1945." *English Historical Review* 119 (2004).

———. "'A Skeleton in Our Cupboard': British Interrogation Procedures in Northern Ireland." In Dover and Goodman, eds. *Learning from the Secret Past.*

Alexander, Keith B. Command Posture Statement. US Cyber Command, House Committee on Armed Services, March 20, 2012; accessed

August 1, 2012, at www.au.af.mil/au/awc/awcgate/postures/
posture_cybercom_20mar2012.pdf.

Alexander, Martin S. "Radio-Intercepts, Reconnaissance and Raids:
French Operational Intelligence and Communications in 1940."
Intelligence and National Security 28:3 (June 2013): 349–51.

Allen, Michael. *Blinking Red: Crisis and Compromise in American
Intelligence after 9/11*. Arlington, VA: Potomac Institute Press,
2013.

Alperovitch, Dmitri, Vice President, Threat Research (McAfee). *Revealed:
Operation Shady RAT*. August 3, 2011; accessed July 24, 2012,
at www.mcafee.com/us/resources/white-papers/wp-operation-
shady-rat.pdf.

Alvarez, David J. *Secret Messages: Codebreaking and American Diplomacy,
1930–1945*. Lawrence: University Press of Kansas, 2000.

Andrew, Christopher. *Defend the Realm: The Authorized History of MI5*.
New York: Alfred A. Knopf, 2009.

———. *Her Majesty's Secret Service: The Making of the British Intelligence
Community*. New York: Viking, 1986.

Andrew, Christopher, and Vasili Mitrokhin. *The Mitrokhin Archive: The
KGB in Europe and the West*. London: Penguin, 1999.

———. *The World Was Going Our Way: The KGB and the Battle for the
Third World*. New York: Basic Books, 2005.

Anthony, Victor B., and Richard R. Sexton. *The United States Air Force
in Southeast Asia: The War in Northern Laos, 1954–1973*.
Washington, DC: Center for Air Force History, 1993.

Applebaum, Anne. *Iron Curtain: The Crushing of Eastern Europe*. New
York: Doubleday, 2012.

Assange, Julian. "The Nonlinear Effects of Leaks on Unjust Systems
of Governance." Interesting Question [weblog]. December
31, 2006; accessed August 12, 2012, at http://web.archive.org/
web/20071020051936/http://iq.org/.

Atkinson, Rick. *An Army at Dawn: The War in North Africa, 1942–1943*.
New York: Henry Holt, 2002.

———. *The Day of Battle: The War in Sicily and Italy, 1943–1944*. New
York: Henry Holt, 2008 [2007].

Babington-Smith, Constance. *Air Spy: The Story of Photo Intelligence in
World War II*. New York: Harper, 1957.

Baer, Robert. *See No Evil: The True Story of a Ground Soldier in the CIA's War on Terrorism.* New York: Random House, 2003 [2002].

Baev, Jordan. "Spying on the West: Soviet-Bulgarian Scientific Intelligence Cooperation." January 2011; accessed May 19, 2012, at Parallel History Project website, www.php.isn.ethz.ch/collections/coll_KGBBulg/intro_baev.cfm?navinfo=126115#_edn28.

Baker, Stewart. Testimony before a hearing on the administration's use of FISA authorities, Committee on the Judiciary, US House of Representatives, July 17, 2013, 9; accessed September 28, 2013, at www.skatingonstilts.com/files/pdf-of-baker-testimony-to-house-judiciary-committee-on-fisa-.pdf.

Ball, Desmond, and Robert C. Toth. "Revising the SIOP: Taking War-Fighting to Dangerous Extremes." *International Security* 15:4 (Spring 1990).

Bamford, Bradley M. "The Role and Effectiveness of Intelligence in Northern Ireland." *Intelligence and National Security* 20:4 (Dec. 2005).

Bamford, James. *Body of Secrets: Anatomy of the Ultra-Secret National Security Agency.* New York: Anchor, 2002 [2001].

———. *The Puzzle Palace: A Report on NSA, America's Most Secret Agency.* Boston: Houghton Mifflin, 1982.

Barrass, Gordon S. *The Great Cold War: A Journey through the Hall of Mirrors.* Stanford, CA: Stanford University Press, 2009.

Barrett, Edward. *Truth Is Our Weapon.* Funk & Wagnalls, 1953.

Barron, John. *Breaking the Ring: The Bizarre Case of the Walker Family Spy Ring.* Boston: Houghton Mifflin, 1987.

Batvinis, Raymond. *The Origins of FBI Counterintelligence.* Lawrence: University of Kansas Press, 2007.

Bauer, Friedrich L. *Decrypted Secrets: Methods and Maxims of Cryptography.* Berlin: Springer, 2006.

BBC. "Jordan 'Not Afraid' after Bombs." November 10, 2005; accessed July 19, 2012, at http://news.bbc.co.uk/2/hi/middle_east/4426458.stm.

BBC News Online. "MI5 Expands to Meet Terror Threat." February 22, 2004; accessed August 20, 2012, at news.bbc.co.uk/2/hi/uk_news/3510611.stm.

Beach, Jim. "'Intelligent Civilians in Uniform': The British Expeditionary Force's Intelligence Corps Officers, 1914–1918." *War and Society* 27:1 (May 2008).

———. "Origins of the Special Intelligence Relationship?: Anglo-American Intelligence Co-operation on the Western Front, 1917–18." *Intelligence and National Security* 22:2 (April 2007).

Bearden, Milt, and James Risen. *The Main Enemy: The Inside Story of CIA's Final Showdown with the KGB*. New York: Ballantine, 2003.

Becker, Jo, and Scott Shane. "Secret 'Kill List' Proves a Test of Obama's Principles and Will." *New York Times*, May 29, 2012; accessed November 12, 2012, at www.nytimes.com/2012/05/29/world/obamas-leadership-in-war-on-al-qaeda.html?pagewanted=all&_r=0.

Belloc, Hilaire, and Basil Temple Blackwood. *The Modern Traveller*. (London: Edward Arnold, 1898).

Benson, Pam. "CIA: Zarqawi Tape 'Probably Authentic.'" CNN, April 7, 2004; accessed July 18, 2012, at http://articles.cnn.com/2004-04-07/world/zarqawi.tape_1_al-zarqawi-zarqawi-organization-abu-musab-zarqawi?_s=PM:WORLD .

Benson, Robert Louis. "A History of US Communications Intelligence during World War II: Policy and Administration." Ft. Meade, MD: National Security Agency Center for Cryptologic History, 1997.

Benson, Robert Louis, and Michael Warner, eds. *Venona: Soviet Espionage and the American Response, 1939–1957*. Washington, DC: Central Intelligence Agency, 1996.

Bergen, John D. *Military Communications: A Test for Technology*. Washington, DC: Center of Military History, 1988.

Berman, Larry. *The Perfect Spy: The Incredible Double Life of Pham Xuan An,* Time *Magazine Reporter and Vietnamese Communist Agent*. Washington, DC: Smithsonian, 2008 [2007].

Bidwell, Bruce W. *History of the Development of the Military Intelligence Division, Department of the Army General Staff: 1775–1941*. Frederick, MD: University Publications of America, 1986.

Birstein, Vadim J. "Soviet Military Counterintelligence from 1918 to 1939." *International Journal of Intelligence and CounterIntelligence* 25:1 (Spring 2012).

Blair, Tony. "Iraq's Weapons of Mass Destruction: The Assessment of the British Government," September 24, 2002; accessed July 17, 2012, at http://news.bbc.co.uk/nol/shared/spl/hi/middle_east/02/uk_dossier_on_iraq/pdf/iraqdossier.pdf.

Blake, George. *No Other Choice*. New York: Simon & Schuster, 1990.

Blau, John. "German Gov't PCs Hacked, China Offers to Investigate." *Washington Post*, August 27, 2007; accessed July 31, 2012, at www.washingtonpost.com/wp-dyn/content/article/2007/08/27/AR2007082700595.html.

Bloche, M. Gregg. "Torture Is Wrong—But It Might Work." *Washington Post*, May 29, 2011.

Boghardt, Thomas. *The Zimmermann Telegram: Intelligence, Diplomacy, and America's Entry into World War I*. Annapolis: US Naval Institute Press, 2012.

Bonilla, Diego Navarro. "'Secret Intelligences' in European Military, Political and Diplomatic Theory: An Essential Factor in the Defense of the Modern State." *Intelligence and National Security* 27:2 (April 2012).

Boscovich, Richard. Microsoft Digital Crimes Unit, "FBI and DOJ take on the Coreflood botnet." Microsoft online blogs, April 13, 2011; accessed August 4, 2012, at http://blogs.technet.com/b/microsoft_on_the_issues/archive/2011/04/13/fbi-and-doj-take-on-the-core-flood-botnet.aspx.

Braden, Thomas W. "I'm Glad the CIA Is 'Immoral.'" *Saturday Evening Post*, May 20, 1967.

Brands, Hal. *Latin America's Cold War*. Cambridge, MA: Harvard University Press, 2010.

Brenner, Joel F. National Counterintelligence Executive. Remarks at the Applied Research Laboratories, University of Texas at Austin. Conference on Business Strategies in Cyber Security and Counterintelligence, April 3, 2009; accessed on January 3, 2010, at www.dni.gov/speeches/20090403_speech.pdf.

Brezhnev, Leonid. Letter to President Carter, February 25, 1977; accessed April 16, 2012, at http://astro.temple.edu/~rimmerma/Carter_Brezhnev_letters.htm.

Broad, William. J. "Computer Security Worries Military Experts." *New York Times*, September 25, 1983.

Burke, Colin. "An Introduction to a Historic Computer Document: Betting on the Future—The 1946 Pendergrass Report on Cryptanalysis and the Digital Computer." *Cryptologic Quarterly* 13:4 (Winter 1994).

Burns, Daniel, trans. "Said Qutb on the Arts in America." In Hudson Institute, *Current Trends in Islamist Ideology* 9 (November 18, 2009); accessed June 10, 2012, at www.currenttrends.org/ research/detail/said-qutb-on-the-arts-in-america.

Bush, George H. W. National Security Directive 42. "National Policy for the Security of National Security Telecommunications and Information Systems." July 5, 1990; accessed April 30, 2012, at www.fas.org/irp/offdocs/nsd/nsd42.pdf .

Bush, George H. W., and Brent Scowcroft. *A World Transformed.* New York: Alfred A. Knopf, 1998.

Bush, George W. *Decision Points.* New York: Crown, 2010.

Butler, J. R. M. *Grand Strategy*, vol. 2, September 1939–June 1941. In United Kingdom Military Series, *History of the Second World War*. London: Her Majesty's Stationery Office, 1964.

Butler, Sir Robin, et al. *Review of Intelligence on Weapons of Mass Destruction: Report of a Committee of Privy Counsellors* [the Butler Report]. London: The Stationery Office, 2004; accessed July 17, 2012, at www.archive2.official-documents.co.uk/document/ deps/hc/hc898/898.pdf.

Butterworth, Alex. *The World That Never Was: A True Story of Dreamers, Schemers, Anarchists, and Secret Agents.* New York: Vintage, 2010.

Byron, John, and Robert Pack. *The Claws of the Dragon: Kang Sheng, the Evil Genius behind Mao and His Legacy of Terror in People's China.* New York: Simon & Schuster, 1992.

Callwell, C. E. *Small Wars: Their Principles and Practice.* London: Harrison & Sons, 1903 [1899].

Camus, Albert. *Algerian Chronicles.* Cambridge, MA: Harvard University Press, 2013 [1958].

Carle, Glenn L. *The Interrogator: An Education.* New York: Nation Books, 2011.

Carlson, Elliot. *Joe Rochefort's War: The Odyssey of the Codebreaker Who Outwitted Yamamoto at Midway.* Annapolis: US Naval Institute Press, 2011.

Carmichael, Scott W. *True Believer: Inside the Investigation and Capture of Ana Montes, Cuba's Master Spy.* Annapolis: US Naval Institute Press, 2009.

Carter, Jimmy. Presidential Directive 59. "Nuclear Weapons Employment Policy." July 25, 1980; accessed May 5, 2012, at http://en.wikisource

.org/wiki/Index:Carter_Presidential_Directive_59,_Nuclear_
Weapons_Employment_Policy.djvu.

Castro, Fidel. "Sixth Summit Conference of the Nonaligned Countries."
Havana Domestic TV. Foreign Broadcast Information Service,
report date September 4, 1979; accessed April 15, 2012, at http://
lanic.utexas.edu/project/castro/db/1979/19790903.html.

Central Intelligence Agency, Center for the Study of Intelligence. "The
Final Chapter in the Hunt for Bin Ladin." CIA Museum website gallery, July 2012; accessed August 19, 2012, at www.cia.gov/
about-cia/cia-museum/experience-the-collection/index.html#!/
story/13.

———. "Panel III: Espionage and Counterintelligence." Recorded at
a conference sponsored by CIA at Texas A&M University
in 1999; accessed June 8, 2012, at www.foia.cia.gov/docs/
DOC_0001445139/DOC_0001445139.pdf.

Central Intelligence Agency, Directorate of Intelligence. "Misreading
Intentions: Iraq's Reaction to Inspections Created Picture of
Deception." January 5, 2006; accessed November 2, 2012, at www
.gwu.edu/~nsarchiv/news/20120905/CIA-Iraq.pdf.

Central Intelligence Agency, Inspector General, Special Report.
"Counterterrorism and Interrogation Activities." September
2001–October 2003. 2003–7123.IG, May 7, 2004;
accessed August 12, 2012, at http://documents.nytimes.
com/c-i-a-reports-on-interrogation-methods#p=1.

Central Intelligence Agency, Office of Scientific and Weapons Analysis.
"Soviet Bloc Computers: Direct Descendants of Western
Technology." SW 89–10023X, June 1989; accessed June 8, 2012, at
www.foia.cia.gov.

Central Intelligence Agency, Office of Scientific and Weapons Research.
"Soviet and East European Computer Networking: Prospects for
Global Connectivity." SW 90–10054X, September 1990; accessed
June 8, 2012, at www.foia.cia.gov.

Central Intelligence Agency, Special Research Staff. "Communist China:
The Political Security Apparatus." Part II, "Destruction and
Reconstruction, 1965–1969." Published as part of the "Polo"
series, November 28, 1969; accessed February 10, 2012, at www
.foia.cia.gov/CPE/POLO/.

Charters, David A. "'Have A Go': British Army/MI-5 Agent-Running Operations in Northern Ireland, 1970–72." *Intelligence and National Security* 28:2 (April 2013).

Churchill, Winston S. *The Second World War,* vol. 3, *The Grand Alliance.* New York: Houghton Mifflin, 1985 [1950].

Cisco. *2011 Annual Security Report.* December 14, 2011; accessed August 4, 2012, at www.cisco.com/en/US/prod/vpndevc/annual_security _report.html?CAMPAIGN=annual+security+report&COUNTRY _SITE=us&POSITION=social+media&REFERRING_SITE= blog&CREATIVE=link.

Clarke, Peter. *Learning from Experience: Counter-terrorism in the UK since 9/11.* London: Policy Exchange, 2007; accessed November 11, 2012, at www.policyexchange.org.uk/images/publications/learning %20from%20experience%20-%20jun%202007.pdf.

Clinton, William J. Address to the US Intelligence Community. Delivered at the Central Intelligence Agency's headquarters, July 14, 1995; accessed June 10, 2012 at www.presidency.ucsb.edu/ws/index.php ?pid=51616&st=langley&st1=#axzz1xP49QrgH.

Clarke, Richard. *Against All Enemies: Inside America's War on Terror.* New York: Simon & Schuster, 2004.

Clausewitz, Carl von. *On War.* Translated by Michael Howard and Peter Paret. Princeton, NJ: Princeton University Press, 1989 [1976].

Cochran, Alexander S., Robert C. Ehrhart, and John F. Kreis. "The Tools of Air Intelligence: ULTRA, MAGIC, Photographic Assessment, and the Y-Service." In John F. Kreis, ed., *Piercing the Fog: Intelligence and Army Air Forces Operations in World War II,* US Air Force, 1995.

Colby, William, and Peter Forbath. *Honorable Men: My Life in the CIA.* New York: Simon & Schuster, 1978.

Commission on the Intelligence Capabilities of the United States regarding Weapons of Mass Destruction. *Report to the President of the United States* [the WMD Commission Report]. Washington, DC: Government Printing Office, 2005.

Commission on the Organization of the Executive Branch of the Government [Eberstadt study panel]. "The Central Intelligence Agency: National and Service Intelligence." January 1949; accessed December 12, 2011, at www.foia.cia.gov/helms.asp.

Cooley, John K. *Green March, Black September: The Story of the Palestinian Arabs.* London: Frank Cass, 1973.

Cordesman, Anthony H., and Emma R. Davies. *Iraq's Insurgency and the Road to Civil Conflict,* vol. 2. Washington, DC: Center for Strategic and International Studies, 2008.

Costello, John, and Oleg Tsarev. *Deadly Illusions.* New York: Crown, 1993.

Cowan, Rosie. "British Suspects Considered Blowing Up London Club, Court Told." *The Guardian,* March 22, 2006; accessed July 15, 2012, at www.guardian.co.uk/uk/2006/mar/23/terrorism.world.

Coyne, J. Patrick. National Security Council to McGeorge Bundy, Special Assistant for National Security Affairs, May 1961. John F. Kennedy Library, President's Office Files, Series 7, Department and Agencies, Foreign Intelligence Advisory Board, Box 94, Briefing Material 5/61. This document contains the "Bruce-Lovett Report" to President Eisenhower. Accessed March 26, 2012, at www.foia.cia.gov/helms.asp.

Cradock, Percy. *Know Your Enemy: How the Joint Intelligence Committee Saw the World.* London: John Moore, 2004.

Craig, Tony. "Sabotage! The Origins, Development and Impact of the IRA's Infrastructural Bombing Campaigns, 1937–1997." *Intelligence and National Security* 25:3 (June 2010).

Crist, David. *The Twilight War: The Secret History of America's Thirty-Year Conflict with Iran.* New York: Penguin, 2012.

Critchfield, James H. *Partners at the Creation: The Men behind Postwar Germany's Defense and Intelligence Establishments.* Annapolis: US Naval Institute Press, 2003.

Crosswell, D. K. R. *The Chief of Staff: The Military Career of General Walter B. Smith.* Westport, CT: Greenwood, 1991.

Crumpton, Henry A. *The Art of Intelligence: Lessons from a Life in the CIA's Clandestine Service.* New York: Penguin, 2012.

Cullather, Nicholas. *Secret History: The C.I.A.'s Classified Account of Its Operations in Guatemala, 1952–1954.* Palo Alto, CA: Stanford University Press, 1999.

Dalton, Curt. "Keeping the Secret: The Waves and NCR Dayton, Ohio, 1943–1946." Privately published, 1997; accessed August 7, 2011, at www.daytonhistorybooks.com/page/page/1482135.htm.

Dandeker, Christopher. *Surveillance, Power and Modernity: Bureaucracy and Discipline from 1700 to the Present Day*. New York: St. Martin's, 1991.

Davies, Pete. "Estimating Soviet Power: The Creation of Britain's Defence Intelligence Staff, 1960–1965." *Intelligence and National Security* 26:6 (December 2011).

Defense Intelligence Agency. "History: 50 Years of Excellence in Defense of the Nation;." accessed April 30, 2012. at, www.dia.mil/history/.

Department of Defense. *The Conduct of the Persian Gulf War: Final Report to Congress*. Washington, DC: Department of Defense, 1992.

Department of Defense. "Verbatim Transcript of Combatant Status Review Tribunal Hearing for ISN 10024 (Khalid Sheikh Muhammad)." March 10, 2007, US Naval Base Guantanamo Bay, Cuba; accessed July 4, 2012, at http://en.wikisource.org/wiki/Verbatim_ Transcript_of_Combatant_Status_Review_Tribunal_Hearing_ for_ISN_10024.

Department of Defense. Inspector General, Audit Report. "Requirements for the TRAILBLAZER and THINTHREAD SYSTEMS." December 15, 2004; accessed http://en.wikipedia.org/w/index .php?title=File%3ARedacted-dod-oig-audit-requirements-for-the .pdf&page=1.

Department of Defense and Inspectors General of other agencies."Unclassified Report on the President's Surveillance Program." 2009–0013–AS, July 10, 2009; accessed August 20, 2012, at www.dni.gov/files/documents/Newsroom/Reports%20 and%20Pubs/report_071309.pdf.

Department of State. *Foreign Relations of the United States, 1945–1950, Emergence of the Intelligence Establishment*. Washington, DC: Government Printing Office, 1996.

———. *Foreign Relations of the United States, 1945–1950, The Intelligence Community*. Washington, DC: Government Printing Office, 2007.

———. *Foreign Relations of the United States, 1950–1955, The Intelligence Community*. Washington, DC: Government Printing Office, 2007.

———. *Foreign Relations of the United States, 1964–1967, vol. 12, Western Europe*. Washington, DC: Government Printing Office, 2001.

———. *Foreign Relations of the United States, 1964–1968, vol. 31, South and Central America; Mexico*. Washington, DC: Government Printing Office, 2005.

——. *Foreign Relations of the United States,* 1969–1972, vol. 2, *Organization and Management of US Foreign Policy.* Washington, DC: Government Printing Office, 2006.

Der Spiegel. "EDV abgezapft." April 14, 1969; accessed June 10, 2011, at www.spiegel.de/spiegel/print/d-45702341.html .

Dillon, Martin. *The Dirty War: Covert Strategies and Tactics Used in Political Conflicts.* New York: Routledge, 1990.

Director of Central Intelligence. "US Intelligence Capabilities to Monitor Certain Limitations on Soviet Strategic Weapons Programs." Special National Intelligence Estimate 11–10–67, February 14, 1967; accessed November 20, 2012, at www.spacebanter.com/showthread.php?t=49729.

Director of Central Intelligence to Heads of Agency Offices. "Distribution of Unclassified Abstract IG Report of Ames Investigation." October 21, 1994; accessed May 27, 2012, at www.loyola.edu/departments/academics/political-science/strategic-intelligence/intel/hitzrept.html.

Director of National Intelligence. *National Intelligence Strategy of the United States of America,* August 2009; accessed August 23, 2012, at www.dni.gov/index.php/newsroom/reports-and-publications/165-reports-publications-2009.

Dover, Robert, and Michael S. Goodman, eds. *Learning from the Secret Past: Cases in British Intelligence History.* Washington, DC: Georgetown University Press, 2011.

Dujmovic, Nicholas. "Extraordinary Fidelity: Two CIA Prisoners in China, 1952–73." *Studies in Intelligence* 50:4 (2006); accessed March 26, 2012, at www.cia.gov/library/center-for-the-study-of-intelligence/csi-publications/csi-studies/studies/vol50no4/two-cia-prisoners-in-china-1952201373.html.

Dziak, John J. *Chekisty: A History of the KGB.* Lexington, MA: Lexington Books, 1988.

Eberstadt, Nicholas. American Enterprise Institute for Public Policy Research. Testimony on US Policy toward North Korea before the US House of Representatives (Committee on International Relations), Hearing on "U.S. Policy toward North Korea." September 24, 1998; accessed November 20, 2011, at www.fas.org/spp/starwars/congress/1998_h/ws924982.htm.

Ebon, Martin. *KGB: Death and Rebirth*. Westport, CT: Praeger, 1994.

Engleman, Eric. "China, Iran Boost Cyber Attacks on U.S., Lawmaker Says," Bloomberg News online, February 14, 2013; accessed September 29, 2013, at www.bloomberg.com/news/2013-02-14/china-iran-boost-cyber-attacks-on-u-s-lawmaker-says.html.

European Union report P6_TA(2007)0032. "Transportation and Illegal Detention of Prisoners: European Parliament Resolution on the Alleged Use of European Countries by the CIA for the Transportation and Illegal Detention of Prisoners." February 14, 2007; accessed August 11, 2012, at www.europarl.europa.eu/sides/getDoc.do?type=TA&reference=P6-TA-2007-0032&language=EN&ring=A6-2007-0020.

Ewell, Julian J. and Ira A. Hunt Jr. "Sharpening the Combat Edge: The Use of Analysis to Reinforce Military Judgment." Washington, DC: Department of the Army, 1995. Accessed November 26, 2008, www.army.mil/cmh-pg/books/Vietnam/Sharpen/.

Fanon, Frantz. *The Wretched of the Earth*. Translated by Constance Farrington. New York: Grove Weidenfeld, 1963.

Farago, Ladislas. *The Tenth Fleet*. New York: Drum Books, 1986 [1962].

Faulkner, Marcus. "The *Kriegsmarine*, Signals Intelligence and the Development of the *B-Dienst* before the Second World War." *Intelligence and National Security* 25:4 (August 2010).

Federal Bureau of Investigation. *The FBI: A Centennial History, 1908–2008*. Washington, DC: Federal Bureau of Investigation, 2009.

———. *Final Report of the William H. Webster Commission on the Federal Bureau of Investigation, Counterterrorism Intelligence, and the Events at Fort Hood, Texas, on November 5, 2009*. July 12, 2012; accessed July 23, 2012, at www.fbi.gov/news/pressrel/press-releases/judge-webster-delivers-webster-commission-report-on-fort-hood.

———. Press release. "Botnet Operation Disabled: FBI Seizes Servers to Stop Cyber Fraud." April 14, 2011; accessed August 4, 2012, at www.fbi.gov/news/stories/2011/april/botnet_041411/.

———. Running memorandum. "British Intelligence Service in the United States." January 1, 1947. States." January 1, 1947.

Fedor, Julie. "Chekists Look Back on the Cold War: The Polemical Literature." *Intelligence and National Security* 26:6 (December 2011).

Feinstein, Dianne. "Feinstein, Levin Statement on CIA's Coercive Interrogation Techniques." April 30, 2012; accessed August 11, 2012, at www.feinstein.senate.gov/public/index.cfm/press-releases?ID=f3271910-3fad-40a5-9d98-93450e0090aa.

Ferris, John R. "'Airbandit': C3I and Strategic Air Defence during the First Battle of Britain, 1915–1918." In Michael Dockrill and David French, eds. *Strategy and Intelligence: British Policy during the First World War.* London: Hambledon, 1995.

———. "The British Army, Signals and Security in the Desert Campaign, 1940–1942." *Intelligence and National Security* (1990).

———. "Reading the World's Mail: British Blockage Intelligence and Economic Warfare." Conference paper, "The Military History of Canada." Kings College London, June 22, 2010.

Finlayson, Andrew R. *Marine Advisers with the Vietnamese Provincial Reconnaissance Units, 1966–1970.* Quantico, VA: US Marine Corps History Division, 2009.

Finnegan, John Patrick, and Ramona Danysh. *Military Intelligence.* Washington, DC: Center of Military History, 1998.

Finnegan, Terence J. *Shooting the Front: Allied Aerial Reconnaissance and Photographic Interpretation on the Western Front—World War I.* Washington, DC: National Defense Intelligence College, 2006.

Finney, John W. "Pentagon Charged with Changing Data to Help Antimissile Plan." *New York Times*, May 15, 1969.

Fischer, Ben B. "'One of the Biggest Ears in the World': East German SIGINT Operations." *International Journal of Intelligence and Counterintelligence* 11:2 (Summer 1998).

———. ed. *Okhrana: The Paris Operations of the Russian Imperial Police.* Washington, DC: Central Intelligence Agency, 1997.

Fisher, Dennis. "DarkComet RAT Used in New Attack on Syrian Activists." *ThreatPost* (Kaspersky Labs), August 16, 2012; accessed August 18, 2012, at http://threatpost.com/en_us/blogs/darkcomet-rat-used-new-attack-syrian-activists-081612.

Flynn, Michael T., Matt Pottinger, and Paul D. Batchelor. "Fixing Intel: A Blueprint for Making Intelligence Relevant in Afghanistan." Center for a New American Security, January 2010; accessed July 15, 2012, at www.cnas.org/node/3924.

Ford, Christopher A., and David A. Rosenberg. *The Admirals' Advantage: US Navy Operational Intelligence in World War II and the Cold War.* Annapolis, MD: US Naval Institute Press, 2005.

———. "The Naval Intelligence Underpinnings of Reagan's Maritime Strategy." *Journal of Strategic Studies* 28 (April 2005).

Franks, Tommy. *American Soldier.* New York: HarperCollins, 2004.

Freedman, Lawrence. *The Evolution of Nuclear Strategy.* New York: Palgrave MacMillan, 2003 [1981].

Freeman, Peter. "The Zimmermann Telegram Revisited: A Reconciliation of the Primary Sources." *Cryptologia* 30:2 (2006).

Friedman, William F., and C. J. Mendelsohn. *The Zimmermann Telegram of January 16, 1917: And Its Cryptographic Background.* Washington, DC: Government Printing Office, 1938.

Frost, Lawrence A. "Balloons over the Peninsula: Fitz John Porter and George Custer Become Reluctant Aeronauts." *Blue and Gray Magazine* 2:3 (January 1985).

Fukuyama, Francis. "The End of History?" *The National Interest,* Summer 1989.

Furse, George Armand. *Information in War: Its Acquisition and Transmission.* London: William Clowes & Sons, 1895.

Fursenko, Aleksandr, and Timothy Naftali. *"One Hell of a Gamble": Khrushchev, Castro, Kennedy, and the Cuban Missile Crisis, 1958–1964.* New York: W. W. Norton, 1997.

Futrell, Robert F. "A Case Study: USAF Intelligence in the Korean War." In Walter T. Hitchcock, ed. *The Intelligence Revolution: A Historical Perspective* [Proceedings of the Thirteenth Military History Symposium]. Washington, DC: Office of Air Force History, 1991.

Gaffney, Glenn A., Deputy Director of National Intelligence for Collection. Press conference on the Camp Williams Data Center, Salt Lake City, October 23, 2009; accessed January 1, 2010, at www.dni.gov/index.php/newsroom/speeches-and-interviews.

Garthoff, Douglas. *Directors of Central Intelligence as Leaders of the U.S. Intelligence Community.* Washington, DC: Central Intelligence Agency, 2005.

Garthoff, Raymond L. "Estimating Soviet Military Intentions and Capabilities." In Gerald Haines and Robert Leggett, eds., *Watching the Bear: Essays on the CIA's Analysis of the Soviet Union.* Washington, DC: Central Intelligence Agency, 2002.

———. "The KGB Reports to Gorbachev." *Intelligence and National Security* 11:2 (April 1996).

Gates, Robert M. *From the Shadows: The Ultimate Insider's Story of Five Presidents and How They Won the Cold War.* New York: Simon & Schuster, 2006 [1996].

———. Testimony on April 1, 1992, at the Joint Hearing, Senate Select Committee on Intelligence and House Permanent Select Committee on Intelligence. "S. 2198 and S. 421 to Reorganize the United States Intelligence Community." 102nd Cong., 2nd Sess., 1992.

Gentry, John A., and David E. Spencer. "Colombia's FARC: A Portrait of Insurgent Intelligence." *Intelligence and National Security* 25:4 (2010).

Gieseke, Jens. "East German Espionage in the Era of Détente." *Journal of Strategic Studies* 31:3 (June 2008).

Gilbert, James L. *The Most Secret War: Army Signals Intelligence in Vietnam.* Fort Belvoir, VA: US Army Intelligence and Security Command, 2003.

Gill, Peter. "'A Formidable Power to Cause Trouble for the Government'?: Intelligence Oversight and the Creation of the UK Intelligence and Security Committee." In Robert Dover and Michael Goodman, eds. *Learning from the Secret Past: Cases in British Intelligence History.* Washington, DC: Georgetown University Press, 2011.

Glaeser, Andreas. *Political Epistemics: The Secret Police, the Opposition, and the End of East German Socialism.* Chicago: University of Chicago Press, 2011.

Goldman, Adam. "Hayden: CIA Had Fewer Than 100 Prisoners." *Associated Press* online, September 7, 2007; accessed August 11, 2012, at www.usatoday.com/news/nation/2007-09-07-502409224_x.htm.

Goldsmith, Jack. *The Terror Presidency: Law and Judgment inside the Bush Administration.* New York: W. W. Norton, 2007.

Gonzales, Alberto, Attorney General, to Senators Patrick Leahy and Arlen Specter. January 17, 2007; accessed August 12, 2012, at www.fas.org/irp/agency/doj/fisa/ag011707.pdf.

Goodin, Don. "Anonymous Takes Credit for Hack that Exposes 2.4 Million Syrian E-mails." *Ars Technica*, July 9, 2012; accessed

August 15, 2012, at arstechnica.com/security/2012/07/
anonymous-takes-credit-for-syrian-emails-hack/.

Goodman, Melvin A. *Failure of Intelligence: The Decline and Fall of the CIA*. Lanham, MD: Rowman & Littlefield, 2008.

Gorbachev, Mikhail. *Memoirs*. New York: Doubleday, 1996.

Gordievsky, Oleg. *Next Stop Execution*. London: Macmillan, 1995.

Gordon, Michael R., and Bernard E. Trainor. *Cobra II: The Inside Story of the Invasion and Occupation of Iraq*. New York: Random House, 2007 [2006].

Goscha, Christopher E. "Intelligence in a Time of Decolonization: The Case of the Democratic Republic of Vietnam at War (1945–50)." *Intelligence and National Security* 22:1 (February 2007).

Gosler, James. "Counterintelligence: Too Narrowly Practiced." In Jennifer E. Sims and Burton Gerber, eds. *Vaults, Mirrors, and Masks: Rediscovering US Counterintelligence*. Washington, DC: Georgetown University Press, 2008.

Gostev, Alexander, Kaspersky Labs. "Back to Stuxnet: The Missing Link." *Securelist*. June 11, 2012; accessed July 24, 2012, at www.securelist.com/en/blog?weblogid=208193568.

———. "The Flame: Questions and Answers." *Securelist*. May 28, 2012; accessed July 24, 2012, at www.securelist.com/en/blog/208193522/The_Flame_Questions_and_Answers.

Grabo, Cynthia M. *Anticipating Surprise: Analysis for Strategic Warning*. Washington, DC: Joint Military Intelligence College, 2002.

Graff, Brian. "American Expeditionary Force Intelligence Sections in World War II: A Failure to Adapt to Open Warfare." Unpublished master's thesis at the Joint Military Intelligence College, Washington, DC, 2006.

Granville, Johanna. "'Caught with Jam on Our Fingers': Radio Free Europe and the Hungarian Revolution in 1956." *Diplomatic History* 29:5 (2005).

Grathwohl, Larry, and Frank Reagan. *Bringing Down America: An FBI Informer with the Weathermen*. New Rochelle, NY: Arlington House, 1976.

Graves, Armgaard Karl. *The Secrets of the German War Office*. New York: McBride, Nast, 1914.

Greely, A. W. "The Military Telegraph Service." In Francis Trevelyan Miller and Robert Sampson Lanier, eds. *The Photographic History of the*

Civil War, vol. 8, *Soldier Life, Secret Service*. New York: Review of Reviews, 1911.

Greenhalgh, William. "Tactical Reconnaissance." In Victor B. Anthony and Richard R. Sexton, *The United States Air Force in Southeast Asia: The War in Northern Laos, 1954–1973*. Washington, DC: Center for Air Force History, 1993.

Greenhouse, Linda. "Computer Security Shift Is Approved by Senate." *New York Times*, December 24, 1987.

Grey, Stephen, and Don Van Natta Jr. "In Italy, Anger at US Tactics Colors Spy Case." *New York Times*, June 26, 2005; accessed August 11, 2012, at www.nytimes.com/2005/06/26/international/europe/26milan.html?_r=1&pagewanted=all.

Grimes, Roger A. "Danger: Remote Access Trojans." Microsoft *TechNet* (reprinted from *Security Administrator*, September 2002); accessed August 17, 2012, at http://technet.microsoft.com/en-us/library/dd632947.aspx.

Grimes, Sandra, and Jeanne Vertefeuille. *Circle of Treason: A CIA Account of Traitor Aldrich Ames and the Men He Betrayed*. Annapolis: US Naval Institute Press, 2012.

Grose, Peter. *Operation Rollback: America's Secret War behind the Iron Curtain*. Boston: Houghton Mifflin, 2000.

Guicciardini, Francesco. *Counsels and Reflections of Francesco Guicciardini*. Nanine Hill Thomson, trans. London: Kegan Paul, Trench, Trubner, 1890.

Gustafson, Kristian. *Hostile Intent: U.S. Covert Operations in Chile, 1964–1974*. Dulles, VA: Potomac Books, 2007.

Habeck, Mary R. "Blessed September: Al-Qaeda's Grand Strategic Vision on 9/11." In Lorry Fenner, Mark E. Stout, and Jessica L. Goldings, eds., *Ten Years Later: Insights on al-Qaida's Past and Future through Captured Records*. Baltimore: Johns Hopkins University Press, 2012.

Haines, Gerald K. "The Pike Committee Investigations and the CIA." *Studies in Intelligence* (Winter 1998/99); accessed March 26, 2012, at www.cia.gov/library/center-for-the-study-of-intelligence/csi-publications/csi-studies/studies/winter98_99/art07.html.

Haines, Gerald K., and Robert E. Leggett, eds. *Watching the Bear: Essays on CIA's Analysis of the Soviet Union*. Washington, DC: Central Intelligence Agency, 2001.

Hamre, John J., Deputy Secretary of Defense. Speech to the Fortune 500 CIO Forum, Aspen, Colorado, July 21, 1998; accessed June 10, 2012, at www.fas.org/irp/congress/1998_hr/98-06-11hamre.htm.

Hanyok, Robert J. *Spartans in Darkness: American SIGINT and the Indochina War, 1945–1975.* Ft. Meade, MD: National Security Agency, 2002.

Harnden, Toby. *Dead Men Risen: The Welsh Guards and the Defining Story of Britain's War in Afghanistan.* London: Quercus, 2011.

Harris, Shane. "The Cyberwar Plan." *National Journal,* November 14, 2009; accessed January 1, 2010, at www.nationaljournal.com/njmagazine/cs_20091114_3145.php.

Hatch, David A. "Before and After June 25: The COMINT Effort." In James I. Matray, ed. *Northeast Asia and the Legacy of Harry S. Truman: Japan, China, and the Two Koreas.* Kirksville, MO: Truman State University Press, 2012.

———. "The Punitive Expedition: Military Reform and Communications Intelligence." *Cryptologia* 31:1 (January 2007).

Hathaway, Robert, and Russell Jack Smith. *Richard Helms as Director of Central Intelligence, 1966–1973.* Washington, DC: Central Intelligence Agency, 1993.

Hawk, David. *The Hidden Gulag, Second Edition: The Lives and Voices of "Those Who are Sent to the Mountains."* Washington, DC: Committee for Human Rights in North Korea, 2012; accessed August 19, 2012, at www.hrnk.org/publications/hrnk-publications.php.

Hayden, Michael V., Director, National Security Agency. Statement for the record to the Joint Inquiry of the Senate Select Committee on Intelligence and the House Permanent Select Committee on Intelligence, October 17, 2002; accessed November 4, 2012, at www.gwu.edu/~nsarchiv/NSAEBB/NSAEBB24/nsa27.pdf.

Haynes, John Earl, and Harvey Klehr. *Venona: Decoding Soviet Espionage in America.* New Haven, CT: Yale University Press, 1999.

Hedley, John Hollister, ed. *The Directorate of Intelligence: Fifty Years of Informing Policy, 1952–2002.* Washington, DC: Central Intelligence Agency, 2002.

Helms, Richard, with William Hood. *A Look over My Shoulder: A Life in the Central Intelligence Agency.* New York: Presidio, 2003.

Hendricks, Steve. *A Kidnapping in Milan: The CIA on Trial.* New York: W. W. Norton, 2010.

Hiley, Nicholas. "Re-entering the Lists: MI5's Authorized History and the August 1914 Arrests." *Intelligence and National Security* 25:4 (August 2010).

Hinnen, Todd. "The Cyber-Front in the War on Terrorism: Curbing Terrorist Use of the Internet." *Columbia Science and Technology Law Review* 5 (2003).

Hinsley, F. H., et al. *British Intelligence in the Second World War.* 5 vols. New York: Cambridge University Press, 1984–1990.

HL Deb 09, December 1993. Vol. 550, cc1024. Accessed June 2, 2012, at http://hansard.millbanksystems.com/lords/1993/dec/09/intelligence-services-bill-hl.

Holden, William J. "Soviet Says West Incited Hungary: Approval of Rebel Plans by 'High U.S. Circles' Alleged." *New York Times*, November 9, 1956.

Holland, Max. "The Lie That Linked CIA to the Kennedy Assassination." *Studies in Intelligence* (Fall/Winter 2001); accessed January 8, 2012, at www.cia.gov/library/center-for-the-study-of-intelligence/kent-csi/vol45no5/html/v45i5a02p.htm#rft0.

Holloway, David. "Soviet Nuclear History." *Cold War International History Project Bulletin*, Fall 1994; accessed November 13, 2011, at www.scribd.com/doc/61520970/7/COLD-WAR-INTERNATIONAL-HISTORY-PROJECT-BULLETIN.

Home Office. "Draft Communications Data Bill." Command Paper 8359. June 2012; accessed August 19, 2012, at www.official-documents.gov.uk/menu/cmd2012.htm.

Hood, William. *Mole.* New York: W. W. Norton, 1982.

Hooper, John. "CIA Methods Exposed by Kidnap Inquiry." *Guardian*, July 1, 2005; accessed August 11, 2012, at www.guardian.co.uk/world/2005/jul/02/usa.italy.

Hoover Institution. "Cold War Broadcasting Impact: Report on a Conference Organized by the Hoover Institution and the Cold War International History Project of the Woodrow Wilson International Center for Scholars at Stanford University, October 13–16, 2004." Accessed January 7, 2012, at media.hoover.org/documents/broadcast_conf_rpt.pdf.

Hopkins, Nick. "UK Developing Cyber-Weapons Programme to Counter Cyber War Threat." *Guardian*, May 30, 2011; accessed November 11, 2012, at www.guardian.co.uk/uk/2011/may/30/military-cyberwar-offensive.

Horne, Alistair. *A Savage War of Peace: Algeria, 1954–1962*. New York: Viking, 1977.

Howard, Michael. "Cowboys, Playboys and other Spies." *New York Times*, February 16, 1986.

Howard, Philip N., and Muzammil M. Hussain. "Egypt and Tunisia: The Role of Digital Media." In Larry Diamond and Marc F. Plattner, *Liberation Technology: Social Media and the Struggle for Democracy*. Baltimore: Johns Hopkins University Press, 2012.

Huckaby, Jessica M., and Mark E. Stout. "Al Qaida's Views of Authoritarian Intelligence Services." *Intelligence and National Security* 25:3 (June 2010).

Intelligence and Security Committee. *Access to Communications Data by the Intelligence and Security Agencies*. London: Her Majesty's Stationery Office, February 2010.

———. *Could 7/7 Have Been Prevented?: Review of the Intelligence on the London Terrorist Attacks on 7 July 2005*. London: Her Majesty's Stationery Office, May 2009.

———. *The Handling of Detainees by UK Intelligence Personnel in Afghanistan, Guantanamo Bay and Iraq*. London: Her Majesty's Stationery Office, March 2005.

———. *Rendition*. London: Her Majesty's Stationery Office, July 2007.

———. *Report into the London Terrorist Attacks on 7 July 2005*. London: Her Majesty's Stationery Office, May 2006.

Intelligence Services Act 1994; accessed June 3, 2012, at www.legislation.gov.uk/ukpga/1994/13/contents.

International Atomic Energy Agency. "Inadequate Control of World's Radioactive Sources." IAEA Press Release 2002/09. June 24, 2002; accessed May 27, 2012, at www.iaea.org/newscenter/pressreleases/2002/prn0209.shtml.

Ireland v. the United Kingdom. 5310/71 (1978) ECHR 1 (January 18, 1978); accessed March 18, 2012, at www.worldlii.org/eu/cases/ECHR/1978/1.html .

Isaacson, Walter, and Evan Thomas. *The Wise Men: Six Friends and the World They Made*. New York: Simon & Schuster, 1986.

Jackson, Robert L. "No Presidential Role Found in CIA Plots." *Los Angeles Times,* July 19, 1975.

Jakub, Jay. *Spies and Saboteurs: Anglo-American Collaboration and Rivalry in Human Intelligence Collection and Special Operations, 1940–1945.* New York: St. Martins, 1999.

James P. Anderson and Co. "Computer Security Technology Planning Study." ESD-TR-73–51. Vol. 2. October 1972; accessed November 11, 2012, at csrc.nist.gov/publications/history/ande72.pdf.

Jeffery, Keith. *The Secret History of MI6, 1909–1949.* New York: Penguin, 2010.

Jehl, Douglas. "CIA Nominee Wary of Budget Cuts." *New York Times,* February 3, 1993.

Jervis, Robert. "Why Intelligence and Policymakers Clash." *Political Science Quarterly* 125:2 (Summer 2010).

Johnson, A. Ross. *Radio Free Europe and Radio Liberty: The CIA Years and Beyond.* Palo Alto, CA: Stanford University Press, 2010.

Johnson, Loch K., and Kevin J. Scheid. "Spending for Spies: Intelligence Budgeting in the Aftermath of the Cold War." *Public Budgeting & Finance* 17:4 (December 1997).

Johnson, Paul. *Modern Times: The World from the Twenties to the Eighties.* New York: Harper & Row, 1983.

Johnson, Thomas R. *American Cryptology during the Cold War, 1945–1989.* 4 vols. Ft. Meade, MD: National Security Agency, 1995.

Joint Chiefs of Staff. *The National Military Strategy of the United States of America.* 2004; accessed July 31, 2012, at www.defenselink.mil/news/Mar2005/d20050301nms.pdf.

Jones, Matthew. "Intelligence and Counterinsurgency: The Malayan Experience." In Robert Dover and Michael S. Goodman, eds. *Learning from the Secret Past: Cases in British Intelligence History.* Washington, DC: Georgetown University Press, 2011.

Jones, R. V. *Most Secret War: British Secret Intelligence, 1939–1945.* London: Hamish Hamilton, 1978.

Kahn, David. *The Codebreakers: The Story of Secret Writing.* New York: Scribners, 1996, [1967].

———. *Hitler's Spies: German Military Intelligence in World War II.* New York: MacMillan, 1978.

Kaplan, Fred. *The Insurgents: David Petraeus and the Plot to Change the American Way of War.* New York: Simon & Schuster, 2013.

Kautilya. *The Arthashastra*. Translated by L. N. Rangarajan. New Delhi: Penguin Books India, 1992.

Keegan, John. *Intelligence in War: Knowledge of the Enemy from Napoleon to Al Qaeda*. New York: Knopf, 2003.

Kerr, Sir Philip [Lord Lothian]. To President Roosevelt, aide memoire. July 8, 1940; accessed April 3, 2013, at www.nsa.gov/public_info/declass/ukusa.shtml.

Khan, Imran. Statement of the defendants read to the media at the Old Bailey on April 30, 2007; accessed August 12, 2012, at www.julyseventh.co.uk/crevice/crevice-imran-khan-statement-for-defendants.html.

Khrushchev, Nikita. *Khrushchev Remembers*. Introduction by Edward Crankshaw. Edited and translated by Strobe Talbott. Boston: Little, Brown, 1970.

Kleinman, Steven M. "KUBARK Counterintelligence Interrogation Review: Observations of an Interrogator Lessons Learned and Avenues for Further Research." In Intelligence Science Board, *Educing Information: Interrogation Science and Art*. Washington, DC: National Defense Intelligence College, 2006.; accessed August 20, 2012, at www.fas.org/irp/dni/educing.pdf.

Kostin, Sergei, Eric Raynaud, and Catherine Cauvin-Higgins. *Farewell: The Greatest Spy Story of the Twentieth Century*. Las Vegas: AmazonCrossing, 2011.

Kotani, Ken. *Japanese Intelligence in World War II*. Oxford: Osprey, 2009.

Kovar, R. D. Affidavit in *General William C. Westmoreland v. CBS Inc. et al.* US District Court. Southern District of New York., July 27, 1983; accessed October 1, 2009, at www.vietnam.ttu.edu/star/images/025/0250147001.pdf.

Kreis, John F., ed. *Piercing the Fog: Intelligence and Army Air Forces Operations in World War II*. US Air Force, 1995.

Kronenbitter, Rita T. (ps.). "Okhrana Agent Dolin." In Ben B. Fischer, ed., *Okhrana: The Paris Operations of the Russian Imperial Police*. Washington, DC: Central Intelligence Agency, 1997.

Laidig, Scott. *Al Gray, Marine: The Early Years, 1950–1967*. Arlington, VA: Potomac Institute Press, 2012.

Lake, Anthony. *Somoza Falling*. Boston: Houghton Mifflin, 1989.

Lambert, Nicholas A. *Planning Armageddon: British Economic Warfare and the First World War*. Cambridge, MA: Harvard University Press, 2012.

———. "Strategic Command and Control for Maneuver Warfare: Creation of the Royal Navy's 'War Room' System, 1905–1915." *Journal of Military History* 69 (April 2005).

Landau, Henry. *The Enemy Within: The Inside Story of German Sabotage in America*. New York: G. P. Putnam's Sons, 1937.

Laqueur, Walter, and Barry Rubin, eds. *The Arab-Israeli Reader: A Documentary History of the Middle East Conflict*. 6th ed. New York: Penguin, 2001.

Latell, Brian. *Castro's Secrets: The CIA and Cuba's Intelligence Machine*. New York: Palgrave Macmillan, 2012.

Lenin, V. I. *What Is to Be Done?: Burning Questions of Our Movement*, 1902; accessed June 28, 2012, at http://marxists.org/archive/lenin/works/1901/witbd/iv.htm.

Levitt, Matthew. *Hizbollah and the Qods Force in Iran's Shadow War on the West*. Washington, DC: Institute for Near East Policy, 2013; accessed April 6, 2013, at www.washingtoninstitute.org/uploads/Documents/pubs/PolicyFocus123.pdf.

Levy, Adrian, and Cathy Scott-Clark. "'One Huge US Jail.'" *Guardian,* March 18, 2005; accessed August 11, 2012, at www.guardian.co.uk/world/2005/mar/19/terrorism.afghanistan.

Lichtblau, Eric, and James Risen. "Bank Data Is Sifted by U.S. in Secret to Block Terror." *New York Times*, June 23, 2006; accessed August 12, 2012, at www.nytimes.com/2006/06/23/washington/23intel.html?ei=5088&en=168d69d26685c26c&ex=1308715200&partner=rssnyt&emc=rss&pagewanted=all.

Lieberthal, Kenneth. *Governing China: From Revolution through Reform*. New York: W. W. Norton, 2004.

Livingston, Robert Gerald. "An Operation Called 'Rosenholz': How the CIA Bought the Stasi Files for $75,000." *Atlantic Times*, March 2006; accessed June 3, 2012, at www.atlantic-times.com/archive_detail.php?recordID=451.

Lizhi, Fang. "Democracy, Reform, and Modernization." *Journal of Democracy* 1:1 (Winter 1990).

Locke, John. *The Second Treatise of Government*. Edited by Thomas P. Peardon. New York: Bobbs-Merill, 1952.

Los Angeles Times. "Hackers Victimize Cal-ISO." June 9, 2001.

Lynn, William S. "Defending a New Domain." *Foreign Affairs* (September-October 2010).

MacEachin, Douglas J. *The Final Months of the War with Japan*. Washington, DC: Central Intelligence Agency, 1998.

Machiavelli, Niccolo. *The Prince*. Translated by Harvey Mansfield. Chicago:

Macintyre, Ben. *Operation Mincemeat: How a Dead Man and Bizarre Plan Fooled the Nazis and Assured an Allied Victory*. New York: Broadway, 2010.

Macrakis, Kristie, Thomas Wegener Friis, and Helmut Müller-Enbergs, eds. *East German Foreign Intelligence: Myth, Reality, and Controversy*. Chicago: University of Chicago Press, 1985.

Maddrell, Paul. "British Intelligence through the Eyes of the Stasi: What the Stasi's Records Show about the Operations of British Intelligence in Cold War Germany." *Intelligence and National Security* 27:1 (February 2012).

———. "The Stasi's View of the Federal Republic of Germany." Paper presented at the International Studies Association conference, Montreal, 2011.

Maddrell, Paul, and Matthias Uhl. "A KGB View of CIA and Other Western Espionage against the Soviet Bloc, 1983." In R. Gerald Hughes, Peter Jackson, and Len Scott, *Exploring Intelligence Archives: Inquiries into the Secret State*. London: Routledge, 2008.

Mandiant. APT1: *Exposing One of China's Cyber Espionage Units*. February 2013; accessed April 6, 2013, at www.mandiant.com/blog/mandiant-exposes-apt1-chinas-cyber-espionage-units-releases-3000-indicators.

Maneki, Sharon. *The Quiet Heroes of the Southwest Pacific Theater: An Oral History of the Men and Women of CBB and FRUMEL*. Ft. Meade, MD: National Security Agency, 1996.

Manwaring, Max G., and Court Prisk, eds. *El Salvador at War: An Oral History of Conflict from the 1979 Insurrection to the Present*. Washington, DC: National Defense University Press, 1988.

Mao Tse-Tung. *On Guerrilla Warfare*. Translated by Samuel B. Griffith. Champaign, IL: University of Illinois Press, 1961.

Marchetti, Victor, and John D. Marks. *The CIA and the Cult of Intelligence.* New York: Knopf, 1974.

Marchio, James D. "Days of Future Past: Joint Intelligence Operations during the Second World War." *Joint Forces Quarterly* (Spring 1996).

Marighella, Carlos. "Popular Support." In *Minimanual for the Urban Guerrilla,* June 1969; accessed February 26, 2012, at www.marxists .org/archive/marighella-carlos/1969/06/minimanual-urban-guerrilla/index.htm.

Markoff, John. "Vast Spy System Loots Computers in 103 Countries." *New York Times,* March 29, 2009.

Marx, Gary T. "Ethics for the New Surveillance." *The Information Society* 14:3 (1998).

Masterman, J. C. *The Double-Cross System in the War of 1939–45.* New Haven, CT: Yale University Press, 1972.

Mastny, Vojtech. *The Cold War and Soviet Insecurity: The Stalin Years.* New York: Oxford University Press, 1996.

Matloff, Maurice, and Edwin M. Snell. *Strategic Planning for Coalition Warfare.* Washington, DC: Department of the Army, 1953.

Mazzetti, Mark. "A Secret Deal on Drones, Sealed in Blood." *New York Times,* April 6, 2013.

Mazzetti, Mark, and Scott Shane. "C.I.A. Abuse Cases Detailed in Report on Detainees." *New York Times,* August 24, 2009.

McChrystal, Stanley A. *My Share of the Task: A Memoir.* New York: Penguin, 2013.

McCoy, Alfred. *Policing America's Empire: The United States, the Philippines, and the Rise of the Surveillance State.* Madison: University of Wisconsin Press, 2009.

McDonald, Robert A., and Sharon K. Moreno. *Grab and Poppy: America's Early ELINT Satellites.* Chantilly, VA: National Reconnaissance Office, 2005.

Melman, Yossi. "Preventive Measures." *BA,* February 17, 2006; accessed March 17, 2012, at www.ba.no/nyheter/urix/article1960706.ece.

Mielke, Erich. Address to the Volskammer. November 13, 1989; accessed January 19, 2013, at www.goethe.de/wis/med/rtv/mpg/ en4430294.htm.

Miles, Milton E. *A Different Kind of War: The Unknown Story of the US Navy's Guerrilla Forces in World War II China.* Garden City, NY: Doubleday, 1967.

Miller, A. Ray. *The Cryptographic Mathematics of Enigma*. Ft. Meade, MD: National Security Agency, 1996.

Miller, Greg. "Plan for Hunting Terrorists Signals U.S. Intends to Keep Adding Names to Kill Lists." *Washington Post*, October 23, 2012.

Miller, Greg, Ellen Nakashima, and Karen DeYoung. "CIA Drone Strikes in Pakistan to Get Pass in 'Playbook.'" *Washington Post*, January 20, 2013.

Minihan, Kenneth A., Director, National Security Agency. "Cyber Attack: Is Our Nation at Risk?" Testimony before the Senate Governmental Affairs Committee. June 24, 1998; accessed on June 10, 2011. at www.defense.gov/speeches/speech .aspx?speechid=704.

Mitrokhin, Vasili. *The KGB in Afghanistan*. Introduced and edited by Christian F. Ostermann and Odd Arne Westad. Cold War International History Project, Working Paper No. 40; accessed April 21, 2012, at www.wilsoncenter.org/publication/ the-kgb-afghanistan.

Molander, Roger C., Andrew S. Riddile, and Peter A. Wilson. *Strategic Information Warfare: A New Face of War*. Santa Monica, CA: RAND, 1996; accessed May 27, 2012, at www.rand.org/pubs/ monograph_reports/MR661.html.

Montague, Ludwell Lee. *General Walter Bedell Smith as Director of Central Intelligence: October 1950–February 1953*. University Park, PA: Pennsylvania State University Press, 1992.

Montefiore, Simon Sebag. *Young Stalin*. New York: Alfred A. Knopf, 2007.

Moorman, Frank. Office of the Chief of Staff, American Expeditionary Force. "Notes on Personnel Required by Radio Intelligence Service, AEF." [n.d.1917]. National Archives and Records Administration, Record Group 120, American Expeditionary Force, Entry 105, Box 5765, unnamed folder.

Morgan, Ted. *A Covert Life: Jay Lovestone—Communist, Anti-Communist, and Spymaster*. New York: Random House, 1999.

Moroni Bracamonte, Jose Angel, and David E. Spencer. *Strategy and Tactics of the Salvadoran FMLN Guerrillas: Last Battle of the Cold War, Blueprint for Future Conflicts*. Westport, CT: Praeger, 1995.

Mudd, Philip. *Takedown: Inside the Hunt for Al Qaeda*. Philadelphia: University of Pennsylvania Press, 2013.

Murphy, David E., Sergei A. Kondrashev, and George Bailey. *Battleground Berlin: CIA vs. KGB in the Cold War*. New Haven, CT: Yale University Press, 1996.

Murphy, Robert. *Diplomat among Warriors*. Garden City, NY: Doubleday, 1964.

Murray, E. C. G. *Embassies and Foreign Courts: A History of Diplomacy*. London: G. Routledge, 1855.

Nakashima, Ellen. "Cyber-Intruder Sparks Massive Federal Response— and Debate over Dealing with Threats." *Washington Post*, December 8, 2011.

———. "Pentagon Computer-Network Defense Command Delayed by Congressional Concerns." *Washington Post*, January 3, 2010.

Nakashima, Ellen, Greg Miller, and Julie Tate. "U.S., Israel Developed Flame Computer Virus to Slow Iranian Nuclear Efforts, Officials Say." *Washington Post*, June 19, 2012.

Nalty, Bernard C. *The War against Trucks: Aerial Interdiction in Southern Laos, 1968–1972*. Washington, DC: Air Force History and Museums Program, 2005.

The Nation. "The War and Aviation." November 12, 1914.

National Commission on Terrorist Attacks upon the United States. *The 9/11 Commission Report*. New York: W. W. Norton, 2004.

National Intelligence Council. "Iran: Nuclear Intentions and Capabilities." November 2007; accessed April 6, 2013, at www.dni.gov/index .php/newsroom/reports-and-publications/167-reports-publica tions-2007/643-iran-nuclear-intentions-and-capabilities.

National Security Agency. "British-U.S. Communications Intelligence Agreement and Outline." March 5, 1946; accessed November 4, 2011, at www.nsa.gov/public_info/declass/ukusa.shtml.

———. *The Friedman Legacy: A Tribute to William and Elizebeth Friedman*. Ft. Meade, MD: National Security Agency, 2006.

———. "Military Construction, Defense-Wide FY 2008 Budget Estimates." February 2007, accessed August 4, 2012, at http:// comptroller.defense.gov/defbudget/fy2008/budget_justification/ pdfs/07_Military_Construction/11 NSA.pdf.

New York Times. "Radio Free Europe Accused by Rebels." November 20, 1956.

Noren, James. "CIA's Analysis of the Soviet Economy." In Gerald K. Haines and Robert E. Leggett, eds., *Watching the Bear: Essays on CIA's Analysis of the Soviet Union.* Washington, DC: Central Intelligence Agency, 2001.

Obama, Barack. "Remarks by the President at the National Defense University." National Defense University, Washington, DC, May 23, 2013; accessed May 26, 2013, at www.whitehouse.gov/the-press-office/2013/05/23/remarks-president-national-defense-university.

O'Connell, Jack, with Vernon Loeb. *King's Counsel: A Memoir of War, Espionage, and Diplomacy in the Middle East.* New York: W. W. Norton, 2011.

Office of the National Counterintelligence Executive. *Foreign Spies Stealing US Economic Secrets in Cyberspace: Report to Congress on Foreign Economic Collection and Industrial Espionage.* October 2011; accessed August 20, 2012, at www.ncix.gov/publications/reports/fecie_all/Foreign_Economic_Collection_2011.pdf.

O'Halpin, Eunan. *Defending Ireland: The Irish State and Its Enemies since 1922.* New York: Oxford 2002 [1999].

———. "The Value and Limits of Experience in the Early Years of the Northern Ireland Troubles, 1969–1972." In Robert Dover and Michael Goodman, eds. *Learning from the Secret Past: Cases in British Intelligence.* Washington, DC: Georgetown University Press, 2011; accessed November 10, 2012, at www.foia.cia.gov/docs/DOC_0001433692/DOC_0001433692.pdf.

Olmstead v. United States. 277 US 438 (1928).

Omand, David. *Securing the State.* New York: Columbia Iniversity Press, 2010.

Omand, David, Jamie Bartlett, and Carl Miller. "Introducing Social Media Intelligence (SOCMINT)." *Intelligence and National Security* 27:6 (December 2012).

Omestad, Thomas. "USIP Conference Assesses Social Media's Role in Conflict." Conference proceedings, US Institute of Peace. September 22, 2011; accessed August 14, 2012, at www.usip.org/publications/usip-conference-assesses-social-media-s-role-in-conflict.

Onley, Dawn S. "Red Storm Rising." *Government Computer News*, August 17, 2009.

Palmer Jr., Bruce. "US Intelligence and Vietnam." *Studies in Intelligence* 28 (1984); accessed November 10, 2012, at www.foia.cia.gov/docs/ DOC_0001433692/DOC_0001433692.pdf.

Panetta, Leon. "Remarks by Secretary on Cybersecurity to the Business Executives for National Security, New York City." October 11, 2012; accessed October 30, 2012 ,at www.defense.gov/transcripts/ transcript.aspx?transcriptid=5136.

Parker, Frederick D. *Pearl Harbor Revisited: United States Navy Communications Intelligence, 1924–1941*. Ft. Meade, MD: National Security Agency, 1994.

Pastor, Robert A. *Condemned to Repetition: The United States and Nicaragua*. Princeton, NJ: Princeton University Press, 1987.

Pavitt, James L. Remarks to the Foreign Policy Association, June 21, 2004; accessed September 28, 2013, at https://www.cia.gov/news-infor mation/speeches-testimony/2004/ddo_speech_06242004.html.

Pedlow, Gregory W., and Donald E. Welzenbach. *The CIA and the U-2 Program, 1954–1974*. Washington, DC: Central Intelligence Agency, 1998.

Perlroth, Nicole. "Cyber Attack on Saudi Firm Disquiets US." *New York Times*, October 24, 2012.

Petersen, Michael B. *Legacy of Ashes, Trial by Fire: The Origins of the Defense Intelligence Agency and the Cuban Missile Crisis Crucible*. Washington, DC: Defense Intelligence Agency, 2011.

Petit, Brian S. "Chechen Use of the Internet in the Russo-Chechen Conflict." Unpublished masters thesis, US Army Command and General Staff College, 2003; accessed September 28, 2013, at www.dtic.mil/dtic/tr/fulltext/u2/a416403.pdf.

Philby, Kim. *My Silent War*. London: Granada, 1980 [1968].

Piette, Diane Carraway, and Jesselyn Radack. "Piercing the Historical Mists of FISA: The People and Events behind the Passage of FISA and the Creation of the 'Wall.'" *Stanford Law and Policy Review* 17:2 (2006).

Pipes, Richard. "Team B: The Reality behind the Myth." *Commentary* 82 (October 1986).

Pollock, John. "People Power 2.0: How Civilians Helped Win the Libyan Information War." *Technology Review*, May-June 2012; accessed August 14, 2012, at www.technologyreview.com/featured-story/ 427640/people-power-20/.

Pollack, Kenneth M. *Arabs at War: Military Effectiveness, 1948–1991.* Lincoln: University of Nebraska Press, 2002.

Popplewell, Richard J. *Intelligence and Imperial Defence: British Intelligence and the Defence of the Indian Empire, 1904–1924.* London: Frank Cass, 1995.

Powell, Colin, with Joseph E. Persico. *My American Journey: An Autobiography.* New York: Ballantine, 1996 [1995].

Powers, Thomas. *Intelligence Wars: American Secret History from Hitler to al-Qaeda.* New York: New York Review of Books, expanded edition, 2004.

———. Thomas. *The Man Who Kept the Secrets: Richard Helms and the CIA.* New York: Alfred A. Knopf, 1979.

Prange, Gordon W., with Donald M. Goldstein and Katherine V. Dillon. *Target Tokyo: The Story of the Sorge Spy Ring.* New York: McGraw-Hill, 1984.

President's Commission on Critical Infrastructure Protection, Final Report. *Critical Foundations Protecting America's Infrastructures.* October 1997; accessed on June 10, 2012, at www.fas.org/sgp/library/pccip.pdf.

Preston, Stephen W., General Counsel, Central Intelligence Agency. "CIA and the Rule of Law." Speech at Harvard Law School, April 10, 2012; accessed April 6, 2012, at www.lawfareblog.com/2012/04/remarks-of-cia-general-counsel-stephen-preston-at-harvard-law-school/.

Pribbenow, Merle L. "The Man in the Snow White Cell." *Studies in Intelligence* 48:1 (2004).

Priest, Dana. "CIA Holds Terror Suspects in Secret Prisons: Debate Is Growing within Agency about Legality and Morality of Overseas System Set Up after 9/11." *Washington Post*, November 2, 2005.

———. "Covert CIA Program Withstands New Furor: Anti-Terror Effort Continues to Grow." *Washington Post*, December 30, 2005.

Rabinow, Paul. *French Modern: Norms and Forms of Social Environment.* Chicago: University of Chicago Press, 1996 [1989].

Rafalko, Frank J., ed. *A Counterintelligence Reader*, vol. 3. *Post-World War II to Closing the 20th Century.* 4 vols. Washington, DC: National Counterintelligence Center, 1998.

RAND Corporation. *Vulnerability of U.S. Strategic Air Power to a Surprise Enemy Attack in 1956.* Special Memorandum 15, April 1953.

Ranelagh, John. *The Agency: The Rise and Decline of the CIA.* New York: Simon & Schuster, 1987 [1986].

Ravid, Barak. "Bashar Assad Emails Leaked, Tips for ABC Interview Revealed." *Haaretz,* February 8, 2012; accessed August 15, 2012, at www.haaretz.com/print-edition/news/bashar-assad-emails-leaked-tips-for-abc-interview-revealed-1.411445.

Reagan, Ronald. National Security Decision Directive 145. "National Policy on Telecommunications and Automated Information Systems Security." September 17, 1984, accessed April 30, 2012, at www.fas.org/irp/offdocs/nsdd145.htm.

Reissmann, Ole, and Marcel Rosenbach. "A Geek Role in the Arab Spring: European Group Helps Tackle Regime Censorship." November 22, 2011; accessed August 15, 2012, at www.spiegel.de/international/world/a-geek-role-in-the-arab-spring-european-group-helps-tackle-regime-censorship-a-791370-2.html.

Riley, Michael, and Dune Lawrence. "Hackers Linked to China's Army Seen from EU to D.C." Bloomberg online, July 26, 2012; accessed August 2, 2012, at www.bloomberg.com/news/print/2012-07-26/china-hackers-hit-eu-point-man-and-d-c-with-byzantine-candor.html.

Rimington, Stella. *Open Secret: The Autobiography of the Former Director-General of MI5.* London: Hutchinson, 2001.

Risen, James, and Eric Lichtblau. "Spying Program Snared U.S. Calls." *New York Times,* December 21, 2005; accessed August 12, 2012, at www.nytimes.com/2005/12/21/politics/21nsa.html?_r=1&ex=1292821200&en=91d434311b0a7ddc&ei=5088&partner=rssnyt&emc=rss.

Risen, James, David Johnston, and Neil A. Lewis. "The Struggle for Iraq: Detainees; Harsh C.I.A. Methods Cited in Top Qaeda Interrogations." *New York Times,* May 13, 2004; accessed August 12, 2012, at www.nytimes.com/2004/05/13/world/struggle-for-iraq-detainees-harsh-cia-methods-cited-top-qaeda-interrogations.html.

Risso, Linda. "A Difficult Compromise: British and American Plans for a Common Anti-Communist Propaganda Response in Western Europe, 1948–1958." *Intelligence and National Security* 26:2–3 (April–June 2011).

Rodriguez, Jose, with Bill Harlow. *Hard Measures: How Aggressive CIA Actions after 9/11 Saved American Lives*. New York: Threshold, 2012.

Rossiter, James, Jonathan Richards, Rhys Blakely, and Richard Beeston. "MI5 Alert on China's Cyberspace Spy Threat." *Times* (London), December 1, 2007.

Rousseau, Jean-Jacques. *A Discourse on Inequality*. Translated by Maurice Cranston. London: Penguin, 1984.

———. *On the Social Contract*. Translated by Judith R. Masters. New York: St. Martins, 1978.

Royden, Barry G. "Tolkachev, A Worthy Successor to Penkovsky." *Studies in Intelligence* (47:3) 2003; accessed May 6, 2012, at www.cia.gov/library/center-for-the-study-of-intelligence/kent-csi/vol47no3/html/v47i3a02p.htm.

Russell, Richard L. "CIA's Strategic Intelligence in Iraq." *Political Science Quarterly* 117:2 (2002).

Safford, Laurance F. "A Brief History of Communications Intelligence in the United States." Part 1. SRH–149. March 27, 1952. National Security Agency.

Sagdeev, Roald Z. *The Making of a Soviet Scientist*. New York: John Wiley and Sons, 1994.

Sands, Philippe. *Torture Team: Rumsfeld's Memo and the Betrayal of American Values*. New York: Palgrave Macmillan, 2008.

Sanger, David. *Confront and Conceal: Obama's Secret Wars and Surprising Use of American Power*. New York: Crown, 2012.

Sargent, Greg. "Private Letter from CIA Chief Undercuts Claim Torture Was Key to Killing bin Laden." *Washington Post*, May 16, 2011.

Saville, Sir Mark, William L. Hoyt, and John L. Toohey. *Report of the Bloody Sunday Inquiry* [the Saville Report], vol. 1, chap. 8. June 15, 2010, National Archives (UK); accessed March 17, 2012, at The Report of the Bloody Sunday Inquiry.

Schecter, Jerrold L., and Peter S. Derabian. *The Spy Who Saved the World: How a Soviet Colonel Changed the Course of the Cold War*. New York: Scribner's, 1992.

Schell, Roger R. "Computer Security: The Achilles' Heel of the Electronic Air Force?" *Air University Review*, January–February 1979; accessed June 10, 2012, at www.airpower.maxwell.af.mil/airchronicles/aureview/1979/jan-feb/schell.html#schell.

Schindler, John R. "Defeating the 6th Column: Intelligence and Strategy in the War on Islamist Terrorism." *Orbis* 49 (Autumn 2005).

Schmeidel, John C. "My Enemy's Enemy: Twenty Years of Co-Operation between West Germany's Red Army Faction and the GDR Ministry for State Security." *Intelligence and National Security* 8:4 (October 1993).

———. *Stasi: Shield and Sword of the Party.* New York: Routledge, 2008.

Schoyen Collection. London and Oslo; accessed September 1, 2012, at www.schoyencollection.com/math.html#4631.

Schroen, Gary C. *First In: An Insider's Account of How the CIA Spearheaded the War Terror in Afghanistan.* New York: Ballantine, 2007 [2005].

Schwarzkopf, H. Norman, with Peter Petre. *It Doesn't Take a Hero.* New York: Bantam, 1993 [1992].

Scott, Len. "Intelligence and the Risk of Nuclear War: Able Archer-83 Revisited." *Intelligence and National Security* 26:6 (December 2011).

———. "Secret Intelligence, Covert Action, and Clandestine Diplomacy." In L. V. Scott and P. D. Jackson, *Understanding Intelligence in the Twenty-First Century: Journeys in Shadows.* London: Routledge, 2004.

Secretary of State for Northern Ireland. "Report of the Committee of Inquiry into Police Interrogation Procedures in Northern Ireland" [the Bennett Report]. March 1979; accessed March 18, 2012, at http://cain.ulst.ac.uk/hmso/bennett.htm.

Serge, Victor. *Memoirs of a Revolutionary.* New York: New York Review of Books, 2012 [1951].

Service, Robert. *A History of Twentieth-Century Russia.* Cambridge, MA: Harvard University Press, 1997.

Shelton, Hugh, with Ronald Levinson and Malcolm McConnell. *Without Hesitation: The Odyssey of an American Warrior.* New York: St. Martin's, 2010.

Sims, William S., with Burton J. Hendrick. *The Victory at Sea.* Garden City, NY: Doubleday, Page & Co., 1921.

Smith, R. Harris. *OSS: The Secret History of America's First Central Intelligence Agency.* Berkeley: University of California Press, 1972.

Smoot, Betsy Rohaly. "Pioneers of US Military Cryptology: Colonel Parker Hitt and His Wife, Genevieve Young Hitt." *Federal History* 4 (January 2012).

Snider, L. Britt. *The Agency and the Hill: CIA's Relationship with Congress, 1946–2004*. Washington, DC: Central Intelligence Agency, 2008.

———. "Unlucky SHAMROCK: Recollections from the Church Committee's Investigation of NSA." *Studies in Intelligence* (Winter 1999-2000); accessed March 25, 2012, at www.cia.gov/library/center-for-the-study-of-intelligence/csi-publications/csi-studies/studies/winter99-00/art4.html.

Solakov, Angel to V. Semichastni. "Acquired Materials from the Italian Embassy in Sofia." November 15, 1965. Todor Zhikov Collection, Cold War International History Project. Accessed November 27, 2011, at www.wilsoncenter.org/digital-archive.

Solzhenitsyn, Alexander. Nobel Prize for Literature Lecture (1970). Translated by F. D. Reeve. Accessed July 10, 2012, at www.columbia.edu/cu/augustine/arch/solzhenitsyn/nobel-lit1970.htm.

Soufan, Ali. "Will a CIA Veteran's Book Save a Terrorist?" *Bloomberg News*, May 8, 2012; accessed August 11, 2012 at www.bloomberg.com/news/2012-05-08/will-a-cia-veteran-s-book-save-a-terrorist-.html.

Spence, Richard B. "Englishmen in New York: The SIS American Station, 1915–21." *Intelligence and National Security* 19 (Autumn 2004).

Stanton, Doug. *Horse Soldiers: The Extraordinary Story of a Band of US Soldiers Who Rode to Victory in Afghanistan*. New York: Scribners, 2009.

Stephen, Robert. "Smersh: Soviet Military Counter-intelligence during the Second World War." *Journal of Contemporary History* 22 (1987).

Stepniak, S. [Sergei Kravchinsky], and Petr Alekseevich Lavrov. *Underground Russia: Revolutionary Profiles and Sketches from Life*. New York: Charles Scribner's Sons, 1885.

Steury, Donald P. *The Intelligence War*. New York: MetroBooks, 2000.

Stokes, Mark A., Jenny Lin, and L. C. Russell Hsiao. *The Chinese People's Liberation Army Signals Intelligence and Cyber Reconnaissance Infrastructure*. Project 2049. November 11, 2011; accessed August 2012, at http://project2049.net/documents/pla_third_department_sigint_cyber_stokes_lin_hsiao.pdf.

Stoll, Cliff. *The Cuckoo's Egg: Tracking a Spy through the Maze of Computer Espionage*. New York: Doubleday, 1989.

Stout, Mark. "World War I and the Invention of American Intelligence, 1878–1918." Unpublished doctoral thesis. School of History, University of Leeds, June 2010.

Sugihara, Seishiro. *Chiune Sugihara and Japan's Foreign Ministry: Between Incompetence and Culpability*. Lanham, MD: University Press of America, 2001.

Sulick, Michael J. "As the USSR Collapsed: A CIA Officer in Lithuania." *Studies in Intelligence* 50:2 (2006).

Sullivan, Brian R. "Soviet Penetration of the Italian Intelligence Services in the 1930s." In Carlo Rastelli, ed. *Storia dello Spionaggio*. Associazione Europea degli Amici degli Archivi Storici, 2006.

Sun Tzu. *The Art of War*. Translated by Samuel B. Griffith. New York: Oxford University Press, 1971 [1963].

Taubman, Geoffry. "A Not-So World Wide Web: The Internet, China, and the Challenges to Nondemocratic Rule." *Political Communication* 15:2 (April–June 1998).

Tenet, George J. Statement by Director of Central Intelligence George J. Tenet before the Senate Select Committee on Intelligence on the "Worldwide Threat 2001: National Security in a Changing World." February 7, 2001; accessed July 10, 2012, at www.cia.gov/news-information/speeches-testimony/2001/UNCLASWWT_02072001.html.

Tenet, George, with Bill Harlow. *At the Center of the Storm: The CIA during America's Time of Crisis*. New York: Harper, 2008 [2007].

Thomas, David. "Foreign Armies East and German Military Intelligence in Russia, 1941–45." *Journal of Contemporary History* 22 (1987).

Thomas, Evan. *The Very Best Men: Four Who Dared—Early Years of the CIA*. New York: Simon & Schuster, 1995.

Thomas, Hugh. *The Cuban Revolution*. New York: Harper & Row, 1977.

Thomas, Martin. *Empires of Intelligence: Security Services and Colonial Disorder after 1914*. Berkeley: University of California Press, 2007.

Time. "One War Won." December 13, 1943.

Treml, Vladimir G. "Western Analysis and the Soviet Policymaking Process." In Gerald K. Haines and Robert E. Leggett, eds., *Watching the Bear: Essays on CIA's Analysis of the Soviet Union*. Washington, DC: Central Intelligence Agency, 2001.

Trotsky, Leon. *Dictatorship versus Democracy: A Reply to Karl Kautsky (Terrorism and Communism)*. New York: Worker's Party of America, 1920; accessed September 1, 2012, at www.marxists.org/archive/trotsky/1920/terrcomm/index.htm.

Truman, Harry S. *Memoirs*, 2 vols. Garden City, NY: Doubleday, 1956.

Tunney, Thomas J., and Paul Merrick Hollister. *Throttled!: The Detection of the German and Anarchist Bomb Plotters*. Boston: Small, Maynard, 1919.

UK AOC Newsletter. "Outstanding NATO Unit 2008: Y Squadron, Royal Marines." January 2009; accessed July 20, 2012, at www.ukaoc.org/newsletters/jan09.htm.

United States v. Anna Chapman and Mikhail Semenko. Sealed Complaint before Hon. Ronald L. Ellis. Southern District of New York. Granted June 27, 2010; accessed July 25, 2012, at www.fbi.gov/news/stories/2011/october/russian_103111/russian_103111.

United States v. "Christopher R. Metsos," et al. Sealed Complaint before Hon. James L. Cott. Southern District of New York. Granted June 25, 2010; accessed July 25, 2012, at www.fbi.gov/news/stories/2011/october/russian_103111/russian_103111.

US Army. "*US v Bradley Manning*—New Charges including Aiding the Enemy." March 1, 2011; accessed August 13, 2012, at www.scribd.com/doc/49908578/US-v-Bradley-Manning-New-Charges-Including-Aiding-the-Enemy.

Usdin, Steven T. *Engineering Communism: How Two Americans Spied for Stalin and Founded the Soviet Silicon Valley*. New Haven, CT: Yale University Press, 2005.

US Cyber Consequences Unit. "Overview by the US-CCU of the Cyber Campaign against Georgia in August 2008." August 2006; accessed August 20, 2012, at www.registan.net/wp-content/uploads/2009/08/US-CCU-Georgia-Cyber-Campaign-Overview.pdf.

US Senate Report 112–173. *National Defense Authorization Act for Fiscal Year 2013—Report to Accompany S. 3254*. June 4, 2012; accessed August 19, 2012, at www.govtrack.us/congress/bills/112/s3254/text.

US Senate, Committee on Foreign Relations. *Intelligence and the ABM*. 91st Congress, 1st Session, 1969.

———. Committee on Homeland Security and Governmental Affairs. Special Report by Sens. Lieberman and Collins. *A Ticking Time*

Bomb: Counterterrorism Lessons from the US Government's Failure to Prevent the Fort Hood Attack. February 3, 2011; accessed July 15, 2012, at www.washingtonpost.com/wp-srv/politics/documents/fthoodsenatereport.html?hpid=topnews.

———. Select Committee on Intelligence. "US Intelligence Community's Prewar Intelligence Assessments on Iraq" [henceforth SSCI Report]. S. Report 108--301, 108th Congress, 2d Session, 2004.

———. Select Committee to Study Governmental Operations with Respect to Intelligence Activities [the Church Committee]. Final Report of the Select Committee to Study Governmental Operations with Respect to Intelligence Activities. 8 vols. 94th Congress, Second Session, 1976.

Valero, Larry A. "From World War to Cold War: Aspects of the Management and Coordination of US Intelligence, 1941–1953." Unpublished doctoral thesis. St. Catherine's College, University of Cambridge, 2001.

Van Hook, Laurie West. *Reforming Intelligence: The Passage of the Intelligence Reform and Terrorism Prevention Act.* Washington, DC: Office of the Director of National Intelligence, 2009; accessed August 19, 2012, at www.fas.org/irp/dni/index.html.

Vassiliev, Alexander, and Allen Weinstein. *The Haunted Wood: Soviet Espionage in America—The Stalin Era.* New York: Random House, 1997.

Vise, David A. *The Bureau and the Mole: The Unmasking of Robert Philip Hanssen, the Most Dangerous Double Agent in FBI History.* New York: Grove, 2002.

Volkogonov, Dmitrii Antonovich. *The Rise and Fall of the Soviet Empire: Political Leaders from Lenin to Gorbachev.* Translated by Harold Shukman. London: HarperCollins, 1998.

Wallace, Bob, and H. Keith Melton, with Henry R. Schlesinger. *Spycraft: The Secret History of the CIA's Spytechs, from Communism to Al-Qaeda.* New York: Plume, 2009.

Waller, Douglas. *Wild Bill Donovan: The Spymaster Who Created OSS and Modern American Espionage.* New York: Free Press, 2011.

Wang, Pufeng. "The Challenge of Information Warfare." *China Military Science,* Spring 1995; accessed June 10, 2012, at www.fas.org/irp/world/china/docs/iw_mg_wang.htm.

Warner, Michael, ed. *Central Intelligence: Origin and Evolution.* Washington, DC: Central Intelligence Agency, 2001.

———, ed. *The CIA under Harry Truman.* Washington, DC: Central Intelligence Agency, 1994.

———. "The CIA's Internal Probe of the Bay of Pigs Affair." *Studies in Intelligence* 42 (1998).

———. "The CIA's Office of Policy Coordination: From NSC 10/2 to NSC 68." *International Journal of Intelligence and Counterintelligence* 11 (Summer 1998).

———. "The Collapse of Intelligence Support for Air Power, 1944–52." *Studies in Intelligence* 49 (2005).

———. "Intelligence and Reflexivity: An Invitation to a Dialogue," *Intelligence and National Security* 27:2 (April 2012).

———. "The Kaiser Sows Destruction: Protecting the Homeland the First Time Around." *Studies in Intelligence* 46 (2002).

———. *The Office of Strategic Services: America's First Intelligence Agency.* Washington, DC: Central Intelligence Agency, 2000.

———. "Prolonged Suspense: The Fortier Board and the Transformation of the Office of Strategic Services." *Journal of Intelligence History* 2 (June 2002).

———. "Sophisticated Spies: CIA's Links to Liberal Anti-Communists, 1949–1967." *International Journal of Intelligence and Counterintelligence* 9 (Winter 1996/97).

Warrick, Joby. *Triple Agent: The Al-Qaeda Mole Who Infiltrated the CIA.* New York: Vintage, 2012 [2011].

Watts, Larry L. "Intelligence Reform in Europe's Emerging Democracies." *Studies in Intelligence* 48 (2004), accessed May 27, 2012, at www.cia.gov/library/center-for-the-study-of-intelligence/csi-publica-tions/csi-studies/studies/vol48no1/article02.html.

Wei, Jincheng. "Information War: A New Form of People's War." *Liberation Army Daily,* June 25, 1996; accessed June 10, 2012, at www.fas.org/irp/world/china/docs/iw_wei.htm.

Weiser, Benjamin. *A Secret Life: The Polish Officer, His Covert Mission, and The Price He Paid to Save His Country.* New York: PublicAffairs, 2004.

Weiss, Gus W. "The Farewell Dossier." *Studies in Intelligence* 39:5 (1996).

Whitehead, Don. *The FBI Story.* New York: Random House, 1956.

Whitehead, Tom. "Hackers Could Be Running Company Computers, GCHQ Chief Warns." *Telegraph*, September 9, 2012; accessed November 2, 2012, at www.telegraph.co.uk/news/uknews/law-and-order/9522969/Hackers-could-be-running-company-computers-GCHQ-chief-warns.html.

Whitehouse, Sheldon. "Cybersecurity." *Congressional Record* (Senate), July 27, 2010; accessed August 1, 2012, at www.fas.org/irp/con gress/2010_cr/cyber.html.

Wiener, Tim. *Enemies: A History of the FBI*. New York: Random House, 2012.

Wilber, Donald. "Overthrow of Premier Mossadeq of Iran, November 1952–August 1953." In *CIA Clandestine Service History*, March 1954; accessed April 27, 2013, at www.gwu.edu/~nsarchiv/NSAEBB/NSAEBB28/.

Wilford, Hugh. *The Mighty Wurlitzer: How the CIA Played America*. Cambridge, MA: Harvard University Press, 2008.

Williams, Dan. "Spymaster Sees Israel as World Cyberwar Leader." *Reuters*, December 15, 2009.

Willing, Richard. "The Nazi Spy Next Door." *USA Today*, February 27, 2002.

Winkler, Jonathan Reed. *Nexus: Strategic Communications and American Security in World War I*. Cambridge, MA: Harvard University Press, 2008.

Winterbotham, F. W. *The Ultra Secret*. London: Weidenfeld and Nicolson, 1974.

Wise, David. *Spy: The Inside Story of How the FBI's Robert Hanssen Betrayed America*. New York: Random House, 2002.

Witcover, Jules. *Sabotage at Black Tom: Imperial Germany's Secret War in America, 1914–1917*. Chapel Hill, NC: Algonquin, 1989.

Wolf, Markus. *Man without a Face: The Autobiography of Communism's Greatest Spymaster*. New York: PublicAffairs, 1997.

Wood, Kevin M., David D. Palkki, and Mark E. Stout. *The Saddam Tapes: The Inner Workings of a Tyrant's Regime, 1978–2001*. New York: Cambridge University Press, 2011.

Wright, Robin. *Sacred Rage: The Wrath of Militant Islam*. New York: Simon & Schuster, 2001 [1985].

Yardley, Herbert. *The American Black Chamber*. Indianapolis: Bobbs-Merrill, 1931.

York, Jillian C. "Syria's Electronic Army: Syrian Computer Hackers Put Their Own Spin on Democracy Protests in Syria." *al Jazeera*, August 15, 2011; accessed August 15, 2012, at www.aljazeera .com/indepth/opinion/2011/08/201181191530456997.html.

INDEX

Note: Page numbers in **bold** represent images and photographs.